Sādhan Samar:

Battles in a Sacred Quest

Devī Māhātmya: Glory of the Goddess

A spiritual Commentary on *Śri Śri Candī*
or *Dūrgā Saptaśati* by

Brahmarṣi Satyadeva

Sādhan Samar:

Battles in a Sacred Quest

Devī Māhātmya: Glory of the Goddess

A Spiritual Commentary on *Śri Śri Caṇḍī*
or *Dūrgā Saptaśati* by

Brahmarṣi Satyadeva

Volume Three

Unraveling the knot of *Rudra*:
Destruction of *Śumbha*

Translated by Narendra Bhadra
2023

Motilal Banarsidass Publications

MOTILAL BANARSIDASS
PUBLICATIONS
4741/23, Ansari Road, Daryaganj, New Delhi - 110002 (India)
Email: mlbd@mlbd.com | sales@mlbd.com | exports@mlbd.com
Website: www.mlbd.com

Sādhan Samar: Vol. III
by
Narendra Bhadra
(Translator)

First Edition Published in 2023

Published in India by Motilal Banarsidass Publications

ISBN : 978-93-91759-75-9 (HB)

Printed and bound in India

This volume is dedicated to
my mentor
Bijoy Ratan Mitra (1916- 2005)

Table of Contents

Foreword to Volume Three

This is an English translation of the Third Volume of *Sādhan Samar*, a spiritual commentary on the *Devī Māhātmya*, (also known as *Dūrgā Saptaśati* or *Śri Śri Caṇḍī*) by Brahmarṣi Satyadeva (1883-1932). The Bengali edition was first published from Kolkata (Calcutta) in the 1920s.

Based on teachings about the six spinal centers (*cakras*), Brahmarṣi says that people usually function from the lower three *cakras.* Ascent through the next center at the level of the heart (*Anāhata)* is difficult. This is the knot of *Brahmā.* To unravel or pierce this knot, Mother destroys *Madhu* and *Kaiṭava*. Spiritual seekers should practice the establishment of Truth to rise to this *cakra*. At the spinal center above this, at *Viṣuddhā*, is the knot of *Viṣṇu.* This knot is pierced when the Goddess destroys *Mahiṣāsura*. To reach this level, spiritual seekers should practice the establishment of life force (*praṇa*).

Volume Three of *Sādhan Samar* is a commentary on the final character (*uttara carit* Chapters Five to Thirteen) of *Devī Māhātmya.* This is piercing the knot of *Rudra* at the *Ājñā cakra.* It is accomplished by Mother destroying the demon *Śumbha* and facilitated by practice of the establishment of Bliss (*ānanda*).

This translation was proposed by Sri Saumyendranāth Brahmacāri (1946-2012), late *Ācārya* of Dev Sangha Āśram, who was in the lineage of Brahmarṣi Satyadeva. The translation follows the words, construction and verse numbers of the mantras from the Bengali text by Brahmarṣi. Textual quotes and verses of *Devī Māhātmya* have been transliterated following IAST (International Alphabet of Sanskrit Transliteration). The choice of English words for much of the terminology used by Brahmarṣi is in accordance with Śri Aurobindo's Glossary to the Records of Yoga (2005). Footnotes were added by the translator to give sources of many of the scriptural texts quoted by Brahmarṣi and occasional English explanations.

Mother's Love: Meeting and Union

paśyastu sarvve amṛtasvarupam|
gacchantu sarvve amṛtaṃ nidhānam||

May all see ambrosial spirit, may all reach their ambrosial home.

O, blissful children! You have been aroused by the sweet call of truth. You have been thrilled by the ambrosial touch of life force. Now come and see my blissful spirit. See that I am sweet, nectar-like, blissful, encouraging and eternally free. See that constant bliss is my nature. See that there is nothing else but completely blissful spirit. Bliss is the content and the ingredient of all that is reflected as visible, as this universe. The ambrosial 'I' is visible everywhere as seer, sight and seen. See that it is 'I' in all sorrow, pain, delusion, needs and cries. Within all this, the eternally blissful being pours a stream of bliss.

Those who have laid their individual spirits at the feet of this valiant nature of immortality will understand me, will see me and merge into me. Those whose ears have heard the call of truth, those who have been revived by the touch of life, let them come forward and see that the heart of the blissful Mother is open for them. Come and be overwhelmed. Enter and merge.

I am here beyond words and thought, only spirit, only the nature of bliss. Here there is no being, no universe, no view, never was, will never be. There is no want, only wholeness and unity.

See that I am engrossed with the bliss of divine play of the multiplicity of creation-maintenance-bliss, the all-knowing, supreme being in all beings. Take a wider look and see that it is I, knowledge-formed, completely blissful, who becomes limited knowledge and bliss, playing the role of worldly persons, who are ignorant and without joy.

Those who will be honored by finding my three-fold nature will look at me with the vision of truth and say, 'Self is nectar in all beings.' They will then look at my worldly form and say, 'truth is nectar in all beings.'

Children, you have been established in truth and life force, in consciousness. Now be established in bliss. Arrive at the principle of the 'one and only, without the relationship of mother and child. Saying 'I am', go beyond spiritual method and effort. May the blessings of the *guru* bring success.

Uttara Carit: The Final Character

ṛṣicchanda – upodghāt sutra[1]

uttaracaritrasya rudra ṛṣiḥ mahāsarasvatī devatā
anuṣṭupa chando bhīmāśaktiḥ bhrāmarībījaṃ
sūryastattvam sāmavedaḥ svarūpam
mahāsarasvatīprītyarthe jape viniyogaḥ||

Translation:

In this final character, the sage is *Rudra*, the goddess is *Mahāsarasvatī*, the rhythm is *Anuṣṭupa*, the power is *Bhīmā*, the seed mantra is *Bhrāmari*, the principle is *Sūrya* (Sun), its nature is the *Sāma Veda*; it is for the pleasure of *Mahāsarasvatī*, and is used for chanting her rosary.

Explanation:

In this final character, the destruction of *Śumbha*, the sage is *Rudra*. He is the god of dissolution. All worldly perceptions, that is, all divided knowledge dissolves into an undivided ocean of knowledge, the intellect formed *Maheśvara*. The last knot of being, or the ego-formed *asura Śumbha*, dissolves in undivided knowledge. So, the god of dissolution, *Rudra* is the sage of the final character.

The goddess is *Mahāsarasvatī*. The pure perception formed nature of Self dissolves, ending one's state as a worldly person, in the knowledge formed, high-natured, pure, form of *Sarasvatī*, of the right attribute (*sattva*).

The rhythm is *Anuṣṭupa*. The life force of a spiritual seeker who bathes in this final character of Mother takes on the calm vibrations of the Vedic rhythm called *Anuṣṭupa*.

The power is *Bhīmā*. The state as worldly person ends in a terrible, destructive force. This power is *Bhīmā*. *Bhrāmari bija*:

1 verses by the seers- introductory lines

the figure surrounded by innumerable bees is called *Bhrāmari*. She destroys the *asura Aruṇāksya*. This will be explained in Chapter Eleven.

The principle is *Sūrya* (the Sun). The meaning of *Sūrya* is that which is expressed or knowledge. Pure perception that removes an eternity of ignorant darkness, this perception is the principle, the main topic of the final character. The *Sāma Veda* is the level-natured *Brahmaṇ*, that is, the nature of a balanced knowledge principle. This final character is applied for the pleasure of the knowledge formed *Mahāsarasvatī*.

Chapter 5
Unraveling the Knot of *Rudra*

Verse 1.

ṛṣiruvāca
purā śumbhaniśumbhābhyāmasurābhyāṁ śacīpateḥ|
trailokyaṁ yajñabhāśca hṛtā madabalāśrayāt||

Translation:

The sage said, 'in ancient times, the two demons *Śumbha* and *Niśumbha*, in their arrogance and strength, robbed the three worlds and the ceremonial offerings of *Indra*, the consort of *Śacī*.'

Explanation:

Mahiṣāsura has been destroyed. Disturbances in the spirit of a spiritual seeker due to stored tendencies of actions have been stopped. There is no longer torment by desires for material things. There is no fear that this might happen in the future. The knot of life force has been removed. A spiritual seeker understands that what is perceived inside as life force, is expressed outside as this world. Wherever the gaze is directed, complete life-natured spirit removes the inert feelings of different names and forms. There is nothing else but dear, supreme life force or consciousness. Whatever is reflected as inert in the eyes of common people, is not truly inert. This is no longer only words or just verbal knowledge. By the establishment of truth over all this world, by the means shown by the *guru*, inert Nature is now perceived as the sentient form of Mother. One does not have to understand by logic and discernment that beings are like unclothed children on the lap of Mother. Memory illuminates the life-natured spirit of Mother. There is nothing to fear. By viewing the rule of Mother all over this world, the sense of control by beings has nearly disappeared. A spiritual seeker is now able to breathe with relief from all the worries of this world. Proper acts over lifetimes and the unconditional grace of the *guru* have brought the seeker to this peaceful place.

But even now, prior tendencies have not been reduced. By the application of some unknown, great force, even with relative unwillingness, actions begin[1]. A spiritual seeker knows that 'the Lord does not create agents or actions for this world'[2], even then, the sense of control reappears momentarily and overshadows everything. Besides this, all efforts to reach Mother and reside in the nature of *paramātmā*, after all the conflicts of joy and sorrow over lifetimes, have not been illuminated. A spiritual seeker may think that all has been found, all has been understood. Yet, something is missing, without which there is no wholeness in life, it has not been fully expressed that, which we may or may not understand. Nothing that can be enunciated. What we know or do not know, we cannot definitely say. It has not yet been clarified. Speaking of which, the sage of the *Upaniṣad* calmly sang, 'those who say they know, do not know'[3], because 'how can one know the one that knows.'[4] Those who say that they 'do not know it' are inexperienced about its nature. It is a lie to say that one does not know the one that is dressed as 'I'. Then who is this 'I'? That which we cannot say we know, nor say that we do not know. However, it may be beyond words and mind, however inaccessible, still we need it. We want it. Can it be found? Yes, it can be.

As long as the puzzle of finding or not finding, knowing or not knowing is not removed, the poverty of the spirit of a spiritual seeker is not gone. At least, it should not be, or cannot be. Beings have appeared from *Brahmaṇ*. Until they reach *Brahmaṇ*, their dissatisfaction cannot be removed. Dissatisfaction is a figure of the movement of Mother. Because Mother always resides in that form in the hearts of all beings, we knowingly or unknowingly,

---

1 *Bhāgavat Gitā*, 3:36

2 *ibid*, 5:14.

3 *no na vedeti veda ca, Kena Upaniṣad*, 2.2

4 *viñjāntaramare kena vijānīyāt, Bṛhadāryaṇak Upaniṣad*, 2.4.14.

day by day move towards Mother. Because of the influence of dissatisfaction, although future and stored actions are eroded until the insurmountable prior tendencies are removed, beings cannot remain still. Until one realizes that the prior actions are not sorrows, that they are but the divine play of bliss, they appear as sorrow. This is the knot of *Rudra* or the knowledge-natured knot. This will be later explained in detail.

The material of this world is bliss. Bliss is its ingredient, bliss is its consequence, bliss is its aim and destination. A spiritual seeker has not yet reached this realization. By the establishment of truth, one has discovered existence (*sat*), by the establishment of life force (*prāṇa*), one has discovered awareness (*cit*). Now by being established in bliss, one can fulfill the great purpose of beloved life as a human.

When one stands in the arena of the intellectual form, this world is illuminated as the nature of perception (*bodha*). As long as it is not felt to be *ātmā*, so long this is seen to be parched, as if without joy. When it is seen that it is not just dry perception, that it is truly blissful, that awareness is congealed bliss, *ātmā*, then the knot of *Rudra*, of knowledge, is pierced. Beings experience prior tendencies but do not think them to be sorrowful. They think that this world is built of bliss, that the material body is a collection of blissful atoms. In this condition, every thought, every action and even every breath is felt to be articulations of the blissful Self.

The intellectual formed *guru* Medhasa is telling Suratha, or, showing him, in connection with the destruction of *Śumbha* and *Niśumbha*, how beings may arrive at this principle, to this blissful arena of Self. At the end of the previous chapter on the destruction of *Mahiṣāsura*, the sage, saying 'I will tell you properly, listen to me', had hinted at this next mystery, the final character. Now he begins to speak of what he had promised. So, this chapter begins with 'the sage said.'

This is the relationship between the *guru* and a disciple. As long as a disciple is not established in blissful nature, the *guru* does not give any opportunity to ask questions. When one acquires the right, when the time comes, then all doubts in the heart of a disciple are answered, without asking. Some disciples may begin to plague the *guru* with questions even before they acquire scriptural rights. It is as if they can remove all doubts in one day. But, that does not happen. These are all things of the heart, they are deep mysteries, difficult to discover. So, just by advice or by reading books, one cannot find Self. When a child is hungry, a mother, more than the child, knows what food is suitable for it. If one does not leave the determination of action on Mother-natured *guru*, but takes it on oneself, then ego remains. As long as this is so, one cannot realize the grace of a *guru*. Without the grace of the *guru*, liberation is not possible.

See how the great spiritual seeker *Arjuna*, whose *guru* was Lord *Kṛṣṇa*, hearing the advice in the *Gitā* up to the chapter on divine splendor, bows down and says, "O god of yoga, O Lord, if you think that I am fit to view your universal form, then show me that imperishable nature."[5] How beautiful it is. Think what lack of ego, what humility and how much respect is expressed in these words by *Arjuna*. When the disciple offers his sense of ownership at the feet of the *guru*, then we see that one has to ask for nothing, the *guru* explains everything that is required. The disciple has to do nothing, the *guru* makes one do all that is necessary. So, it is not surprising that if one enters the arena of the higher spiritual quest with impatience or malfeasance, results are delayed. But that is another matter.

The destruction of *Śumbha*, or the final character of Mother is profound and full of variety. It appears that without high privileges and pure intelligence, it is difficult to enter into these mysteries. So, let us first bow down at the feet of Mother, our only sanctuary and ask for her grace. She will purify our intelligence and we will be able to properly understand this incredible mystery.

O, Mother! We have heard that without the grace of *guru*, scriptures and Self, without these three, no one can enter the

5 *Bhāgabat Gitā,* 11:4.

kingdom of liberation. Only you appear as all these three. You are the *guru*, you are the scriptures and you are grace. The words of the scriptures are not inert letters; they are life-formed, awareness-formed, the eternally aware Mother. You appear as the words of the scriptures and remove the ignorant blindness of our eyes with *kohl* of knowledge. Understanding this, we remember your mercy. You are the form of mercy, the affectionate Mother. You will take us to the arduous principle of *paramātmā.* As long as you do not confer on beings the ability to realize the words of the scriptures, even with scholarship, their ignorance is not removed. Mother, emerge as intelligence (*dhi*) and grant us the ability to immerse in this very deep principle. Let us go beyond all doubt and ignorance. O, Mother.

Śumbha: Ego (*asmitā*); The word '*Śumbha*' is formed from the root '*śunav*' meaning appearance. This varied world, this family of spouse and children, all this wealth, honor and fame, this material and subtle body, all these reside in ego. The materials of this world are all layers of ego. What is *asmitā*? The feeling of 'I, I' is *asmitā*. Everything that beings do, whatever they think, this feeling of 'I' is closely enfolded into each of them. This world or this universe is based on this feeling of 'I.' Remember that this is not the pride of perception of a material body. This is the sense of 'I' of the intellectual formed (*vijñanmaya*) sheath. When a spiritual seeker can withdraw his sense of 'I' into the intellectual formed sheath, that is, when just as a general person thinks of the physical body when saying 'I', one thinks of the intellectual formed 'I', when the intellectual percept is as strong as the physical one, then the nature of this ego is perceived. The center at which a spiritual seeker has been repeatedly advised to travel in Volumes One and Two of *Sādhan Samar*, when those areas are under their control, when they can willfully enter into the intellectual arena, they discover the nature of this ego. This is further explained below.

In the philosophy of Pātañjali, it has been said that the faculty of sight is the male principle (*puruśa*) and the power of seeing is intelligence (*buddhi*). The perception that these two are nondifferent is ego (*asmitā*). When intelligence appears to be *ātma,* it may be called *asmitā.* This also is a burden. Ignorance, ego, anger, jealousy and close attention are the five great burdens. Broadly, the perception of nondifference between intelligence and *ātmā* is the burden called *asmitā.* In the language of *Devī Māhātmya,* this is the great demon, the *asura Śumbha.* Material things, senses and mind terminate in intelligence. The disturbances and power of action of materials of form and flavor perceived by the senses, the eyes and other senses and mind, end in intelligence. There is no connection with materials and senses above intelligence. This intelligence and ego are nondifferent. There is no difference between the perception of 'I'-ness and definitiveness. It is by noticing differences in results and actions that intelligence and ego are differentiated.

When spiritual seekers, by the establishment of truth and life force, are able to withdraw the sense of Self into the principle of intelligence, and remain there for some time, for a short duration, they feel intelligence or this ego to be Self. But, those who have taken sanctuary at the feet of Mother, do not hold on to this error or disturbance for too long. Mother destroys this subtle *asura* and expresses her proper nature. Even then, until this fortunate moment comes, a spiritual seeker suffers torment. However, no one can understand or see this torment frin outside. A spiritual seeker realizes the nature of this burden of ego in the heart and suffers. Arriving at this arena of ego, one thinks that one has found everything, understands everything and that the puzzle of life and death of many ages has been solved. One has attained something special, compared to common people. All this is true, but reaching the place where there is nothing that is 'all', where every burden is gone, where ignorance vanishes forever, has not yet been reached. That is the lap of affection of my Mother, the blissful heart of my Mother beyond all perceptions, without the three attributes. It is the reassuring, ambrosial feet of my Mother, reaching which, the riddle of this universe, ends forever. It is the heart of my Mother, where there is nothing called the world, or being, never was, or never will be. Oh! What a happy, sweet, blissful place it is. It is 'I' without I. As long as you do not reach this place, as long as you cannot merge this divided self into the heart of Mother that is beyond the spirit of this world, until then, even if you receive control of all this universe, the power of creation-maintenance-dissolution, and the wealth of all comprehension, the dissatisfaction in your heart will not cease, will not be cooled, the pain will not end. Until then you will willingly or unwillingly suffer the torment of the *asura*.

Whatever that is, with the piercing of the knots of *Brahmā* and *Viṣṇu*, the place that a spiritual seeker was to reach, the self that was advised to be attained, in this final character is described as an *asura*, who has also to be destroyed. What has before been advised to be a delectable attainment, is here to be discarded. This is what happens in the spiritual quest. If day by day, this feeling of rejection does not appear, then what is a spiritual quest? Spiritual enterprise is the abandonment of multiplicity and reaching unity. As long as one does not reach this principle of nonduality, so long, willingly or unwillingly, one has to accept this desertion. For children who have surrendered at the feet of Mother, this abandonment does not have to happen by treacherous resolve, it happens by the grace of Mother. Whatever it is, the nature of this ego or the *asura Śumbha* will be explained in detail later, where it will be easier to understand.

Niśumbha: attachment, the feeling of 'my' or 'mine' is attachment (*mamatā*). But this is not attachment as is generally understood. This is the attachment by the intellectual sheath. The attachment that develops in the subtle principle is *Niśumbha*. Those who have not discovered the intellectual sheath may not understand the nature of this attachment correctly, because this cannot be understood only by thought. This has to be realized. This is the attachment that is hinted at when saying, 'my knowledge' or 'my perception.' Just as ego (*asmitā*) is the subtle form of 'I'-ness, this attachment is a subtle feeling. They are brothers. Where there is ego there is attachment. So *Śumbha* and *Niśumbha* are often mentioned together.

Sacipati: consciousness covered by *māyā*. Although

commonly, *Sacipati* refers to the king of gods *Indra*, here the word is used as an indicator of *Brahmaṇ* or *paramātmā*. The *śrutis* also say that *Indra*, that is *Brahmaṇ* became many because of *māyā*. The word '*saci*' means *māyā*, so the consort (*pati*) is 'consciousness covered by *māyā*.' In case using the word '*indra*' could mean the attribute-less (*nirguṇa*) *Brahmaṇ* instead of the one covered by *māyā*, sage Medhasa used the word '*sacipati*.' In the words of *Sānkhya* philosophy, '*sacipati*' refers to the persona reflected by the supreme principle. In the words of the *Bhāgabat Gitā,* it is the eternal being. In the language of *Vedānta,* it is root consciousness (*kūṭaśtha*). Many may think that this meaning given to the word *Sacipati* is contrived. But it may be seen in the references to the texts given above that the word '*indra*' refers to *Brahmaṇ*. The *śrutis* have used the word '*indra*' to mean *Brahmaṇ* in many places. Besides this, referring to the three worlds of *Sacipati* cannot mean *Indra*, because he is only the king of the gods, not of the three worlds. The king of the three worlds is *Īśvara*. The significance of the word '*triloka*' (three worlds) is threefold expression, material, subtle and causal. This threefold expression can be called the three worlds. The ruler of this threefold expression can only be the consciousness covered by *māyā*, *Brahmaṇ* with attributes.

We see in the mantra that the demons *Śumbha* and *Niśumbha* are both opposed to the gods. By their arrogance and strength, they have overtaken the three worlds and all the offerings of ceremonial worship. The word '*mada*' is arrogance or pride and '*vala*' is power or ability. The characteristics of ego and attachments are arrogance and power. It is natural for *Śumbha* and *Niśumbha* to have pride that all this universe resides in them. Those who think that they control this world put a high value on their power and abilities.

As few now understand the three worlds of *Sacipati* and the appropriation of the ceremonial offerings, we will give an idea of the meaning of this first mantra. This is a little difficult, so it is discussed in detail. The ruler of the three worlds, material, subtle and causal is *Sacipati*, the consciousness covered by *māyā*, not ego (*asmitā*). Ego is part of the intelligent principle, so it too is visibly inert, or illusory. Its nature is derived from that of consciousness, otherwise, there can be no separate nature of ego, cannot be. But *asmitā* is an *asura*. It sees itself as the great ruler. Thinking that this universe is situated in it, that it establishes everything, it cannot imagine that there is anything else that expresses it. So out of ignorance, it takes over the three worlds. Not only this, it takes over all ceremonial offerings. All varied acts that are being performed in the ceremonial house of this universe, it sees all of that and the results in itself. It sees everything in itself, saying everything is born of it, lives in it and dissolves in it. It does not understand that 'I' refers to the nondual nature of Self without 'I.' Because that which is properly 'I', that *paramātmā* is being discarded, that is, supreme Self is not accepted, only ego is reflected as Self. This is the mystery of the *asura Śumbha*. The ceremonial offerings mean divine nectar (*amṛta*). In the commentary of the *Upaniṣads*, Sankaracārya has given the meaning of the word '*amṛta*' as the results of actions. The ego nature *asura* sees in itself, all the results of action of ceremonial offerings or the divine nectar. So, the mantra says that he 'robbed the three worlds and ceremonial offerings.' This is made clear in the next mantra.

Verse 2.

tāveva sūryatāṁ tadvadadhikāraṁ tathaindavam|
kauberamatha yāmyañca cakrāte varuṇasya ca||

Verse 3.

tāveva pavanarddhiñca cakraturvahnikarma ca||

Translation:

The two demons usurped the rule of the Sun, Moon, *Kuvera*, *Varuṇa*, wind and fire.

Explanation:

When a spiritual seeker arrives at ego, it is perceived that the various gods are special expressions of oneself. (The principles of deities have been explained in detail in Volume Two.) The senses which are doorways to receiving things and the awareness established in them are arrays of ego. By the establishment of truth and life force in external things, a spiritual seeker arrives where things of form and flavor, or the eyes and other senses, or memory and imagination are not understood to be different from 'I.' They are all different expressions of 'I'. Even the distant Sun, Moon and stars reside in me. These spouse, children and family, this material body is enlivened by my spirit. I am expressed as all these multitudes. I perceive them, so they are here. They have no separate existence from my perception. I am their ruler, maintainer and destroyer. By proper effort and severe enterprise, a spiritual seeker reaches this divine arena. Alas! This too is of the nature of an *asura*, of ignorance; because that from which this universe appears, by which it is held, where it dissolves is not ego, it is *ātmā*, my Mother. Ego is also envisioned, it is animated by *ātmā*. But ego does not look at true spirit, thinking itself to be the ruler of this universe. It is an *asura*.

This condition may seem like the intellectualism of 'transience'. Some intellectuals say that 'there is no such separate thing as this universe that is perceptible; it is momentary intellect that appears as this visible universe.' Whatever that be, as long as a spiritual seeker is unable to grasp 'I', such errors are inevitable. This happens to most spiritual aspirants.

Let me clearly say that the word 'I' has two meanings. One is the verbal meaning (*vyācārtha*) the other is the directed meaning (*lakṣyārtha*). The perceptual, intellectual formed 'I' that is intimately united to me when we say 'I' is the verbal meaning. Whatever we do or think in the awakened, dreaming or dreamless states, are all united with a sense of 'I. The sense of 'I' mixed with all these perceptions is the verbal meaning of 'I.' It may be of concern that in dreamless sleep, we do not do anything or think of anything, so the sense of 'I' does not remain. In reality, it is not so. Even in dreamless sleep, the thought 'I do not know' remains. So, the knowledge that 'I am ignorant' remains. Whatever it is, 'I' that is intimately blended with perceptions in these three states is the verbal meaning of 'I.'

There is another meaning of 'I' that is the directed meaning. This is beyond all percept. It does not appear that there is, was or will be any relationship of it to perception. That there is a Self-formed 'I', beyond words and mind, is explained within this 'I' united with all percepts. So, 'I' points to this pure, perception form of *paramātmā*. Remember that the percept of 'I'-ness is also not there, because there is no you or they, a complete absence of visible or knowable things. What remains there though is by its nature 'I'. That is why, before this, I have explained the matter of Self as 'I' without 'I'-ness.

Let us try to understand this with an example. Someone says that there are a hundred elephants on the tip of a finger. Here, because it is impossible to have a hundred elephants on a fingertip, one understands it to be the piece of land pointed to by the finger. In the same manner, the perceived ego, pointed to by the word 'I' is not the proper Self (*ātmā*). Self expresses it. When a spiritual seeker thinks this ego to be Self, then it robs the glory of Self, the powers of Self, as the *asura Śumbha*. In this condition, the seeker believes that Self is without characteristics, finding or not finding it is the same. This ego is true God; all the characteristics of God are reflected here; what is the use of searching for Self that is inert, bereft of all percepts? In this manner, a seeker is cheated by ignorance, by demonic percepts. Maybe sometimes, leaving ego, trying to realize the principles of Self, one makes a faint discovery of a nature beyond perception. Then one understands that faint, inert perception to be the nature of *Brahmaṇ* beyond words and thought, and thinks that there is nothing more to see or understand. But alas, the seeker does not realize that this too is a perception of the *asura*.

The intellectual sheath or the intelligent principle that in previous chapters has been mentioned as a close refuge is here declared by the great sage Medhasa as an *asura*. When this great *asura Śumbha* together with his companions like *Niśumbha* are all destroyed, then only will the state as a worldly person properly end, the last roots of the tree severed. When this knot of intellect is pierced, beings arrive at the abode of bliss. It does not appear that this knot can be pierced by any spiritual effort other than the grace of the *guru* or Self. Here, all spiritual effort is based on the kind glance of Mother, or her strong attraction and affection.

We will discuss the matter of the *asura Śumbha* robbing the control of the gods. It has been mentioned in the mantra that *Śumbha* stole the control by the gods, the Sun, Moon, *Kuvera, Varuṇa*, the wind and fire. We have said that the special aspects of consciousness are the named gods. Now when ego is taken as *ātmā*, as God, then the divinities, that is awareness established on the senses are chastised or covered by ego. The gods are removed from their percepts of awareness and are reflected as part of visible and inert ego. Think of the Sun; it is the ruling deity of life force (*prāṇa*). The part of Self by which the specific perception of life force is expressed is the Sun-god (*Surya deva*). This specific perception of *ātmā* is the 'sun'-ness of the Sun. This perception of Self has been censured by *Śumbha*, the ego. The rights of the Sun god have been removed. One has to understand this about the other gods too. When inert ego understands itself to be *ātmā* or consciousness, then the Sun, Moon and other residing deities of life force, mind, etc. are overcome by inertness. This is the significance of *Śumbha* overcoming the rule by the deities.

---

tato devā vinirdhūtā bhraṣṭarājyāḥ parājitāḥ|

Verse 4.

hṛtādhikārāstridaśāstābhyāṁ sarve nirākṛtāḥ||
mahāsurābhyāṁ tāṃ devīṁ saṁsmarantyaparājitām||

Verse 5.

tayāsmākaṁ varo datto yathāpatsu smṛtākhilāḥ|
bhavatāṁ nāśayiṣyāmi tatkṣaṇāt paramāpadaḥ||

Translation:

Hereafter, the host of divinities, who had been driven away from their kingdoms and overpowered by the two great demons, began to pray to the undefeated goddess. Because (at the end of the battle with *Mahiṣāsura*), the goddess had given them an assurance that whenever any danger appeared, if they called on her, she would appear and remove their hazards.

Explanation:

Because of the torment by *Śumbha* and *Niśumbha*, the host of gods were tortured, defeated, frightened, had lost their kingdoms, and were without ownership. It has been said that the gods are specific expressions of consciousness. Consciousness is the power of awareness or Mother. The gods know that we are established on the lap of Mother, or in awareness. It is the nature of the gods to reside in the field of awareness or the kingdom of heaven. Now, ego has understood itself to be *ātmā*, so when the gods look at their ownership, they see that instead of being specifically expressed as consciousness, they appear as encirclements of ego. Ego is not proper awareness, so it cannot offer the gods any taste of awareness. The divine nectar, which the gods were consuming to be immortal, is now censured by inert ego. The gods are banished from the kingdom of heaven or the arena of spirit.

Let me say this more clearly. Whenever any matter of the senses like seeing and hearing takes place, this feeling of ego arises. The sense-based consciousness, even for a moment, cannot reside independently without leaving this ego, or 'I' natured *asura Śumbha*.

A spiritual seeker should see that in whatever condition one resides, there is the unbearable, subtle torment of this 'I' natured *asura Śumbha* towards sense-based consciousnesses. Even after understanding for a thousand times that 'there is nothing else but Mother', who knows from where this 'I' rises in the heart. Then there is an inseparable barrier between the two. Whether you practice meditation and concentration, or you are in a state of absorption, this subtle 'I', keeps you far away from the pure heart of Mother. You cannot remove this distance even after hundreds of attempts. Who will find, not only today but from what eternal times, this ego-natured *asura Śumbha* is sitting on the throne of your heart and driving you away from the kingdom of Self? This torment is always present in the heart of beings, but as long as one is engaged in removing the persecution by *Madhu*, *Kaitava* and *Mahiṣāsura*, that is by desire, anger and the other passions, one has no opportunity or power to pay attention to this. Until now, a spiritual seeker had understood that one was tormented by the attacks of *Madhu*, *Kaitava* and *Mahiṣāsura*. Now, by the grace of Mother and the selfless blessings of the *guru*, attacks by external enemies, the material senses have been quietened. One now has the opportunity to observe one's present condition with a calmer spirit.

The gods, laying eyes on their rights, see that the feelings of demons that had been tormenting them, for so long, were very elementary. Now they observe a subtler attack. This is the torment by intelligence or ego. Our proper privileges have been stolen. We were in the shelter of Self or the power of spirit. Alas! What do we now see? The inert 'I'-ness now appears to be our sole refuge. What can be more terrible than this?

Truly, this subtle 'I'-ness can be a terrible thing. What is this foe that does not die when killed? First, the material 'I'-ness based on the physical body, or the materialistic ego is weakened by bowing at the feet of the *guru* or by complete surrender. Then it is established in the thought-formed body (*manomaya koṣa*), or the subtle body. In this condition, much spiritual enterprise and worship are conducted. The ego that 'I am engaged in searching for God', 'I am a spiritual seeker' is slowly nurtured. Even if by the unconditional grace of the *guru* or by the incredible bravery of the seeker, this can be driven away, it is seen that this 'I', more powerful than before has taken shelter in the arena of intelligence. This is the great *asura Śumbha*. Destroying him is a difficult enterprise.

It will be seen later that the intelligence or intellect with which spiritual effort was being conducted, is also tainted by the sense of 'I.' From the beginning, the seeker has learned that Mother will not appear if 'I' does not disappear. So, one takes care to remove 'I.'

Being driven from the physical body, it crosses the borders of the senses and mind, to stand in the arena of intellect. Arriving here, a spiritual seeker sees that the 'I'-ness of the intellectual body is great and big, nearly like God. Much of the divine rights are within its grasp. It is not easy to get rid of. It is by this 'I'-ness that the kingdom of Self is chastised. At first, a spiritual seeker does not grasp that intelligence and intellect are also part of the inert or visible world. Only those who have pierced the knot of *Viṣṇu* can perceive the inertness of intelligence. Whatever it is, under this condition, the sense-based divinities of the seeker, with no other recourse, begin to pitifully call on the undefeated Goddess, the affectionate Mother. They appeal to the undefeated one.

One day, it is this Mother who had saved us from the powerful demon *Mahiṣāsura*. If we now seek her refuge to be relieved of the torment of the *asura Śumbha*, she will save us. Not only that, Mother had before this, told us, no, assured us, that whenever we were in trouble, we could call on her and she would appear and save us from all danger. So, what is there to fear? Come, let us also, like the gods, cry for Mother. Our pitiful cries will bring a flood of affection in the heart of Mother. The affectionate Mother will descend from the arena beyond words and thought and relieve us from this terrible danger. Mother will appear when we cry for her. Mother knew of our danger from before, so she began relief for the future. Knowing that we will have supreme danger, that is, that our supreme condition will be in danger, that we will be far from our supreme Self, Mother had assured us of relieving us. Come, let us all, with focused heart, call on Mother.

Verse 6.

iti kṛtvā matindevā himavantaṁ nageśvara|
jagmustatra tato devīṃ viṣṇumāyāṁ pratuṣṭuvuḥ||

Translation:

The gods, their intelligence stilled, in the manner mentioned, traveled to Himālayā, the king of mountains and began to sing praises to the goddess *Viṣṇumāyā*.

Explanation:

The spiritual mystery of the gods traveling to the Himālaya is the descent into the sense of the physical body. The sense of the physical body is the Himālaya mountains. (This was explained in Volume Two.) Realizing the torment of the demons in the intellectual sheath, the gods descend to the material, the sense of the physical body. One cannot call on Mother if one does not descend to the physical body. The singing of praises (*stava*) is function of the speech organs. Without a physical body, one cannot carry out any special spiritual practice like singing praises.

Let me here mention something else. The physical body is the arena of action. All acts are carried out based on the physical body. That is why it is called the arena of *dharma* or Kurukṣetra. Actions cannot be carried out with the subtle body. That is why such movement has to be created from actions by the physical body. As a result of it, one may cross the subtle arena and arrive at the pure, perception-natured arena of supreme Self. Those who pretend to be without action are surely cheated of the upward speed of spirituality. Whatever it is, one can see here that even the gods have to descend to the physical body to remember the undefeated one, that is, sing praises to Mother. That the singing of hymns is a great spiritual enterprise was mentioned in Volume Two in the explanation of the 'accolade by the gods.' The meaning of *Viṣṇumāyā* will be seen later.

Verse 7.

devā ūcuḥ
namo devyai mahādevyai śivāyai satataṁ namaḥ|
namaḥ prakītyai bhadrāyai niyatāḥ praṇatāḥ smatām||

Translation:

The gods said, "We bow down to the goddess. We always bow

down to the great goddess *Śivā*. We bow down to *bhadrā prakṛti*. Calmly, we bow down to her (one beyond words and thought).

Explanation:

Look. The gods, beginning to sing the praises of the goddess, saying '*namoḥ*' in the beginning, subdue their sense of 'I.' All of us know something about bowing down (*praṇām*). Children from Hindu households are used to this from childhood. First to our parents and other seniors, then to deities and temples. We think that by touching our hands to our forehead, or our head to the ground, or by laying down, we have accomplished *praṇām*. But is that correct? Have we ever discussed the principles of deep science *praṇām* is based on? There does not seem to be an easier way to lower the head of 'I'-ness than *praṇām*. The proud head of our sense of physical body does not bow down, so, night and day, we are slaves of worldly life and are tormented by sickness, sorrow, regret and poverty. Our countrymen are trampled on by all because they have forgotten the secret of *praṇām*. Those who know how to do *praṇām*, never bow their heads at the door of people. They do not appear at the door of people saying 'give me alms.'

To bow down in the best way is *praṇām*. The load of ignorance called 'I' that in the pride of knowledge, we raise our heads high with, lowering that sense of 'I', that load of ignorance in front of knowledge is proper *praṇām*. One who cannot lower this ignorance, and the inability, poverty and weakness closely allied to it at the feet of the knowledge-formed arbitrator of all, cannot do *praṇām*. This is why the Lord has said, 'know how to bow down, question and give service.'[6] One has to receive this three-fold knowledge of principles. Bowing down and removing control by the knowledge of 'I' is proper *praṇām*. As long as it does not occur, understand that one has not learned *praṇām*. So, I say to a spiritual seeker, before discussing the knowledge of *Brahmaṇ*, analyzing the principles of this universe, discovering the presence of Self, and other high-level words, for some time, just practice

6 *Bhāgavat Gitā*,4:34

praṇām. If after a lifetime of severe spiritual enterprise, one can bow down for one time, just once in life, if for a moment one can bow down, then life will be successful. The supreme goal of human life will be accomplished.

But how, can you do this? One may try to lower it, but the high head of 'I'-ness does not want to bow down. Try. Beginning with the smallest microbe to God. All are your teachers, all are your Mother and all are to be worshipped by you. In this manner, with a thousand heads, in a thousand ways, bow down to Mother. Do not be afraid. You do not have to become a lowly beggar to bow down. Instead, if you can bow down to the Lord of this universe in this manner, you will not have to bow your head down to anyone else. It is because you do not bow down to the Lord of this universe, that you have to knock on the doors of people, of material things, yet scarcity is not removed.

If one thinks calmly, one will understand how by bowing down, one can achieve progress in life. As soon as you bow down to somebody, there arises in you a sense of the teacher. (We are speaking about bowing down with respect and devotion; not about what is done to maintain civility.) The feeling that 'the one I bow down to, is greater than me', arises in our hearts. Together with this, the feeling that I am lower also arises. What happens as a result? In bowing down, you gain. On one side of your spirit, greatness appears, on the other, the ego is a little subdued. In this manner, the one you bow down to, may or may not benefit, but you gain much. Because, in bowing down in this fashion, the spirit is packed with high feelings and the great enemy ego is taken down.

In connection to this, let me say something here. Some modern people, proud of their Western education, think that accepting someone to be a teacher and bowing down as if to God is stupidity. Alas, they do not know that those who are truly trying to find God, have to take someone in human form as the *guru* or divinity. By direct worship, by bowing down with the perception of divinity, one subdues the sense of 'I.' This is a gate for entry to the spiritual kingdom. Just as when children learning the alphabet agree to the advice of a teacher without argument, so has a seeker traveling in the kingdom of Self, acknowledge one with human form to be divine and offer the great burden of 'I' stored over many lifetimes. This is the way to discover God. The *śrutis* say that those who have found a *guru* will know Self. We have to also say here that just receiving some special advice or initiation from a visionary person does not mean one has found a *guru*. One who in the heart is always aware the *guru* is divine and most desirable is rightly honored by finding a true *guru*. One who has found a right *guru* can have no fear or worries. To find such a *guru*, one has to first learn how to bow down.

The more innocent and natural is the manner in which one can learn *praṇām*, the faster and easier is one able to reach one's goal. This is the secret of *praṇām*; this is the greatness of it. So, before you begin to hear words of great principles, learn how to bow down with simplicity. Try to offer your 'I'-ness at the feet of the *guru*. Your life will turn blissful.

Whatever that is, let us now, like the gods saying, 'we bow down to the goddess, we always bow down to the great goddess', sing praises to Mother and offer our sense of ego at her feet.

namoh devai: we bow down to the goddess. The resplendent one, the playful one, the one who acts out creation-maintenance-dissolution, who is always expressed as the form of all beings in this world, we bow down to that eternal self-expressed physical form of Mother.

mahādevyai śivāyai satataṁ namaḥ: we bow down always to the great goddess *Śivā*. That which is subtler than this expressed universal form, the undefined subtle supreme power that covers this world, we bow to that great Goddess.

To bow down to the physical form, one needs external actions like touching the foreheads with the hands, so it may not be possible all the time. But the subtle, supreme universal form of Mother, can be bowed to by all knowingly or unknowingly at all times. Whatever actions that one carries out in the awake, sleep or dream state, are for the worship or *praṇām* to that supreme power. So, one bows down to her always. Today we knowingly bow down to the beneficial great goddess who is to be bowed to at all times. Mother accept our *praṇām*.

namaḥ prakītyai bhadrāyai: We bow down to the beneficial *prakṛti* (nature) *Bhadrā*. What is the causal behind the before mentioned material and subtle, that root nature formed Mother is *Bhadrā*, who is beneficial to the children. It is by her grace that beings go beyond nature, and the material and subtle, to the great arena of liberation. One cannot bow down all the time to this *Bhadrā* nature because she is nonmanifest. Some lucky seekers find her and bow down to her.

niyatāḥ praṇatāḥ smatām: We control ourselves and bow down to her. Completely controlling the senses, we bow down to the one who is beyond words and mind. What she is cannot be expressed by language, conceived by the mind, understood by intelligence. The one beyond the material, subtle and causal, we bow to that unknowable Mother.

We see in this mantra, that the gods, saying '*namo devai*', bow down to the material form of Mother. With '*mahādevyai śivāyai satataṁ namaḥ*' they bow down to the subtle form of Mother. With '*namaḥ prakītyai bhadrāyai*' they bow to the causal form and with '*niyatāḥ praṇatāḥ smatām*' they bow to the one beyond the material, subtle and causal, the one without characteristics (*nirguṇa*). One cannot get even a hint of that form without controlling the senses. So, in bowing down to her, having to control the senses, the word '*niyatā*' is used.

This chapter is about bowing down; only *praṇām*, only *praṇām*. Come let us practice *praṇām* all the time.

Verse 8.

raudrāyai namo nityāyai gauryai dhātryai namo namaḥ|
jyotsnāyai cendurūpiṇyai sukhāyai satataṁ namaḥ||

Translation:

We bow down to *Raudrā* the fiery one. We bow down over and over again to the eternal fair one *Gourī* and the nurturer *Dhātrī*. We always bow to the Moon and the Moonlight formed Mother, the one who is always happy.

Explanation:

Roudrā: The power of *Rudra,* is the great destructive force. One cannot reside for long with Mother mentioned in the previous mantra, who is beyond the three attributes. In a moment, one has to descend to the perception of this world. In descending from that arena without attributes, to the perception of this world, one first remembers the static (*tāmasa*) form of Mother. Because it is by way of this *tāmasa* form that one has to land on the spirit of this world. That is why the gods saying '*roudrāyai namo*', bow down first to the destructive power of *Rudra*. Behind all the feelings overcome by destruction, what is realized is eternal. It does not increase, decrease or degrade. Then, in that eternal thing, one observes the appearance of right attribute (*sattva*). That nature is beautiful. So, Mother is here called *Gourī*, the fair one. Then appears the form of the one who nourishes this world, so she is the nurturer (*dhātrī*). After this, one bows down to Mother in the form of moonlight and the Moon. The Moon (*Indu*) is mind, and moonlight is its extension or directional spirit, all illuminated matters of this world. (It has been said before that the mind and materials of this world are the same.) In this manner, to those, who can bow to Mother or see her through all perceptions, under all conditions, she appears in the form of happiness, '*sukhāyai satataṁ namaḥ*.'

'That which is immensity (*bhumā*) is happiness.[7]' What is great is happiness. When Mother imagines herself as mind and time, she is expressed as the Moon and moonlight, her nature as happiness is especially expressed. Happiness is the experience of greatness. On the other hand, what is neither atomic nor great, although of the nature of happiness, cannot be enjoyed as there is

7 '*yo vai bhumā tat sukham*' *Chandogya Upaniṣad*, 7.23.1

no separation between the enjoyer and enjoyed. So, to specifically enjoy happiness, one has to experience greatness. When Mother imagines herself to be the great mind, that is, when beings arrive at Godhood, then they can taste this supreme nature of immense happiness. Worldly persons only get a taste of small joys through the materials of the senses. So, knowingly or unknowingly, all look for happiness and serve it. All beings bow down to it always. Pointing to this, the gods say '*sukhāyai satataṁ namaḥ.*' Such an interpretation may also be made.

Whatever it is, spiritual seekers perceive Mother level by level. First in the form of the material world, then as the subtle supreme power, then as the nonmanifest seed or causal form and finally as the one beyond attributes, as pure spirit. This mantra describes how seekers go down from nature without attributes. From it, they first descend to the destructive power of *Roudrī* and at the same time, realize the eternal state with the arousal of the right principle (the form as *Gourī*), then as the seed of this universe (as *Dhātrī*), then as mind and materials (this is the Moon and moonlight), the things of this world. Then, whether as the perception of this universe or as beyond this universe, discovering the undivided spirit of happiness inside and out, perceiving the spirit of happiness in the manifest and non-manifest, in material and subtle, the seeker is honored to say, 'we bow down to the spirit of happiness.'

We are always searching for happiness. Holding on to a false belief that there is no happiness without desire and wealth we are running after happiness like a thirsty deer. In the service and saving of desire and wealth you have been much wounded, but have you found happiness? No, you have not. You have not understood this thing called happiness. First, look on the one who is the spirit of happiness, then not only from desire and wealth, but you will taste immense happiness even from the dust of this Earth. How much longer will you live in error? Come and find happiness, you will be pleased. You will in joy, like the gods say, 'we bow down always to the one who is happiness' (*sukhāyai satataṁ namaḥ*). Look, the gods are saying this even though they have been defeated and have lost heaven. You have to be like this. Even if this universe is destroyed, say '*sukhāyai satataṁ namaḥ.*' When you have control of all this universe, say '*sukhāyai satataṁ namaḥ*', because, there is nothing else but happiness. Not understanding that what you think to be unhappiness is nothing but happiness, you run from fear of unhappiness and blindly search for happiness. Come here, you can find happiness, eternal happiness, unchanging happiness which is never unsatisfying, to bring complete satisfaction. What would you want?

Verse 9.

kalyāṇyai praṇatā vṛīddhyai siddhyai kurmo namo namaḥ|
nairṛtyai bhūbhṛtāṁ lakṣmyai sarvāṇyai te namo namaḥ||

Translation:

We bow down to the blessed one, *Kalyāṇī*, we bow down to Mother who is growth and the nature of success. You are *Nairṛtī*, *Lakṣmī* of the *bhūbhṛīt* and *Sarvāṇī*, we bow down to you repeatedly.

Explanation:

The one who brings good fortune is *Kalyāṇī*. If you can bow down once to joy-formed Mother, there is nothing that can be misfortune. Then, wherever seekers lay their eyes, they see good fortune. Those to whom Mother appears in the form of good fortune, for them, growth or emergence, success (*siddhi*) and fulfillment of goals are inevitable. In this manner, whether in this material world or the arena of spiritual effort, Mother emerges as growth and success. So, a spiritual seeker cannot but bow down to her. When worldly ascent or success of goals happens to common beings, they do not or cannot notice that it is only Mother who appears as growth and success. So, very soon, they lose these things. Mother, to bring the light of knowledge to her children, appears to them as an adverse controlling figure. Then she is called *Nairṛtī*, the demoness (*rākṣasī*). When Mother sits with her children on her lap in the form of a demoness, then their behavior becomes that of demons. On the lap of the demoness form of Mother, desires for material things of the children are not curbed. They derive great pleasure from their animal tendencies of eating, sleeping, fear and so on. The *Bhāgavat Gitā* has said, 'those who ignore my human form, they find demonic natures.' We see that on one hand, Mother manifests in her beneficial form and offers growth and success. On the other, she appears as the demoness *Nairṛtī* and nurtures demons. Only in the indefinable Mother is it possible for such opposite tendencies to reside together. Mother, we bow down to you again and again.

bhūbhṛītāṁ lakṣmyai: some have given the meaning of this as the royal *Lakṣmī*. We have no conflict with them. It is only Mother who appears in the form of royal beauty. But Mother, by your grace, we find another meaning in this. The word '*bhu*' means the principle of earth and '*bhṛt*' means one who bears. Those that bear the earth principle, that is, cover the sense of self with the earth principle, are *bhūbhṛīt*. So '*bhūbhṛtāṁ lakṣmyai*' means the presiding consciousness of those who are beings with pride for their physical bodies. The word *Lakṣmī* means beauty or wealth. Awareness (*cit*) is proper beauty. As long as consciousness is expressed in beings, they appear as beautiful. On the other hand, dressing a corpse with fine clothing and ornaments will not make it attractive. That is why one uses the term '*Śrī*' signifying *Lakṣmī*, before the name of a living person. So I say, Mother, you appear as consciousness, as life force, as *Lakṣmī* to beings proud of their material form. Mother, this is your form as *bhūbhṛt Lakṣmī*. As *Sarvāṇī*, as the power of the god of dissolution *Śiva*, you hold everyone in a grasp of destruction. Mother, in this way, on one side you are *bhūbhṛt Lakṣmī*, that is you appear as the consciousness of beings in hundreds of births, and then in the form of *Sarvāṇī* send everyone into the terrible grip of death. On one side, as *Kalyāṇī* you bring growth and success, on the other, as *Nairṛtī* you are of the form of life and death of worldly existence. We bow down to your two opposing forms.

The word '*te*' in this mantra means 'to you.' One cannot use 'to you' if one does not see Mother in front of oneself. So, it is of concern, that those who are not established in truth can be capable of easily understanding this principle.

Verse 10.

durgāyai durgapārāyai sārāyai sarvakāriṇyai|
khyātyai tathaiva kriṣṇāyai dhūmrāyai satataṁ namaḥ||

Translation:

We bow down always to *Durgā*, to *Durgapārā, Sārā Sarvvakāriṇī, Khyāti, Kriṣṇā* and *Dhumrā*.

Explanation:

Mother, you are *Durgā*. The nature of your principles is difficult to understand. As long as there is the perception of knower and known, until then, one does not understand your true nature. You are *Durgapār*ā. You take us across this fortress (*durga*), this worldly existence. As long as one does not seek shelter in you who is the one beyond all perceptions, one cannot be saved from this arduous worldly life. Again, your nature that appears in all the perceptions of this world, is restless, changeable and insensate. But, you are sensate, the form of stillness. The tranquil spirit on which this varied, restless universe is established is also you. So, you are *sārā*, that is eternal, the form of *sadcidānanda*.

Mother, you are the cause behind all things (*sarvvakāriṇī*). You express all percepts of creation-maintenance-dissolution of this universe, so when one says *Sarvvakāriṇī*, only your form as the supreme goddess comes to mind. Those who say that you who is the form of the power of awareness is by nature without attributes, and cannot be the cause behind anything, that *māyā* is the universal cause, see you separate from *māyā*. In practice, this uniqueness is rejected. One can try to save uniqueness by saying that *māyā* is without spirit, undefined, and the nature of ignorance, but can it free anyone from doubt? The modern world searches for logic. What cannot be accepted by logic and argument, even if it be the words of the *Vedas*, is not accepted gladly. That is why today we try to understand you with the yardstick of our divided knowledge. Mother, I have said before (in Volume Two) that I do not have the audacity to believe that just by discussing you, I will understand you or make anyone else understand you. Discovering you, understanding you, does not transpire by anything other than your grace. Then why do I still discuss it? There is an advantage. At least, sluggishness of tongue and murkiness of intelligence may improve.

Come spiritual seeker, let us try to understand what Mother is. Bliss is the nature of Mother. The *śrutis* say that the nature of *Brahmaṇ* is nothing else but bliss. All beings have some notion of bliss. When one acquires things of desire in this world, for a moment, a feeling of bliss appears in the heart. Try to remember that feeling. That moment of bliss is a 'bliss because of', that is, it is a momentary change in the spirit because of the connection with material things. That the bliss from material things is a hint of the bliss of spirit has been mentioned before in Volumes One and Two. Whatever that is, if you could be taken to a state, where there is no connection with material things, no thoughts, no worries, no refusal or receiving, no hearing or seeing, but only bliss, then the spirit that you would land on, understand that to be the nature of Mother. Try to go forward calmly. Bliss is a feeling or perception. When our feeling appears as only the spirit of bliss, then we can perceive this thing called bliss. It is of the nature of perception. There are no divisions in the nature of bliss. That is, there is no other thing that can be called bliss. There is no perception that there is anything that is or can be that is separate from this bliss. There is no separation within it, that is, there is no separation of enjoyer and enjoyed within it. Only bliss, only bliss, pure bliss. This is what the *śrutis* have called 'one without a second.' The other name for this bliss is love (*prema*) or nectar. The gods have indicated this to be 'that which is nectar'[8]. Here there is no division between love, lover and beloved. No difference between enjoyer, enjoyment and enjoyed. Only love, only nectar. How can I express this in language? Oh! It is beyond words. It is beyond understanding. Still, we have to try to understand. From time

8 *'raso vai sah' Taittiriya Upaniṣad*, 2:6

immemorial there has been this attempt to understand. The *Vedas* said 'not sound, not touch, not form, not material, not large, not small' and tried to explain it by negatives. Remember, this is the nature of my Mother without attributes (*nirguṇa*). Here there is no other attribute but bliss. Here Mother is pure and eternal.

It is in this pure nature of Mother without attributes, that the two-fold nature of Mother is revealed; one is Godhood the other is that of a worldly person. Of these two, we will first discuss the supremacy of the Godhood of Mother. The *Upaniṣad* says, 'only from bliss do all beings appear[9]' and so on. All beings arise from bliss, they reside in bliss and only in bliss do they disappear. A doubt may arise here. The bliss that has been said to be only happiness, or without any percept, without attributes, and this bliss which is the cause of creation-maintenance-dissolution of this universe, are they the same or different? In response to this concern, some say that what you call bliss without attributes is just words, because bliss cannot be without attributes. The word '*nirguṇa*' (without attributes), means attributes without distinctions. Bliss is an attribute or characteristic, like the sun and its rays they are both the same and different. Others say that bliss is the power of delight (*hlādinī*). The one with this power is God. So, bliss cannot be God. In this way, many different doctrines are prevalent. The solution to all these doctrines is simple. If we take all these that people say are true, then there is no conflict, because one cannot define what *Brahmaṇ* is. It is complete, one cannot imagine any incompleteness in it. So, whatever anyone says about it is true. In whatever manner *Brahmaṇ* is expressed to someone, so is the language that appears. Even if someone says that there is no *Brahmaṇ*, that also is true because here it is expressed in its form as 'not being.' It is the specialty of *Brahmaṇ* that one cannot acknowledge it. Not only is it beyond one's capacity and denial, but it is also the only vessel bearing the opposing characteristics of light and darkness, knowledge and ignorance, *vidyā* and *avidyā*, with and without attributes, sorrow and joy. These opposing characteristics can reside together only in *Brahmaṇ*. Another

9 *Taittiriya Upaniṣad,* 3.6.1

specialty that was mentioned before is this, even though these characteristics are always expressed in *Brahmaṇ*, they are no hindrance to its pure nature. The purely blissful form of *Brahmaṇ* can keep its purity intact in all cases and appear simultaneously as God and worldly being. This is the nature of *Brahmaṇ*.

Now let us try to understand how this bliss-natured substance without attributes can express itself as God or one with all characteristics. Can you say that this bliss without attributes does not or cannot have something called perception? Can it be that there is bliss but no perception? If you say that accepting such power in something without attributes, makes such bliss seem to be self-divided, that is not so. When bliss expresses and perceives itself, there is no perception of any divisiveness of enjoyer and enjoyed. So, one can say that in that pure bliss, there is no perception of enjoyer and enjoyed.

Let me say something else here. Even if you have some doubt, even then agree that there is something that is pure bliss without attributes in which there are no divisions. Ācārya Śankara in balancing something with and without attributes had to use the term 'indefinable.' The use of this word signifies agreement. Lord Gouranga using the term 'divided-undivided beyond comprehension' (*acintya vedāveda*), indirectly expressed this agreement. If you can agree to this now, or if you wish to find it through the scriptures and by the directions of a *guru*, then by grace, you will one day understand that bliss can be without attributes.

It has been said in Volumes One and Two, that undivided knowledge and supreme energy are nondifferent. Knowledge is energy or energy is knowledge. Those who have not understood this properly, may not be able to grasp this principle of bliss.

What you have understood before to be pure knowledge, now try to understand that it is not just knowledge, but bliss. Awareness (*cit*) is not just awareness, its nature is bliss. When we say bliss, the percept of bliss and its spirit are perceived together. This perception is awareness (*cit*) and its spirit is existence (*sat*). So, in defining the meaning of the word 'bliss' (*ānanda*), one finds that existence, awareness and bliss (*sat*, *cit*, *ānanda*) is the same gentity with three names. This has been said many times before. Where this bliss resides in its nature, when it is pure, even then, there is awareness or the power of perception and spirit in it. When the power of perception or expression of consciousness, without which there is no discernment of bliss, is especially manifest, then on the sides, doer and action are seen. That is, perception, the perceiver and the matter of perception, these three feelings are expressed. Even though these three are expressed in bliss, there is no alteration in it. One bliss perceives itself. That is, when bliss perceives itself, then in one with no second, self-difference is noticed, and these are known as the right, active and static tendencies (*sattva*, *rājasa* and *tāmasa*). The first pulsation of *sadcidānanda* is existence (*sat*) or *sattva*, the enjoyer of bliss, the second pulsation is awareness (*cit*) or *rājasa*, the power of perception of bliss and the third pulsation of bliss is *tāmasa* or the perceived form of bliss. Remember that even if these specificities are expressed, the form of bliss remains pure.

You can name it 'I', no not 'I', say *ātmā*. The author of the *Pañcadaśi* says, 'this knowledge natured *ātmā* is the receptacle of love.' Because it is the receptacle of love, *ātmā* is of the nature of bliss. The one who is the supreme source of love, the one who we love the most, for the pleasure of who we bear this burden of being for lifetimes and can forsake this world, how can I express in words, how densely blissful its nature is?

Whatever it is, when *ātmā* perceives itself in the aforementioned manner, it is said to be with attributes (*saguṇa*). In the language of the philosophers—this can be, distortion, result, transformation, error, imagination or assignment. Whatever you may call it, nothing is lost. Only understand that with or without attributes, both are true and one without attributes becomes one with attributes. Even if it comes with attributes a thousand times, there is no change in its form without attributes, it remains intact. When cotton is transformed by name and form, into thread or cloth, there is no change to its nature as cotton. When gold is changed into bangles and earrings, its nature as gold remains intact. When water is changed into oceans, rivers and ponds, there is no change in its nature as water. When a snake is coiled into a spiral, it remains a snake. When an oyster shell appears to be like silver, it remains an oyster shell, it does not turn into silver. When space is confined inside pots and containers, it remains unspecified space.

Look. When bliss perceives itself or envisions itself, it is with characteristics. *Vedānta* calls this a superposition of illusion (*māyā*). It is called a relationship with nature (*prakṛti*) by *Sānkhya*. The *Upaniṣads* have indicated this spirit with attributes as *ātmā* or *Brahmaṇ*. In this bliss with attributes, the perception of multiplicity is also expressed. Do not ask why or how. Understand it to be divine play or wish. I am of the nature of bliss. Enjoying myself as One feeling bliss, when I wish to enjoy myself as many, then I am called God (*Īśvara*). The perception of 'One becoming many' is called God. When in this bliss formed *ātmā*, the origin, residence and dissolution of many perceptions occur, it is called *Īśvara*. You may ask, 'Is *Brahmaṇ* without bliss? Why does it find bliss in multiplicity?' No, that is not so. The nature of *Brahmaṇ* is bliss, there is never any lack of bliss in it. But, just as its oneness and uniqueness are true and natural, so is its multiplicity or Godhood in its viewing of this universe. Just as *Brahmaṇ* is without attributes in its state beyond this universe, in a state of viewing this universe it is with attributes, yet holds on to both its natures, with and beyond attributes. One is not changed or damaged by the other. When this supremely loving, blissful *ātmā*, enjoys itself by dividing up, then it is *Īśvara*. If we remember this, we can understand the supremacy of *ātmā* as God.

There is another pre-eminence in Self (*ātmā*) and that is the state as general beings. The great statements in the *śrutis*, 'you are that', 'everything is *Brahmaṇ*', 'Self is all', and 'it is everything', establish that worldly persons are completely non-different from *Brahmaṇ*. What are they? They are the individual expressions of the bliss of *Īśvara*, that is the bliss of the expressed totality. The One in the many are beings. Therefore, beings are by nature nothing but bliss. Remember the examples of water and cotton given before. Just as the waves in the ocean are nothing but water, just as the cloth built of thread is nothing but cotton, beings with different names and forms are nothing but bliss. In this manner, different kinds of beings, placental, born from eggs, microbial or plant-like, are created from the bliss of God, reside in it and disappear in it. So, bliss is the nature of beings. Now, think and see that *ātmā*, Mother is only bliss, as the cause of everything, it is the bliss of God, and as all beings, the bliss of all beings.

Look and see where you have reached. What in Volume One, you understood to be existence (*sat*) or truth, you understood in Volume Two to be life force or awareness (*cit*). Now you can see that what is life force (*prāṇa*) is supreme love, the nature of supreme bliss, Self (*ātmā*). You have arrived from bliss, every mark of you is bliss. Every atom in your body is nothing but bliss. Bliss is your constituent, bliss is your nature and you are established in bliss. All around you, above and below, there is nothing but bliss. Every thought inside you is blissful, your birth and death are bliss. Your sickness and grief are bliss. Your sorrow and poverty are bliss. Look at the tree standing in front of you. It is formed of bliss. A dense spirit of bliss has taken the form of a tree. Look at an inert piece of rock; it is your blissful Self that appears as a piece of rock. Your spouse, children and relatives that you think to be separate entities from you, see that they are your many formed spirits of bliss. Your bliss appears as these figures of joy. Wherever you look, whatever you receive by your senses, all are bliss. The earth and five elements, the five matters of the senses, the Sun, Moon and stars, are all nothing but supremely loving, supremely blissful Self. If you do not taste the bliss-filled nature of this Self, your life will be incomplete. You are immersed in an ocean of bliss, you are serving bliss night and day, yet you are blindly searching for bliss. The moment that you discover this bliss-filled form, from that moment, this world will appear to you as bliss formed. Then, your desire to specifically enjoy this world will disappear.

Let me say this more clearly. If you rightly understand that bliss is your nature, will you collect or enjoy objects of desire to find bliss any longer? Never. Renunciation will appear naturally. When you properly understand that it is the bliss-filled 'I' that is expressed everywhere as material things, then there will be no more reception or rejection. Then one can learn to move in the joy of material things without discrimination. Recall the words of the *Gitā*, 'free from aversion and attraction, moving in the objects of the senses'[10]. Whatever it is, in discussing the principles of bliss, we have moved far away from our subject matter. Come, let us in tune with the gods, saying '*sārāyai sarvakāriṇyai*' bow down at the feet of the blissful Mother. *Ātmā*, the blissful Mother in the form of my awareness without attributes is expressed in the form of the Goddess of all causes.

khyātyai tathaiva kriṣṇāyai dhūmrāyai satataṁ namaḥ–: Other than fame or eminence, the word '*khyāti*' means the establishment of conscience (*viveka khyāti*). A firm perception of the difference between *prakṛti* and *puruśa*, or between the inert and the conscious, has been called *viveka-khyāti* in *Sānkhya* philosophy. It seems that *Sānkhya* philosophers have called Nature (*prakṛti*) inert. In fact, it is not so. Nature is not inert, it is a perception of inertness in consciousness. Inertness is but a perception (*bodha*). Perception is not inert but conscious. Not only is it conscious, bliss is its true nature. We have said, how that which is blissful, without attributes, takes on the percept of things with attributes, that is, is expressed as formed by *sattva*, *rājasa* and *tāmasa*. The three attributes (*guṇas*) are the spirit of Nature. Realizing that bliss is shaped into the three attributes, is the conscience of *prakṛti* and *puruśa* or *viveka-khyāti*.

Mother, it is you who express yourself as fame (*khyāti*). When you, the pure, blissful *puruśa*, perceive yourself, then you are called *prakṛti*. You are the proper realization of this principle of *prakṛti* and *puruśa*. This realization is fame or establishment of conscience. Mother, we bow down to you as the establishment

---

10 *Bhāgavat Gitā*, 2:64

of conscience. Again, opposing this fame, *Krișṇā*, the ignorant-natured dark form is also you. Wherever we see that perceptions do not arise, nothing arises after spiritual effort, the nature of Self as bliss does not appear, then we understand that you reside in your ignorant natured dark form. Mother, we bow down to *Krișṇā*.

Between these two forms of *Khyāti* and *Krișṇā* you have another form that is *Dhumrā* (murky). In this form, appears a nature of ignorance, slightly tinged by knowledge. Mother, whenever we see that some of your children are experts in explaining your nature as expounded in the *Vedas*, skilled in analyzing the principles of the states with and without attributes, are well versed in the scriptures, yet completely deprived of any perception of your blissful nature, we understand that you hold them to you in your murky form, with that form of ignorance tinged by knowledge. We bow down to your incredible form as *Dhumrā*.

We see that you hold all beings to yourself in your forms as *Khyāti*, *Krișṇā* and *Dhumrā*. When we accept material things, then these three forms are specially expressed. 'I know this' is the nature of accepting things. In this, 'I' am the form of *Khyāti*, 'know' the form of *Dhumrā*, and 'this' is the form of *Krișṇā*. These three forms of you are expressed everywhere. We bow down to your three forms with devotion.

Verse 11.

atisaumyātiraudrāyai natāstasyai namo namaḥ|
namo jagatpratișṭhāyai devyai kṛtyai namo namaḥ||

Translation:

We bow down to a very placid and a very angry form. Then we bow to that beyond these two, beyond words and thought. We bow repeatedly to the creator Mother and the goddess *Kṛti*.

Explanation:

Mother, before this, we have seen your opposing forms as *Khyāti* and *Krișṇā*. They are here called very placid (*atisoumya*) and very enraged (*atiroudra*) and are being addressed by the gods. Mother, on one side you are very calm, a loving, happy, kind Mother, on the other you are very angry, appearing in your terrible dark form as *Kriṣṇā*. Mother, in this visible world we often see the play of both your forms. What do we see? On one side, you appear in your angry form as famine, plague, and floods, driving your children to extreme sorrow. On the other side, you appear as mercy in the hearts of your children and bring help in your very placid form. You appear to remove their sorrows. Mother, wherever we look, we see your terrible form and your form of mercy. Mother, on one hand, being pained by the atheism and unruly behavior of your children, you appear as punishment and control. On the other hand, you appear as the form to remove pain and wipe the tears of your children. This is your motherhood. All over this world, we see this play of your motherhood.

Where does one go to look for Mother? What spiritual exercise, devotion, yoga or austerity will you carry out to see Mother? If you have to undertake such labor to see Mother, her name will be defamed. Wherever you look, the form of Mother is completely illuminated. There is a saying, 'those who cannot see Mother with eyes open, will never see her even with a thousand eyes.' Truly, Mother is simple and straightforward. When beings can truly see Mother everywhere like the gods and bow down to her, then they can in tune with the gods, say, 'we bow down to her in the form beyond words and thought.' Do not disagree with this. Where is bliss in this terrible form? If you have vision, you will see where there is bliss. Bliss is spirit. It is bliss that appears as happiness and sorrow. Look from the point of view of beings. When they weep, they find a trace of bliss in it, so they weep. They find bliss through sorrow and poverty, so they suffer. This has been discussed in more detail in the book 'Sorrow and Peace' (*Śok-Śānti*). Remember that just as bliss formed Self appears in the laughter of beings, so does it in tears. Although to see or understand the bliss within tears, one has to have the eyes of a yogi or the grace of Mother. But that is something else.

What stages one has to pass to understand these placid,

terrible and unthinkable forms of Mother, is declared in the other half of the mantra. '*namo jagatpratiṣṭhāyai devyai kṛtyai namo namaḥ*.' The word '*pratiṣṭā*' means refuge. One first has to bow down to, or understand and realize the refuge of this universe, that is, the cause and constituent form of the conscious bliss formed spirit. Then one has to pay attention to the Goddess as *Kṛti*, that is the power of action that shapes the divided world from undivided bliss. Come let us also bow down to the non-different cause and constituent form of Mother. Then let us bow repeatedly to the Goddess as *Kṛti*, the supreme power of creation-maintenance-dissolution

---

Verse 12.

yā devī sarvabhūteṣu viśṇumāyeti śabditā|
namastasyai namastasyai namastasyai namo namaḥ||

Translation:

We bow down to the Goddess who is known as the *māyā* of *Viṣṇu* in all elements, we bow down to her, we bow down to her, we bow down to her over and over again.

Explanation:

Viṣṇumāyā: The universal, supreme power of stability. The meaning of the word '*devī*' is the manifest, self-expressed, supreme force of awareness. When the formerly mentioned silent, untouched, unformed, undefined nature of bliss, is formed into all elements, expresses itself as all elements, sees, feels and perceives, then it is called the *māyā* of *Viṣṇu*. We bow down to that Mother who is the *māyā* of *Viṣṇu*, who in the material world, appears in the shape of all beings. After this, we bow down to *Viṣṇumāyā* Mother who in the subtle form is expressed as the divine supreme power. Then we bow down to the causal form of *Viṣṇumāyā* who is beyond the material and subtle. Finally, we bow down repeatedly to Mother who is beyond the material, subtle and causal, unseen by words and thoughts.

From here, each mantra in the praise applies the word

'*namastasyai*' three times. Other than this, the terms '*namo namaḥ*' is also added. With the first '*namastasyai*', we bow down to the physical form, that is, our respects are directed to the material expression of Mother. In this case, the *praṇām* is expressed verbally and physically. Then the second '*namastasyai*' is directed to the subtle form of Mother. It is directed to the subtle power of awareness that appears on the material plane and takes on a specific name and form. This second is the subtle state of *praṇām*. It is called a bowing down of the mind. Then the third '*namastasyai*', is bowing down to the causal form. This third *praṇām* is directed at that causal nature of Mother, the primal cause from which the material and the subtle are expressed. This bowing down occurs in the causal body. Although causal spirit is seated in the principle of intelligence, this *praṇām* is expressed by intelligence, directed at the causal form beyond intellect. So, this is called a *bouddha praṇām*.

The fourth *praṇām* is '*namo namaḥ*.' This is expressed in the pure arena of perception of the loving *paramātmā* beyond the material, subtle and causal. Although here there is no three-fold separation of receiver, supplicant and *praṇām*, those who are from the beginning, surrendered seekers, arrive in this nondual state and still say '*namo namaḥ*.' In surrender, they merge into the supreme love of the supreme bliss of *paramātmā*. This is the fourth, or *turiya praṇām*.

In this manner, those who are able to bow down, paying attention to the material, subtle, causal and state beyond, are truly gods. It may be because the host of gods, tormented by *Śumbha* and *Niśumbha*, could bow down in this manner, that Mother soon appeared on the battlefield and destroying the demons, protected them. A spiritual seeker has to practice in the same manner. One has to practice *praṇām* keeping one's attention to the four states. Focusing the power of spiritual enterprise in that direction, one can, like the gods be freed from all torment by demons.

The ancient scriptures describe four levels of liberation, *sālokya, sāmīpya, sārūpya* and *sāyujya*. Going beyond inertness and reaching the level of consciousness is *sālokya*. Getting near the unified consciousness in which it is situated is *sāmīpya*. Alighting on the subtle causal formed center from which this is expressed, is named *sārūpya*. A spiritual seeker arriving here becomes one with it. There is still distinctiveness here. Then there is *sāyujya*. In this condition, there is no distinction. Beings alight on the undivided nature of consciousness. Another name for it is *nirvāṇa*. In your daily practice, you have to give attention to these four conditions. In the four *praṇāms*, there are indications of keeping attention to these four conditions. Those who are unable to give attention to the four states should try to give attention to at least two or three of them. This is proper spiritual enterprise. Every day, one has to taste a tiny fragment of liberation. Only this will give a taste of freedom from the state of being.

In the next mantras, there is no need to explain this portion about *namastasyai*. The smart reader will easily understand it. Although in the division of the 'seven hundred' verses, the last part '*namastasyai namo namaḥ*' is defined as a separate mantra, there is no harm in separating the last '*namo namaḥ*' from the third '*namastasyai*' as a fourth *praṇām*. The third *praṇām* is aimed at the causal form. When one reaches the causal state, it is easy to enter the state beyond it. So, it is being said that one enters the state beyond the causal one saying '*namo namaḥ*.'

Verse 13.

yā devī sarvabhūteṣu chetanetyabhidhīyate|
namastasyai namastasyai namastasyai namo namaḥ||

Translation:

We bow down to the Goddess who is consciousness in all beings, we bow down to her, we bow down to her, we bow down to her repeatedly.

Explanation:

In the material plane, consciousness is expressed in the form of names. In the subtle, it appears as life force and in the causal, it is nonmanifest. Material consciousness is this world (*viśva*), the subtle one is *taijasa* and the causal is known as *prājña*.

Consciousness formed Mother, as the consciousness of this world, you are expressed every day, taking the names and forms of this world. We offer our physical and verbal *praṇām* to this material, conscious form. Then, the supreme power that is called *taijasa* consciousness that is always engaged in creation-maintenance-dissolution of this universe, to that subtle, divine form of power, we offer our mental *praṇām*. Beyond that, what resides as the seed of the material and subtle, eternally as the causal, that intellectual, conscious form of yours that is nonmanifest, we offer *praṇāms* with our intellect. Finally, that pure, consciousness, that is beyond words and thought, beyond the material, subtle and causal, to that eternal, supreme nature, saying '*namo namoḥ*', we merge into that sweet, loving nature of Self.

A spiritual seeker should see that the one who appears in the heart as consciousness is Mother. The one you ignore all the time, look, the gods are bowing down to that Mother who appears as consciousness in all beings. You should also, in tune with the gods, paying close attention to the consciousness of Self, bow down, saying '*namastasyai.*' May your physical and verbal *praṇām* be worthy. Understand that this consciousness in the heart appears as a physical body, as a sense of body. Offer your first *praṇām* to it. Then perceive that all-pervading, sentient Mother, resides as the ruler of all perceptions, saying '*namastasyai*' offer her your second *praṇām*. Next, attend to the very subtle condition, in nonmanifest causal consciousness, where there is no variety of name and form. Offer her your third *praṇām* from intelligence. Keeping your attention on this causal state, by the grace of Mother, you will find her state beyond the causal. Keeping your focus on this pure state, saying '*namo namoḥ*', you will merge into nectar formed spirit.

Verse 14.

yā devī sarvabhūteṣu buddhirūpeṇa saṁsthitā|
namastasyai namastasyai namastasyai namo namaḥ||

Translation:

We bow down to the Goddess who resides in all beings as intelligence, we bow down to her, we bow down to her, we bow down to her over and over again.

Explanation:

There is no need to explain the words '*yā devī*' repeatedly. By saying 'that', it means the one beyond words and thoughts, yet is of the nature of truth, in whose spirit there is no doubt or disbelief about expression, because of whose existence this universe exists. Because one cannot express what that one is clearly, we use indirect terms, '*yā devī*' and '*tasmai*.' In using the term '*sarvabhūteṣu*' (all beings), a spiritual seeker should not forget to give special attention to one's self. It is needless to repeat this.

Mother! You are in the form of intelligence. You reside as divided intelligence in each being, as the united intelligence in supreme principle, and as the seed of intelligence in the unexpressed arena. We offer our physical, verbal, and mental *praṇāms* to your three natures. Then your pure form, where there is no such thing as intelligence, though intelligence resides in it, that which expresses intelligence, that pure nature of yours, which is also my pure nature, we bow down to it repeatedly, saying '*namo namoḥ*.' Mother accept our *praṇāms*. Let us alight on Self.

A spiritual seeker reading this mantra should first bow down to one's intelligence. It is Mother in the form of intelligence (*buddhi*). To find this intelligence (*dhī*), *brāhmiṇs* reciting '*dhiyo yo naḥ pracodayāt*', pray three times daily. This *dhī* is Mother. If you can properly bow down to it, then you can find the supreme spirit, the united intelligence in which your divided intelligence resides. Offer it your second *praṇām*. Then offering your *praṇām* to the unexpressed seed of the divided and united intelligence, what is known as the root nature (*mulā prakṛti*), move on to pure spirit. Merge into the spirit beyond perception, beyond the three attributes, into the nature of the *guru*, of Self. May the weight of 'I' disappear forever when one says '*namo namoḥ*.'

Verse 15.

yā devī sarvabhūteṣu nidrārūpeṇa saṁsthitā|
namastasyai namastasyai namastasyai namo namaḥ||

Translation:

We bow down to the Goddess who resides in all beings as sleep, we bow down to her, we bow down to her, we bow down to her over and over again.

Explanation:

Mother, you appear in the form of sleep. When all matters of our senses and internal features are halted, then you, knowledge formed Mother, reside there, with 'I do not know' held in your heart. This is the nature of your form as sleep. It is you who is expressed as a break in all perception. That is why the philosophy of Patañjali has indicated this form as the faculty of a lack of certainty. When you appear as a lack of certainty, then we are embraced by your loving, nectar-filled form as sleep and rest from the labor of matters of the senses. We find supreme satisfaction. There is so much love in your heart, that when we, your beloved children, are tired of roaming in these three worlds filled with sorrow, then you embrace us in your form as sleep and with your ambrosial touch, make us forget all our pain and disturbance. Spiritual seekers looking for Mother, where do you run about searching for her? See how close to us the sage of *Devī Māhātmya* has brought Mother. Every day, we can find her in sleep. Mother is me (*sva*), because we find this self, another name for sleep is *svapiti*. By a touch from her one can be saved from all pain, Mother comes and holds us every night in her loving embrace.

Come, Mother, come my sleep formed Mother, we bow down at your feet. Accept our physical *praṇām* of body and words.

Then, by your grace, we extend our vision and see that in a great united form of sleep, you hold all beings in you. Mother, that form of your sleep as Goddess, that supreme form as ignorance resides in all this universe. We bow down to that supreme form. Seeing it, our bodies and mind are stilled. How dense is that dark form of sleep? We bow down a thousand times at your feet.

After this, the cause of this divided and united sleep form, we offer our third *praṇām* to that unexpressed, causal form that is the seed of sleep and goes beyond to the pure form that is beyond sleep. In it, there is nothing such as sleep, yet its spirit is the spirit of sleep. That ever awake, perceptual nature of your pure spirit expresses sleep. We bow down to it over and over again. May our *praṇāms* bring us success.

Verse 16.

yā devī sarvabhūteṣu kṣudhārūpeṇa saṁsthitā|
namastasyai namastasyai namastasyai namo namaḥ||

Translation:

We bow down to the Goddess who resides in all beings as hunger, we bow down to her, we bow down to her, we bow down to her over and over again.

Explanation:

Mother, you exist as hunger in all beings, as the desire to eat. The weariness that comes to us because of the loss of blood, fluid and other elements, brings a need for food. This is your form as hunger. Not only in the physical body, the *annamaya koṣa*, do we see the expression of your form as hunger, we see this form in all the other sheaths. There is the desire to feed all the five sheaths. The food for the *prāṇamaya koṣa* is life force; that of the intellectual sheath is knowledge, and of the blissful sheath is joy and happiness. In this manner, because you express yourself as the form of hunger in the five sheaths, knowingly or unknowingly to appease our hunger, we approach you in this fashion every day. Blessed is the wonderful, attractive expression of your form as hunger. First, saying *namastasyai*, we bow down to your eternal form as the hunger for material food, your individual, material form as hunger. Then, by your grace, we extend our view, we see a universal, undivided form of hunger residing in all beings. Your form is not satisfied with only the before-mentioned five forms of food. This whole universe exists as food to satisfy your supreme form as hunger. Who else but you know from what eternal times, you have expressed yourself in this form? Mother, we bow down at your feet. We have heard that those who can truly bow down at the feet of your form as hunger, have their worldly hunger satisfied forever. Mother, for how many lifetimes have we been enjoying this world? We have come through so much pain and suffering. Even then, our worldly hunger is not satisfied. Mother, you have to satisfy our hunger. You are Mother; it is for you to give us food to satisfy our hunger.

The children are just playing, they have forgotten about food. Mother comes to feed them. This is her maternity. Come and satisfy our hunger. We cannot look for food anymore. We have been looking for ages, but we do not eat, our hunger is not satisfied. But now that we understand that you are in the form of hunger, you have to come and satisfy it. Mother, seeing your children pained by hunger, how can you, the one who feeds this world (*Annapūrṇā*), remain silent? Can that be? You are *Annapūrṇā*, we are your children. How can we stand this prospect? Accept our *praṇāms* and end our hunger for material things forever. My hunger formed Mother, we did not recognize you for so long, we ignored you, we looked at you with disgust. But no more. We recognize you today. Come, Mother, accept our *praṇāms* to the physical, subtle and causal. May your children be honored. Then, saying '*namo namoḥ*' we will move to your pure spirit, where there is no hunger, no food. The one who expresses all hunger, that which ends all hunger, that is your pure spirit. Mother, accept our final *praṇām*. May the bright light of your maternal pride light up this world. May millions of beings move towards you, calling you Mother.

Verse 17.

yā devī sarvabhūteṣu chāyārūpeṇa saṁsthitā|
namastasyai namastasyai namastasyai namo namaḥ||

Translation:

We bow down to the Goddess who resides in all beings as shadows, we bow down to her, we bow down to her, we bow down to her over and over again.

Explanation:

The word 'shadow' (*chāyā*) means worldly persons. Ācaryā Śankara in his commentary on the *Upaniṣad* gave the meaning of 'shadow' as a worldly person. Shadows have three states, material, subtle and causal. In different bodies, one can make out these differences. A shadow is a reflection. The reflections of awareness are beings. The shadow as the physical body or its reflection of awareness is the material form of shadows. The shadow of the subtle body (the five action organs, five sense organs, mind and intelligence) is the subtle form of shadow. In the same manner, the reflection of *avidyā* in the causal body is the causal form of shadows. The mantra mentions three *praṇāms* to bow down to these three forms of shadows. The fourth *praṇām* is directed at the nature beyond shadows.

Here, there is something to be said about shadows. Just as common shadows cover expression, this shadow of worldly persons is a cover over the nature of *paramātmā.* It is to move this cover that there is all this bowing down and seeking shelter. It is by bowing down that false pride is removed. When ego is removed, one does not perceive the state as a worldly person to be an entity with a separate existence. One then correctly perceives that the reflection has no separate existence, the spirit of the reflection is that of the reflected. The easy way to realize that there is only *ātmā* is to see shadows in all beings. Those who have had their intelligence aroused, see this world of beings as shadows. Like a great city reflected in a mirror[11], one truly sees this physical

11 *Dakṣiṇāmurtti stotram*

world of name and form as shadows. However much the modern *Vedāntist* may try to drive away this shadow of existence as error, mistake or assignment, as long as there is a physical body, even trying a thousand times, one cannot remove it by calling it false.

The Lord has said in the *Gitā*, 'God resides in the hearts of all beings and directs them like machines'[12]. This specially proves that beings are but shadows. Just as when one stands in front of a clean mirror and gestures, the reflected image makes the same gestures. The reflection of existence in the form of beings, being directed by God in the heart, acts similarly. I have heard in a song, 'I say what you make me say, laugh as you make me laugh.' This is very true.

We may have the concern here that, if beings are reflections of God and all actions by them are directed by God, then there can be no place for sin and sanctity. Yes, those who have truly reached this point, who realize themselves to be shadows of the supreme one, to them there is no sin and sanctity. But, before such a state, as long as ego exists, one has to discern right and wrong. Even after a thousand reiterations, *saṁskaras* of sin and sanctity will arise.

We however know, that you are reflected and you are the reflection. It is you who as *paramātmā* is the reflected and cast a reflection of awareness in the intelligence as being or shadow. That is why the gods bow down to you in the form of shadows. Mother, you are sentient, so whatever is encroached upon by your shadow also acquires sentience. When the shadow of inert matter falls on inert matter, there is no sentient behavior. But by the shadow of my consciousness-natured Mother, the material body, intelligence and senses all acquire consciousness. Mother, you are the form of 'I', so by your shadow, this inert body prides itself as 'I.'

Mother, with the first *namastasyai*, we bow down to your existential shadow reflected in our intelligence. Then, the shadow in the united form or supreme principle (*mahat*), which the

---

12 *Bhāgavat Gitā*, 18:61

scriptures called *Hiraṇyagarbha*, we offer our second *praṇām*. Then saying '*namastasyai*', we bow down to that nonmanifest shadow in the causal plane. Finally, in the pure arena, saying '*namo namoḥ*', we bow down repeatedly where there are no shadows, yet gives spirit to shadows, who express all shadows. Let shadows and illusions vanish forever.

Verse 18.

yā devī sarvabhūteṣu śaktirūpeṇa saṁsthitā|
namastasyai namastasyai namastasyai namo namaḥ||

Translation:

We bow down to the Goddess who resides in all beings as energy, we bow down to her, we bow down to her, we bow down to her over and over again.

Explanation:

When we speak of energy, we first notice our bodies. If we follow this thought calmly, we perceive that this body is nothing but energy. Looking at the power of sight, hearing and other sensory powers, we notice the material part of this body formed of blood, muscles and so on. Then we see that innumerable atoms and molecules are held together by some unknown force and appear as the body. Looking at the molecules, we see that they are minute centers of energy. This body appears to be a conglomeration of energy. Mother, we bow down to your form as physical energy.

Mother, modern materialists, view this physical form of your expression as energy to be inert. They do not understand that energy that is expressed in all beings, in physical bodies, in materials, in light, heat, electricity, in the sun and Moon, are all the sentient power of your inclination. They do not agree that power is nothing but consciousness. Mother, open their eyes of knowledge. Let them feel that physical materials are but flows of energy.

What is it Mother? Energy is not at all dissimilar. The power to see and hear does not appear to be different energies. Supreme energy takes on different names and forms and carries out different functions. This seems to be so not only in our bodies, or special things in this world but everywhere in the immense universe that our intelligence can fathom. Whatever is in here, we cannot take it to be just material. It is one energy. What vastness, what supremacy! Our minds and intelligence fall silent. That supreme energy that is expressed as all elements, as this infinite universe, in which the three-fold vibrations of creation-maintenance-dissolution are observed, that united great energy is Mother. On this insurmountable, great ocean of energy, beings appear as waves momentarily and then disappear. We bow down to your divine form as energy. Mother, as supreme energy, accept our *praṇām*.

Then, the seed of these individual and united energies, the great energy appears from a nonmanifest arena. We bow down to that form of energy and move on to pure spirit. Here there is no perception of energy, yet without it, there is no energy. Appearing as energy, there is no change to its nature. Saying '*namo namoḥ*' we bow down repeatedly to that which is beyond words and thought.

Mother, we hear that some of your learned children say that your nature as supreme Self is without energy and try to establish this by logic and argument. By your grace, express your nature to them. Let them see that *paramātmā* is not something inert, without energy, without flavor, without bliss. It is the vessel of all energies, it is of the nature of bliss.

Verse 19.

yā devī sarvabhūteṣu tṛṣṇārūpeṇa saṁsthitā|
namastasyai namastasyai namastasyai namo namaḥ||

Translation:

We bow down to the Goddess who resides in all beings as thirst, we bow down to her, we bow down to her, we bow down to her over and over again.

Explanation:

Mother, you express yourself in all beings as thirst or the desire to drink. In remembering this thirst in all beings, we first notice our thirst. Mother, you are not only the desire to drink water. You are always awake in the heart as unfulfilled needs. For how many lifetimes have we tried to satisfy this form of you as thirst, but failed. Even with the ownership of all this universe, this thirst is not satisfied. For so long, we did not understand that this thirst was you, did not cherish it as Mother. Today, by your grace, we see that it is you who express yourself as thirst, as intense desire. Come, my thirst-formed Mother, my unfulfilled desires, let me bow down to you and go beyond all thirst, my heart filled with hope.

Looking at your individual forms of thirst, our eyes fall on your united form as thirst in all beings. How great it is! Wherever we lay our eyes on this world, we see your unfulfilled form of desire. What is this Mother? What is this form with which you carry all beings? This is your form as supreme divinity. You are the united form of thirst. Finding a drop of this, beings are overwhelmed, suffer births and deaths for eons. How will we understand this great form of thirst of yours, by which you have engaged in this play of multiplicity, from that one and only form of bliss? Understand or not, we bow down to you. Do not appear to us as the desire for worldly things. Come to us as the intense thirst to find you. May we be honored.

Then we bow down to the unexpressed cause from which this great thirst appears. Saying '*namo namoḥ*' we bow down repeatedly to that form of you beyond thirst, beyond feeling, that is your pure perceptual nature. There is no thirst in there, but thirst gets spirit from it. Appearing as thirst, it is unchanged and untouched. That is your pure spirit, take us there.

Verse 20.

yā devī sarvabhūteṣu kṣāntirūpeṇa saṁsthitā|
namastasyai namastasyai namastasyai namo namaḥ||

Translation:

We bow down to the Goddess who resides in all beings as forgiveness, as endurance, we bow down to her, we bow down to her, we bow down to her over and over again.

Explanation:

Mother, you reside in the hearts of all beings to some degree as forgiveness. To be tormented by others and quietly tolerate it, despite being able to prevent it, is *kṣānti*. Just as we can tolerate the trouble given to us by near ones, when we can tolerate all kinds of trouble, we understand that you hold us in your form as *kṣānti*. The rise of that tendency that lets us tolerate trouble from others is your form as forgiveness. When this form is expressed, we find peace.

Then, when the united nature of your all-encompassing form of mercy rises in our perception, our hearts fill with courage from happiness and enthusiasm. Mother, that world-encompassing form of forgiveness is you. We bow down to you a million times. You Mother, are in the form of forgiveness. You are in that form of *kṣānti*, where there is nothing that is a crime, nothing that is wrong, where your permissiveness is an outer expression of affection. Let alone other lifetimes, even in this one, we have neglected you so much, ignored your silent orders, your blessings. Yet you have never cast even a glance of annoyance at us. You, the always smiling, ever forgiving Mother, keep looking at us, as to when we will end our error, when we will listen to you, when we will truly call you Mother. From eternal times you hold this world of beings at your breast. Otherwise, such an ungrateful world would not exist. That this world of beings that does not accept your spirit exists, is an incredible example of your form as *kṣānti*. We offer innumerable *praṇāms* to your great united form of forgiveness.

Then we offer our third *praṇām* to the unexpressed seed form of mercy and move on to the pure arena, where there is nothing known as mercy or not mercy, whose nature is that of forgiveness, the one who appearing as forgiveness does not at all move from its nature. We bow down repeatedly to that form beyond attributes.

Verse 21.

yā devī sarvabhūteṣu jātirūpeṇa saṁsthitā|
namastasyai namastasyai namastasyai namo namaḥ||

Translation:

We bow down to the Goddess who resides in all beings as race or nation, we bow down to her, we bow down to her, we bow down to her over and over again.

Explanation:

Mother, that which is grouped as many, although it is eternal, is your form as race. Race or caste is evident from birth. As *brahmiṇs*, *kṣatriyas,* etc. or as humans, gods and animals, you hold all to yourself as races. Just as young children seated on the lap of their mother are proud to say, 'I am a child of my mother', so in this world, some say 'I am a *brahmiṇ*', 'I am a man', 'I am a god', and introduce themselves. Mother, we see that you are holding them in your form as race or lineage. Mother, we bow down to this form of you as race.

Mother, all of your children who are today trying their best to remove the differences of race, need to know that it is you who is expressed as race. This form of you as race is eternal. As long as there are beings, as long as there is creation, differences in race will remain. It cannot be removed by trying a hundred times. But with changes in time, place, and nation, the differences in race will change. Mother, let them know and understand that the nature of race is true. As long as this world remains, it will not be destroyed.

In bowing down to this individual form of you as race, we notice your form in that collective form as race. Then we see that individual races are waves of the unity of races. We bow down to that great spirit as race of the supreme form of all beings. After this, we bow down to the seed formed, causal spirit, of your form as race. When this universe disappears at the time of dissolution, the seeds of race remain. That is your causal form as race. Finally, where there is no race, no form, no dissolution, yet in which everything resides, that is unchanged by appearing as race, we bow down repeatedly to that nature beyond words and thought. Mother accept our *praṇāms*.

Verse 22.

yā devī sarvabhūteṣu lajjārūpeṇa saṁsthitā|
namastasyai namastasyai namastasyai namo namaḥ||

Translation:

We bow down to the Goddess who resides in all beings as shame, we bow down to her, we bow down to her, we bow down to her over and over again.

Explanation:

Mother, because you appear in the form of shame in the hearts of all beings, your children refrain from carrying out forbidden acts. Our hair stands on end to think that if this shame was not expressed in the hearts of beings, then this world would truly be just a land of animals. On one hand, with your form as mercy, you have given beings freedom to act as they desire, on the other hand, with your form as shame, you have controlled their unruliness. Blessed is your grace. Mother, we bow down to your individual form as shame. Then, when we see this form as shame exists in all beings in its divine, united form as shame, we understand that taking the form of control, with a thousand hands, you hold all unruly beings to your heart. It is through this form of shame that your maternity and affection are expressed. We bow down to this combined form as shame. Then we offer our third *praṇām* to the seed or causal form of this material, subtle, individual and combined form as shame.

There is something that is to be noted here. Although you restrain the desires of all beings in your form as shame, and if by the force of habits some carry out forbidden acts and try to hide them from others, there is no shame in front of you. There can be no wish to hide anything from you. What cannot be said to anyone else in this world, what is to be hidden from all, can be said to you with an open heart. You are in a form as shame, yet the children have no shame in coming to you and telling you the secrets of their hearts. This is your specialty. Mother, another truth is that this is the external sign that we love you the most. However much we may be engrossed with this world, however we may love our spouses, children, wealth and fame, we love you the most. Otherwise, why can we not hide anything from you? Why do we not wish to hide anything from you? As long as one does not understand that you are the most favorite thing in this world, one is engrossed by this world. When by your kindness, you reveal this principle in the hearts of beings, the attachment to worldly things begins to diminish.

Where there is no shame, no hesitancy, no willfulness, no restraint, yet in whose spirit all these are expressed, and by their expression who is not changed at all, we bow down repeatedly to that 'one and only' principle formed Mother.

Something else is needed to be said here. Many disciples are ashamed to express their weaknesses in front of their *guru*. This is a hindrance to development. The scriptures say that one should declare one's sins and weaknesses without any barrier to a teacher. As long as that does not take place, one has to understand that one has not properly found a *guru*, or there is a lack of sense of divinity in one's *guru*. Whatever that is, we now bow down to that which is beyond the material, subtle and causal, saying '*namo namaḥ*.'

Verse 23.

yā devī sarvabhūteṣu śāntirūpeṇa saṁsthitā|
namastasyai namastasyai namastasyai namo namaḥ||

Translation:

We bow down to the Goddess who resides in all beings as peace, we bow down to her, we bow down to her, we bow down to her over and over again.

Explanation:

Mother, although there is no peace in enjoying worldly materials, only a trace of peace, although one cannot find peace until the spirit is calm, yet in this enjoyment and collecting of material things, the trace of peace that occurs through disturbances of the spirit and for a moment purifies our hearts, that form of peace is you. It can be seen more or less in all beings. It is your form as peace. Mother, when you sit with us in this form as peace and hold us, only then, even though we perceive the nature of peace only for a moment, it is wonderful. Mother, let all your children who are searching outside in the hope of finding peace understand that it is not outside but inside. Come, Mother, let us bow down to you in your form as peace. Then, let us go and look at your great form of peace, where there is nothing but endless peace. Reaching this, the heart wounded by the troubles of the world heal forever. Come, Mother, let us go there. What a sweet place it is. Oh! How extraordinary, only peace, only peace. There is no sorrow, no heat, no burning, only heart-filling peace. We cannot hold that ocean of peace in our tiny hearts. Mother, we bow down repeatedly to that united form of you as peace. Do not remove us for even a moment from this supreme form of you as peace. As long as the desire for worldly things is not removed, one cannot discover this indefinable form of peace. Bowing down to this form of you as supreme peace, we reach a nonmanifest arena where peace does not have such supremacy, extent or specialty. It exists as the unexpressed seed of peace, from which the individual and united forms of peace arise. We offer our third *praṇām* to this causal form of you as peace. Then, where there is nothing, yet there is no lack of anyhing, where one cannot understand anything to be peace, yet there is nothing that is turmoil, to that pure form of you beyond all tendencies, beyond words and thought, we bow down repeatedly saying '*namo namoḥ*.' Take us to that place of eternal peace.

Verse 24.

yā devī sarvabhūteṣu śraddhārūpeṇa saṁsthitā|
namastasyai namastasyai namastasyai namo namaḥ||

Translation:

We bow down to the Goddess who resides in all beings as respect, we bow down to her, we bow down to her, we bow down to her over and over again.

Explanation:

Mother, when we say respect, our eyes first fall on your individual form as respect. Although firm faith in the words of *guru* and *Vedānta* has been called respect, we should know the meaning ascribed to the word by *Yāska* in *Nirukti*. The belief that always holds the truth is properly ascribed to the word respect (*śraḥ satyam dhiyata iti śraddhā*). Mother, those that you free from this imagined bondage of *māyā*, respect first appears in their hearts. They have firm faith in the words of *guru* and *Vedānta*, and their goal in life is the establishment of truth. Seeing these external signs, we can understand that you have appeared in their hearts in your form as respect. You appear always in the hearts of beings, whether little or much, in your form as respect. Mother, we bow down to you.

The *Gitā* says 'the respectful find knowledge.' Respect comes before knowledge of Self. As long as respect is not present, hopes of entry into the kingdom of knowledge are futile. Respect and definite knowledge are similar. There is no definite knowledge as long as there is doubt. So, one has to understand that as long as there is doubt, Mother has not appeared in her form as respect. Once respect is acquired, it is not destroyed. Generally, we think that we respect some other thing or person. It is not so. Respect is a wonderful condition of our knowledge, it is expressed as truth, as freedom from doubt. Spiritual exercise and worship are to acquire respect. Those that find it are honored. Bowing down to the individual form of Mother as respect, we see in the united form that is under a great, pure sky, without any disturbances, this great universe existing in the form of supreme respect. All beings exist in this supreme form of the Goddess as respect. Mother, we bow down at the feet of this great, united form of respect.

Beyond this, what is a seed of this individual and united form of respect, that unexpressed causal form of respect, we bow down to it with our third *praṇām* and arrive at what is beyond attributes. Here there is nothing that is respect or disrespect, whose spirit is respect, who is unchanged by the appearance of respect. Saying '*namo namoḥ*', we bow down to this repeatedly. Mother, appear in our hearts in the form of respect. Let us be honored by finding knowledge.

Verse 25.

yā devī sarvabhūteṣu kāntirūpeṇa saṁsthitā|
namastasyai namastasyai namastasyai namo namaḥ||

Translation:

We bow down to the Goddess who resides in all beings as beauty, we bow down to her, we bow down to her, we bow down to her over and over again.

Explanation:

Mother, you are expressed in all beings as beauty or attractiveness. However ugly or hideous a being may be, there is in each something called beauty. Everyone realizes a portion of this beauty. Besides this, there is something in a flower, a lotus, the Moon, a child or a woman's face that we are happy to see. That Mother, is the expression of your form as beauty. As long as you are established as consciousness in the bodies of beings, one can perceive this form of you as beauty. Not just in the bodies of animals, but, in plants and vines, mountains, rivers, planets and stars, one can see this special form of your beauty. Mother, these are the individual forms of your beauty. We bow down to them.

Then, as we leave the individuals and cast our eyes on your supreme form as ruler of all beings, we see the whole universe turn beautiful, attractive and nectar-like. As far as our tiny intelligence can expand, seeing your expansive all-encompassing beauty, we do not know what to feel. Then our 'I'-ness merges into this ocean of beauty. How can I express what happens when 'I' immerses in that formless ocean of form? This is the beauty, seeing which the women of *Vraja* ran out mindlessly. Seeing which grazing cattle forgot to graze and stared at you. Beauty that made the river *Yamunā* flow with life. This is that beauty. This is truly a beauty to blind all eyes. Beauty to engross heart and mind. Once this beauty falls on the eye, there is nothing else in this world, in this universe, that can remove memories of this beauty. Mother, we bow down to that universal, infinite beauty of yours.

Beyond this, we bow down to that unexpressed seed, the causal form, from which this individual and united form of beauty are expressed. Finally, saying '*namo namoḥ*' we bow down to you as that pure nature, where there is nothing that can be known as beauty, yet is that which expresses beauty, and in doing so, its undefined form is unchanged. We bow down again and again to that supreme and beautiful nature of Self.

Verse 26.

yā devī sarvabhūteṣu lakṣmīrūpeṇa saṁsthitā|
namastasyai namastasyai namastasyai namo namaḥ||

Translation:

We bow down to the Goddess who resides in all beings as *Lakṣmī*, we bow down to her, we bow down to her, we bow down to her over and over again.

Explanation:

Before, it has been said that the meaning of the word *Lakṣmī* is life (*prāṇa*). As long as there is life in the body, one is united with *Lakṣmī* or *Śrī*. Whatever meaning you ascribe to the word *lakṣmī*, splendor, riches or beauty, life is its only container.

Mother, you are established as life in your form as *Lakṣmī* in all beings. Even though this may not be observed by our senses, it is always perceptible. No living person ever experiences any lack of it. This perceptible nature of life, in all beings, at all times, is your form as *Lakṣmī*. We offer thousands of *praṇāms* to the feet of this life-formed Mother.

What you always feel in your heart as life is the individual form of Mother as *Lakṣmī*. First bow down to that individual form of Mother as life, saying '*namastasyai*.' Then view the universal combined form of Mother as great life. Look. In this ocean of life, beings appear as individual waves. You have ignored it for a long time. Do not do so anymore. Today, bowing down to it saying '*namastasyai*', pour your tiny life force into that great ocean of life. Let your individuality end. After this, what is at the center of individual and united life force, bow down to that unexpressed subtle and causal spirit of life. Arriving at the arena of purity, saying '*namo namoḥ*', be engulfed with joy, find Self.

Verse 27.

yā devī sarvabhūteṣu vṛttirūpeṇa saṁsthitā|
namastasyai namastasyai namastasyai namo namaḥ||

Translation:

We bow down to the Goddess who resides in all beings as vocation, we bow down to her, we bow down to her, we bow down to her over and over again.

Explanation:

The word '*vṛtti*' means vocation or tendencies of the spirit. When nonmanifest consciousness appears in the present by occupying something, is expressed, it is known as *vṛtti*. Vocation or occupation is a special expression of this consciousness.

Mother, every day we experience this nature of you as *vṛtti*. Whether as the nature of the senses, or inner natures, you are always manifest in all these forms. We have never cherished this form, never adored it as Mother. By your grace, you have expressed yourself today. You have given us the ability to realize you as *vṛtti*. Today, in penance for that ungratefulness, we offer you a tiny *praṇām*, saying '*namastasyai*.' Vocation formed Mother, accept our *praṇām*.

Then, when we look at the subtle, we see that in this world, there is one undivided *vṛtti*. Single sparks from that supreme, vocation formed Goddess, appear through each being as different professions. O vocation formed Mother, we bow down a million times at your feet.

After this, the most subtle, nonmanifest cause from which all these individual and united vocations are expressed, and in which they disappear, we bow down to that causal form of you, we enter into your purest principle. In it, there is nothing that is *vṛtti*, only pure awareness. Arriving there, all vocations disappear, we bow down to that nature that is beyond attributes. Mother, when will you accept our *praṇāms*? Vocation formed Mother, when you discard the material, subtle and causal natures and appear as pure perception, in the form of *Brahmaṇ*, then our *praṇāms* will be worthy.

Verse 28.

yā devī sarvabhūteṣu smītirūpeṇa saṁsthitā|
namastasyai namastasyai namastasyai namo namaḥ||

Translation:

We bow down to the Goddess who resides in all beings as memory, we bow down to her, we bow down to her, we bow down to her over and over again.

Explanation:

Mother, after vocation, your form as memory is lit up. The feeling that first appears as vocation is later brought to the spirit as tendencies (*saṁskāra*). When that feeling is aroused in the spirit, then they are called memories. Mother, it is you who holds these drops of knowledge over lifetimes as memory. If with each death, we lost all this acquired wisdom, then there would be no hope of ever finding complete knowledge. We would never taste freedom. We would decompose in ignorance forever. But, loving Mother, to free us from this eternal ignorance, you reside in the hearts of all beings as memory. That is why, residing in your heart as memory, we collect knowledge over lifetimes. As a result, we will finally arrive at 'I am *Brahmaṇ*.' This riddle as worldly persons will end. Come my memory formed Mother, we bow down to you.

Then, by your grace, appearing near your form of memory as the empress of all beings, we see that a supreme form of memory holds this universe together. The memories expressed in different beings are different waves on this united ocean of memory. Mother, we bow down to your form as the Goddess of memory. After this, we bow down to the unexpressed causal form and arrive at your pure nature. When our memory as worldly person vanishes, the memory of 'I am *Brahmaṇ*' is continuously aroused, then we can discover this form of you without attributes. We bow down repeatedly to this nature where there is no such thing as memory, yet in whose spirit memory is expressed and in doing so, its state without attributes is undisturbed.

Verse 29.

yā devī sarvabhūteṣu dayārūpeṇa saṁsthitā|
namastasyai namastasyai namastasyai namo namaḥ||

Translation:

We bow down to the Goddess who resides in all beings as compassion, we bow down to her, we bow down to her, we bow down to her over and over again.

Explanation:

Mother, the desire that arises in you to remove sorrow, seeing it in beings, is your form as compassion. Your form as compassion can be seen to be expressed in the hearts of all beings. Mother, we bow down to this form. Mother, let your dear children know that when feeling compassion for someone's sorrow they donate something, or try to help in some other way, that they do not do so thinking 'I am compassionate to those in sorrow.' That they do not help with the knowledge 'I am helping others' because one does not help others, one helps oneself. When some blind, lame or needy person prays to someone in hope of help, then by viewing that need, a feeling of compassion is aroused in the donor. Maybe one was busy with work, but seeing such a poor or disabled person, compassion is aroused in the heart. This compassion is your form. You appear in the form of compassion in the heart. If the giver can recognize this and bows down to you saying '*namastasyai*', then one will have gratitude for the poor person. Will one not be grateful to the person who shows the giver the form of Mother as compassion? What may be given in return for this in gratitude will be small in comparison. So, whatever the receiver is helped by it, the giver is helped a thousand-fold. Compassion is the right attribute. The more one practices it, the happier one is. There is no doubt that we are indebted to those, however poor they may be, who give us the opportunity to practice this right attribute. Whatever may be given in return for this, is bound to be small in comparison.

Look. When you donate something to the poor, on one hand, it is Mother who taking the form of poverty stands in front of you and piteously begs for something. On the other, it is pity that makes Mother take the form of compassion in your heart. You were busy with worldly thoughts, and within moments you see Mother as compassion. How indebted are you for it? Can you repay it by giving anything you have? It is in this way that donations are worthwhile. Remember that when a wish to remove the sorrow of others appears in your heart, do not ignore it as just an attribute of the spirit. Understand it to be Mother. Like the gods, bow down at her feet, at the feet of the compassion-formed Mother. You will find supreme bliss.

Now we will leave the individual form of compassion and move to its united form. Nearing that form, wherever we look in this world, we see nothing but compassion. All these uncountable beings reside in the heart of this form of compassion. In all conditions, sorrow, joy and all else, beings reside in the heart of compassion. Who will say, where there is the end to that compassion which gives us life. Whose compassion and love give us this thing called life? Mother, we offer hundreds of *praṇāms* to your supreme compassion. Those who do not see this form of you as compassion tormented by sickness, sorrow and poverty, only see cruelty, are blind. Let me tell you a story.

In a dense forest, there was a man who was severely affected by leprosy. His whole body was covered by sores so that no one went anywhere near him. At the end of each day, a distant relative brought him some food, so he was kept alive. He spent his days as if death was the only thing desirable. By divine fate, one day, a traveling monk (*fakir*), came there and seeing his pitiful condition, moved by compassion, said to him, 'O, how cruel is God, giving you so much suffering; there is not a spot on your body that is not affected.' Hearing this, with a smiling face, the man replied, "No esteemed sir, don't say that God is cruel. He is very kind. My throat is still unharmed. Even now I can sing his divine name to my heart's content. Honored is the compassion of one by whose grace I can still sing such praises, even when I am in such dire straits." Pleased by this response, the *fakir* healed the man.

Truly, those that under all circumstances, cannot but think of the kindness of God instead of his cruelty, are never tormented or downed by sorrow. But that is something else.

Mother, wherever we look in this world, we see the dense form of your compassion. There is nothing but the expression of your compassion in every being. What we saw before as forgiveness, is but an expression of your form as compassion. We offer uncounted *praṇāms* to your form as the supreme form as compassion. Then from the nonmanifest center from which this individual and united compassion appears, we bow down to that causal form of compassion and move into the pure field. In it, there is nothing known as compassion, yet its spirit is that of compassion. Appearing as compassion, it is eternally unchanged. Saying '*namo namoḥ*' we bow down to it over and over again.

Verse 30.

yā devī sarvabhūteṣu tuṣṭirūpeṇa saṁsthitā|
namastasyai namastasyai namastasyai namo namaḥ||

Translation:

We bow down to the Goddess who resides in all beings as satisfaction, we bow down to her, we bow down to her, we bow down to her over and over again.

Explanation:

Mother, you are in the form of satisfaction. On finding the desired, or on ending the undesired, the feeling that for a moment arises in the heart, is your form as satisfaction. You reside with this form, individually in all beings. We bow down to you. Then when we lay our eyes on your united form as satisfaction, we see an undivided ocean of satisfaction over all this world. We move around in it. The pitiful cries of the sorrowful, the pain of the diseased, the fire of hunger, in all of this, you reside endlessly as satisfaction. If we did not find satisfaction even when weeping, we would not do so. Knowingly or unknowingly we worship satisfaction, serve it and suffer the weight of innumerable lives and deaths for it. Mother, we bow down to this supreme form of you as satisfaction. You have said in the *Gitā* that a person who is 'always satisfied', is your favorite devotee. But, Mother, those who have not found your form as satisfaction, can they be always satisfied? It is seen in this world, that the lack of satisfaction is due to different expectations from past actions (*prārabdha*), or due to a wish for quick results. These two are the roots of all dissatisfaction. What is due from past actions be different, and nothing can happen before the time is set for the results. If people understood this, there would be no lack of satisfaction, there could not be. Mother, as long as you appear in the hearts of beings as dissatisfaction, how can they discover contentment or satisfaction? Mother, express your supreme form as the nature of satisfaction and remove the false discontent of beings. May this world be honored to reside in your form as contentment. Let our *praṇām* to these individual and united forms be worthwhile. Then we can enter into the causal principle.

Bowing down to that causal form of you as satisfaction in the nonmanifest arena, we arrive at the pure spirit where there is nothing such as contentment or discontent. Its spirit is that of contentment, but it is unchanged in being so expressed. We bow down to it repeatedly.

Verse 31.

yā devī sarvabhūteṣu mātīrūpeṇa saṁsthitā|
namastasyai namastasyai namastasyai namo namaḥ||

Translation:

We bow down to the Goddess who resides in all beings as Mother, we bow down to her, we bow down to her, we bow down to her over and over again.

Explanation:

O Mother, we bow down to you in your maternal form. You hold all beings as seeds in your womb. To manifest them, you apply your enterprise or willpower. Then one can observe a separate spirit called a worldly person. In this manner, you express them, that is give them birth. You feed them at your breast and nurture them with divided knowledge. Through innumerable births and deaths, you the affectionate Mother, keep looking at their faces. You satisfy the false, imagined needs and desires of your children. The children nurtured at your breast, slowly acquire belief in the nature of Mother. They forget independent control, embrace you and lose themselves. Then, you merge them with you and take them to an unknowable principle beyond Mother and child. This is your well-expressed form as Mother. Seeing your maternal form in the physical, subtle, causal and pure planes, Mother, my Self, we bow down to you over and over again.

Has any spiritual seeker found such words of protection anywhere else? Do you remember what is in the *Gitā*? 'Even those who are wicked, they worship me with one mind'[13]. In it, there is the advice for worship. What do we see here in *Devī Māhātmya*? In singing the praises of Mother, the gods say something that is not to be found so clearly anywhere else. What can be stronger words of support than that 'my Self is Mother?' Whatever condition I may be in, I am on the lap of my Mother. Even as I think myself to be a separate being, as I am engrossed by multiplicity, even then, I am on the lap of my Mother. I am honored. Honored is my life. I have nothing to search for, I have no wants, I have no right and wrong to discern. I am on the lap of my Mother. Not only me, all beings, this universe, are in the lap of Mother. If you pass it away as *māyā*, as inert Nature, as false, there is no harm, I know I am on the lap of my Mother. This universe is on her lap. Again, where there is no 'I', no universe, Mother is there, as unexpressed causality. Beyond that? What can I say what is beyond that? I cannot even think of it. By using the words, 'is, is, is' or 'bliss, bliss, bliss' I establish again and again that I do not know or understand it, I have not found it.

Mother, on the physical and individual levels you are my Mother. On the subtle and united you are Mother of all, Mother of this world, because you have given birth to me and all this world. Beyond that, in the *turiya*, where there is no difference between you, me or this world, you are only Mother, Self, *Brahmaṇ*. We bow down to you on the physical, subtle and causal levels, saying '*namastasyai. namo namoḥ.*' Accept our *praṇāms*.

Verse 32.

yā devī sarvabhūteṣu bhrāntirūpeṇa saṁsthitā|
namastasyai namastasyai namastasyai namo namaḥ||

Translation:

We bow down to the Goddess who resides in all beings as

13 *Bhāgabat Gitā*, 9:30

error, we bow down to her, we bow down to her, we bow down to her over and over again.

Explanation:

No other scriptural text or philosophy has probably had the courage to spread such a word of truth. If we discard all parts of *Devī Māhātmya* except these last two mantras (form as mother and form as error), the truth that they bring to this world is incomparable. What you want to brush off as error, that figure as error is Mother. Oh! I have only one mouth, one pen and a single mind. They are all tiny. With my feeble spiritual effort, how can I explain what these two mantras have to give to the world? If one can bring into one's heart the purport of these two mantras, one can well see why *Devī Māhātmya* is recited all over this land. I do not think that such strength for the weak, hope for the hopeless, such words of safety have ever been painted in the hearts of beings. The truth that is covered by language in the *Veda* and *Upaniṣad* is illuminated in *Devī Māhātmya*.

Listen to how error can be Mother by looking at a famous example. Like the error of perceiving a rope to be a snake, we erroneously see this world in *Brahmaṇ,* which is without attributes or characteristics. We agree that the rope is never the snake, never was the snake. Similarly, this world is not *Brahmaṇ*, never was *Brahmaṇ*. If I here ask, whose error is it? You will answer, the one who asks the question. There is no error in *Brahmaṇ*, it is of the nature of pure awareness. It is beings who are in error. Good. The rope is an inert object. When one attributes it to be a snake, it is correct that it has no knowledge of snakes. But think, what if the rope was sentient, then the attribution of snake-ness, would that not be reflected in its perception? It has to be, because, whatever you bring in front of perception, that will be expressed. That is the nature of perception. So, the awareness-formed entanglement of attribution of the snake-like world, on a rope-like *Brahmaṇ*, is expressed by *Brahmaṇ*. The perception of humans remains unchanged. Some modern interpreters of the theory of *māyā*, do not agree with this. They say, that only in the existential part of

Brahmaṇ is attributed the inertness of *māyā*. Even agreeing to this, can one imagine an existential part without awareness? That cannot be. This existence and awareness are indistinguishable. So, what is perceived as this world, even if we say thousands of times, that it is an error, this error is expressed in *Brahmaṇ*, that is, in awareness. Whatever is expressed in *Brahmaṇ*, under any condition, is nothing by *Brahmaṇ*. So, error is also *Brahmaṇ*. Let us leave these arguments, all these are characteristised by thought. Not understanding the proper conditions under which the great *Ācārya* interpreter tried to explain why this world is an illusion, his conquering words, in the hands of some followers, have now to be deplored. We pay our respects to the great interpreter, he appeared as a teacher of this world.

Whatever it is, we know Mother, that as long as there is this a world, as long as there is a body, your indefinable form of error will remain. Without error, there will be no worldly games. You who are knowledge-formed, are carrying out this unthinkable worldly game in the form of error. We want to blow it away as error, so we can never be rid of it. Mother, night and day, we forget you, forget ourselves and are occupied with transient worldly things. This mistake, this error is also you. As long as you express yourself as error, no one has the strength to perceive your true nature. Then, when you express the nature of your spirit, that day, your form as error will make us forget this world, this knowledge of differences. How will we forget this world without the presence of error? All these games, all this tedium, this immense distance from you, there is hope that you will one day, wipe all this away in your form as error. Mother, as you reside always in the heart in your form as error, by your grace, one day, we will leave and forget everything and remain only as you and me. Mother, how far away is that day?

Mother, every day you express yourself in the three states in your form as error. We do not look and see. All the 'I'-ness and care while in the waking state is forgotten when we enter into the kingdom of dreams. There we move about with a new 'I'-ness in a new world. When we enter dreamless sleep (*suṣupti*) then we forget about the waking and dreaming states. There, alone and naked, we travel in some unexpressed kingdom. In this way, every day, you show yourself in your form as error. So, I hope, I wait with great hope in my heart, that one day, I will forget everything and discover you. Just as now, forgetting you, we are busy with worldly things, we will one day forget all this world and be with you, only you.

Dear seeker! Where do you run looking for Mother? She is here. Look, here is Mother. She is expressed every day in your heart as error, as ignorance, from wakefulness to dreams, from dreams to dreamless sleep, and then to awakening. In all these perceive Mother, enjoy her. Do not blow this away as error, as insignificant. Cherish it as Mother, ask for it like a simple-hearted child. Surrender your Self to it, this form as error will express itself in its form as *ātmā* and carry you across all errors.

According to *Vedānta*, error is of two kinds, *saṁvādī* and *visaṁvādī*. The error that is not a hindrance to finding a desired goal is called *saṁvādī* error. Like when one sees a glimmer and makes the error of thinking it to be a jewel and goes after it. Yet, one may as a result be able to find a jewel. This is an example of *saṁvādī* error. If one is under the error that a red hibiscus is a ruby and goes looking for it, then one does not find a ruby but a hibiscus flower. This is *visaṁvādī* error. If this universe is viewed in error as *Brahmaṇ*, it brings one to *Brahmaṇ*, because this is a *saṁvādī* error. I do not know why we had *visaṁvādī* error in this world for so long. The Mother, appearing as *visaṁvādī* error kept beings away from their desired goals. But now, a flood of affection has come to her heart, so she has now appeared in the form of *saṁvādī* error, so that one may find the desired goal. This is the preparation. This is why the sounds of success of the establishment of truth remove all *visaṁvādī* error, arousing this sleeping land. It is taking us all beyond error to the truth.

Error formed Mother, will our errors go away if we bow down at your feet? We will understand that under all conditions, we are the eternal, pure, knowledge of Self. So first we bow down to your individual form. We bow down repeatedly to your special form as error that resides in each of our hearts, by whose influence, we forget you. Then, bowing down to your united, divine form as error, we arrive at an unexpressed area. There, bowing down to your seed form as error, we go on to the pure arena. Here there is nothing known as error, yet, error resides in it, being expressed as error, it is not itself error. We bow down innumerable times to its pure perceptual spirit. Remove our errors.

Verse 33.

indriyāṇāmadhiṣṭhātrī bhūtānāñcākhileṣu yā|
bhūteṣu satataṁ tasyai vyāptyaidevyai namo namaḥ||

Translation:

To the all-pervading deity of the senses and the elements in all beings, we bow down again and again to that extensive Goddess.

Explanation:

Only Mother is expressed as eyes and other senses, the earth, water and other elements. Although the deities residing in each of the senses are given different names, to a spiritual seeker, they are evident as consciousness. In this connection, we name the deities of the senses here: *Dik* (direction) for hearing, *Vāyu* (air) for touch, the Sun for sight, *Varuṇa* for taste, the *Aśvinikumārs* for smell, *Agṇi* (fire) for speech, *Indra* for the hands, *Viṣṇu* for the feet, *Maitra* for the bowels, *Prajāpati* for the genitals, the Moon for the mind, *Acyuta* for intelligence (*buddhi*), *Caturmukha* for ego (*ahaṁkāra*) and *Śankara* for the spirit. The power of consciousness that is expressed as the senses, is given all these names. In the same manner, consciousness that appears as the elements are its reigning deities. Although these residing consciousness associated with the senses and elements is given different names in connection to different titles, it is one united consciousness. This is the all-pervading form of Mother.

Mother, wherever we look in this world, we see your great

pervasive form. A united, dense supreme spirit pervades this world. We are born, reside and disappear in its womb. Mother, seekers who can see this pervasive form of you, have any narrowness of their hearts, hesitancy of their spirits removed. Seeing the spread of this supreme life force, all life expands. This is the significance of seeing your all-pervasive form. Mother, we bow down uncountable times at your feet.

Verse 34.

citirūpeṇa yā kṛtsnametad vyāpya sthitā jagat|
namastasyai namastasyai namastasyai namo namaḥ||

Translation:

One who pervades the universe as the power of spirit, we bow down to her, we bow down to her, we bow down to her over and over again.

Explanation:

We had bowed down before this to Mother, who in the form of consciousness was special awareness, one that is perceived by the senses. In this mantra, the word '*citi*' is used, pointing to consciousness without attributes (*nirguṇa*). By the word '*citi*', is meant *Purūṣa* of *Sānkhya*, *Brahmaṇ* of *Vedānta*, *ātmā* of the *Upaniṣad* and our Mother. One may be concerned here that if the word '*citi*' means one without attributes, how can the words, 'pervades the whole universe' be correct. How can it be without attributes, if it has the character of pervading this universe? Before answering this, one has to understand that the substance of consciousness is nothing but energy. The philosophy of Pātañjali has also used the word '*citiśakti*' to explain this. On the other hand, although *Sānkhya*, says that *Purūṣa* being the cause of inert Nature is only important by its proximity, in practice, *Purūṣa* without attributes has been said to be energy. An intelligent reader has to think whether the one by the proximity of which, inert nature acts consciously can itself be other than energy. Even *Vedānta*, says 'from which birth and all else' (*janmadyāsya yataḥ*), and expressed the energy of consciousness. Even if this universe is false and creation is imaginary, it resides in *Brahmaṇ*. What gives shelter to something else or is of the nature of a shelter of something else, cannot be other than energy.

You may say, if the Self is of the nature of energy, it cannot be without attributes. In answer, it has to be said that when there is no activity observed in awareness it may be said to be without attributes. If you say, how can something without expression of activity be called energy, because activity is the sign of energy? It has to be said that even in a state without attributes, subtle energy of action remains. Even in its state, *Brahmaṇ* is self-expressed, that is, it expresses itself, or enjoys itself. It is nothing other than energy. It is needless to say that when perceptual seekers realize or try to realize *paramātmā* through intelligence, so long the Self expresses itself as the energy of intelligence. We know that *ātmā* is energy (*śakti*). In the material world, energy may appear separate from the one with it, but in the arena of Self, energy and the one with it are one. The difference is seen only in language, but the energy of awareness does not need any other residence. If one agrees with this conclusion, there is no conflict with other scriptures, philosophies or ancient texts. One can without any doubt solve this conflict between with or without attributes. Doubts as to how this universe is created from the one without attributes are also removed.

If you want to prove that there is any state without energy, give it a place above one without attributes. It is beyond words and mind, so *Vedas* and *Vedānta* are silent in describing its nature. What is established by this world 'one without second', and 'not this, not this', is only for One without attributes. So, agree to it that there is an entity beyond words and mind that is neither with attributes nor without. That unknowable principle has two supremacies or expressions, one with and the other without attributes. What is with attributes has two great expressions, one is God the other, worldly persons.

How the power of awareness without attributes, takes on a

perception of attributes and expressed in this way has no change to its attribute-less nature, has been explained in discussing the principle of bliss. It is not necessary to repeat it here.

That this universe is energy is agreed to by all. Even with an infinite variety of names and forms, those who have eyes, see it as nothing but one energy. One who knows well about water will know nothing but water when seeing ice. Just as seeing an ornament one perceives gold, or seeing a pot one perceives clay, so do the many names and forms of this universe, appear as one energy of awareness to those who have eyes to see. This world is built of awareness and resides in awareness. The substance of awareness is nothing but perception (*bodha*). This perception and bliss are nondifferent, This universe is bliss. I have said before and say again, that this universe is built from bliss, resides in bliss and will dissolve into bliss. By the grace of Mother, if eyes of knowledge are opened, one sees this universe as bliss.

Whatever that is, Mother, we bow down to you who is expressed as this world of name and form. Then, we bow to your supreme form as the sentient Goddess, who is expressed as the energy of awareness in the creation-maintenance-dissolution of this universe. After this, we bow down to the unexpressed causal power that is beyond the physical and subtle. Finally, saying '*namo namoḥ*', we bow down to the pure nature beyond words and mind. May our *pranāms* be worthy.

Open your eyes and see that Mother as awareness fills all this universe. There is nothing else but Mother. All that you see and think is my Mother.

Verse 35.

stutā suraiḥ pūrvamabhīṣṭasaṁśrayā
ttathā surendreṇa dineṣu sevitā|
karotu sā naḥ śubhaheturīśvarī
śubhāni bhadrāṇyabhihantu chāpadaḥ||

Verse 36.

yā sāmpratañcoddhata daityatāpitai
rasmābhirīśā ca surairnamasyate|
yā ca smṛtā tatkṣaṇameva hanti naḥ
sarvāpado bhaktivinamramūrtibhiḥ||

Translation:

The Goddess was worshipped for many days by *Indra* and the other gods (in connection with the destruction of *Mahiṣāsura*). We (the gods), now being tormented by proud demons, with devotion, bow down to that supreme Goddess. We call on the one by remembering whom, all our dangers are immediately removed. May the supreme Goddess, who is the cause of good fortune, bless us and remove all our difficulties.

Explanation:

See how much faith the gods have. They say, 'by remembering whom, all our dangers are immediately removed' (*yā ca smītā tatkṣaṇameva hanti naḥ*). Truly when one has faith like this, one is never downcast in danger. When belief is firm that 'I have an all-powerful Mother', however much one may be in danger, there is such hope and faith in the heart, that dangers become inconsequential. What is so surprising in the fact that if we can properly remember the one who is our Self, one who expresses us, who has given us life to perceive joy and sorrow, then all dangers are immediately removed. But there is one thing, '*bhaktivinamramūrtibhiḥ*', bowed by devotion. Our 'I'-ness has to be lowered. The degree to which our 'I'-ness is lowered, our body-sense weakened, to that extent Mother appears in her form as the supreme Goddess. It is true when beings can realize the form of Mother as the supreme Goddess, their worldly dangers are removed.

Many have seen examples of people in deep danger, with pitiful hearts, crying to God and thus being saved. Many persons with incurable diseases are healed by surrendering at the feet of God. The secret of this is that by bowing down with devotion, this worldly 'I'-ness is weakened and God-like 'I' is expressed. By remembering the all-knowing, all-powerful supreme Lord, a small amount of that power is inducted by the body of a worldly person. As a result, dangers are removed. This is also the secret of finding medicines in dreams or by supplication at temples.

The word '*sarvāpadaḥ*' has another special meaning. Everything (*sarvvai*) is danger (*āpad*), meaning, as long as there is a perception of everything, of multiplicity, so long a spiritual seeker is in danger. To be freed from this danger in the form of everything, all need to bow down with devotion at the feet of God. As long as multiplicity is not removed and a sense of oneness is not perceived, so long one is inexperienced about the nature of Mother. In *Bhāgavat Gitā*, the Lord has advised us to forsake all religions and seek refuge in the undivided one[14]. Only by seeking refuge, that is, by devoted *praṇāms* can this be easily achieved.

Before this, the *stotra* by *Brahmā* in connection with the destruction of *Madhu* and *Kaitava*, and the *stotra* by the gods after the destruction of *Mahiṣāsura* have been explained. The present *stotra* has many special characteristics from the other two. In the two previous hymns, the supremacy, kindness and power of Mother were described. This *stotra* is about *praṇām*. Here, Mother is seen in her appearances as hunger, thirst, sleep, error, etc. and is offered *pranām*. As knowledge emerges, one understands that the 'I' is an insurmountable ignorance. So, to be free of this ignorance, whatever appears, existent or nonexistent, the seeker sees as Mother and tries to offer the sense of 'I'-ness at her feet. In this manner, the higher the seeker rises in knowledge, the lower one offers oneself. Acquiring knowledge means understanding the extent of ignorance. Understanding the nature of ignorance makes it easier to offer it at the feet of knowledge without hesitation. So, the gods by bowing down repeatedly, make a path to success easy. After this, with the destruction of *Śumbha*, we will see the praises sung to *Nārāyaṇī*, which is also about *praṇām*. This is a

---

14 '*sarva dharmān parityajya māmekaṁ śaraṇaṁ vraja*' *Bhāgavat Gītā*, 18.66

secret of spiritual effort. One can achieve everything by devoted *praṇām*. The gods are children in the heart of Mother, nurtured at her breast, so they are always bowing down.

We are beings with a sense of physical bodies, smallest of the small, yet our heads refuse to bow down. We do not understand that the more we try to honor this false 'I', the more we abuse it. Our sad condition is because we do not understand that if this 'I' lowers itself at the feet of God, then it will achieve divine glory. Even now, in this country, Hindus true to their religion bow down to foremost *brāhmiṇs*. Why do they do so? One day these *brāhmiṇs* lowered their 'I'-ness at the feet of the queen of this universe, as a result, even today their children receive the *praṇāms* of all the Hindu race. Even thinking of this, my eyes fill with tears. One day, a *brāhmiṇ* who bowed at the feet of Mother, was powerful. They had such faith in the spirit of Mother that they considered even a state as *Viṣṇu* to be negligible.

Let us briefly discuss the different forms of Mother that are mentioned in this hymn. Beginning their praises, the gods first bow down to the form of Mother as *Viṣṇumāyā* that resides in all beings. In turn, they repeatedly bow down to Mother as consciousness, intelligence, sleep, hunger, shadow, energy, thirst, forgiveness, race, shame, peace, respect, beauty, *Lakṣmī*, profession, memory, mercy, satisfaction, maternity and error. You see Mother every day in all these aspects. But you cannot believe that it is truly Mother. Because of a lack of faith, you cannot truly bow down at her feet. Even if you do you cannot do it faithfully. You are at a distance from the pleasure and grace of Mother. Mother is always present inside you as consciousness, intelligence, sleep hunger and so on. Bow down to her. The establishment of truth spoken of in Volume One, the establishment of life force in Volume Two, is now illuminated by bliss. Understanding that an undivided blissful perception keeps us in its living embrace as the before mentioned intelligence, sleep, etc. removes ignorance. The knot of *Rudra*, of knowledge, is pierced.

These *praṇāms* are not just this. They are a high form of

spiritual enterprise. If one can bow down in the manner indicated, that is, keeping attention to the physical, subtle, causal and beyond, which are the individual, combined, unexpressed and pure spirit, the restrictions of knowledge are removed. This is the principle of knowledge. In Volume Two it was advised to perceive life force as the principle of earth, water, energy and all. Here the spiritual enterprise has advanced to a subtler stage. By viewing each attribute and bowing down to it, a path appears to the immensity of an undivided ocean of perception. The undivided blissful perception that was given as an explanation for the mantra '*sārāyai sarvakāriṇyai*', understanding it to be expressed as individual intelligence, sleep, etc. one has to offer a first *praṇām*. The significance of the first '*namastasyai*' is to realize the attributes of each individual spirit as the nature of bliss. Then one has to offer a second *praṇām*, taking that individual attribute to a unified principle, that is to the divine principle. A realization of the supremacy of God is the secret of this second *praṇām*. After this is the discovery of the causal or nonmanifest arena and finally the nature beyond all perceptions. These are the secrets of the third and fourth *praṇāms*. Bowing down in this manner is the goal of this hymn. To a seeker without perceptions, this may appear to be a puzzle. Those who have been blessed by the grace of the *guru* will, without a doubt, find these principles fulfilling.

Verse 37.

ṛīṣiruvāca|
evaṁ stavābhiyuktānāṁ devānāṁ tatra pārvatī|
snātumabhyāyayau toye jāhnavyā nṛpanandana||

Translation:

The sage said, 'O royal child! When the gods were singing praises in this fashion, the goddess *Pārvatī* arrived, to bathe in the waters of the river *Jāhṇavī*.'

Explanation:

The gods finish reciting the hymn. So, the words 'the sage

said' are used again. The great sage Medhasa addresses king Suratha as '*nṛpanandana.*' One who protects or looks after people is '*nṛpa.*' The great spiritual seekers can be properly said to be *nṛpa*. Occasionally, great spiritual seekers like Suratha appear in this world and the society of humans remains stable. Ideal spiritual seekers with a heart of *dharma*, who are dedicated to *Brahmaṇ* are the backbone of the greater race of humans. Being roused by their example, humans keep their eyes on truth and *dharma*. Otherwise, the society of humans would turn into one like animals. The lower the number of spiritual seekers in a land, the more other people are addicted to material things, the more they are of the nature of animals. But that is something else. Those that show the light of truth in this world and stabilize society, are truly *nṛpa*, protectors of people. Even now, in the Western parts of India, people address great souls with an honorary word similar to *nṛpa*, such as '*mahārāj*' (emperor). One who brings joy to great spiritual seekers is *nṛpanandana*. Here the great sage Medhasa is ready to explain the principles of bliss (*ananda*). So he addresses Suratha as '*nṛpanandana*'.

When the gods were singing praises to Mother in this fashion, she appeared there in the form of *Pārvatī*, to bathe in the waters of the river *Jāhṇavī,* the Ganges of heaven. While singing praises, feelings of *sattva* arose in the hearts of the truth-united gods, so their spirits were moistened and tears of love flowed from their eyes. These were the waters of *Jāhṇavī*. Repeatedly remembering the name of Mother, viewing her splendor in all manners, crying for her with a pitiful voice, and bowing to her with devotion over and over again, the inevitable results of these actions are the holy waters of *Jāhṇavī*. Mother appeared to bathe in it, to be honored by it. When the children cry for her, Mother appears in this manner to remove their sorrow. The tears of devotion of the children are holy. They are the waters of *Jāhṇavī*. Mother cannot bathe or be sprinkled with any other water. To cool the heart of Mother, to move her by the terrible cries of her tormented children, needs such unrestrained tears of love. The gods have accomplished this today with their hymns. Mother has appeared.

Mother has appeared in the form of *Pārvatī*. Before this, the gods had descended to Himālayā or the ego of the physical body to sing praises. So, Mother appears physically in the form of *Pārvatī*. That is, Mother appears in this physical world, her blissful spirit is expressed. The gods saw that the visible world is not inert, it is the blissful form of Mother. Each atom of this universe is an expression of bliss. This cluster of bliss, being built of the holding power of Mother, appears as this world. Materials are not just materials, they are dense forms of bliss. Mountains are not just mountains (*parvvat*) they are the dense blissful form of *Pārvatī*. The forms and flavors enjoyed by the senses are but the blissful nature of Self. Wherever we lay our eyes, up, down, right, left, front or back, as far as perception extends, everywhere is of the dense spirit of bliss. Coming here, the gods were honored. They understood that their desires would be fulfilled.

Verse 38.

sāhbravīttān surān subhrūrbhavadbhistūyatehatra kā|
śarīrakośataścāsyāḥ samudbhūtābravīcchivā||

Verse 39.

stotraṁ mamaitatkriyate śumbhadaityanirākṛtaiḥ|
devaiḥ sametaiḥ samare niśumbhena parājitaiḥ||

Translation: The Goddess *Pārvatī* with beautiful eyebrows, asked the gods, "Who are you singing praises to?" Appearing from her body sheath, *Śivā*, a beneficial form of the goddess, appeared and said, "tormented by the *asura Śumbha* and defeated by the *asura Niśumbha*, the gods have come together to sing praises to me."

Explanation:

Like an innocent girl, 'feigning' innocence, as if she knows nothing, she asks. "Who are you singing praises to?" My Mother is like this. A simple child, daughter *Gourī*, my mother *Umā*, is like this. The children are in trouble, tormented by demons. With anxious hearts, they call on Mother. But on the calm, simple, pure face of Mother, there are no signs of concern. It is as if nothing has happened. So, with a pleasant look, she asks, "What has happened?"

Oh, you may see in these words signs of poetry. But it is not so. There is no trace of poetry in this. Truly this arena of Self is steady, quiet and peaceful. Worldly vibrations do not reach here. Material things reach up to intelligence; they cannot come to this blissful arena of Self. How can material vibrations remain where even inert things are illuminated as blissful percepts? Nothing has happened here. She is always our, eternal, pure, undisturbed, steady Mother. So, she asks, "What has happened? Who are you singing praises to?"

From the body sheath of *Pārvatī* appeared a beneficial form, *Śivā*. The form of the goddess *Śivā* arose from the blissful figure of *Pārvatī*. The gods saw her appear while they sang praises. We have said that the blissful form of *Pārvatī* appears based on the material world. When this blissful spirit expresses itself after discarding its material basis, then it may be said to discard its body sheath and appear in the form of *Śivā*. The bliss, based on which this universe is manifested, that expresser and enjoyer of attributes (*guṇas*), which is attribute-less, this basic spirit has been here named *Śivā*. It is the divinity of this final character in *Caṇḍī*, the goddess *Sarasvatī*, the seed form of speech and this world, the form as *Gourī*.

Let one not think of a goddess holding a *viṇā*[15], when we say *Sarasvatī*. The word '*saravān*' means ocean (*arṇav*) or causality (*kāraṇ*). In the mantras of creation principles in the *Ṛk Vedas*, the word is meant as the causal ocean. The power of *sarasvān* is *Sarasvatī*. The power that is expressed as causality is called *Sarasvatī*. In this final character, the final union of this world of beings with causal-natured supreme divinity is going to be explained. This has also been mentioned in the introductory verse[16]. This *Sarasvatī* is of the form of knowledge. All percepts

15 stringed musical instrument

16 *upodghāt sutra*

dissolve in it. This goddess, emerging from the body sheath of *Pārvatī* will soon destroy all the demons like *Śumbha* and *Niśumbha*, and be established as the one and only, nondual nature. These events begin here. For so long, she was sheltered in the body sheaths, that is, was expressed in the inert material world in the form of *Pārvatī*. But now, with the hymns of the gods, by their pitiful prayers, because of mercy and affection, she leaves the body sheaths, the connection with inertness and is expressed as pure power of awareness.

She is the sentient nature of self-expression. All perceptions are expressed by her. There is nothing unknown to her. She describes the cause and nature of the worship by the gods. 'The gods tormented by *Śumbha* are singing my praises.' It is true. Where there is nothing else but 'I', then whatever one does, knowingly or unknowingly, all worship is directed to me. In the *Rajaguhya* yoga of the *Gitā*, the Lord has said the same thing. 'I am indeed the enjoyer and Lord of all ceremonies'[17]. Here in *Devī Māhātmya*, the working form is expressed. Mother expresses her true nature by saying 'singing my praises' (*stotraṁ mamaitatkriyate*). In the *Gitā*, speaking about the worship of other gods, the indirect worship of Self was mentioned. Here the gods have sung praises to the power of awareness, or Self, so there is no question about anything else.

A spiritual seeker should remember that, as long as not only spiritual enterprise but all actions are not directed to the awareness-natured Self, they are unprescribed acts. They are the cause of birth and death, of worldly existence. To truly relieve oneself from the insurmountable hands of *māyā*, like the gods, one has to seek the help of Self. With all percepts, at all times, one has to serve 'I.' All acts have to be carried out directed at 'I.' If you can do this, (all humans have the right), then one will undoubtedly conquer both worlds.

'Seek shelter only in me'[18]; how this final, invaluable advice

17 *Bhāgavat Gitā*, 9:24

18 *'māmekaṁ śaraṇaṁ vraja' ibid* 18:66

is brought to a successful state in the life of a spiritual seeker is directed in *Devī Māhātmya*. All this is being repeated as a reminder. Something else to be mentioned here is that, when the words 'I' and 'mine' are used here, they are not attachment and ego (*Śumbha* and *Niśumbha)*. It is *ātmā*, Mother, *guru*. Perceptible seekers will be able to understand the difference.

Verse 40.

śarīrakośādyattasyāḥ pārvatyā niḥsṛtāmbikā|
kauśikīti samasteṣu tato lokeṣu gīyate||

Translation:

Because the goddess *Amvikā*, appeared from the body sheaths (*koṣa*) of *Pārvatī*, in all these worlds, she was named *Kouṣikī.*

Explanation:

The Goddess is the shining form of self-expression of the power of awareness. She is expressed based on the material sheaths of the body. Sometimes, condensed by the chill of devotion of a spiritual seeker, she leaves the material sheaths and expresses herself as awareness. This is a renouncement of the body sheath (*koṣa*), so she is known by the name *Kouṣikī*. This name of Mother is sung in all the worlds. Remember that as long as Mother appears in the form of the five sheaths, she is known as *Pārvatī*. When she leaves the connection with the sheaths and appears in her sentient form, my Mother is known as *Kouṣikī* .

Verse 41.

tasyāṁ vinirgatāyāntu kṛṣṇābhūtsāpi pārvatī|
kāliketi samākhyātā himācalakṛtāśrayā||

Translation:

Because of her (*Kouṣikī*) leaving the body sheaths in this manner, the goddess *Pārvatī* turned dark in color and was known as the *Kālika*, sheltered by Himālayā.

Explanation:

When my Mother, *ātmā*, the power of awareness, leaves her connections with the five sheaths and expresses her pure nature of Self, then the five sheaths turn dark (*kriṣṇā*), that is of the nature of ignorance. Because it is of the nature of ignorance, this dark form is known as *Kālikā*. Because it resides in the very inert, this form of *Kālikā* is said to be sheltered by Himālayā.

Let me say this more clearly. When spiritual seekers see the pure, sentient form of Mother, they forget material percepts of the body. Not that they are questioning at this time, they are not subject to knowledge. This ignorance about the physical body is here *kriṣṇā*, in the form of *Kālikā*. In this condition, when one resides in pure perception, although one's percept of material states is absent, in the view of others one appears in a material form. This is the mystery of *Pārvatī* appearing in the form of *Kālikā*, sheltered by Himālayā. When intelligence is purified, that is, when the active and inert *guṇas* are overcome, one discovers *paramātmā* beyond intelligence. There appear hints of its appearance and the difference between inert and conscious is perceived more clearly. On one side intensely dark, on the other, self-expressed awareness. A spiritual seeker reaches this point as a result of much piety.

Verse 42.

tatoḥambikāṁ paraṁ rūpaṁ bibhrāṇāṁ sumanoharaṁ|
dadarśa caṇḍamuṇḍaśca bhṛtyau śumbhaniśumbhayoḥ||

Translation:

After this, the servants of *Śumbha* and *Niśumbha*, named *Caṇḍa* and *Muṇḍa* saw the very pleasing and beautiful *Amvikā*.

Explanation:

The form as *Kauṣikī* that was mentioned before, is expressed here as the form of *Amvikā*. The form appearing from the body sheaths of *Pārvatī* is the pure power of awareness *Amvikā*. When the power of awareness leaves any connection with inertness and is expressed in its own nature, then inertness turns into a black form covered by darkness. This was named *Kālikā* in the previous mantra. When consciousness or the power of awareness is expressed materially, it is named *Pārvatī*. When the pure awareness is expressed separately from the body of *Pārvatī*, it is named *Amvikā* or *Kouṣikī*. The remaining part is named *Kṛṣṇā* or *Kālikā*.

Amvikā: Mother, the maternal form that gives birth to this world; '*sumanohara*' means extremely pure, untainted by matters of this world. Or, that which can rob or remove the mind (*man*) is *sumanohara*. Or, the word '*sumanā*' means divinities. That which can rob even the *sumanā* is '*sumanohara*.' My Mother had taken a form of supreme beauty. By this great form, the mind and even the divinities established in the senses are deprived of any expression. The mantra says, 'saw the very pleasing beauty *Amvikā*.'

Truly my Mother *Amvikā* is very pleasant, supremely beautiful. Where all perceptions have disappeared yet by which all things are expressed, that is truly supreme beauty. If the mind is not stolen, supreme beauty is not expressed. On the other hand, if supreme beauty is not expressed, the mind is not lost. When this supreme beauty is illuminated, mind vanishes.

That living plant or vine that you see, a special form is visible in it because it has life. The difference that is seen between a living and a dead tree, the difference between living and dead, the one that makes the difference, is the supreme form. It is this which on being expressed, makes this world so beautiful, so pleasing. A spiritual seeker should try to envision this form when one leaves any connections to inertness. That is the supreme form. When one sees this beauty, will the mind not be lost? That is why I have said many times, do not try to still the mind by spiritual enterprise. Look at supreme beauty, the mind will be stilled, will disappear. When the mind is stolen, the divinities residing in the senses, will dissolve into that supreme form. That is why the word '*sumanā*' can also mean divinities.

First, the servants of *Śumbha* and *Niśumbha*, named *Caṇḍa* and *Muṇḍa* discover this supreme form. *Caṇḍa* is inclination and *Muṇḍa* is disinclination. The word *Caṇḍa* is also used for one who is wrathful or irritable. Wrathfulness is a movement by inclination. As we proceed, we will enter into more subtle principles. What we have seen before as material tendencies of desire, anger, etc. coming here, we see as flows of subtle energies, a root tendency named inclination (*pravṛtti*). With it, we see another subtle flow of energy named disinclination. Both inclination and disinclination are expressed in the shelter of ego (*asmitā*) and attachment (*mamatā*). So, the sage calls them the servants of *Śumbha* and *Niśumbha*. Just as *Śumbha* and *Niśumbha* are of similar minds, so are *Caṇḍa* and *Muṇḍa*. Where there is inclination, there is disinclination.

A spiritual seeker should not here understand inclination and disinclination to have their common meanings. Here the words *Caṇḍa* and *Muṇḍa* mean the inclination towards *paramātmā* and the disinclination of the end of the ego. You have carried out much spiritual enterprise to find such inclination and disinclination. By much piety and spiritual effort, your inclination seeks only *paramātmā* and your disinclination wants the end of the matters of ego. This is the result of much good fortune, but these too are demons. They too have to be destroyed. There should be nothing that is inclination or disinclination. There will no longer be ego and attachment. Only the pleasing, beautiful Mother, *paramātmā* will remain

It is needless to say that this is not about the inclination towards matters of the world. The topic here is not about a dual inclination towards worldly things and *paramātmā.* Only the inclination towards *paramātmā* is meant by the demons *Caṇḍa* and *Muṇḍa*. When inclination is towards *ātmā*, that towards worldly matters is prevented. This also is a feeling of the demons, of non-Self. When there is anything other than *paramātmā*, there is inclination and disinclination. There is nothing else but the nondual *ātmā*, so it is seen that as long as spiritual seekers seek *paramātmā* and want to end worldly matters, they have feelings of non-Self. These have to be also destroyed. A spiritual seeker does not have to make any special arrangement for this. Mother has expressed her supreme form. One by one, she will offer *Caṇḍa*, *Muṇḍa* and the other demons to the supreme fire of nondual knowledge and so destroy the eternally stored *saṁskāra* of a spiritual seeker. These are a preparations for it. *Caṇḍa* and *Muṇḍa*, the servants of *Śumbha* and *Niśumbha*, have seen the form of *Amvikā*. There is no longer any delay, they will be soon destroyed.

First, the inclination towards Self discovers a hint of *paramātmā*. So, before *Śumbha* sees *Amvikā*, his servants *Caṇḍa* and *Muṇḍa* saw her.

Verse 43.

tābhyāṁ śumbhāya cākhyātā atīvasumanoharā|
kāpyāste strī mahārāja bhāsayantī himācala||

Translation:

They (*Caṇḍa* and *Muṇḍa*) came to *Śumbha* and said, 'O great king, an extremely pleasing, indefinable female form resides, lighting up the Himālayās.

Explanation:

It is with the help of inclination and disinclination that ego discovers the nature of *paramātmā.* Because he establishes all percepts, *Caṇḍa* and *Muṇḍa* address *Śumbha* as the great king (*mahārāja*). Then, describing the feminine form of *Amvikā*, they first say that she is extremely pleasing. When the nature of Mother is expressed, even for a very brief moment, mind, intelligence, senses, inclination and disinclination, all feelings of non-self are lost. That is why my Mother is truly pleasing. *Caṇḍa* and *Muṇḍa* also say that the form resides, illuminating inertness (the Himālayās).

One day, inclination that attracted you to murky areas of worldly matters, that you made so many arrangements to subdue, that you saw as great sorrow, today you see that inclination discover a very pleasing, supreme beauty. Inclination that one day took you towards bondage, today opens the locks on the doors of the temple of liberation. What is the fault of inclination? As long as it did not discover supreme beauty it ran towards worldly things. What is the fault of disinclination? As long as it did not discover the nature of supreme Self it was engaged with the practice of ending worldly things. It practiced abandonment and renunciation. But today they have seen *Amvikā*. They have discovered the supreme beauty situated beyond intelligence. So, they run ahead and inform ego that 'an indefinable female form resides, illuminating the Himālayās.'

Until now a spiritual seeker had thought the Himālayās, that is inertness, to be a place of expression of consciousness. It understood that consciousness was expressed as inert matter. But what does it see today? Consciousness is self-expressed. It can be seen without any connection to inert matter, can be enjoyed completely isolated. Consciousness expressing inert matter is today independently illuminated. So *Caṇḍa* and *Muṇḍa* said, separate from the Himālayās but illuminating it. The *Upaniṣad* says, 'all that is bright is a shadow of its brightness, all these shine by its light'[19].

Before this, a spiritual seeker only viewed Mother in the form of *Pārvatī*, that is, by the establishment of truth and life force, perceiving the nature of consciousness as the manifest world. Today there is the opportunity to perceive it independently from this world. Oh! How can I write what it is? How many times have we said 'that from which birth and everything else' (*janmadyāsya yataḥ*).[20] From that which we are born, in which we reside, in which we will merge again, yet that which does not have birth-residence-dissolution; how can I state the joy of perceiving it, or meeting it? Because its nature cannot be described, the mantra uses the word '*kāpi*' meaning undefined. And, to explain that the pure consciousness natured Self is energy, the word 'feminine'

---

19 '*tameva bhāntam anubhāti sarvvaṁ tasya vāsā sarvvamidaṁ vibhāti*' *Kaṭha Upaniṣad*, 2.2.15

20 *Brahma Sutra*, 1:1

is applied. That energy is always indefinable. It is by action that energy is defined. When a spiritual seeker discovers even a trace of this energy unconnected to action, it brings him enormous bliss.

Verse 44.

naiva tādṛk kvacidrūpaṁ dṛṣṭaṁ kenaciduttamam|
jñāyatāṁ kāpyasau devī gṛhyatāñcāsureśvara||

Translation:

No one has ever seen such exquisite beauty. O king of demons, you have to find out who this goddess is. You have to get her.

Explanation:

These words of *Caṇḍa* and *Muṇḍa* are beautiful. Truly, who has ever seen such beauty? Whoever sees her will become the same. There is no means of remaining separate. So, *Caṇḍa* and *Muṇḍa* say 'no one has ever seen such beauty.' It is untouched. One cannot explain its nature to anybody. One cannot speak. It is the enjoyment by someone who is dumb.

They also told *Śumbha*, 'find her and then get her.' The *Gitā* has also said, first one has to know, then see and then enter[21]. The *Upaniṣad* calls this hearing, thinking and practice.

The word '*gṛhyatām*' used in the mantra means to receive. This receiving and going in are the same because to receive Mother is to be with her. One cannot take Mother, one has to be taken oneself. Mother cannot be taken or known. Mother herself is the nature of knowledge. How can one know the knower or take it? To know her, one has to go beyond knower and known.

Verse 45.

strīratnamaticārvaṅgī dyotayantī diśastviṣā|
sā tu tiṣṭhati daityendra tāṁ bhavān draṣṭumarhati||

---

21 *jñātuṁ draṣṭuñca tattvena, Bhāgabat Gitā,* 11.54

Translation:

O king of demons, she is a jewel among women. Her form is extremely beautiful. The horizons are lit up by the glow from her body. You have to see her.

Explanation:

Although these are the words of enticement by inclination, there is not a shred of untruth in them. Truly, she is a jewel among women. She is the indefinable center of infinite energy. The word 'jewel' (*ratna*) also means knowledge. So, the words 'jewel of a woman' can also point to the knowledge-formed nature of energy. We have mentioned this power of awareness before. By saying 'jewel of a woman', *Caṇḍa* and *Muṇḍa* give a hint to *Śumbha*. Truly her limbs were beautiful. She was the charmer of the god of love. Truly, seeing her, 'the god of love swoons.' She is a storehouse of infinite beauty. She is the supreme form of love, the supremely loved Self. She is so charming, so beautiful, that 'even looking at her beauty for a lifetime, eyes are not satisfied.' Such is the beauty that 'looking at her always, we still look for her.' It is the beauty of the one beyond beauty, incredible splendor. What language is there to express this? If one could imagine the feeling of collecting all the beauty of this world, putting together all the happiness in this world, then one could get a hint of that undivided bliss, the immense happiness. Oh! It is nectar, it is ambrosia, it is sanctuary!

'*dyotayantī diśastviṣā*': The splendor of her body lit up the horizons. The *Upaniṣad* says, 'by its light, everything is lit up'[22]. This universe, this multiplicity, this 'I', all that is expressed by it, one that after expressing all, resides as only bliss, she is *Amvikā*, *ātmā*, my Mother. To explain that Mother is only bliss and the energy of awareness, *Caṇḍa* and *Muṇḍa* use the words, 'beautiful form' and 'jewel of a woman.' How else will the demons express the nature of the bliss of Mother? Bliss has no specific form. It is in the form of perception.

---

22 *Kaṭha Upaniṣad*, 2.2.15

There is something else in this mantra. *Caṇḍa* and *Muṇḍa* told *Śumbha* that 'you have the capability of looking at her.' As long as one does not discover ego (*asmitā*), one cannot understand this 'nature of beauty beyond beauty.' But, by the grace of the *guru*, a spiritual seeker, after all this time, discovering truth and life force arrives at the center of 'I'-ness. So, one now has the capability of realizing the nature of supreme bliss. This is the way inclination entices the ego.

Look! As long as inclination faces worldly things, it takes us along a path towards hell. But it is inclination that opens the locks on the doors to the temple of liberation. So, I say, do not criticize inclination, it is truly a well-meaning friend.

Verse 46.

yāni ratnāni maṇayo gajāśvādīni vai prabho|
trailokye tu samastāni sāmpratam̐ bhānti te gṛhe||

Translation:

O Lord, all the greatest gems, elephants and horses in these three worlds, now grace your home.

Explanation:

Caṇḍa and *Muṇḍa* are doing their best to try to entice *Śumbha*. O Lord, all the best in this universe adorn your house.

Although all percepts are expressed based on ego, although all things best and worst should be in the house of *Śumbha*, to describe the greatness of *Śumbha*, *Caṇḍa* and *Muṇḍa* only mention jewels and other great objects. In the material sense, all the greatest objects in the three worlds, elephants, horses, gems and jewels are in the house of *Śumbha*. Other than this, in a spiritual view, one can see that jewels mean the greatest thing, knowledge. The *Gitā* too says, 'nothing here exists as pure as knowledge'[23]. In the same manner, elephant means bondage and horse means movement. (These have been previously explained.) The knowledge formed

23 *Bhāgavat Gitā,* 4:38

jewels, the elephant formed bondage of actions and the horse formed movement towards heaven or hell are all in the residence of ego.

The last portion of the mantra says, '*samastāni sāmpratam̐ bhānti te gṛhe.*' There is some mystery in the word '*sāmpratam̐*' (presently). Up to now, all things in the three worlds are owned by ego. Later it will all be of *ātmā*. When knowledge arises, it is seen that only *Brahmaṇ* is the causal and constituent reason for this universe. Ego is not the universal cause. The universal cause of this universe by ego appears for the present. Later, such ignorance will not remain. Whether *Śumbha* understood the deep meaning of the words of *Caṇḍa* and *Muṇḍa* will have to be decided by spiritual seekers.

Verse 47.

airāvataḥ samānīto gajaratnam̐ purandarāt|
pārijātataruścāyam̐ tathaivoccaiḥśravā hayaḥ||

Translation:

You have taken the prize among elephants *Airāvata*, the *Pārijāta* tree and the horse named *Uccaiḥśravā* from *Indra*.

Explanation:

In the next six mantras, *Caṇḍa* and *Muṇḍa* develop the statement in the previous mantra. Before they had said that all the wealth and gems of the three worlds are in your house. Now being specific, they tell *Śumbha*, 'Look at all the great things of *Indra* you have taken, *Airāvata*, *Pārijāta* and *Uccaiḥśravā*.'

The terms *Indra* and *Airāvata* have been explained in Volume Two. '*Pārijāta*' is the tree of wish fulfillment. When the wishes of a seekers are fulfilled just by resolution, then one has to understand that the *Pārijāta* tree resides in their homes. '*Uccaiḥśravā*' is the power of divine hearing. The power to hear from great distances or the finest sounds is called *Uccaiḥśravā*.

As the right tendency becomes pure, the true nature of ego is revealed. A spiritual seeker then sees that 'I'-ness closely united with all percepts is its only residence. Everything is contained in 'I'-ness. Whatever is in this world, subtle or material, is owned by ego. Although *Airāvata* and the others are powers of *Indra, paramātmā*, they are understood by inclination and disinclination to be expressions of ego. This is the percept of the demons. Not understanding that self-expressed power of awareness (*cit*) is the residence of all, thinking that the expression of ego is holding them. This is the percept of a demon.

Verse 48.

vimānaṁ haṁsasaṁyukttametattiṣṭhati tehaṅgane|
ratnabhūtamihānītaṁ yadāsīd vedhasohadbhutam||

Translation:

The extraordinary, bejeweled craft of *Brahmā* has been taken by you and sits in your courtyard.

Explanation:

Vedhā: *Brahmā*, the great mind; *haṁsa*: worldly person; *vimāna*: a flying craft; *haṁsayukta*: drawn by swans. The minds of worldly persons travel in space or the principle of the sky. So, mind is called *vimāna* or a space-craft. The great mind, whose resolution is this world is *Vedhā* or *Brahmā*. Our minds are also his special resolve. This individual mind is the extraordinary aircraft of *Brahmā*. If one understands how individual and collective minds reside, one can understand the mystery of the swan-connected *vimāna* of *Brahmā*. The manner in which collective mind or *Prajāpati* travels by riding on individual minds or the swan-connected *vimāna* is extraordinary. This is the greatest gem or power of *Brahmā*. We have discussed this before but it may be done here again.

You see a tree. You do not see the great mind whose resolve is this tree. The tree is of the form of resolve, of perception of bliss, because the imagination of a blissful *parameśvara* is expressed as a tree. It is formed of bliss. That sentient bliss-formed tree is unknowable to you. Then, what tree do you see? From that awareness-blissful tree form, a vibration comes to the senses and arouses your mind, the swan connected *vimāna* of Brahmā is molded by the form of a tree. In this manner, you see a tree. According to your *saṁskāra*, you only see a material, physical tree. The tree of bliss-formed material is hidden by your elemental tendencies. This is the strange *vimāna* of *Brahmā* or the mysterious diversity of creation. In this manner, although the creation by God is by nature awareness-bliss, it appears to be covered by elemental tendencies. Although *Brahmā* is the nature of awareness, he can transform his imagination into inert, physical matter. The swan-connected craft or the minds of beings is what helps this transformation, So *Brahmā* rides on a swan. From eternal times, we have kept our individual minds, to be able to receive forms and flavors only of materials. We have lost the ability to enjoy this awareness-bliss of the universe. So *Prajāpati Brahmā* rules over us. We are beings, we are swans, the carriers of *Brahmā*. Because our individual minds are experts at receiving physical things, he shows us the material play of this indefinable creation, all the time.

This strange craft of *Brahmā* has been stolen by *Śumbha*. Now, these extraordinary matters of creation are no longer those of *Brahmā*, they are owned by *Śumbha*. Arriving at the true nature of ego, a spiritual seeker sees that it is 'I' who holds all resolutions and vibrations of individual and collective minds. It is from 'I' that individual and collective minds appear. Without 'I', the spirit of mind does not exist. This is the mystery of *Śumbha* acquiring the *vimāna* of *Brahmā*. The mind is an enclosure of ego (*asmitā*). This is well realized by a spiritual seeker with practices directed by a *guru*.

Verse 49.

nidhireṣa mahāpadmaḥ samānīto dhaneśvarāt|
kiñjalkinīṁ dadau cābdhirmālāmamlānapaṅkajām||

Translation:

You have received the treasure named *Mahāpadma* from the ruler of wealth *Kuvera*. The ocean has given you the garland named *Kiñjalkini*, of never-fading lotus flowers.

Explanation:

The words 'treasure named *Mahāpadma*' mean pure right attribute (*sattva*). The *Mārkeṇḍya Purāṇa* has said, the treasure named *Mahāpadma* is the repository of pure attribute. So, persons who are of the right attribute (*sattva guṇa*) are fit to receive this treasure. When active and static (*rājasa* and *tāmasa*) tendencies are overcome, right attribute is purified. Here, right attribute is called the treasure *Mahāpadma*. It has been said that all treasures or special powers appear from right attribute. If the active and static principles are not subdued, if one cannot reside in pure right attribute, a spiritual seeker cannot realize the nature of ego. This treasure, *Mahāpadma* is in the house of *Śumbha*.

The god of wealth is *Kuvera*. Life force is the proper ruler of wealth, so the word '*dhaneśvara*' means life. If one can perceive the nature of life force that exists in this world, then right tendency is purified. The great lotus (*Mahāpadma*) or pure right tendency may be said to be sheltered by life force. A spiritual seeker who arrives at ego has by the practice of establishment of life force, already realized its presence everywhere. So, one has the right to the treasure of the great lotus of pure right attribute. Because pure right attribute is found by the establishment of truth, this verse speaks about receiving this treasure from *Kuvera*, the god of wealth.

Besides this, *Śumbha* had received a garland of never-fading lotus flowers, named *Kiñjalkini* from the ocean. The ocean is the reservoir of actions. A spiritual seeker who arrives at ego, has only a meager mass of actions, because stored and future actions have been removed, yet, as long as past tendencies (*saṁskāra*) are not eroded, some (though small) actions remain. Although one does not see any binding actions of desire in such seekers, there is no way to deny that as long as the body remains, tendencies of prior actions (*prāravdha*) remain. One has to understand this to be a store of prior actions. We have spoken before about stored and future actions. They will later be explained as parts of the four battalions of warriors of *Caṇḍa* and *Muṇḍa*.

By the garland of never-fading lotus flowers, one has to understand the ready-to-bloom prior tendencies. Until now they have not eroded, so they are never fading. The word '*pañka*' means sins or ignorance. They are born from the ignorance-natured clay (*pañka*) so they are called '*pañkaja*.' The word '*kiñjalka*' means pollen. The one with pollen is called *kiñjalkini*. The garland of ready-to-bloom prior actions is '*kiñjalkini*.' Just like yellow pollen inside a lotus, the strong seeds of prior actions keep a seeker from residing in the nature of Self. As long as strong, adverse prior tendencies are not eroded, the knowledge of Self is not obtained. As long as one does not see Mother emerge as the nature of Self, one has to realize that the garland of unfading lotus flowers remains an obstacle. One has to wait calmly for the erosion of prior tendencies. Anxiety will result in delay. One has to rely on the mercy of Mother and cry to her tenderly.

Whatever that is, the store of actions appeared to be an independent entity before. Now one can see it as an expression of ego. *Caṇḍa* and *Muṇḍa* tell *Śumbha* that the lotus garland owned by the ocean has been received by him.

The explanation of the ocean as differences between the connections of the three tendencies (*guṇas*) given in Volume Two is not in conflict with the meaning of 'ocean' given here. An insightful reader will understand this.

Verse 50.

chatraṁ te vāruṇaṁ gehe kāñcanasrāvi tiṣṭhati|
tathāyaṁ syandanavaro yaḥ purāsīt prajāpateḥ||

Translation:

The golden umbrella given by *Varuṇa* and the superior chariot that was owned by *Prajāpati* are in your house.

Explanation:

Chatra: umbrella, that which covers; *kāñcanasrāvi*: that which brings wealth. When the sense of self is withdrawn into ego, on one side, the true nature of Self is covered. On the other, the nature of ownership of all percepts is expressed. Wealth and special powers are manifested. This is the golden umbrella. Because it covers *paramātmā*, it is called an umbrella. Before this was owned by *Varuṇa*, the god of flavor (*rasa*). Now it is in the house of *Śumbha*. A spiritual seeker used to think that desires, wealth and special powers were each of separate natures. One now sees them as special manifestations of one's self. So *Caṇḍa* and *Muṇḍa* say, what was before owned by *Varuṇa* is now yours. Because a spiritual seeker has subtle desires for godliness and greatness, they cover *paramātmā* like a golden umbrella.

The chariot (*syandanavara*) of *Prajāpati*: are the faculties of spirit. It is by these faculties (*vṛtti*) that mind-natured *Prajāpati* moves about, that is, carries out acts of creation. These faculties are the chariot. It was owned by *Prajāpati* before, now it is in the house of *Śumbha*. A spiritual seeker used to know these faculties to be characteristics of the mind. Now one sees that they are nothing but different expressions of one's ego (*asmitā*). The word '*syandan*' is also used in the sense of exudation. Because the steady feeling of *paramātmā* is exuded, the faculties may be called '*syandan*.' In the beginning, a spiritual seeker used to think of these faculties as obstacles to finding Self. Now that feeling is no longer there. One sees everything as an expression of Self. As long as the faculties are seen to be separate from Self, one attempts to control them. When one arrives at the knowledge that the faculties are 'expressions of myself', one does not harbor adverse feelings towards them. The faculties are neither adverse nor helpful. When attention falls on the One by whose spirit they acquire spirit, their harmfulness is removed.

Verse 51.

mṛtyorutkrāntidā nāma śaktirīśa tvayā hṛtā|
pāśaḥ salilarājasya bhrātustava parigrahe||

Verse 52.

niśumbhasyābdhijātāśca samastā ratnajātayaḥ|
vahnirapi dadau tubhyamagniśauce ca vāsasī||

Translation:

Lord, you have taken away the power of death called *utkrāntidā*. A snare from the king of the waters and all the treasure from the oceans are now owned by your brother *Niśumbha*. Besides this, the god of fire has given you a pair of golden attire.

Explanation:

The power of death is '*utkrāntidā*.' It is the job of death to make life exit the body (*utkrāman*). This is its power or ability. Before arriving at ego, a spiritual seeker thought that death was a visiting entity, that *Yama* forcefully makes life exit from the body. Now that feeling is no longer there. Now one sees that death is not separate. When I wish to exit from the body, something called death takes place. This is the significance of removing from death the power to make life exit.

There is a beautiful story about the exit of life in the *Upaniṣad*. To determine who was the greatest among the eyes, ears, other senses and life, it was arranged for them to leave one by one. First, the senses began to leave, but this did not harm life, there was only some pain due to the loss of the senses. Finally, life began to exit, and the senses fearing the loss of their existence became disturbed, acknowledged the greatness of life and sang its praises. Understanding that the exit of life is 'my desire', any fear of death by a seeker is removed. This knowledge is easy and natural for those who have arrived at ego.

The snare of the king of the waters and the treasure from the oceans were taken by *Niśumbha*. The word '*paśa*' means affection. The meaning of the *paśa* of *Varuṇa* was explained in Volume Two. Here, one should not understand 'affection' to mean a love of material things. This affection is the attachment to ego (*asmitā*). Where there is attachment, there is affection. Generally, in the case of any love for material things, the desired objects appear to be separate from the enjoyer, so there is an attachment to them. But this is not so for the affection for the ego. Whatever feelings appear here, they do so as expressions of the ego. So, my attachment to my multiplicity of feelings can be called affection. This is the mystery of the demon *Niśumbha* taking the snare of the king of the waters. The seeker may not understand this until arriving at ego.

The treasures of the oceans signify all the yogic powers. Before all these appeared as separate entities or powers. Now, by the grace of Mother, a spiritual seeker understands that they are all expressions of one's own self. This multiplicity of feelings of ego are expressions of attachment. This is the significance of the treasures received by *Niśumbha*.

The wealth mentioned by *Caṇḍa* and *Muṇḍa* to entice *Śumbha*, are all in his grasp, only two are *Niśumbha*'s (the snare of *Varuṇa* and the treasures of the ocean). A spiritual seeker will understand by this that although affection and special powers are of ego, they are taken over by attachment (*mamatā*). So, the mantra says 'taken by your brother.'

Fire gave dresses purified by it. The root '*vas*' means covering. That which covers *paramātmā* is *vas*. The word '*agṇiśouca*' means purified by a fire of knowledge. Delusion (*māyā*) and lesser knowledge (*avidyā*) are the pair of dresses purified by fire. I remember a song saying 'covering the body with a cloth of *māyā*, always hidden.' Standing in the arena of ego, a spiritual seeker realizes the proper nature of *māyā* and *avidyā*. In the nature of *paramātmā*, there is no *māyā* and no *avidyā*. Before arriving at ego, what the seeker knew about *māyā* and *avidyā* was only a vague, verbal knowledge. Now it has been purified by fire, by a fire of knowledge. Without standing in the intellectual sheath (*vijñanmaya koṣa*), one does not understand what *māyā* and *avidyā* truly are and where their centers are.

Verse 53.

evaṁ daityendra ratnāni samastānyāhṛtāni te|
strīratnameṣā kalyāṇī tvayā kasmānna gṛhyate||

Translation:

O Lord of the demons! You have acquired all these jewels. Why are you not taking this jewel among women?

Explanation:

The words of enticement by *Caṇḍa* and *Muṇḍa* end here. This is the manner in which inclination and disinclination provoke beings to receive Mother. When the sense of Self is drawn into ego, a spiritual seeker understands that all expressions with different forms are jewels. The world consists of great jewels of the forms of 'I.' All that is formed by 'I'-ness, appear to me as favored things. All that one sees, all that one perceives by the senses, are all my 'I'-ness. The great jewel of 'I'-ness is reflected as various forms. So, the mantra says 'all the jewels.'

This is the inevitable result of the establishment of truth and life force. By establishing life force all over this world, a spiritual seeker sees that it is 'I' that is expressed as all this world and covers all this world. It is the jewel of 'I' that appears as everything. This realization is very attractive and very joyous. Many seekers arrive here and thinking that they have achieved the finality of life become inactive. It is such a nectar-like state. But one has to move on. My Mother appears as *Caṇḍa* and *Muṇḍa*, as inclination and disinclination of the power of awareness, brings news of *paramātmā*, and entices spiritual seekers, attracting them strongly towards *paramātmā.* One might think that only *Caṇḍa*, inclination towards *paramātmā* entices a seeker, disinclination does not entice the seeker. The answer is that although disinclination does not directly attract the seeker towards *paramātmā*, it removes the strong attraction of previously acquired treasures or special powers and helps attraction by inclination. If *Śumbha* was engrossed by the treasures in his house, would he move forward to find *Amvikā*? It is by the influence of disinclination that *Amvikā* is discovered. So, *Caṇḍa* and *Muṇḍa* say to *Śumbha*, "When everything is yours, then why do you not also bring this beneficial form?" When all treasures are yours, why will this treasure among women not be yours? Take this as yours. Being enticed by *Caṇḍa* and *Muṇḍa*, *Śumbha* gets ready to receive *Amvikā*. Alas! He does not know that to make *Amvikā* his own, 'I' will not remain, only *Amvikā* will. To receive the power of awareness, ego has to be destroyed. Soon, this wonderful principle will become clear.

A spiritual seeker has to be enticed like *Śumbha*. Let inclination entice you to the beneficial Mother. Let disinclination remove your desires for treasures. You too should lose yourself in finding Mother and discover the greatest purpose of human life.

Verse 54.

ṛṣiruvāca|
niśamyeti vacaḥ śumbhaḥ sa tadā caṇḍamuṇḍayoḥ|
preṣayāmāsa sugrīvaṁ dūtaṁ devyā mahāsuram||

Verse 55.

iti ceti ca vaktavyā sā gatvā vacanānmama|
yathā cābhyeti samprītyā tathā kāryaṁ tvayā laghu||

Translation:

The sage said, 'hearing these words of *Caṇḍa* and *Muṇḍa*, *Śumbha* sent a demon named *Sugrīva* to the Goddess.' *Śumbha* told him, "You will go there and, speak to the goddess with amity. Take proper action to see that she arrives here quickly."

Explanation:

Śumbha was enchanted by the words of *Caṇḍa* and *Muṇḍa*. Inspired by inclination, ego was ready to discover Self. The first effort of *Śumbha* was to send a messenger named *Sugrīva*. The one whose neck (*grīvā*) is beautiful (*su*) is named *Sugrīva*. The ability to apply beautiful words or verbal knowledge is *Sugrīva*. *Śumbha* trying to understand the nature of *paramātmā* is the mystery of his sending the messenger *Sugrīva*.

The feeling always rises in a spiritual seeker who has landed on the arena of ego, that I am the one who expresses this universe. Who else is there to express me? Even if there is one, it can only be an empty, inactive, unsupported, sleep-like state that can be described negatively as not large, not small, not short, not long and so on. What is the use of going there? I am fine just I am. Only verbal discussions of an attribute-less nature, as propounded by *Vedānta*, will serve our goals. That condition, nature beyond words and thought, cannot be realized, or need not to be realized, as long as one has a physical body. Now, one only needs to know it in words. Alas! A spiritual seeker does not understand that this knowledge about *paramātmā* is an indirect one from the scriptures and is conjecture. There has not been direct perception. If inclination for *paramātmā* did not provoke it, then one would not even discuss the nature of spirit beyond thought. It is as if one is forced to discuss it. Such a temporary inactiveness occurs in all seekers.

Such a failing comes to all who are spiritual seekers, because, after efforts of many lifetimes, one arrives at this subtle arena of ego and finding the establishment of all perceptions, one discovers complete certainty. One does not feel the need to go on beyond this. Just because of the force of inclination, one discusses it to some extent. One does not want to advance towards pure spirit with any great effort. So, one wants to accomplish things by sending a messenger named *Sugrīva*. This is a wonderful notion.

Many in the modern *Vaiṣṇava* community consider such a condition to be the greatest fulfillment of life. They call this the 'play beyond nature' or 'eternal *Vrindāvan*.' On the other hand, considering the nature of *paramātmā* to be rather dark and torpid, they say that 'it is better to taste sugar than be sugar.' Alas, they do not know that as long as there is a shred of difference, one cannot know the true nature of Self. One cannot taste continuous bliss or supreme love. Do they not know that monistic knowledge is immortality, divided knowledge is death? Although as long as the physical body exists, one cannot reside in that monistic for very long, still, as long as one does not arrive at it, as much as one may taste divine play, one does not find divine nectar. One is not established at the feet of assurance.

Verse 56.

sa tatra gatvā yatrāste śailoddeśehatiśobhane|
sa devī tāṁ tataḥ prāha ślakṣṇaṁ madhurayā girā||

Translation:

There in a very beautiful mountainous area, where the Goddess was residing, he (*Sugrīva*) arrived and using very soft, sweet words, spoke to her (the Goddess).

Explanation:

'*atiśovana śailoddeśe*': a very beautiful mountainous area; *Sahasrār*: arena of unlimited knowledge. A commentary of the *Caṇḍī*, called *Tattva Prakāśikā*, gives the meaning of '*śailoddeśe*' as 'the top of a mountainous area.' Truly, in the topmost part of this Himālayā of the body, there is a thousand-petalled lotus (*Sahasrār)*. There is no beauty in this world that can be compared to it because worldly beauty is mostly mingled with inertness. That place is a pure sentient zone. It is 'the form of bliss, pure perception, eye enchanting.' So, the mantra uses the word 'very beautiful' (*atiśovana*).

On hearing the word '*sahasrār*', those who think that there is a lotus with a thousand petals in the head, may not be able to grasp this mystery. When one advances towards this pure arena of sentience, there is an incredible perception that appears in the head. This perception is all-encompassing, ever manifest and the center of unlimited power. Just as the spokes are connected to the center of a wheel, in the same manner, from that arena of perception, there extends unlimited expansions, expressions and power. So, it is called '*sahasrār*', the word '*sahasra*' (thousand) implying uncountable.

Today, many spiritual seekers know something about the actions of the six centers (*cakras*). and advice others about them. This may be quite useful for early learners. But, if the practice of the various colors of the cakras, or thoughts of various forms, or chanting of various mantras, or the actions of the breaths in various cakras are without perception, do not arouse consciousness. One cannot hope that these acts will let the knowledge of Self be expressed. There are secrets to these different cakras. They are centers of spiritual principles. To advance to subtler levels, they are great shelters for a seeker. A learned *guru* expounds these secrets to those with proper rights. They do not express it to those who will not understand. Their purpose is not just to be secretive.

'*ślakṣṇaṁ madhurayā girā*': Using very soft, sweet words, the messenger of *Śumbha* tried to enchant the Goddess. Very sweet repetitions of the *Praṇava* and other mantras, sweet recitals of hymns, sweet readings of the *Upaniṣad* and other scriptures, with all these means, *Śumbha* tries to bring Self, *Amvikā*, into his house, the arena of the ego. That is not to happen. *Śumbha* has to sacrifice himself, otherwise Self will not come. Until ego is ended, Self will not be expressed. To bring Mother, one has to lose 'I.' It is true that as long as 'I' remains, Mother does not arrive. Here the seeker should remember the words of the truth seeing sages, 'that Self is not discovered by great words, not intelligence, not listening[24]. One will understand the futility of *Śumbha* sending a messenger.

Verse 57.

dūta uvāca|
devi daityeśvaraḥ śumbhastrailokye parameśvaraḥ|
dūtohahaṁ preṣitastena tvatsakāśamihāgataḥ||

24 *nāyamātmā pravacanena labhyo, Kaṭha Upaniṣad*, 1.2.23.

Verse 58.

avyāhatājñaḥ sarvāsu yaḥ sadā devayoniṣu|
nirjitākhiladaityāriḥ sa yadāha śṛṇuṣva tat||

Translation:

The messenger said, "O goddess. The lord of the demons, *Śumbha*, is the supreme god of all three worlds. I have come to you as a messenger, sent by him. The one whose orders all the gods carry out with bowed heads, the one who has overcome all foes of demons, please listen to what he (*Śumbha*) has to say to you."

Explanation:

Sugrīva said that *Śumbha* is the god of all three worlds. The three-fold expression of creation, existence and dissolution resides in ego. It appears as the supreme god who is the ruler, keeper and destroyer of all perceptions. The verbal knowledge-formed messenger *Sugrīva* comes to the Goddess and describes these supreme powers of *Śumbha*, that is, the great powers of ego. Thus, if all that is this universe is established in me, then why will you, the Goddess, the self-expressed, self-natured, power of awareness, not come to me? My power is established over all the gods, they are now powered by my spirit. They have no control over me, I keep them powerless. If they are all only different expressions of me, then you are also for me. Why will you not be mine? These are the feeling of *Śumbha*, as expressed by the messenger.

When beings first enter into the arena of spiritual effort, they think that they will find God, that is, they understand that God is something very valuable and very different from them. Slowly by spiritual effort, the dull coverings of doubt, distrust, pride, desire and anger are removed. 'I' is dressed in valuable robes of respect, faith, mercy, forgiveness and humility. Then, by the grace of the *guru*, one arrives at a point where one sees nothing but 'I.' One sees all multiplicity, all good and bad as expressions of 'I.' Then hope increases and even Self is sought to be brought under the influence of 'I.' In practice, this too is ignorance or the feelings of an *asura*.

We say 'my Self.' This is ignorance. *Ātmā* is never mine. 'I' is of the nature of Self. Not understanding this, when beings try to bring Self into 'I', they arrive at a supreme ignorance. This is the great demon *Śumbha*. Ignorance is the nature of *Śumbha*. He tries to bring *ātmā*, Mother under the influence of 'I.' This attempt first appears as the sending of a messenger.

Verse 59.

mama trailokyamakhilaṁ mama devā vaśānugāḥ|
yajñabhāgānahaṁ sarvānupāśnāmi pṛthak pṛthak||

Translation:

These entire three worlds are mine. All the gods are under my control. I enjoy all the ceremonial offerings.

Explanation:

These words of *Śumbha* are very true. Arriving at ego, a spiritual seeker will understand how true these words are. The three worlds are mine. The gods are under my control. I accept all ceremonial offerings (*yajña*). It has been mentioned before that, physical, subtle and causal, or creation, maintenance and dissolution, these three-fold expressions are the three worlds. The word '*loka*' also has the meaning of 'expression.' *Ātmā* is reflected in intelligence (*buddhi*). Relatively inert intelligence seems to be reflected as *ātmā*, as 'I.' *Ātmā* as the power of sight, and *buddhi*, the power of seeing, although separate, appear to be the same. This is ego (*asmitā*) or the demon *Śumbha*. The physical-subtle-causal or creation-maintenance-dissolution, three-fold expressions are perceived in ego. So, the mantra says 'the three worlds are mine.'

How the gods are under the control of ego, and how the results of ceremonial offerings are taken by ego have been discussed before. Here we will just mention them again. The word '*yajñabhāga*', residuals of the ceremonial offerings, means the results of actions. Actions are ceremonial offerings. This universe is action, so this universe is a house of ceremonial offerings. The products of actions, or consequences, are the results of ceremonial worship. These results of worship are owed to the gods because the Sun and other ruling deities of the eyes and other senses accept the results of actions of form and flavor of worldly things. Let me explain. You are happy to see a flower. Think about what is happening in this case. A vibration appears from the resolution about a flower that is from the great mind and activates your sense of seeing. Immediately, your eyes accept this external form of the flower and present it to mind. Mind illuminates it in the light of intelligence (*buddhi*) and accepts the beauty of the flower. By this, the sense of sight is satisfied. This satisfaction of the sense of sight means the satisfaction of the residing deity of the eyes, that is, of the consciousness that is expressed as the sense of sight. This satisfaction is the result of a ceremonial offering. It is the residual or nectar of the ceremonial offering of accepting worldly things of form and flavor. This is allocated to the gods. But now, it is under the control of ego, because now, the gods are not expressed as portions of pure consciousness. Instead, they appear as special appearances of a reflected awareness in intelligence. In this manner, the gods are removed from their individual rights and are deprived of the results of ceremonial offerings.

In *Bhāgabat Gitā*, the Lord has said, 'One has to satisfy the gods with actions. If one accepts the results of ceremonial offerings of action oneself, then it is theft.'[25] This theft occurs because of the feelings of a physical body. As long as one is not a spiritual seeker, one roams in the feelings of a physical body and enjoys matters of form and flavor, satisfying body and mind. One does not then understand that these results of satisfaction, the ceremonial offerings are owed to the gods. Entering a kingdom of spiritual enterprise, one at first thinks that the mind is *ātmā*. Even then, these results of ceremonial offerings are not offered to consciousness. Then, ascending to the intellectual plane (*vijñan*), one satisfies the intellectual formed ego (*asmitā*). From worldly persons to seekers in the intellectual plane, all are knowingly or

25 *Bhāgabat Gitā,* 3:12

unknowingly stealing the fruits of ceremonial offerings. This is the mystery of the theft of the results of ceremonial offerings by the demons. The mantra mentions the word '*pṛthak*' (separately). Even in the intellectual plane, matters of form and flavor acquired by the senses are imbibed separately. If they were offered to Self, then they would no longer be separate. All differences would be removed and they would be taken together. Calmly think of this principle and see that the fruits of ceremonial offerings are not to be stolen. Be mindful that they are offered to *Hari*, the Lord of ceremonial offerings, so all sins are removed.

Verse 60.

trailokye vararatnāni mama vaśyānyaśeṣataḥ|
tathaiva gajaratnāni hṛtvā devendravāhanam||

Verse 61.

kṣīrodamathanodbhūtamaśvaratnaṁ mamāmaraiḥ|
uccaiḥśravasasajñaṁ tat praṇipatya samarpitam||

Verse 62.

yāni cānyāni deveṣu gandharveṣūrageṣu ca|
ratnabhūtāni bhūtāni tāni mayyeva śobhane||

Translation:

The greatest jewels from the three worlds are under my control. Even the carrier of the king of gods, the jewel of elephants *Airāvata*, who appeared by the churning of the oceans, and the great jewel of a horse *Uccaiśravā* have been brought from *Indra* by the gods and respectfully offered to me. O beautiful one, the greatest gems from all the gods, celestial beings (*gandharvas*) and serpents (*nāga*) are all under my control.

Explanation:

In the previous mantra, the abilities of *Śumbha* were described. In these three mantras, his wealth is spelled out. The terms *Airāvata* and *Uccaiśravā* have been explained before. Through the messenger, *Śumbha* is describing his wealth. His intention is that when all earthly and other worldly wealth is under my control, then why should you, pure awareness natured great jewel, not come under my control too?

The word '*ratna*' means gem. Also, the one who is the greatest in a nation is called a gem. The word gem is here aimed at great worldly and heavenly enjoyment. The ego is reflected through and as this world, so there are not many grievances, not much give and take, or attraction or detraction about others. Just as a person does not feel the lack of one's limbs and try to acquire them, a seeker landed in ego has no acceptance or rejection because of any sense of division. When all is 'I', how can there be acceptance or rejection? All things are formed from me, so all the jewels in all these worlds, divine, celestial or under the earth, are all under my control.

This is a honeyed state. Think. Everything in this world is enjoyed by me. All beings in this world, all enjoyment is formed of me. I am one and only. All beings are like my senses. So, all that is being enjoyed by nature is done by me. Such is the arena of ego. I have said before, that it is by great good fortune that a spiritual seeker gains the ability to enter this plane.

Śumbha sends word by the messenger, 'O beautiful one, the supremely beautiful power of awareness, everything is me. So why do you also not be expressed through me? Looking at you, thinking of you, it appears that you are separate from me. Why should you be separate? Be mine.'

After one arrives at ego, one begins to notice the one who is expressing ego, the one whose spirit is that of ego. A spiritual seeker makes all the effort to acquire this. The attempt by *Śumbha* to take the goddess *Amvikā* is following an eternally fruitful path of spiritual enterprise.

Verse 63.

strīratnabhūtāṁ tvāṁ devi loke manyāmahe vayam|
sā tvamasmānupāgaccha yato ratnabhujo vayam||

Verse 64.

māṁ vā mamānujaṁ vāpi niśumbhamuruvikramam|
bhaja tvaṁ cañcalāpāṅgi ratnabhūtāsi vai yataḥ||

Translation:

We think that in this world, you are the one woman who is a gem. We enjoy all jewels. So, you should also seek shelter with us. You, the one with fleeting glances, should worship, either me or my very powerful brother *Niśumbha* (whomever you wish), because you are such a jewel among women.

Explanation:

Every word *Śumbha* says is true. My Mother is rightly a jewel of a woman. It has been said before that the word 'woman' (*strī*) means energy. Of all the energies, the energy of awareness is the greatest. Others, like the powers of creation, maintenance, and destruction are nothing but expressions of supreme energy. So, my Mother *Amvikā* is a jewel of a woman. As long as beings do not discover this blissful energy of awareness, they do not find proper peace. Now, after millions of births, when it has been found, then it needs to be acquired in some fashion. It is by considering this that *Śumbha* is trying to acquire her. He said, 'because we are the ones who have rights to all the jewels, why should you, the jewel among women be beyond our influence? It cannot be. Come to us. We want to find you through my 'I'-ness. Come and complete my incomplete 'I'. It is only the lack of you that keeps this precious 'I' incomplete. Goddess, come and remove this need. Let this incomplete 'I' become complete.'

You can choose one of us. You can seek shelter with me or my brother, the powerful *Niśumbha*, whomever you wish. You will bring us success. You are Self, express yourself through 'I'-ness and there will be nothing lost. Or else, be expressed as my 'I', there is no loss in that too. We cannot grasp you through our

'I'-ness. This 'I' is only a reflection. How can a reflection grasp what is reflected?

If this is not possible, seek the shelter of *Niśumbha*. He also is very powerful. This world is also under the rule of *Niśumbha*, that is attachment. If you, *ātmā*, are with *Niśumbha*, even that will be very profitable for us. We say a thousand times, 'my *ātmā*', but it has never been mine. If *ātmā* could be mine, then we could enjoy it, but it does not happen. In trying to get *ātmā*, my 'I' is lost, there is no 'I' and no 'mine.' So, we do not find you. But no longer, we will see you through our 'I'-ness, or we will enjoy you as our 'I'-ness. You are the one with fleeting glances. Remove your volatility, be constant and pay homage to us.

My Mother is the one with fleeting glances. *Śumbha* is very right. In the blink of an eye, Mother will vanish. She is calm expression, the one which appears through everything, that which is expressed beyond word and thought. Oh! She disappears within a fraction of a moment. She is my Mother beyond all percepts, beyond 'I.' There is no means to view her for any length of time, as long as this body remains, as long as the mind remains. Although Mother appears after the complete dissolution of body, mind and other percepts, their seeds remain. So, like something capricious, like a bolt of lightning, before the corner of the eye can be lit up, Mother disappears. Is it truly that? My Mother is the one who is eternally still, eternally of the nature of expression. Then why this restlessness? We are very restless, so Mother appears to be restless. We love our 'I' and do not want to leave it. We are afraid that if Mother appears, then 'I' will not remain. So, after a glance at Mother, we again embrace 'I.' Oh! When will you understand that Mother is 'I', there is nothing else as 'I'? O, Mother! We may not want you, we may not be present near your appearance that destroys everything else. Still, we ask you to be kind and express yourself. Let our 'I'-ness disappear.

Spiritual seeker, those you see seated in yogic postures, in *samādhi* for a long time, in mountain caves, do not think that they view Mother all the time. That does not happen. To view Mother all the time, the body cannot remain. Within a short time, *ātmā* leaves any connection to the body. If the perception of non-Self is completely gone, it is no longer possible to reside in the body. Such vision is like a flash of lightning, life is honored by it and one is freed from the state as a worldly person. One is blissful, of the nature of *Brahmaṇ*. Once one has met this, it is never lost from memory. One can view it whenever one wishes. This is bliss condensed knowledge. How can this be forgotten? What can be lost? It is 'I', it is *ātmā*, my Mother. What is it about seeing or not seeing her, finding or not finding her? Still, we want to see, we have to see, we have to find. That is proper fulfillment.

Śumbha said something else to Mother, 'you should worship (adore) us' (*bhaja tvaṁ*). It is very true. Not only does *Śumbha* say this. The *śrutis* say, 'they discover it, those whom *ātmā* accepts.'[26] *Bhāgabat Gitā* says, 'whoever wants me in whatever manner, I worship them in the same manner'.[27] We see that the *Veda*, *Gitā* and *Caṇḍī* say these words in the same tune. It is *ātmā* that worships beings. These words appear contradictory and are difficult to explain, but they are undoubtedly true.

Let a spiritual seeker, who is advancing towards discovery of Mother by spiritual effort and worship understand that it is but an echo of Mother. Mother worships you, that is why you worship her. When Mother worships you, then there are external signs of worship that appear in you. It is *ātmā* that worships beings and wants them. So, beings act as if they want *ātmā*. These words are to those who have acquired the rights to pierce the knot of *Rudra*. Those who have never for once seen Mother, will raise much opposition. Let it be, it is very true.

O, Mother! Whatever anyone may say, like *Śumbha*, we say a hundred times, a thousand times, 'you worship us', you accept us. O! If you worship me, my false 'I' will be lost. If I go to worship you, then it remains. So, I say with all my effort, 'Mother accept me, take me. I cannot come to you, you take me.'

---

26 *yamevaiśa vṛṇute, Kaṭha Upaniṣad* 1.2.23

27 *taṁ tathaiva bhajāmyaham, Bhāgavat Gitā*, 4.11.

The sages have also said that 'you express yourself, you appear' (*āvirāvirma edhi*[28]). Mother, from eternal times you have adored beings. You are Mother. If you will not adore us, can the children adore you? Mother, from the day that I became separate, you have adored me. Whether I do not see or understand, you have slowly at your breast of knowledge, adored me. Now, end this adoration. How much longer? You have cared for us, adored us and nurtured us for so long. Has your desire to nurture your children not been fulfilled yet? Now pick us up. Let us, torn by divisions come to your pure heart and for one last time be overjoyed by calling for you. Let the division between mother and child end forever. Let us reside in the unique nature of the 'one without second.'

There is something else that *Śumbha* said to Mother. 'You are of the nature of a jewel.' You are that jewel, by finding which, one has no desire for anything else, all tears of longings are removed[29]. How can we find you if you do not come? Although the poet has said, a jewel does not seek anyone, all seek the jewel. We know that the jewel appears to people. People cannot seek and find the jewel. If the jewel could be found by search, then everyone could be successful. But, that does not happen. Only those that the jewel searches for are honored by finding it. So, not only *Śumbha*, we also with tearful hearts say to you, 'adore us, O one with fleeting glances.' You are the one who is the core jewel, so we ask you to adore us. You have to with kindness, come and adore us. We are honored by finding the jewel.

Verse 65.

paramaiśvaryamatulaṁ prāpsyase matparigrahāt|
etadbuddhyā samālochya matparigrahatāṁ vraja||

28 *Ṛk Veda, śānti mantra* (peace evocation).

29 *yaṁ labdhvā chāparaṁ lābhaṁ, Bhāgavat Gitā*, 6.22.

Translation:

If you accept me, you will find supreme wealth, so critique this by intelligence and be accepted by me.

Explanation:

Ego has immense wealth, as all this world is in it. It entices the Goddess with its wealth. But the *asura* does not know that its nature is that of Mother. It thinks that bringing the power of awareness under the control of this world will be an advantage to power itself, he entices it with wealth. Alas! *Śumbha* does not know that this is useless. There was nothing in him that is this universe, nothing was, nothing will be. If she comes, that is, when she appears, within a moment, the entire universe will lose itself. She is the creator-maintainer-destroyer of this universe. But that is something else.

The messenger of *Śumbha* tells Mother, 'critique this by intelligence.' Critique is described as actions of the eye and other sense organs in *Sānkhya* philosophy. Here, *Sugrīva* tells *Amvikā* to critique by intelligence. The actions of the senses and the mind cannot be carried out without intelligence. There is no critique by pure perception. Mother, who is of the nature of pure perception, has to descend to the level of intelligence. The mystery of the messenger using the word 'intelligence' will be clear after one more mantra, so it is not necessary to say much more here.

Verse 66.

ṛṣiruvāca|
ityuktā sā tadā devī gambhīrāntaḥsmitā jagau|
durgā bhagavatī bhadrā yayedaṁ dhāryate jagat||

Translation:

The sage said, when the messenger spoke to the Goddess in this manner, she who was *Durgā*, *Bhagavatī* and *Bhadrā*, who holds this universe, although a little amused, spoke in a gentle, serious voice.

Explanation:

Hearing the words of *Śumbha* from the messenger, that is, knowing the intentions of *Śumbha*, Mother smiled a bit. The reason is this. Although *Śumbha* wants me, he does not know that if he finds me, his separate existence will not remain. If I, *ātmā* express myself, where is the existence of ego? Knowing the intention of *Śumbha* and its result, Mother is amused.

There are a few names of Mother in this mantra. *Durgā*: she who saves from what is difficult (*durgam*); *Bhagabatī*: she who has the six powers or treasures; *Bhadrā:* who is beneficial; *Jagaddhātrī:* one who holds this world. Mother will soon save *Śumbha* from a difficult and unfortunate state, and open infinite stores of knowledge and wealth. She is eternal good fortune and embraces this universe, the power of awareness that will remove the ignorance of *Śumbha* and express his nature as knowledge. She smiled a little, knowing the intentions of *Śumbha*.

The mistake of *Śumbha* that he holds this universe will be soon removed. Ego does not hold this universe. It is Mother, the power of awareness, that holds this universe. Here, one may have the misgiving that the power of awareness, being without attributes (*nirguṇa*), could not be the holder of this universe. Also, how could the one without attributes, possibly do physical things like smiling? In answer, understand that all these designations, all percepts confined to the faculty of intelligence, being assigned to consciousness without attributes, makes it appear to behave like one with attributes (*saguṇa*). When a container is moved, the space inside also appears to move, understand this to be the same.

The one who is equally able to reside with anger and satisfaction at the same time is '*gambhirā*' (serious). My Mother is eternally unchanging. Under no condition does one observe any change, so she is *gambhirā*. The word '*antaḥsmitā*' means, that inside, she was amused. We have remarked on the significance of the smile before this. The word '*jagou*' means she sang. That is, the words Mother uttered were said with such a sweet voice, that they seemed to pour nectar-like music into the ears of the messenger.

Truly the words of Mother are sweet. Although without music, the words are melodic notes, like nectar.

Verse 67.

devyuvāca|
satyamuktaṁ tvayā nātra mithyā kiñcittvayoditam|
trailokyādhipatiḥ śumbho niśumbhaścāpi tādṛśaḥ||

Translation:

The Goddess said, "(O messenger) what you say is true, there is nothing false. *Śumbha* is the sovereign of the three worlds, and *Niśumbha* is also like him."

Explanation:

This mantra has different meanings, we will discuss them in turn. Mother *Amvikā* tells *Sugrīva* that *Śumbha* and *Niśumbha* (ego and attachment), both think that they are the rulers of the three worlds. What you have said is true, you have not spoken falsely. Or, when parsed another way, '*tvyā satyaṁ na uktaṁ*', messenger, you have not spoken the truth, there is something false in what you have said. *Śumbha* and *Niśumbha* are not truly the rulers of the three worlds. You said before, 'the supreme deity of the three worlds.' The proper ruler of the three worlds is *ātmā*, not ego. The Self is the spirit of the three worlds. Without *ātmā*, nothing else can be its nature, so what you have said is not true. Another meaning can be taken. I, *ātmā* as *Śumbha* and *Niśumbha*, as ego and attachment are rulers of the three worlds. So, messenger, what you have said is true. You have not spoken falsely. The *Taittirīya Upaniṣad* says, 'all this that is perceived is truth.' Truth and falsity, all being equal to existence natured *ātmā* are all truth (*satya*). The authentic *Upaniṣads* and the *Brahma Sutra* have not used the words false and error. The great commentator himself used the word 'false' in the sense of indefinable. Even falsity is established on truth, because there is nothing but *sat*-natured *ātmā*. Everything is truth. So, messenger, you have spoken the truth and not said anything false.

Verse 68.

kiṁtvatra yatpratijñātaṁ mithyā tatkriyate katham|
śrūyatāmalpabuddhitvāt pratijñā yā kṛtā purā||

Translation:

I have sworn something about this matter, how can that be denied? Listen to a resolution that I have made with my limited knowledge.

Explanation:

Mother says, 'O messenger, *Śumbha* and *Niśumbha* are the rulers of the three worlds and are able to enjoy all wealth. It would be my duty to accept them. But, before this, due to my limited knowledge, I had made a resolution.

Here, one may have the misgiving. Did Mother lie? She who is the nature of knowledge, who the gods have said to be 'established in knowledge', who will later be sung to as 'one who is established in all hearts as the nature of knowledge', she is saying today, 'I had sworn, because of my limited knowledge.' Is this not a lie? No. There is no trace of untruth in this. Truth is her essence. Because there is no falsity under any circumstances with her, she is uncovered, unclothed. Assigning any untruth on her is painful. Then what is this? Listen. Let me explain. The principle of knowledge is insignificant. Even the *śrutis* say that only in a little part of *ātmā* does this universe, that is, knowledge reside. What is expressed by something is its limit. *Ātmā* is the unlimited expresser. Knowledge is expressed, limited and so is little. Knowledge is always slight. My Mother, *ātmā*, being expressed as knowledge, has become small. Before this, we understood the negative words, untrue, transient and *avidyā*, to mean lesser. When *ātmā* Mother, becomes small and is expressed in this manner, it is called intelligence (*buddhi*). There is nothing false in the words 'limited knowledge.' Also, this matter of resolution occurs in intelligence. The first resolution of Mother was, 'the one I will become many.' With that resolution, *ātmā* Mother, first manifested as supreme intelligence. To resolve it, Mother has to become small and has to be expressed as intelligence. Percept is self-expressed, complete. When it has to be expressed as knower and known, then it becomes small or limited. So, Mother tells the messenger of *Śumbha* and *Niśumbha*, 'before this, due to limited knowledge, I had made a resolution.' We will now discuss the resolution. It is very beautiful and surprising. Listen to what Mother has to say.

Verse 69.

yo māṁ jayati saṅgrāme yo me darpaṁ vyapohati|
yo me pratibalo loke sa me bhartā bhaviṣyati||

Translation:

One who can be successful in battle over me, can remove my pride and who will be equal to me in power, may become my spouse.

Explanation:

There are three parts to this resolution by Mother. The first, winning a battle. This is a battle of the senses. At all times, the senses accept inert matters of form and flavor. Even if it is explained a thousand times that it is awareness-natured Mother who travels by the paths of the senses as the matters of form and flavor, the senses from prior habit, accept them as inert materials. This is the battle of the senses. Beings are always defeated in this battle. My consciousness-natured Mother, acting as if inert, appears as senses, as worldly materials and defeats them. Worldly persons do not understand that matter is not just physical but condensed bliss, senses are but energy flows of condensed bliss. So they are defeated. But, Mother says, those who can defeat me in this battle, that is, who can understand, realize that it is I, bliss condensed *ātmā* who resides in each of the senses, they will be able to defeat me in the battle of the senses.

The second part is destroying my pride. The meaning of the word '*darpa*' is pride. Desire (*kāma*) can also be the meaning of the word *darpa*. Understand the word '*kāma*' to mean desire instead of an attribute. Mother said, the one who can remove my pride, that is, who can rightly understand that it is I, condensed bliss of *ātmā* that appears as pride, ego, attachment or desire, that I cover *ātmā* with this pride, those who can lift this cover of pride, they will be able to remove it. One has simply to understand this to mean the destruction of pride and desire.

The third part is equality of strength. Mother said one who is equal to me in power. What is the power of Mother? They are unity, bliss, supremacy and lack of any attributes. Worldly persons, who will have these powers, have properly realized *Brahmaṇ*.

'Such a one will be my spouse (*bharttā*).' One who achieves the previous three parts, only such a one can be my spouse. The word '*bharttā*' means one who supports. The root '*bhṛ*' means to support or bear. To hold and support the supremely loving percept of *paramātmā* is called being the '*bharttā*' of Mother.

Now, understand the meaning of the mantra in brief. Mother said, persons who with contact by the senses, receive bliss condensed Self, whose pride and desire have disappeared, who have realized the unity and bliss of Self, only such a person can be my spouse, can bear and care for *Brahmaṇ*. The *śrutis* have also said, 'that Self is not found by one without strength' (*nā ayamātmā valahinena labhyaḥ*). The significance of the words 'the knower of *Brahmaṇ* becomes *Brahmaṇ*'[30], is expressed through this resolution of Mother. The one who knows *Brahmaṇ* becomes of the nature of *Brahmaṇ*. The one for whom the previous three parts are achieved discovers the nature of *Brahmaṇ*. Without winning this battle, the end of pride and equal power, the hope of finding Mother is not fulfilled. Pride is removed by accepting matters from the senses as the nature of Self. Feelings such as 'I am the doer of my duties' are removed. Then characteristics of *ātmā*, unity, eternity, etc. are realized, so one becomes equal in power. When this takes place, there is nondifference between *ātmā* and *Brahmaṇ*. Then, saying 'I am *Brahmaṇ*' (*ahaṁ brahmāsmi*), a

30 *brahmavid brahmaiva bhabati, Muṇḍaka Upaniṣad* 3.2.9

spiritual seeker goes beyond all disparity. The nature of *Brahmaṇ* is illuminated.

Some think that the three parts are alternatives. That is, a lack of previous parts can still allow the other part to be the '*bharttā*.' The mantra does not have any such alternative words, so why do we have to construe this? The 'complete' meaning is fine. We will understand it to mean that when all three parts are accomplished, one can become the *bharttā*. We see that when the first is achieved, the others happen by themselves. When the battle is won, pride is destroyed, when pride is destroyed, one is of equal power. With equal power, one has the ability of the knowledge of Self.

Different people say different things in trying to understand the meaning of this mantra. We do not want to mention all of them and increase the size of this text. Some say that the words '*so me bharttā bhabiṣyati*' signify the conquering of nature (*prakṛti*). Some say that the first part, winning the battle is the yoga of action (*karma*), the second part, destruction of pride, the yoga of devotion (*bhakti*), and the third part, equal power is the yoga of knowledge (*jñanam*). We have no conflict with these statements. They are all true and so are all appealing. All will agree that one cannot find Self without overcoming the senses and the unification of action, devotion and knowledge.

Verse 70.

tadāgacchatu śumbhohatra niśumbho vā mahāsuraḥ|
māṁ jitvā kiṁ cireṇātra pāṇiṁ gṛhṇātu me laghu||

Translation:

Let the great demons *Śumbha* and *Niśumbha* come here immediately, win over me in battle and accept my hand.

Explanation:

In this mantra, there is an echo of the beautiful words in the *Upaniṣad*; ' only those who welcome Self can discover it; Self reveals itself to them'.[31] Just as a bride welcomes her husband, those who welcome Self, pray for it intently, are honored by meeting it. They are wed to it. Mother tells the messenger, 'if *Śumbha* or *Niśumbha* have the abilities according to my resolutions, let them come and accept my hand. The power of receiving is of the hand (*pāṇi*). To receive is called *pāṇigrahan.* The deep desire to accept *ātmā*, is the significance of the words 'accept my hand.' Let *Śumbha* or *Niśumbha* by their deep desires, come and get me. There is no harm in taking the meaning of the words 'accept my hand' in the sense of marriage. Without intense addiction for *ātmā*, there is no marriage or union or meeting with it. Because ego-natured *Śumbha* was very keen to find awareness-natured *ātmā*, and discard his one-ness, he found Self. To lose oneself and become the desired is the ultimate result of desire or longing. Intense longing is the crux of spiritual enterprise. If there is longing, nothing else is required. But, one has to remember something. Intense longing and unruliness are not the same things. Leaving everything for finding Self and running about here and there, is not intense longing, but only temporary arousal. Intense longing does not make one lose the sense of duty. To let the movement of life, through all conditions and actions, towards the same goal is the true nature of intense longing. But that is something else.

Here, a deep mystery will be introduced to any spiritual seeker. So that the longing for God may increase day by day, so that it overflows, wise persons in this land carried out spiritual enterprise with five approaches. These five attitudes (*bhābas*) are named *śanta* (calm), *dāsya* (servitude), *vātsalya* (parental), *sakhya* (companion) and *madhura* (sweet). To serve God as a son or a daughter is *śanta bhāba*. The service like the servant to a master is *dāsya*. The manner of affection of a parent to a child is *vātsalya*. Worship as a friend or companion is *sakhya*. Worship as a spouse is *madhura*. Worship as romance without social mores is the apex of *madhura* worship. Examples of worship with *śanta bhāba* are *Dhruva* and *Prahlāda*; those with *dāsya bhāba* are

31 *Kaṭha Upaniṣad*, 1.2.23.

Hanuman and *Garuḍa*; of *vātsalya* are *Nanda, Yashodā, Kouśalyā* and *Menakā*; and of *madhura bhāba*, *Rādhā* and the other *gopis*. The more intensity there is in *bhāba*, the more it grows. Although the *Vaiṣṇava* literature has said of the previous ways to be 'all this is outside, move forwards[32]' and given *madhura bhāba* the greatest position, still, those that have discovered the supreme love of *ātmā*, have united with it by all *bhābas* and enjoyed the bliss of union. There is no special percept without which one cannot go near *ātmā*. Self is our all, mother, father, master, friend, daughter, wife or husband. To relate to *ātmā*, all *bhābas* are equal.

The *Vaiṣṇava* community by worship in *madhura bhāba* takes the example of the *gopis* of *Vraja* as their ideal. *Kṛṣṇa* is the only supreme male and all else is *prakṛti* (Nature) so are all females. In trying to worship in this manner, they think themselves to be the dearest companions of God. Even the male worshippers, to arouse this special sense of companionship, sometimes dress and behave and dance like women. Although some may think this to be unnatural, these are not to be condemned. In this land of contemplatives and connoisseurs, it is greatness and honor for the land to have seekers with all varieties of sentiments. Whatever it is, imagining *paramātmā* as husband and worshipping in *madhura bhāba* is equivalent to worshipping it as one's wife. But *Vaiṣṇava* scriptures have not accepted this sentiment. It appears that for male worshippers, worship with these sentiments may be easier than the one mentioned before as a female companion. No text has had the courage to mention this sentiment explicitly. One can get a hint of this in the words of *Śumbha* in *Caṇḍī*. Besides this, in the *Prāṇatoṣiṇī* and other *Tantra* texts, there are indications of this in some places. I know that many will oppose and criticize this kind of worship. But, it is correct that one can assign all sentiments to the one who is Self, who is 'me', who is my all, without who I do not exist. Just as there is no diminution in the glory of Self in showing affection to it as son or daughter, or embracing it as a friend or companion, there is not the least lowering of its greatness, in loving it with all one's heart as one's wife, one's dearest spouse.

32 *Caitanya Caritāmṛta*

Those people in this world, who have given their hearts to their wives, whose aim in life is to find happiness and satisfaction for their wives, if they have a similar love for *paramātmā,* then their lives would be honored. In this *madhura bhāba*, the extra-social sentiment is natural and great. But there are other things we have found in this nature beyond sentiment when moving towards it. So, it is not necessary to bring up things about this world of sentiment and annoy the reader.

Mother said, to accept my hand, one will have to conquer me. Just as I am one, unique, without change and beyond all percepts, the one who wants to wed me will also have to have the same characteristics. There is another mystery in the words 'win me' (*māṁ jitvā*). One has to vanquish 'I' to discover Self. As long as there is an 'I', *ātmā* does not emerge, cannot emerge.

I know Mother, to find you, one has to win the battle of the senses. One has to hold you in the path of the senses. One has to see your al-encompassing, united control and destroy pride of personal control. Then becoming as powerful as you, realizing unity and self-sufficiency, appear in front of you. In this manner, we can love you with our lives, I can lose my Self in you, my 'I'-ness will vanish forever. Then, only you will reside in your unique presence. That is why I have said before this, we do not need liberation if before being liberated we could love you with our lives. Those who say that they do not seek liberation, devotion is the only thing desirable, alas, they do not know that proper devotion cannot appear before liberation. How much devotion can a bound being have for free Self? Can there be love between those not equal? There cannot be love as long as there is even the least difference. One-pointed devotion is the only thing for beings to pray for. Devotion that comes out of a sense of difference is only a spiritual enterprise towards devotion.

Verse 71.

dūta uvāca|
avaliptāsi maivaṁ tvaṁ devi brūhi mamāgrataḥ|
trailokye kaḥ pumāṁstiṣṭhedagre śumbhaniśumbhayoḥ||

Translation:

The messenger said, "Goddess, do not be so arrogant. Tell me who is there in the three worlds who can confront *Śumbha* and *Niśumbha*?"

Explanation:

The messenger of *Śumbha*, *Sugrīva* had before this said many words of enticement. Failing, he now begins to employ fear. The mindset of the messenger is that by speaking about the power of *Śumbha*, Goddess *Amvikā* may accept him and so his goal might be achieved. Whatever it is, in a spiritual view, one can see that whatever is reflected in front of ego, appears as special encirclements of ego. The multiplicity of percepts does not appear to be different from ego. So what man (*purūṣa*) can be there who can confront *Śumbha*? *Purūṣa* is another name for *paramātmā*. Because it lies in the home (*pura*) of the body, it is called *purūṣa*. Ego thinks that is self-expressed. It cannot imagine that there could be some other *puruśa* that could confront it. This is the mystery expressed by the words of the messenger. On the other hand, when no man can stand in front of *Śumbha*, how can you, a woman, be so proud and claim to fight with *Śumbha*? This is strange. (We have before this, explained the word '*trailokya*').

Verse 72.

anyeṣāmapi daityānāṁ sarve devā na vai yudhi|
tiṣṭhanti sammukhe devi kiṁ punaḥ strī tvamekikā||

Verse 73.

indrādyāḥ sakalā devāstasthuryeṣāṁ na saṁyuge|
śumbhādīnāṁ kathaṁ teṣāṁ strī prayāsyasi sammukham||

Translation:

The gods cannot stand in battle even in front of the other demons. O, Goddess, how can you fight alone? One who the gods *Indra* and others cannot stand in front of, how can you, a woman, go into battle with *Śumbha* and the other great demons?

Explanation:

When the gods are unable to battle with the other demons, that is *Dhumralocana*, *Caṇḍa*, *Muṇḍa*, *Raktavija* and other followers of *Śumbha*, then how can you a powerless, lonely woman battle with *Śumbha* and *Niśumbha*? (The nature of *Dhumralocana* and others will be explained later.)

Why *Indra* and the other gods cannot stand in front of *Śumbha* has been explained before in the explanation of the acceptance of the offerings of ceremonial worships, and will not be repeated. It will be sufficient to understand here that the gods appear as special encirclements of the ego. So their conscious parts are admonished or covered. When the gods try to stand with their special consciousness, they appear to be reflected as parts of ego, so they cannot stand in front of *Śumbha*. A spiritual seeker should note that in the first mantra, there is no mention of the word 'battle', only about standing in front. The gods lose their special characteristics as soon as they come in front of *Śumbha*, such is his influence. Then, in the third mantra, a battle is mentioned. Even if *Indra* and the gods appear in battle, they are subdued. If such is the condition of the gods, how will you, only a woman stand in front of *Śumbha*?

Sugrīva, the messenger of *Śumbha*, always sees that all that is expressed as anything, this world and gods, all appear as sparks of ego. Nothing appears to have a nature separate from ego. Only this form of a woman, this power of awareness appears to be separate from ego. If this can be taken in front of *Śumbha* by some means, it will be accepted by him. Alas! The messenger does not know that this show of terror will also fail. To accept this form of a woman, the *Śumbha*-ness of *Śumbha* will also disappear. We will see this slowly unfold.

Verse 74.

sā tvaṁ gaccha mayaivoktā pārśvaṁ śumbhaniśumbhayoḥ|
keśākarṣaṇanirdhūtagauravā mā gamiṣyasi||

Translation:

So, as I say, you should come to *Śumbha*. It will not be great if I take you there, dragging you by your hair.

Explanation:

This is the conclusion of the words of the messenger. He expresses his final wish. If you do not on your own, want to go to *Śumbha* or *Niśumbha*, then there is the chance of your honor being destroyed by you being dragged there by your hair. That is, you will be taken in front of *Śumbha* by force. This is the broad meaning of these words. What do we see here with spiritual insight?

First, we must understand the words 'dragged by the hair' (*keśākarṣaṇa*). The terms (*ka+ā+īśa = keśa*), the sound '*ka*' stands for *Brahmā*, the '*ā*' for *Viṣṇu* and '*iśa*' for *Maheśvara*. This difficult assignment of meaning using the unit letter dictionary was not devised by us. Previous teachers have shown this method. In giving the meaning of the meditation mantra of *Kālī*, with the words '*muktakeśiṁ caturvūrjaṁ*[33]' some ancient and well-known commentator has said, 'the one who liberates *Brahmā*, *Viṣṇu* and *Maheśvara* is '*muktakeśiṁ*' (free locks of hair). The *Tattva Prakāśikā* commentary of the *Caṇḍī*, also gives the meaning of '*keśa*' (hair) as *Brahmā-Viṣṇu-Maheśvara*.

Brahmā and the other gods, that is, the forces of creation-maintenance-dissolution, is the meaning of the 'hair' (*keśa*) of Mother. If these three forces can be attracted, then the power of awareness will lose its strength and its glory will be lost. So, it will lose its honor. Reasoning in this manner, the messenger uses the previous words. He thinks that if creation—maintenance-destruction of this universe by *ātmā* can be removed, that is, if

33 'one who is with flowing hair and four armed' *Daksinā Kālikā dhyāna*.

ego is able to carry them out, then awareness will have no power. Then awareness will be easy to overcome.

Alas! The messenger does not know that nobody can attract the powers of creation of Mother. However powerful a spiritual seeker one may be, no one has the power to drag Mother by her hair. That is why Vyāsadeva in *Vedānta Darṣaṇa* has mentioned a special aphorism saying '*jagad vyāpāra varjjam*[34]' (excluding matters connected with this universe). The significance of it is that liberated souls may have all the powers, but they have no hand in the matters of this universe. That is, the creation-maintenance–dissolution of this universe cannot be carried out by anything else but *Brahmaṇ*. Liberated souls, if they wish, can reside in this universe and have partial control over it; under no conditions, can they have control over the creation-maintenance-dissolution of this universe. So, dragging Mother by her hair is not possible. One will have to destroy oneself, to carry this out.

In the material world, one may see that in trying to destroy the honor of a woman, one destroys oneself. That *Śumbha* wants to accept the hand of *Amvikā* is only for matters of this universe. I will speak more clearly. A spiritual seeker who has landed on ego sees oneself as Lord of this universe and can have some control over individual things. Some characteristics of God may be expressed. One's wishes may be carried out. But, one cannot lay hands on creation-maintenance-dissolution. So, it is forced to go to the power of awareness, where creation-maintenance-dissolution occurs. If one can remove it, then one may have control over this universe. This is the hope of *Śumbha*. So, he does all this to take *Amvikā*.

Verse 75.

devyuvāca|
evametad balī śumbho niśumbhaścātivīryavan|
kiṁ karomi pratijñā me yadanālocitā purā||

34 *Brahma Sutra.*

Verse 76.

sa tvaṁ gaccha mayoktante yadetat sarvvamādṛtaḥ|
tadācakṣvāsurendrāya sa ca yuktaṁ karotu yat||

iti śrīmārkaṇḍeyapurāṇe sāvarṇike manvantare devīmāhātmye devyādūtasaṁvādaḥ|

Translation:

The Goddess said, it is true that *Śumbha* is very powerful and *Niśumbha* is also very strong; but what can I do? I have resolved all this without much deliberation. So, if you can go to the king of the demons and say with affection, these words that I have said. Then he can do what he thinks would be appropriate.

Here ends this episode of the words between the Goddess and the messenger, in *Devī Māhātmya*, in the era of *Sāvarṇi*, in the *Mārkeṇḍeya Purāṇa*.

Explanation:

Hearing these words from the messenger, Mother said, it is true that both *Śumbha* and *Niśumbha* are very powerful. Both ego and attachment are great warriors who have won the three worlds and subdued the gods. As long as a spiritual seeker does not discover them, they do not understand their potential. But, today, by the grace of Mother, the sense of Self of a seeker has come to ego. All acknowledged and accepted powers are reflected as special waves. One has the hint about the nature of God. Although proper reception, that is, the true nature of knowledge is not that of ego, but only that of the power of awareness, despite that, ego illuminated by awareness, seeing itself separate from awareness, wants to take it as the strength of acceptance. That is, it sees itself as the receiver and the Self as received. This is the desire of *Śumbha* to have the hand of *Amvikā*.

Whatever it is, Mother is not doubtful of the potential of *Śumbha* and *Niśumbha*. She has not used any words of ridicule with the messenger. Mother does not know how to mock anything. There is no mockery here. What is true, what is eternal, is always revealed.

Truly, power and potential are expressed in ego. Although Mother has special power over it, there is no doubt about the power of *Śumbha* in conquering the three worlds. It is in the combined arena of ego that the three worlds of creation-maintenance-dissolution, are expressed. This is the direct perception of seekers.

Mother said '*yadanālocitā purā*', before the advent of creation, she had made her resolutions without any special deliberation. This may be doubted because the *śrutis* have spoken of creation by will or deliberation. Then why does Mother say there was no deliberation? It may be said in answer, that there had not been any deliberation before, that to take the hand of *Amvikā*, one has to win in battle, remove her pride and be her equal. The nature of my Mother is eternal. Mother is always there. Mother cannot imagine that there has to be any special effort to discover her. That worldly persons, forgetful of their Self would not discover the nature of Mother, is unthinkable, surprising. But now, in practice, it is seen that beings thinking themselves to be of separate natures from Mother, in the shelter of error, want to acquire Mother by battle, by spiritual enterprise. Mother is eternal knowledge and clarity. How can she have this error in her? Yet, beings assign their vision to her. So, although she is the spirit of truth, sentience and bliss, that she could have to be the viewer of error, had not been imagined before this. So, the mantra says, 'without previous deliberation.' From another aspect, discussion or deliberation is a characteristic of the senses. My Mother is beyond the senses. Before creation, Mother was residing in her nature beyond deliberation.

The Goddess said something else. "Do not say these words to the king of the demons with disrespect. Speak to him warmly." Say them, just as I did. I have not shown any doubts about the power of *Śumbha* or shown him any disrespect. He is my reflection. I can have nothing but affection and mercy for him. I cannot and do not have any anger or disregard for him.

Śumbha has been called the king of the demons. He is the guest of all feelings of non-self, opposed to the divinities (*suras*).

All the seeds of tendencies (*saṁskāra*) are established in ego, so it can be called the king of the demons.

Does a spiritual seeker understand this principle? If you have established truth and life force, if you have met the principle of intelligence, if you have acquired the ability to stay even for a moment in the arena of pure intellect, then you must have landed on your sense of ego. Closely united with all perceptions, yet separate from all perceptions, that which is your 'I'-ness, appears as *ātmā*. It is not in fact *ātmā*, just a reflection of *ātmā*. This ego shrouds the nature of *ātmā*. Arriving here, do not be engrossed by the view of your powers. On finding hints of you Godhood, do not think this to be your supreme home. Look once at that form, that *paramātmā*, the blissful, awareness-powered Mother, seeing the reflection of which, you think yourself to be so high and great. Move forward with much enterprise. Practice thinking of this as a perception by the demons. Remember, as long as there is a trace of division, one cannot discover divine nectar, cannot find true bliss. With the great enthusiasm by which you accepted physical things as Mother, with the great pain in your heart that made you go forward in your spiritual enterprise, with the same interest and keen sense of loss keep your eyes on the 'one and only' principle of bliss. You will be honored to discover divine ambrosia. With a sad heart, keep saying, Mother, 'when will you destroy these great demons of stored tendencies and appear as the pure spirit of awareness and bliss?' From what eternal times do we bear this burden as worldly persons, engrossed by mirages of error, running for lifetimes with our hopes. We look on for a chance that we may find you, lay our dim sight on your self-expressed eyes and be overcome crying 'Mother.' Come, Mother! Save us from this torment by demons and take us to the pure nature of perception, where there is no difference between Mother and child. Bring forth your spirit beyond perception, without the three tendencies. Let us be honored. A spiritual seeker needs to weep in this fashion. This will make one realize the grace of Mother. When this grace is realized, the destruction of *Śumbha* and *Niśumbha* will not be far away.

In this chapter, in the message between the Goddess and the messenger, we discover another mystery. First, *Caṇḍa* and *Muṇḍa* encouraged *Śumbha* in various ways to accept *Amvikā*. Then, at the instigation of *Śumbha*, the messenger applied fear and inducements so that the Goddess would accept *Śumbha*. Our literature on proper conduct is filled with such words of enticement and terror. The purpose of such words as 'ceremonies will land one in heaven' and 'jealousy will take one to hell', are to make outward-facing beings turn towards Self and learn about their own nature. People generally unmindful of the injunctions in the texts are motivated to follow them by such inducement and peril, so that their spirits may be purified. Finally, they meet the nondual blissful Self. They go beyond injunctions and ordinances.

Chapter 6

Destruction of *Dhumralocana*

Verse 1.

ṛṣiruvāca|
ityākarṇya vaco devyāḥ sa sa dūtohamarṣapūritaḥ|
samācaṣṭa samāgamya daityarājāya vistarāt||

Translation:

The sage said, "Hearing these words of the Goddess, the messenger was angered and going to the king of the demons, described everything in detail."

Explanation:

Verbal knowledge and prayers failed. The power of awareness was not acquired by ego without a battle. The messenger came and made *Śumbha* listen to the resolutions of the Goddess. She may only be taken by a one who can defeat her in battle, remove her pride, and who is equal to her in power.

In this mantra, the messenger is said to be filled with anger (*amarṣapūritaḥ*). Learning of the previous firm resolutions of the Goddess, the messenger of *Śumbha* was angered. He had to be. Verbal knowledge is not able to discover Self. Nowadays, there is a lot of discussion in many places on the principles of Self, *Brahmaṇ* and this universe. These verbal discussions do not let one discover Self. Some think that understanding by verbal discussion and argument 'I am *Brahmaṇ*' gives one knowledge of *Brahmaṇ*. That does not happen. Such knowing is not real. It is just a hint of knowledge. As long as it is not perceived, it cannot be termed knowledge. *Ātmā* is of the nature of perception. It is impossible that one discovers *ātmā*, yet there is no perception. Do you all know happiness, sorrow, winter and summer? This knowing means perceiving. You know these things, that is, you have perceived them. As long as these do not reach perception, saying these words a thousand times does not let you know their true nature. When it is this about worldly things, then how can *ātmā*, which is the nature of perception, be found only by verbal discussion? Shouting 'water, water' a thousand times does not satisfy one's thirst. This is the spiritual mystery of *Sugrīva*, the messenger of *Śumbha* coming back unsuccessful and angered.

Verse 2.

tasya dūtasya tadvākyamākarṇyāsurarāṭ tataḥ|
sakrodhaḥ prāha daityānāmadhipaṁ dhūmralochanam||

Verse 3.

he dhūmralocanāśu tvaṁ svasainyaparivāritaḥ|
tāmānaya balād duṣṭāṁ keśākarṣaṇavihvalām||

Translation:

Hearing these words from the messenger, the king of the demons was angered. He said to *Dhumralocana*, the general of many *asura* warriors, 'O *Dhumralocana*, travel with speed, surrounded by your army and by force overcome this impudent woman and drag her here by her hair.'

Explanation:

The first general of *Śumbha* is *Dhumralocana*. He is the first one sent by *Śumbha* to bring the Goddess by force. *Dhumralocana*[1] means sight filled with smoke or distorted view. Not knowing the true nature of something and viewing it differently is distorted knowledge. Philosophers call this error. The rule of the three worlds by ego is based on this error or distorted knowledge. Not knowing the true nature of Mother, *ātmā*, perceiving the ego as Self is because of this distorted knowledge. Let us make this clearer. First, take *ātmā*. It is recognized by intelligence (*buddhi*); recognized meaning reflected (*pratisamvedan*). Think of a mirror by which light is reflected and is returned to the place from where it came. In the same manner, *ātmā* is reflected in the mirror of intelligence and returns towards *ātmā*. By the reflection of *ātmā* on

1 *dhumra*: smoke; *locana*: eyes

intelligence, the sense of 'I'-ness appears. That which is the center of that 'I'-ness, that is, the center from which the image appears and is reflected in intelligence as 'I'-ness, the reflection turns back towards that center. In this way, at each moment, *ātmā* is reflected in intelligence. This reflection is called recognition. The center of this recognition is *ātmā*. The reflection of *ātmā* in intelligence is called ego (*asmitā*). This has been mentioned before. Even though ego is not very different from *ātmā*, it is not the same. A spiritual seeker has to understand and recognize *ātmā*. One has to find that which is to be recognized, from recognition itself. When by the grace of a *guru*, a seeker lands on ego, for some time they do not discover the nature of *ātmā* that is recognized by intelligence. From this point on, the great *asura Śumbha* foils every attempt by a seeker. A follower of *Śumbha*, is distorted knowledge, *Dhumralocana*. It is the action of *Dhumralocana* to make what is not the proper nature of something, appear as its nature. It is distorted knowledge that makes the ego appear as *ātmā*. Just as in the beginning, the physical body appeared to be 'I', now the ego appears to be 'I.' In fact, the ego is not 'I', it is a reflection of 'I.' But here, it is difficult to know it as a reflection. Because, just as when light comes from a clear mirror, at first sight, one cannot see the mirror, similarly, when one first comes on ego, it is not easy to recognize that the 'I' one sees is not the proper 'I' but a reflected one. The influence by which this happens is *Dhumralocana* or smoke-filled sight. Because a mascara of little learning (*avidyā*) is on the eyes, the reflection of *ātmā* appears to be itself. If one does not understand this well, it will be difficult to enter the mystery of this final character.

It is *Dhumralocana* or distorted knowledge who is first sent to Mother. The purpose is to bring the Goddess dragging her in by her hair. The meaning of dragging her by her hair has been explained before. If the power of creation-maintenance-dissolution of this universe is attracted or taken, then the Goddess *Amvikā* who is the nature of the power of awareness will be overcome, that is made powerless. It is by his decision in this manner that the great *asura Śumbha* sent *Dhumralocana* to the Goddess.

Verse 4.

tat paritrāṇadaḥ kaścid yadi vottiṣṭhatehapara|
sa hantavyohamaro vāpi yakṣo gandharva eva vā||

Translation:

If anyone appears to protect her, be they god, *yakṣa* or *gandharva*, kill them too.

Explanation:

In this mantra, *Śumbha's* intentions are spelled out. He says, 'O *Dhumralocana*. I have heard from the messenger that the woman is alone. You should be able to bring her here by force with ease. If anyone else appears there to try to save her, whoever they are, god, *yakṣa* (nature spirits) or *gandharva* (celestial being), destroy them also.

When distorted knowledge tries to get near *ātmā*, it thinks it is easily available, because it thinks that ego is greater than *ātmā*. Distorted knowledge knows that this universe is established in ego. Therefore, what appears to be the power of awareness, why should that too not be expressed by ego? Remember, this is the knowledge that is *Dhumralocana*.

Śumbha knows that the Goddess is alone, there is no other companion. It should not be difficult to bring her. So, he orders *Dhumralocana* that if she takes the help of anyone else, that is if any gods or *yakṣa* or *gandharva* appear there to help her, destroy them too. Wherever special presences are expressed, they are under the influence of ego. Without ego, the gods and *yakṣas* cannot express themselves, because they are special encirclements of ego. It is easy for followers of ego to destroy them. *Yakṣas* and *gandharvas* are also of divine origin.

Verse 5.

ṛṣiruvāca|
tenājñaptastataḥ śīghraṁ sa daityo dhūmralochanaḥ|
vṛtaḥ ṣaṣṭyā sahasrāṇāmasurāṇāṁ drutaṁ yayau||

Translation:

The sage said, "On being ordered by *Śumbha*, the giant *Dhumralocana*, surrounded by sixty thousand demons, quickly began his assault."

Explanation:

Dhumralocana has sixty thousand soldiers. It is in distorted knowledge that birth, growth and the other six seeds of change reside. Appearing by the ten senses, they become sixty. Then because of innumerable worldly things, these sixty seeds of change are expressed in innumerable ways. That is why the mantra uses the word 'thousands' for innumerable. Do not doubt the fact that because the six-fold changes have previously been described as the army of *Mahiṣāsura*, now calling them the army of other demons is a blunder of repetition. That is not what it is. What has been mentioned before, was in the physical world, in that of action. This is now manifested in the causal field. It is because the seeds of change reside in the causal field, that they appear as actions in the material world. Before this, the destruction of the action natured changes was described. Now seeds of the sixty thousand changes are ready to be destroyed. Remembering steadily the principle, that demons like *Dhumralocana*, described in this final character are all of the sense of non-Self, opposed to the gods, will stem all kinds of doubts. Now, the nature of Self is ready to be revealed, so even the most subtle seeds of change are ready to be burnt in the flames of battle.

Verse 6.

sa dṛṣṭvā tāṁ tato devīṃ tuhinācalasaṁsthitām|
jagādoccaiḥ prayāhīti mūlaṁ śumbhaniśumbhayoḥ||

Verse 7.

na cet prītyādya bhavatī madbhartāramupaiṣyati|
tato balānnayāmyeṣa keśākarṣaṇavihvalām||

Translation:

Seeing the Goddess seated on the Himālayā mountains, *Dhumralocana* in a loud voice said, "Come to *Śumbha* and *Niśumbha*. If you do not appear before my lord with affection, then I will by force, drag you there by your hair."

Explanation:

Distorted knowledge discovers the power of awareness based on the material body, so the mantra uses the words 'seated on the snowy mountains' (*tuhinācalasaṁsthitām*). All perceptions of non-Self are destroyed based on a material body. Those who think that knowledge of duality can only occur after death are mistaken. One has to be liberated during life. If death occurs, then birth is inevitable. Whatever it is, *Dhumralocana*, seeing Mother from a distance, tries to bring her within the boundaries of ego. Knowing that finding Mother will bring true godhood, he tells her to appear before *Śumbha* with affection. There is no means to be in front of Mother, because being in front of her, all sense of duality is destroyed. So, demons carry on trying to enjoy her through all their perceptions. If it is impossible to have her, then they will be forced to drag her by her hair. Removing control of this world, stealing the power of creation–maintenance-dissolution, and bringing them into ego will give one Godhood. This is the hope of *Śumbha* in this enterprise. Alas, he does not know that this can never succeed. A spiritual seeker does not understand that when one tries to acquire Mother, one's 'I'-ness is completely lost.

Verse 8.

devyuvāca|
daityeśvareṇa prahito balavānbalasaṁvṛtaḥ|
balānnayasi māmevaṁ tataḥ kiṁ te karomyaham||

Translation:

The Goddess said, "You have been sent by the king of demons. You are strong. If you take me by force, what can I do?"

Explanation:

Distorted knowledge is stored over many lifetimes and sustained by a perception of differences. It cannot be destroyed even after much effort. So, Mother tells *Dhumralocana* that he is powerful. If one tries to take her by force, Mother does what she has to do, saying, "What can I do?" This event plays out for all spiritual seekers. First, one tries to get Mother with distorted or lesser knowledge (*avidyā*). All scriptural prescriptions, spiritual work, worship, ceremonies, rules, *Veda* and *Vedānta* are functions of lesser knowledge. Scriptural knowledge, yogic power and devotional attraction are all in the arena of lesser knowledge. Aiming at all these efforts to find Mother, she said "If you try to take me by force." Truly, as long as there is an attempt to find Mother by spiritual effort or worship, one has to understand that a spiritual seeker is trying to attract Mother by force. The result of such attempts to find knowledge, that is meet Mother by lesser knowledge is expressed by 'What can I do?' Remember, however long and dense the darkness of ignorance is, it does not take a moment to be removed by the grace of Mother. This is expressed in the next mantra.

Verse 9.

ṛṣiruvāca|
ityuktaḥ sohabhyadhāvattāmasuro dhūmralocanaḥ|
huṅkāreṇaiva taṁ bhasma sā cakārāmbikā tataḥ||

Translation:

The sage said, 'when the Goddess spoke in this manner, the demon *Dhumralocana* rushed towards her. With a loud roar, Goddess *Amvikā* turned him to ashes.'

Explanation:

When lesser comprehension comes in front of knowledge, it is destroyed in a moment in this fashion. Just as darkness disappears with light, however powerful distorted knowledge may be, it is destroyed as soon as it comes in front of the power of awareness. However long and dense ignorance may be, its existence disappears as soon as it comes in front of knowledge. Ignorance exists as long as the light of knowledge does not fall on it.

Her loud roar (*huṅkār*) is an expression of anger. It has been described in *Tantra* as a seed of destruction. I am the eternal, pure knowledge of the establishment of self, how and from where can distorted knowledge appear before me? It is by such knowledge that ignorance is destroyed. So, this mantra expresses feelings of anger. There is a mystery expressed in the words 'turned to ashes.' No trace of the demon remained. Ignorance is destroyed and can never reappear. One may doubt this. Even in persons who have knowledge of Self, one can see ignorance. Even knowledgeable persons carry out acts of lesser knowledge (*avidyā*). They conduct actions like teaching people, creating texts and observing rules and regulations. If ignorance is destroyed and is never again resurrected, then how are these acts, such as maintaining the body possible? In answer, it has to be said that only by the effects of past tendencies, such acts of ignorance can be carried out. Just as when the axle of a wheel is removed, the former rotation continues for a little time, when the light of knowledge destroys ignorance by its roots, former fruits of ignorance, the body and its actions continue for little while.

Whatever it is, until Mother *Amvikā* turns the distorted knowledge of a spiritual seeker into ashes, how can one find Mother? That is why I say, whatever it be, good or bad, pious or sinful, knowledge or ignorance, hold everything in front of Mother, send everything to Her. Just as *Śumbha* sent *Dhumralocana* and other followers to Mother one by one, you too should send whatever you have to Mother. Mother will deal with them. Why would you tear up your life with unnatural processes of destroying error and ignorance, dissolving spirit, controlling tendencies, and still live with trouble? You are a child of Mother, you do not know anything but Mother. Whatever comes, good or bad, like a naked child take everything indiscriminately to Mother. Mother will remove all percepts and express the nature of her Self. Your hopes will be fulfilled. The puzzles of lesser knowledge, of ignorance, will be removed forever.

Verse 10.

atha kruddhaṁ mahāsainyamasurāṇāṁ tathāmbikām|
vavarṣa sāyakaistīkṣṇaistathā śaktiparaśvadhaiḥ||

Translation:

Thereafter, (because of this event), the huge army of demons, being angered, began to shower sharp arrows and other weapons upon *Amvikā*.

Explanation:

The spiritual mystery of arrows and other weapons has been previously explained in Volume Two. There is no need to do it again. But spiritual seekers should understand that most of what was said in Volume Two was aimed at the subtle body. In this Volume, much will be said aimed at the causal or blissful body. Inclination and disinclination, love and distaste, divisive knowledge and duty, all that has been mentioned before, will be repeated here. One has to understand them, not as repetition, but at a more refined level. Now we are leaving the material and subtle and moving towards the causal. At this level, everything that is in the material or subtle level exists, only in nonmanifest form. If one can pay attention to this nonmanifest form, then the seeds of the material and subtle are destroyed. When the seeds of worldly existence are destroyed, the discovery of Mother is inevitable.

Whatever it is, lesser knowledge has been destroyed. The distorted knowledge formed *Dhumralocana* has been turned to ashes, so there is no doubt that his followers will soon be destroyed. The actions of lesser knowledge should be destroyed with it, and that is what takes place. But, a seeker needs time to realize this. Like persistent habits, actions of destroyed lesser knowledge from prior tendencies, linger for a time. Even though the fear of snakes is removed, palpitations from that fear continue for a time. Even though a circling flame stops, the image persists. The actions of lesser knowledge stop. How they are destroyed, is pointed out by the sage Medhasa to king Suratha. The demons who will be destroyed now are all actions of lesser knowledge.

After *Dhumralocana* was destroyed, his sixty thousand soldiers threw sharp arrows and power weapons at Mother. That is, the percepts of six-fold changes tried to cover self-expressed Mother. Another name for this six-fold change is a state as a worldly person. It has previously been called a shadow. Even though one can understand that a shadow cannot exist without the original, it tries to cover the original. The followers of *Dhumralocana* tried to cover Mother.

Verse 11.

tato dhutasaṭaḥ kopāt kṛtvā nādaṁ subhairavam|
papātāsurasenāyāṁ siṁho devyāḥ svavāhanaḥ||

Translation:

At this, the carrier of the Goddess, the lion, shaking its mane in anger and with terrible growls jumped in among the demon warriors.

Explanation:

When distorted knowledge is destroyed, worldly persons discover pure perception and with lion-like valor resolve to destroy past tendencies. It has been said before that a worldly person wishing to change its state is a lion. By the grace of Mother, it has now understood what the state of worldly person is and how it can be removed. Now, understanding that by quickly applying effort and destroying the followers of the demon it can end its state as a worldly person. It goes after the demon warriors. The efforts of a spiritual seeker increase from a hint of the true nature of Mother. Then, with courage in heart and with terrible roars one decides to destroy the demons, because it understands that it is a carrier of the Goddess. Even before, it was so, but there was a more distant relationship. As Self-nature, there is now no other specialty of Mother but her nature as bliss. So, a seeker is now the carrier of bliss. One is full of power in the heart. By great good actions and grace of the *guru*, seekers understand that they are carriers of the Goddess. Now truly, a seeker is a figure of bliss. When will we arrive at such a condition?

Verse 12.

kāṁścit karaprahāreṇa daityānāsyena cāparān|
ākrāntyā cādhareṇānyān jaghāna sa mahāsurān||

Verse 13.

keṣāñcitaṁ pāṭayāmāsa nakhaiḥ koṣṭhāni kesarī|
tathā talaprahāreṇa śirāṁsi kṛtavān pṛthak||

Verse 14.

vicchinnabāhuśirasaḥ kṛtāstena tathāpare|
papau ca rudhiraṁ koṣṭhādanyeṣāṁ dhūtakesaraḥ||

Verse 15.

kṣaṇena tadbalaṁ sarvaṁ kṣayaṁ nītaṁ mahātmanā|
tena keśariṇā devyā vāhanenātikopanā||

Translation:

The lion killed some of the demons by swiping at them with his paws, some with his mouth, and some with his lips, that is by biting them. In this manner, the lion tore the abdomen of some demons with his claws. It severed the heads of some from their bodies by swiping with his limb. In the same manner, some demons lost their arms and legs. After this, the lion, shaking its mane, (in glee) drank blood from the bodies of some demons. Within a short time, the carrier of the Goddess, the very angry and powerful lion, destroyed the army of demon warriors.

Explanation:

How the demon army was destroyed is described in these four mantras. The lion does not have other weapons. His body is his weapon for destroying an enemy. He destroyed the *asura* warriors by 1) blows from his limbs, 2) with his mouth, 3) with his bite, 4) his claws, 5) slapping them with his paws and 6) frightening them by shaking his mane. It was said that *Dhumralocana* set out for battle with sixty thousand warriors. This was aimed at the innumerable different birth and other changes multiplied by the ten *indriyas*. Here it is seen that the lion using six methods, brings down the sixty thousand warriors. We will here try to understand these birth and other changes.

1) Birth (*jāyate*): The perception that we had birth and have to be born, is not real. Yet, such a percept is always with us. This is the first alteration (*vikāra*). Now, by the grace of Mother, distorted knowledge has been destroyed. These former perceptions, the past tendencies of birth are going to be easily destroyed. This is the mystery of some of the demons being felled by being beaten by the paws of the lion.

2) Existence (*asti*): It is perceived that I exist after I am born. This is the second alteration. This sense of special nature is also the result of distorted knowledge. My spirit is eternal and uniform. There is no percept of other changes in it. Until now, a spiritual seeker has not been able to understand this, or understanding it, has not realized it. Today, by the grace of Mother, the distorted knowledge natured *Dhumralocana* has been destroyed. As an inevitable result of it, this eternal nature is being expressed. On the other hand, the alterations of specific natures are also destroyed. This is described in the mantra as the lion opening its mouth to bite the demon warriors.

   In this connection, I cannot resist quoting a few lines that I composed when I was a student. My levity should be forgiven.

   "Mother, the word *asti* that is seen used in this world, the great sages, the great ones who have met *paramātmā*, apply only to you. The word 'exist' cannot be used for anything but you. Because at the end of this dream of error, one sees that true spirit is only you. But Mother, because of delusion and engrossment, we cannot understand this world to be without spirit, without existence. O, all-forgiving Mother, grant us true knowledge."

There is no other separate existence as a worldly person or a universe. It is only the spirit of Mother that is known as the universe. Not realizing this, beings are repeatedly pained by the scourge of death. But now my Mother has appeared to save them. She is rending the chains of being. We can now hope that this world of beings will be honored by discovering the nature of Mother.

3) Growth (*varddhate*): That I grow and my age increases every day, is a perception that is the third alteration. The reason for the perception of this alteration is ignorance of the nature of Self. It is based on distorted knowledge. But, this time, Mother has destroyed distorted knowledge. The alterations based on it will be easily removed. The part of the mantra, saying that some demons were destroyed when attacked by the lips, is describing the destruction of this third alteration.

4) Extinction (*vipariṇamate*): I have an end. At the end of growth, I will no longer increase. Such perception is the fourth alteration. This too is removed with the destruction of distorted knowledge. This is the mystery of innumerable soldiers of *Dhumralocana* being downed after being hit by the claws.

5) Diminution (*apakṣīyate*): I decline. I keep on reducing. Such a perception is the fifth alteration. When Self is illuminated, such alterations do not remain. The words in the mantra saying 'severed the heads of some from their bodies by swiping with his limb', indicates the end of this alteration.

6) Termination (*naśyati*): I am impermanent. I have to face death. This is the sixth alteration. When distorted knowledge is removed, when one meets ambrosial

Mother, fear of death is removed. Understanding properly that this sixth alteration is also not in us, beings are freed from the attack of the fear of death. Today the carrier of the Goddess, the lion, destroying the followers of *Dhumralocana*, finds relief from the torment of these demons. This is the significance of arousing fear by shaking its mane and drinking blood from the corpses.

When distorted knowledge is destroyed, the six alterations of Self, the army of *asura* soldiers, do not take long to be destroyed. This is why the mantra uses the term 'in moments' (*kṣaṇena*). Besides this, the lion has been called a great soul. As long as beings do not discover Self, greatness is absent. That one is truly 'great, universal, extraordinary' is not understood. But now, by the grace of Mother, the dream of error is ended. So now one can realize the greatness of Self. The mantra uses the word '*mahatmanā*' (great soul). A spiritual seeker has to remember that if one does not become a carrier of the Goddess and has not surrendered, then these powerful demons cannot be destroyed so easily. We have explained in Volume Two that a seeker who has surrendered is a lion, a carrier of the Goddess.

Verse 16.

śrutvā tamasuraṁ devyā nihataṁ dhūmralochanam|
balañca kṣayitaṁ kṛtsnaṁ devīkesariṇā tataḥ||

Verse 17.

cukopa daityādhipatiḥ śumbhaḥ prasphuritādharaḥ|
ājñāpayāmāsa ca tau caṇḍamuṇḍau mahāsurau||

Translation:

Hearing about the death of *Dhumralocana* and the destruction of all the soldiers by the lion, the demon lord *Śumbha*, his lips quivering in anger, gave orders to the great demons *Caṇḍa* and *Muṇḍa*.

Explanation:

When distorted knowledge and the six alterations by it are removed, ego is concerned that if those that are with me are destroyed in this manner, how will I exist? Being angered, to keep his nature intact, *Śumbha* sends inclination and disinclination to Mother.

The six alterations that have been mentioned before are not only about the material body. A spiritual seeker should not forget that there is very little in this part of the episodes, about the material body. But one may wonder, when the material body is forsaken, where are the actions of the six alterations? In answer. one has to understand that the alterations were seen in the material body. That one is born, grows and declines were perceived in the physical body. All these are also felt in the subtle body. This knowledge present in the subtle body resides as seeds in the causal body. Not only in the physical one but subtle versions of these alterations reside unexpressed in the causal body. So not only the material, but the subtle and causal bodies also house these alterations. But only *ātmā*, Mother is the owner.

Let us now try to understand the commands of *Śumbha* or ego. We have said that the reflection of awareness in intelligence is ego. What is truly 'I' is not a reflection, it is awareness itself. That this awareness is not understood as 'I', and the reflection is taken as 'I', is at its root, because of distorted knowledge. It creates knowledge of non-existent material. This distorted knowledge is destroyed at the death of *Dhumralocana*. Now, ego is going to be destroyed. There is nothing that can save it. But ego is not simple. It is a percept from many lifetimes and ages. It is not easy to destroy. This is the same as when, even after the head of a poisonous snake is cut off, its tail tries to beat the attacker.

Now, *Śumbha* thinks and sees that even though *Dhumralocana* has been killed, the generals *Caṇḍa* and *Muṇḍa* with their huge armies are still here. They are the ones who told me about this woman, so let me send them to battle.

A spiritual seeker has to remember that when distorted perception is destroyed, it does not take long for inclination and disinclination to be destroyed. Although these things may happen in moments, recording them and explaining them to someone takes much effort.

In reality, even after distorted knowledge is destroyed, because of their previous velocity, inclination, disinclination and the other tendencies continue for some duration. By the repeated practice of establishment in Self for a long time, they slowly vanish.

Verse 18.

he caṇḍa he muṇḍa balairbahubhiḥ parivāritau|
tatra gacchata gatvā ca sā samānīyatāṁ laghu||

Verse 19.

keśeṣvākṛṣya baddhvā vā yadi vaḥ saṁśayo yudhi|
tadāśeṣāyudhaiḥ sarvairasurairvinihanyatām||

Verse 20.

tasyāṁ hatāyāṁ duṣṭāyāṁ siṁhe ca vinipātite|
śīghramāgamyatāṁ baddhvā gṛhītvā tāmathāmbikām||

iti mārkaṇḍeyapurāṇe sāvarṇike manvantare devīmāhātmye dhūmralochana vadhaḥ|

Translation:

O, *Caṇḍa*! O, *Muṇḍa*! Go with many warriors and quickly bring that Goddess here dragging her by her hair or bound. If there is any doubt during the battle with her, then with all the demons, use your weapons to kill her. Destroy that wicked woman and her lion and return here quickly. Or, bind *Amvikā* and bring her here.

Here ends this episode on the destruction of *Dhūmralocana*, in the era of *Sāvarṇi*, in the *Mārkeṇḍeya Purāṇa*, in the *Devī Māhātmya*.

Explanation:

The inspirations of ego are the orders by *Śumbha*. Now inclination and disinclination will go with many followers to bring

Amvikā. There are three things ordered by *Śumbha* that they have to do when they reach her. The first, drag her by the hair, or bind and bring the Goddess. The second one is, if there is any doubt, that is, if it is impossible to drag her here by her hair, then kill both the Goddess and her lion. *Śumbha* gave a third order, try to bind her and bring her here. In these three orders by *Śumbha*, his anger toward the Goddess, his wish to kill her and his keenness to bring her are expressed.

If powers of Godhood, like creation and others, are removed from the powers of awareness, then it will be easier to acquire them. Maybe then, Godhood can be expressed through ego. It is with this hope that *Śumbha* gives orders to drag the Goddess in by her hair. *Śumbha* may be doubtful as to the success of this order because Godhood is never separate from the power of awareness. That is why without hope he gives the order to kill. The significance of killing the power of awareness or *ātmā* is to declare final principle to be empty. In the period following the Buddha, Buddhist philosophy came to stand on this void. Some Buddhists tried to annihilate *ātmā*. The teachings of Buddha turned into a nihilistic philosophy. The meaning of liberation or *nirvana* became the destruction of Self and arriving at a principle of emptiness. Alas, they did not know that *ātmā* was indestructible. *Ātmā* cannot be destroyed. What stays on after attempts to destroy the Self, remains as Self. Here it may not be out of context to very briefly discuss this philosophy.

The scriptural saying, '*asadevedamagra āsīt*' is the mainstay of this thought. The meaning of it is that before creation, this universe was not covered by '*asat*', that is by name and form. Some Buddhists interpret a different meaning. They say that before creation, what existed was '*asat*, that is deficiency or emptiness. So, emptiness is the final principle. Also propounded by them is a science of moments (*kṣaṇik-vijñan*). The external world does not exist. What appears to be this universe is our tendencies (*saṁskara*), a momentary existence. This science is of two varieties. With all matters of form and flavor that we accept at each moment, there is associated a feeling of 'I.' I see, I hear, I do. With these, there is a momentary flow of 'I.' This is the science of flow (*dhārā*). Beneath this flow of 'I', there is an undivided 'I', on which these momentary 'I' appears and disappears. This is known as the science of '*ālaya.*' From these conclusions, some Buddhists by methods of yoga, first try to shut off any science of flow. Later by removing the science of *ālaya* they arrive at emptiness, or the matter of nothingness and call it *nirvana* or liberation.

Ācārya Śankara countered these ideas with various arguments and logic. It is unnecessary to mention them here. We will understand that what the Buddhists called a complete absence of 'I', still had a remaining 'I' to express it. The one who knows the absence of 'I' is also Self. So, the elimination of the Self is not possible. On the other hand, we do not have any conflict with this Buddhist philosophy. Whatever conflict there appears to be, is one of language, that is application of words. There is no conflict over the material content. Buddhist science of flow is our 'pride' and Buddhist science of containment is our 'ego.' There is no loss in accepting that an external world exists as the intention of God and that this universe enjoyed by beings is transient. Then there is the matter of emptiness. Truly, there is no distinction apparent in pure spirit. So, Buddhists have applied the words 'void' or 'emptiness' pointing to that which is complete. Whatever it is, we have come far away from our topic. Let us get back to it.

What *Śumbha* said in the third part, when sending *Caṇḍa* and *Muṇḍa* to battle, appears to be that the death of *Amvikā* was not his intention. It was his desire to get her to be his consort. If it was not possible, then her death was preferable.

Listen. Ego does not agree that there is something else that expresses it other than its own self. If there is something called Self, then let it be known as being expressed by ego. This is the intent. Spiritual seekers at very high levels will easily understand this mystery. But those for whom intellectual principle is not illuminated may find these things appear to be a riddle. It is hoped that those who with interest move on a path of establishment of truth and life force, will soon arrive at the principle of intelligence and easily understand these mysteries of Self and ego. There is no conflict between this establishment of truth and life force and communal methods of worship. Everyone can practice this keeping their special distinctions intact. After a period of practice, one will find success on this path. One has to remember that as long as lesser knowledge or the distorted knowledge formed *Dhumralocana* is not killed, the bonds of being are not removed. Today, seekers who have established truth by the grace of Mother, come to this point where they understand what 'destruction of lesser knowledge (*avidyā*)' means.

The demons of distorted knowledge, attacking the children who had taken refuge at the feet of Mother were turned to ashes by a loud roar from Her. This is the seed of unraveling the knot of *Rudra*. It was said that this is called the knot of *Rudra*. The knowledge of this world, this perception of 'I', all this is based on distorted knowledge. This pile of ignorant knowledge is based on inexperience about the nature of Self. By the grace of Mother, it is now removed. Therefore, what remains as actions of ignorance will now destroyed.

Come, spiritual seeker, let us cry 'Victory to Mother' and move on. Let us see how Mother destroys the demons *Caṇḍa*, *Muṇḍa*, *Raktavija* and others and establishes herself in her own nature. We offer uncounted *praṇāms* at her feet.

Chapter 7

Destruction of *Caṇḍa* and *Muṇḍa*

Verse 1.

ṛṣiruvāca|
ājñaptāstu tato daityāścaṇḍamuṇḍapurogamāḥ|
chaturaṅgabalopetā yayurabhyudyatāyudhāḥ||

Translation:

The sage said, "After this, by order of *Śumbha*, with *Caṇḍa* and *Muṇḍa* in front, four battalions of demons, began their campaign for the Goddess."

Explanation:

By encouragement from ego, inclination and disinclination with their armies went towards the power of awareness. Spiritual seekers will see that they also want to acquire Mother with their inclination and powered by disinclination try the end of material things to increase movements towards Mother. Not only this, but inclination and disinclination move with innumerable perceptions and actions. This is the campaign of *Caṇḍa* and *Muṇḍa* with their armies. Now they will all be destroyed. It has been said that Mother appears after the destruction of inclination and disinclination.

The four battalions have been explained in Volume Two. Pain, action, misfortune and fate are the four divisions. Just as you understood them in the subtle body, understand them to be similar in the causal body. Because they reside as unexpressed seeds in the causal body, they germinate in the subtle body and bear fruits in the material body. By the grace of Mother, the tendencies of material and subtle bodies have been destroyed. Now the unexpressed seeds in the causal body are ready to be eroded. So, Mother makes *Caṇḍa* and *Muṇḍa* appear for battle with their four battalions.

Verse 2.

dadṛśuste tato devīmīṣaddhāsāṁ vyavasthitām|
siṁhasyopari śailendraśṛṅge mahati kāñcane||

Translation:

After this, they saw the Goddess with a slight smile on her face, sitting on her lion, on the great golden peaks of the Himālayās.

Explanation:

My Mother seated on her lion of worldly person, on the golden peaks of the Himālayās, has a slight smile on her face. Mother expresses her divine play of the death of *Śumbha*, based on a golden body. It is the golden nature of *Hiraṇyagarbha* by which various plays of *ātmā* or the pure power of awareness is expressed. My Mother is smiling a little. All these armies, the noise of battle and the powerful demons *Caṇḍa* and *Muṇḍa* ready for war, yet, my Mother is smiling. Truly, Mother with her slight smile is untouched under any circumstances. As this visible universe, during repeated conflict, residing in frictions of joy and sorrow, the blissful state of Mother is never changed. Just as a figurine made of sugar is sweet all over, so is the bliss-filled form of my Mother, always blissful under all percepts. This bliss-formed Mother is blissful in sickness, sorrow and terror.

All are formed from bliss. When will a spiritual seeker discover this spirit of bliss and be honored? The all enchanting *Amvikā*, the smiling Mother is expressed everywhere. She is not hidden. For once, I look at Mother. Your 'I'-ness, every atom of your material body will be revived by nectar of bliss.

Verse 3.

te dṛṣṭvā tāṁ samādātumudyamaṁ cakrurudyatāḥ|
ākṛṣṭacāpāsidharāstathānye tatsamīpagāḥ||

Translation:

Seeing her (*Amvikā*), some of the demons holding bows and

swords went forward to grab her. Some other demons also moved toward her.

Explanation:

Analyzing the meaning of this mantra, we see that the demon warriors approached in two groups to capture the Goddess. One was armed, the other unarmed. The group of inclination, using swords and bows, that is by concentration, meditation and so on, try to acquire Self. The group of disinclination is unarmed, that is they forsake all materials and negate everything and try to get close to *ātmā*.

Remember, the action of inclination is spiritual effort and that of disinclination is renunciation. By both of these, one can get close to Mother, but cannot obtain her. Because, both spiritual enterprise and renunciation are features of the inner spirit. Mother is established above this. To make this clear, the sage said 'went forward' (*ādātumudyamaṁ cakru*) and 'moved towards her' (*tatsamīpagāḥ*). The group of inclination attempted to get Mother, but could not. The group of disinclination only went near Mother. They did not find her. This has to be said more clearly.

Both *Gitā* and *Pātañjali* have said that disturbances of the spirit can be removed by practice and renunciation. But, preventing these tendencies (*vrittis*) and discovery of Self is not the same. It is true that discovery of the Self results in an end to these tendencies. But, just by stopping tendencies, one does not find Self. There is no direct connection between stopping tendencies and finding Self. *Ātmā* is above intelligence. The matter of restraining tendencies, at the most, goes up to the level of intelligence. Look, action by inclination is spiritual enterprise, that is practice. Action by disinclination is renunciation. These can get close to Mother, advance a spiritual seeker, but cannot rightly find Self. The results of these practices and of renunciation are not very high. If an arrow aimed at a target misses it and then flies ten feet further on, it has not served its purpose. Coming close to a target does not accomplish one's goal.

The goal is to find Self, supreme bliss. Practice and renunciation cannot bring supreme bliss, they can only end sorrow. It is very true that spiritual effort and renunciation can diminish sorrow, but they do not bring supreme joy. Happiness appears due to the end of sorrow. Removing an unbearable load from the shoulders brings happiness due to an end of sorrow, but does not bring supreme joy.

Worldly persons advance by such spiritual enterprise and renunciation, but they do not find supreme joy. That is, they get near *ātmā*. We see here that the warriors of *Caṇḍa* and *Muṇḍa* get close to Mother. Mother will soon destroy them. Mother, Self is beyond all perception, so she will destroy all spiritual effort and renunciation carried out by perception and then appear as the nature of her Self. Those who are true seekers will be surprised and enchanted by learning this mystery in *Caṇḍī*. Those hearing this and thinking that renunciation is unnecessary will undoubtedly be greatly mistaken. There are no other means to get close to Mother than these two. Only after getting near Mother can one receive her. The hopes of finding Mother, for those who have not come near her are futile. Thinking that spiritual effort and renunciation are unnecessary would be a great error.

Verse 4.

tataḥ kopaṁ cakāroccairambikā tānarīn prati|
kopena cāsyā vadanaṁ maṣīvarṇamabhūttadā||

Translation:

Thereafter, *Amvikā* displayed great anger toward these enemies. Her visage turned dark from wrath.

Explanation:

My mother *Amvikā* was very angry at these enemies. Are inclination, disinclination and their followers not true enemies? They are obstacles to the expression of the nature of Mother. One might argue, who can be friend or enemy of Mother? We have answered this before. My Mother is eternal, undisturbed, there are no changes of perception in her. All this is true, but these are used by entitlement. Whoever appears in front of her with whatever feeling, she expresses herself in the same manner. *Caṇḍa* and *Muṇḍa* have appeared as enemies, so undistorted Mother also appears to be inimical. So, the mantra says 'to enemies' (*arīn prati*).

The demons have come near Mother, so their destruction is inevitable because all percepts disappear near *ātmā*. The *śrutis* say, 'there the Moon and Sun are not expressed',[1] and 'this universe is its nourishment; death itself is its ingredient.' Her expression pierces everything and destroys all percepts. The demons do not know that they do not have any separate nature. Even this utilitarian spirit that is observed is established on that of Mother. As soon as the nature of Mother is expressed, the destruction of demons is inevitable. Whatever happens when darkness moves to catch the light is now taking place for these demons. This natural dissolution, this disappearance into existence (*sat*) of what is not, its prior form, is the anger of Mother. So, the sage says she was angry.

We see in this world that anger turns the visage red. Here, the sage says that the visage of Mother turned dark with anger. Mother will soon appear in her destructive, dark, *tāmasa* form. This is its first indication. Generally, anger is the expression of the *rājasa* tendency, but here it is not so. It is the expression of *tāmasa* of the superior nature (*parā prakṛti*). The color of *tāmasa* is black, so my Mother turns dark. All perceptions disappear into *tāmasa*. It has been said in Volume Two that the final result of *tāmasa* is the stopping of all tendencies. This stoppage and destruction are the same. When all percepts are destroyed, my Mother will be expressed in her pure nature. The word '*vadan*' means front. The one who's true nature is the power of awareness, is the very beautiful, all blissful form of *Amvikā*. Destruction of all percepts resides in front of this form of *Amvikā*, of Mother. This is made clearer from the next mantra.

---

1 *Kaṭha Upaniṣad, 2.2.15.*

Verse 5.

bhrukuṭīkuṭilāttasyā lalāṭaphalakāddrutam|
kālī karālavadanā viniṣkrāntāsipāśinī||

Verse 6.

vicitrakhaṭvāṅgadharā naramālāvibhūṣaṇā|
dvīpicarmaparīdhānā śuṣkamāṁsātibhairavā||

Verse 7.

ativistāravadanā jihvālalanabhīṣaṇā|
nimagnāraktanayanā nādāpūritadiṅmukhā||

Translation:

From her furrowed brow (of *Amvikā*), the very terrible form of *Kālī* emerged. In her hands were a sword, net and an unusual mace. She was adorned with a garland of human skulls, wearing a tiger skin, emaciated, looking very fierce, mouth agape. Her lolling tongue made her look fiercer. Her eyes were sunken, and she filled the horizons with her terrible howls.

Explanation:

The anger of *Amvikā* emerged as a devastating, destructive fierce form. From the center of her brows, a great destructive force emerged. Spiritual seekers will also understand that by focusing on the *Ājñā* center between the brows, all states of this world may vanish. So, the mantra uses the term 'center of the brows' (*lalāṭaphalakā*). The terrible form of *Kālī* appeared from the brow of Mother.

Kālī is the power of time (*kāla*). The consciousness formed great power that is inspired by the percept of time is called the power of *Kālī*. To enter into the nature that is to go beyond time, spiritual seekers have to go through this form of *Kālī*. My Mother *Kālī* is a terrible, destructive force. All this time, we have not seen this form. Until one is keen to reside in the pure nature of Self, one cannot perceive this destructive form of Mother. Now a seeker has discarded perceptions of this world, sacrificed one's specific 'I'-ness and is ready to stabilize in the nature of Self. Today one is keen to leap onto the lap of Mother by destroying inclination and disinclination. So, Mother, graciously expresses herself as a destructive force, to remove *Caṇḍa* and *Muṇḍa*, to end all states.

The power of awareness first envisions in itself time and direction, then slowly an infinitely varied universe is created. It is from the power of awareness that the power of time appears. This is why the emergence of *Kālī* is depicted from the brow of *Amvikā*. Time is the container for this universe. Because it destroys all states, it is called *Kālī*. Time (*kāla*) and *Kālī* are nondifferent. With an intellectual eye, a spiritual seeker can see that this universe appears in the womb of time and then sets into it. From the first moment of creation, acts of destruction begin. One day it ends, that is, it is completely withdrawn. The time that is taken, or needed to destroy a created object is its duration of existence. There is nothing that is at rest, all are moving towards death. What is at rest resides in truth-natured Mother. Time and movement are nondifferent. In theory time itself is moving very fast.* Therefore, all that appears in the container of time are all mobile. Just as a rider in a fast-moving vehicle is not able to stop his movement, in the same manner, this world of beings, even by much effort, cannot for a moment stop the movement towards destruction.

[* Note by Author: It has been said that time is undivided and immobile. Here we say that time and movement are nondifferent. In principle, there is no conflict between these two views. Because looked at as the container for actions, time may be said to be still. Pointing at time as action, it may be said to be moving. *Mimāṁsā* philosophy views time as action.]

In whichever direction you look in this world, you will see uncounted beings, at every moment, rushing towards death. One who is today a child is tomorrow a youth. All see the child's age increase. The child is losing its span of life and moving towards destruction. In this way, trees, vines, insects, flies, animals, birds, gods, demons, humans, planets and satellites, in other words, from

Brahmā to the tiniest atom, all are unknowingly moving toward death. Who will say by what strong attractive power this world of beings is approaching death? Look. This universe is moving fast to enter the terrible mouth of *Kālī*. Look. Just like insects rushing into a flame, beings appear to be mesmerized by apparitions and rush quickly towards self-immolation in a fire of destruction. Look how every atom of your body is drawn by the terrible attraction of *Kālī* and is drawn to disappear into the heart of this force of destruction. Oh! What a condition we are in! Look. Above, below, in front, behind you, right and left, inside and outside, *Kālī* is everywhere, death is everywhere. Not only you, all those you hold close to your heart, look at them. They too are moving fast to leave you and embrace death. At each in-breath and out-breath, this movement towards death is articulated. The breath that you think to be a sign of life, is at each moment attracting you to be a guest at a house of destruction. Death is your nature, you are born to die. How do you remain so assured? Do you not see the destructive, terrible form of Mother, this form of *Kālī*?

But, have no fear. Do not try to run away crying death, death. There is no running away. Understand it to be Mother. The way you are traveling, call that embrace of death Mother and leap into it. You will see that you have found the spirit beyond time, divine nectar. *Kālī* will bring you to that place where there is no such thing as death. Then you will see that you are eternal, you are ambrosial, you are bliss. But that is something else.

Kālī has a terrible visage. This face of my Mother is terrifying. My Mother swallows all states of non-Self, so *Kālī* is of terrible visage. My Mother is dark, black-hued. Where there is a lack of all colors, all states, where there is nothing, how can one express in words how dark, how black that is? Only if one has met the dense, dark, destructive form of Mother, one will understand how terrifying Mother is. This is the place where 'I' cannot be found, let alone body and senses. We are in a dark, moonless night, in a deep, dreamless sleep. No, not even this exists. There will be no action of life or breath in it. No physical body, no senses, no mind, no imagination, nothing. No thing, not even 'I.' Then slowly if you can find the 'I'-less 'I', then you will understand how terrifying *Kālī* is. It cannot be expressed by language. Whatever you say, 'emaciated, looking very fierce, mouth agape', it cannot be expressed.

Those who on seeing an image of *Kālī* are frightened to even bow down to it and try to seek refuge of the flute holding love of *Rādhikā*, do not know that without traveling across death, that is, without crossing the power of time, one cannot see the heart-warming view of the beauty of *Śyāma* (*Kṛṣṇa*). The one who is *Kālī* is in the nature of the one beyond time, the blissful *Śyāma*. When one understands this, there is no more fear. But this moves us away from the topic here.

My Mother is holding a sword, a net, and an unusual mace. The sword is an instrument to cut, the net one to attract and the mace to break. By cutting, attracting and breaking, in these three ways all conditions, all states of non-Self disappear in that terrible face. Separating objects from the supreme spirit based on which the working existence of visible things appears, is the first action of this power of Time. The sword in the hand of Mother is its sign. When the imaginary part is separated, the supreme part that is expressed is attracted and united with supreme spirit. This is the second act. This is the mystery of the net in the hand of Mother. Finally, all visible conditions are broken, are destroyed. This is the third act. The mace in the hand of *Kālī* is the representative of this action. Mother destroys non-Self in these three ways, that is why she is said to be wielding a sword, a net and a mace.

Kālī wears a garland strung with fifty skulls. What are fifty skulls? The fifty letters of the alphabet, sixteen vowels and thirty-four consonants are the fifty letters of the alphabet. This is the garland of Mother. Let me make this clearer.

This universe that you see is a diversity of sounds. This was explained in the principle of *nādas* during the commentary on the destruction of *Mahiṣāsura*. Moon, Sun, humans, animals, trees, vines and such sounds (words) are visible as this universe. By saying 'water-pot' we find a name, although it has no other nature but that of clay. In the same way, this universe is name and sound. That is why the sage of the *Upaniṣad* calmly sang that this universe is but a transformation of name and sound. Words are nothing but groups of letters. These letters are demons because they group together and express the state of non-Self of things. As long as the letters express specific states, they stay alive. But when Mother appears in her all-consuming form of *Kālī*, then the fifty letters are unable to produce special states. They are lifeless. The ability to express different things is the living state of letters. When there are none of these states, then letters vanish, that is, their ability to produce conditions is destroyed. They die. This is featured as the garland of skulls around the neck of the great destructive force. Because they reside as the seeds of future creation, they remain as an ornament for Mother. When seekers arise from *samprajñāta* (with distinctions) *samādhi*, this principle appears in their hearts.

dvīpicarmaparīdhānā: wearing a tiger skin. *Kālī* is usually naked. The power of destruction has no covering or hesitation. But here we see that Mother is wearing a tiger skin. At this point, *Caṇḍa*, *Muṇḍa*, *Raktavija* and other demons have not been killed, that is, the fine seeds of tendencies in the causal body have not yet been destroyed. These varied seeds are still on Mother as a covering cloth. This is a tiger skin. The variety of colors, black, yellow and red of the tiger skin, stay as a covering for Mother. So, she appears in her terrible form as *Cāmuṇḍā*. When all states are destroyed, my dark Mother will again appear in her naked form.

Some spiritual seekers sit on a tiger skin and conduct worship and meditation. Whatever the scientific reason that is given, (that it is a nonconductor of electricity), it cannot be denied that it is used as an external sign of a host of subtle tendencies. Maybe because the sight of the tiger skin reminds one of the varied tendencies of actions, aggressive seekers of old, made use of it. This is just a side note.

śuṣkamāṁsātibhairavā: emaciated and dangerous. Before all past tendencies are eroded, my Mother remains emaciated. Only when she has fed on the entirety of tendencies, will her body be nourished. Now my Mother keeps her hungry look. Before dissolution, this power appears to be hungry. When she is ready to destroy all states, my Mother appears lean and terrible. This destructive force is truly terrible.

ativistāravadanā: mouth wide open; *jihvālalanabhīṣaṇā*: with lolling tongue. Mother will soon need this to destroy *Raktavija*. We will discover this mystery in the right place.

nimagnāraktanayanā: her eyes red and sunken; *nādāpūritadiṁmukhā*: her roars filling the horizons. The arousal of anger is a source of destruction. Its external signs are bloodshot eyes and loud sounds (*nada*). The powers of special expression are nearly gone, so the eyes are sunken. Other than this, the roars from Mother fill the horizons. There is no way to know such specific states. These are descriptions of a destructive force.

A spiritual seeker should not think that such destructive forces are needed just to extinguish the state of this world, that is, the names and forms of this world. When even a small. clear space of awareness appears, material states are obliterated. But Mother needs to appear as a special form, to destroy the subtle states, subtle seeds of a state as a worldly person. Without the appearance of this destructive force, the subtle tendencies, the causes of birth, death and movement of worldly states are not destroyed. The center from which all states are expressed, to destroy that unexpressed central seed, Mother needs to appear in her terrible form as *Cāmuṇḍā*.

Those who have not observed this nature of Mother have to understand that the means for ending their worldly movement has not yet taken place. One can truly see this form. This destructive force appears. If one weeps for Mother, if one is keen to merge oneself into the heart of Mother, then she appears in this manner to end all tendencies as a worldly person. Do you, a spiritual seeker want to see this destructive form of *Kālī*?

Verse 8.

sā vegenābhipatitā ghātayantī mahaasurān|
sainye tatra surārīṇāmabhakṣayata tadbalam||

Translation:

Kālī, slaying the great demons, fell on the enemies of the gods and began to devour the strength of the demon forces.

Explanation:

As soon as the power of destruction is expressed, the variety of states of the demons begins to expire. It is a beautiful sight. On one side, the terrible, dark form appears, on the other, the expressed and unexpressed states of spirit are annihilated. The great seeker *Arjuna* too was one day overcome by fear and wonder by a view of this.

The demon warriors that Mother fell upon and began to devour were the soldiers of *Caṇḍa* and *Muṇḍa*, that is followers of inclination and disinclination. Past tendencies that are roused by the movement of inclination towards worldly things were destroyed at the death of *Mahiṣāsura*. Here, inclination moves towards *ātmā* and disinclination helps it by moving away from worldly matters. Besides this, they have other actions. Where there is action, there is a sense of control and duty. Although these are at subtle and higher levels, they support the state of non-Self. Even with a decline in the sense of non-Self, the true nature of Self is not revealed. Mother appears in her terrible form and moves a spiritual seeker to tears and devours the followers of inclination and disinclination.

Verse 9.

pārṣṇigrāhāṅkuśagrāhi yodhaghaṇṭāsamanvitān|
samādāyaikahastena mukhe chikṣepa vāraṇān||

Translation:

With one had she picked up elephants decorated with bells,

the warriors accompanying and riding them, and their guides, and threw them into her mouth.

Explanation:

It has been said that *Caṇḍa* and *Muṇḍa* arrived for war with four battalions of warriors. The elephants are in the first division. Warriors at the side of the elephants are called *pārṣñigrāha* and the conductor or *mahout* is called *āñkuśagrāhi*. With her hand, my *Cāmuṇḍā* mother took these warriors, riders and elephants with their bells and decorations and threw them into her mouth. A surprising battle. Who can stand in front of this destructive power? All that is expressed as non-Self is all taken down to become extinct. In Volume Two, speaking of the four battalions of the warriors of *Cikṣura*, it was said that these four were pain, action, misfortune and fate. There it was aimed at the subtle body. Here the seeds in the causal body are the four battalions of *Caṇḍa* and *Muṇḍa*.

The elephant represents pain or labor. Because seeds of pain, of sorrow and happiness, reside in the causal body, they appear also in the subtle one. The consciousness in which these seeds of pain, conducted by inclination and disinclination reside and are protected are the side warriors and riders of the elephants. Although there can be no divisions in consciousness, by the effect of different titles, they appear to take different states. Removing such specificities is the destruction of these demons. These special states are being thrown out by destructive power. Then there is no more perception of pain. With the emergence of that true destructive, dark power, the subtle states begin to disappear. It appears in this condition that these states enter a black, terrible mouth. By the powerful attraction of *Kālī*, the finest seeds of tendencies disappear into the nonmanifest arena. To explain this, the mantra says 'with her hands.'

Verse 10.

tathaiva yodhaṁ turagaiḥ rathaṁ sārathināsaha|
nikṣipya vaktre daśanaiścarvayatyatibhairavam||

Translation:

In the same manner, throwing the horses with their riders and the chariots with the charioteers into her mouth, she ground them with her teeth.

Explanation:

The previous mantra spoke of elephants, this one speaks about horses and chariots. It has been said that horses and chariots signify action and the store of actions respectively. Consciousness that is expressed as action and its store are the riders and charioteers. My Mother threw all these into her terrible mouth and ground them up with her teeth. That is, she destroyed the unexpressed seeds of action and their stores in the causal body.

The great devotee *Arjuna*, seeing the universal form also said the same thing. 'All the sons of *Dhṛtaraṣtra*, with all the other kings, *Bhiṣma, Droṇa* and our chief warriors, are entering into your mouth, which has terrible, fearful fangs. Some stick between the teeth with their heads crushed'[2]. There too, the warriors were being crushed by terrible teeth. There too, the Lord, because of the prayer of *Arjuna*, described himself as 'Time that destroys people.' The one who is *Kāla* (Time) in *Gitā* is *Kālī* in *Caṇḍī*. *Gitā* speaks of the destruction of material tendencies. In earlier volumes of *Devī Māhātmya*, the destruction of the subtle tendencies was described. In this one, tendencies of the causal body are described. Just as spiritual seekers advance from level to level of knowledge, tendencies also are divided by levels. To ascend into the levels of knowledge, surrender is the one easy and definitive method. The degree to which a seeker surrenders, that is, seeks shelter in God, knowledge flowers to that degree. Surrender is completed with the knowledge of Self. When there is no one left as 'I', but only 'I' remains, then surrender is complete. Belief in existence is the mainstay of surrender. The degree to which one has belief in the existence of the nature of God, states of surrender increase to the same degree. We who are readers of *Devī Māhatmya* always try to surrender, so we see Mother appear in her destructive form

2 *Bhāgavat Gitā*, 11:26,27.

and destroy all seeds of our tendencies of non-Self, our divided knowledge. We are honored.

Verse 11.

ekaṁ jagrāha keśeṣu grīvāyāmatha cāparam|
pādenākramya caivānyamurasānyamapothayat||

Translation:

Thereafter she held some by their hair and some by their necks. She crushed some with her feet and some with her chest.

Explanation:

Three of the four battalions of *Caṇḍa* and *Muṇḍa*, elephants, horses and chariots have been destroyed. Now the end of the fourth, the remaining foot soldiers are being described. Fate or the results of actions are foot soldiers. They bring stored seeds of action towards germination. Because they reside in subtle planes, they appear in the material as race, life-span and fulfillment of desires. 'I am of this race. I am this age. I go through joy and sorrow.' These are actions of this power of fate.

Mother appears here in her destructive form and holds them by their hair, that is, takes their heads. Taken by the destructive one means annihilation. What is special is that once the heads of tendencies are removed, there is no chance of their reappearance. Generally, the seeds of tendencies are hidden in a nonmanifest arena, appearing in connection with time, place and person. Mother is now ready to remove them from their nonmanifest arena.

Even if by the grace of Mother, stored and future actions have been ended, one is not yet free from the hands of senses of differences due to race, life-span and desires. At each moment one sees their expression because as yet all four battalions of *Caṇḍa* and *Muṇḍa* have not been destroyed. But now, Mother will take a spiritual seeker beyond all knowledge of differences. This is why all these preparations, all these cruel acts, all these dances of destruction. Mother destroys the demons in numerous fashions, some held by the neck, some crushed by her feet, some by her chest. In broad words, all kinds of tendencies were being destroyed by the appearance of the power of dissolution. It is because of the variety of tendencies that this variety of procedures is observed and various methods are described. This is the mystery in the next three mantras.

Verse 12.

tairmuktāni ca śastrāṇi mahāstrāṇi tathāsuraiḥ|
mukhena jagrāha ruṣa daśanairmathitānyapi||

Translation:

The demons used their strongest weapons. The Goddess took them into her mouth and ground them up with her teeth.

Explanation:

Even when they are being destroyed because of their former velocity, the foot soldiers of unexpressed fate do not stop applying their strength. A spiritual seeker can perceive this mystery of applying their strongest weapons. As much as one might practice devotion and knowledge, as much as one may be immersed in the spirit of Mother, one cannot be freed from the clutches of race, life-span and desire. Repeated reappearances of fate are the weapons of these demons. But now they will fail. Mother has appeared in her destructive form. Now when perceptions of fate reappear, they will be covered by nondual spirit. By this happening repeatedly, they become powerless.

It is seen that *sannyāsis* and renunciates, remove caste signs like hair and sacred threads to end any cognizance of race. They receive food from all castes. To remove discernment of their life-span, they never speak of their age. To end fulfillment of physical desires, with great effort, they tolerate sorrow and joy, winter and summer, hunger and thirst. All this is very good. *Sannyāsis* are to be revered by us. But, I do not know, how many of them can save themselves from the hands of these demons by practices of indescribable severity. Even after forsaking signs of caste and taking food from all, inside, there is still a percept of 'I am of this race.' Even without discussing about age, one retains the knowledge of childhood, youth and old age. And, desires remain. The physical body is the burning proof. Only when the nondual nature of Self is expressed, are these divisions removed. Otherwise, they do not go away even after a thousand attempts. One might be concerned that even after the discovery of true knowledge, if these things remain, then what is the worth of Mother appearing in her form as *Kālī*? Do not fear. Mother truly devours all, appearing as Self. Even after the expression of Self, they may still follow for a little time. It is a forced following. They are as if not there. We will discuss this in more detail later.

Verse 13.

balināṁ tadbalaṁ sarvvamasurāṇāṁ mahātmanā|
mamarddābhakṣayaccānyānanyāṁścātāḍayattathā||

Translation:

In this manner, Mother crushed some demons, devoured some, and drove some away.

Explanation:

Those who were crushed or devoured will not reappear again. Those who were driven away will reappear as forced followings. The fates that are greatly opposed to realizing Self were devoured and crushed by the power of destruction. Those who were not truly obstacles were driven away by Mother. Think about race, life span and fulfilling desires. These perceptions appear as soon as one moves away from the nature of Self. Only when one is residing in the nature of the Self are they driven out. When my Mother appears, one cannot find their existence. It does not even seem that they ever were or will be. But they reappear as one moves away. Even if a seeker has no special knowledge of his race, lifespan and desires, those about others remain. Perceptions that do not remain for oneself, are of concern because they remain about others. So, one has to say that even when they are driven away, they can come back. Here, the question is that, if race, life-span and desires remain, then what is the worth of Mother appearing in her destructive form? Yes. It is still worthwhile. Any supreme worth of these things is lost. A knower of Self does not value these things in the way that worldly persons think of them as having some supreme worth. The words, 'I am a *Brāhmaṇ*, I have so much life left, my joy and sorrow' remain as applications of words, without any real spirit. They understand this so well that even when perceptions of race and life-span appear, their perception of nonduality is not hindered.

But remember something. Those for whom Mother does not appear and wipe out pain, action and fate, cannot remove any sense of definitive worth by discussing scriptures or by advice. It is only Mother by her grace who can make one understand that only *ātmā*, Mother is of supreme worth. Nothing else remains. Other than supreme spirit, everything else is only operational. Without complete realization, only learning and inference, cannot remove ignorance.

Verse 14.

asinā nihatāḥ kecit kecit khaṭvāṅgatāḍitāḥ|
jagmurvināśamasurā dantāgrābhihatāstathā||

Verse 15.

kṣaṇena tadbalaṁ sarvamasurāṇāṁ nipātitam|
dīṣṭvā caṇḍohabhidudrāva tāṁ kālīmatibhīṣaṇām||

Translation:

Some of the demons were killed with a scimitar, some beaten with a mace, and the rest were destroyed by her teeth. In this manner, within a short time, all the warriors fell. Seeing this, the great *asura Caṇḍa* raced towards *Kālī* with great speed.

Explanation:

The significance of the sword and mace has been explained before. There are innumerable demon warriors. First, from the knowledge of race, tendencies of the characteristics of caste, class and prescribed actions appear. From the knowledge of life span, stages of childhood and youth and their associated actions appear. In the same manner, unnecessary tendencies associated with desires are called up. Together, all these become the innumerable warriors of inclination and disinclination. But, however innumerable they are, the power of the demons is overcome within moments. How long can they stand in front of this destructive force? Just as darkness disappears with the appearance of light, ignorance and any divisiveness due to it are destroyed immediately by the rise of knowledge. Seeing his warriors destroyed in this fashion, *Caṇḍa* (inclination) moves towards Mother for battle.

Verse 16.

śaravarṣairmahābhīmairbhīmākṣīṁ tāṁ mahāsuraḥ|
chādayāmāsa cakraiśca muṇḍaḥ kṣiptaiḥ sahasraśaḥ||

Translation:

The great demon *Caṇḍa* threw a shower of arrows at the powerful-eyed goddess and covered her. *Muṇḍa* threw thousands of discs at her.

Explanation:

Now the battle begins with *Caṇḍa* and *Muṇḍa*. One shoots a terrible shower of arrows, and the other throws thousands of sharp discs (*cakra*). Arrows are *Praṇava*. The strong attempt to keep spirit steady by mental repetitions of *Praṇava* mantra, or the natural rise of the sound of *Praṇava* from the heart (*Anāhata*) center, is the shower of arrows from *Caṇḍa*. This is the final act of inclination moving towards Self. The weapon of *Muṇḍa* or disinclination is the discus (*cakra*). It is the action of disinclination to counter the cycle of worldly life. In this fashion, inclination and disinclination apply their powers to save themselves from the destructive force. A spiritual seeker has to understand that as long as there is spiritual effort, worship, the repetition of mantra, meditation and concentration, so long the nature of Self is not expressed. Again, as long as there is renunciation, non-desire of worldly things, and such senses, Mother has not shown herself. This is the significance of a shower of arrows and discs. This will be clearer later on.

Verse 17.

tāni cakrāṇyanekāni viśamānāni tanmukham|
babhuryathārkabimbāni subahūni ghanodaram||

Translation:

The many discs closing in on the face of the Goddess, adorned it like innumerable rays of the Sun streaming out of a cloud.

Explanation:

Dissolution of the efforts of inclination and disinclination by the terrible destructive power took on a special beauty. The poet of *Devī Māhātmya* uses the words 'Sun rays' and 'clouds', as similes. The face of *Kālī* is compared to a cloud and the weapons to the rays of the sun. When the discs thrown by *Muṇḍa*, abandonment, renunciation, control, rules, nonviolence and all acts of disinclination, were destroyed by *Kālī*, disappearing in her cave of destruction, it appeared as if these bright states, like rays of the sun, were appearing from a dark cloud. When the greatest components of humanity, pure expression of the right principle, the greatest expressions of divinity, when all these bright features get near the dark, black, terrible face, their natural brightness is enhanced. Just as bright stars disappear behind dark clouds, the greatest features of humanity, disappeared one by one.

Until this time, a spiritual seeker acquired divine features and moved towards Godhood. Now, the time has come to dissolve them. Now the seeker has to land, not on Godhood, but *Brahmaṇ*. So, Mother is also destroying all the right characteristics (*sat guṇas*). She will not let even a drop of specialty or divisiveness remain. Without separation of right or wrong, she will remove all *bhāba* and only then reveal her nature as *Amvikā*. All this is preparatory to that. This is a beautiful principle.

Verse 18.

tato jahāsātiruṣā bhīmaṁ bhairavanādinī|
kālī karālavaktrānta durddarśadaśanojjvalā||

Translation:

Angered, *Kālī* gave forth loud roars and terrifying laughter. At that time, the brilliance of the fearful teeth in her wide-open mouth made it sparkle.

Explanation:

With her loud laughter, terrifying roars and the whiteness of her teeth, the dark form of my destructive Mother is enhanced. All these are conditions for dissolution. Mother needs such a figure to destroy inclination and disinclination. One can with ease leave aside lust, anger, jealousy, and other wicked states. But, no one wants to leave proper states of spiritual effort, worship and renunciation. Mother appears in her terrible form with a wide-open mouth and destroys them by force. Seekers might be fearful seeing this. Viewing such a form, *Arjuna* said 'my mind is filled with fear.' I have said that all spiritual seekers have to go past this destructive form. Those who worship the beautiful form of *Śyama* and are afraid to even utter the name of *Kālī* or harbor enmity towards her, have to know that one day, the beautiful *Śyama* will also emerge saying 'I am the destroyer of all,'[3] and appear in the terrible form of *Kālī*. Until all is destroyed, the beautiful *Śyama* cannot appear. As long as anything visible remains, that supreme form cannot appear. This destruction is necessary. The loud laughter and roars from Mother help this obliteration in worldly persons.

The expression of this figure is beautiful and joyous. However terrifying it may be, this is the form that is beneficial to spiritual seekers. This is the proper figure of *Caṇḍī*. My Mother needs to appear in this form as *Caṇḍī* to destroy *Caṇḍa* and *Muṇḍa*. If Mother is not terrifying and filled with anger, then this false playhouse will never be torn down. My Mother has demolished

3 *Bhāgavat Gitā*, 11.32.

two rooms and is now preparing to break down the third. This is the value of her form as *Caṇḍī*. Fear not. Do children of a lioness fear the wide-open mouth of their mother? It is Mother. Be she terrifying, be she destructive, calamitous, she is Mother. If one is afraid of the terrible face of Mother, one has to hide one's face on her chest, wrap one's hands around her neck, be engrossed by her and call her 'Mother.' Although here, there is no connection of mother and child, no affection and mercy for any material view, still, until the point of dissolution, we will not be moved from the relation between Mother and child. We began calling the material earth and water Mother. We will call her Mother to the end of all our states. Then when 'I' will no longer be, I will no longer call her Mother. This incredible, divine play by Mother will end.

Even now, *Kālī* is worshipped in many parts of this land. In practice, it is not the worship of *Kālī* but that of the dark one, *Śyāmā*. When *Kālī* is called Mother, she is no longer *Kālī* but *Śyāmā*. We are not able to worship *Kālī*. In worshipping her, we call her Mother. In case our cherished position as her child vanishes, we call her Mother, with that fear in mind. To maintain duality, she appears as Mother. From the *saṁskāras* of very long duration, many lifetimes, we cannot let go of this duality. But now this will not continue. Mother has become *Caṇḍī*. Mother has appeared in her destructive form to end multiplicity and establish oneness. Now, we will land on a supreme nature beyond word and thought, without any relationship as mother and child. Even thinking about this is thrilling.

Verse 19.

utthāya ca mahāsiṁhaṁ devī caṇḍamadhāvata|
gṛhītvā cāsya keśeṣu śirastenāsinācchinat||

Translation:

After this, the Goddess, in much anger raised her great sword and raced towards *Caṇḍa*. Holding him by his hair, she cut off his head.

Explanation:

The word '*mahāsiṁhaṁ*' in the mantra has two parts. One is '*mahāsiṁ*' and the other is '*haṁ*.' The part '*haṁ*' signifies anger. A great sword is a weapon to destroy perceptions of duality, it is knowledge of nonduality. The great Vedic statements establishing the non-difference between beings and *Brahmaṇ* are great swords. The four great statements in the *Vedas*, 'intellect is *Brahmaṇ*, Self is *Brahmaṇ*, I am that and I am *Brahmaṇ*[4]', are seeds for the destruction of percepts of duality. This nondual knowledge, in the language of *Caṇḍī,* is a great sword in the hand of the Goddess.

The word '*mahāsi*' (great sword) can have another meaning. The great statement in the *Sama Veda* also has the term '*asi*.' The meaning of the root '*as*' is spirit or nature. The word '*mahāsi*' can also mean great spirit. When the great or supreme spirit is revealed, the operational or worldly spirit disappears. The annihilating Mother, raising her great sword, cuts off the head of *Caṇḍa* with it. That is, by expressing supreme nature, she destroys the root inclination of perception of duality. Knowledge of nonduality is the reason for all inclination. When nondual knowledge is firmly established, there is nothing of inclination that remains.

There is another idea in this mantra. Mother holds *Caṇḍa* by his hair. The mystery of the hair has been explained before. The significance of the Goddess holding the hair is the removal of any enticement of landing on the states of *Brahmā*, *Viṣṇu* or *Śiva*. My Mother removes any desire for Godhood, before destroying inclination. There are no other wishes left, cannot be left. When Mother raises her great sword, that is, when great spirit is firmly perceived, then differences between receiver and received, attempter and attempt are no longer discerned. Inclination is removed by its roots. Do not think that just analyzing the meaning of the great statement like 'I am that' will bring an end to inclination and discovery of the supreme state. As long as Mother does not raise her great sword and destroy the *asura Caṇḍa*, hopes of liberation remain only a hope.

---

4 *prajñānaṁ brahma; ayamātmā brahma; tat tama asi; ahaṁ brahmāsmi.*

Verse 20.

atha muṇḍohapyadhāvattāṁ dṛṣṭvā caṇḍaṁ nipātitam|
tamapyapātayadbhūmau sā khaḍgābhihataṁ ruṣā||

Translation:

Thereafter, seeing that *Caṇḍa* had fallen, *Muṇḍa* rushed towards the Goddess. In anger, the Goddess felled him to the ground with her scimitar.

Explanation:

With the end of inclination, disinclination also ends. I have said before this, that they are of similar states. Destruction of one brings the inevitable end of the other. These are the ones who first brought the news of Mother to ego. Their work has ended. The need for inclination and disinclination is over. They sacrifice themselves to complete the arrangement for the expression of the nature of Mother.

The great sword that was mentioned before, was used to down *Muṇḍa*. The great swords of the great Vedic statements are infallible ways of removing all perceptions of divisiveness.

A spiritual seeker has to think about how much effort, severity and enterprise one had to expend to turn inclination from worldly things towards *paramātmā*. Then, because the desire for worldly things did not go away and disinclination did not appear, many techniques of yoga had to be applied and much sorrow ensued because hopes were not fulfilled. Tears were silently shed at the feet of Mother. Then, when hopes were fulfilled, when inclination was turning towards Mother, when disinclination was ending the desire for worldly matters, you sighed a breath of relief. My Mother appeared in the form of *Kālī* and engulfed inclination and disinclination, your spiritual enterprise and renunciation. Think yourself to be honored. Because Mother took all your renunciation and rejection into her wide-open mouth in an instant, will you feel sad? No. You are a seeker of the principles of *Caṇḍī*. You are a lion who destroys worldly persons. You are a seeker of nondual knowledge. Why will you be sad? You will go forward saying 'Hail *guru*. Hail Mother.' Inclination and disinclination are gone. Now hold up to Mother whatever is left. Mother in her form as *Cāmuṇḍā* will engulf your completeness and bring you to nonduality. That is why I have said from the beginning that the principles of *Caṇḍī* are very deep. Even the *Upaniṣad* says that 'it is like traveling in darkness, on an arduous path on the edge of a razor,[5].' Truly, are these principles not deep?

Verse 21.

hataśeṣaṁ tataḥ sainyaṁ dṛṣṭvā caṇḍaṁ nipātitam|
muṇḍañca sumahāvīryaṁ diśo bheje bhayāturam||

Translation:

Seeing that *Caṇḍa* and *Muṇḍa* had both fallen, the remaining warriors escaped.

Explanation:

Most of the followers of inclination and disinclination had been previously destroyed. Those who remained ran away in fear, at the appearance of this destructive force. Those who reappear again as repeating natures have been named the escaped warriors in this mantra. Let me make this clearer.

Even after the destruction of inclination and disinclination, spiritual seekers remain in their physical bodies. Inclination is seen in their acts of eating, sleeping or teaching people and disinclination in not conducting acts forbidden in the scriptures. If inclination and disinclination remain, some of their followers will also be there. It is aimed at these that return that the mantra says that they ran away in fear. It may be of concern that if inclination, disinclination and some of their followers reappear, then how have they been destroyed? True, but this has been answered before. Although inclination and disinclination remain in use, their supreme knowledge is destroyed. Only during the duration that

5 *Kaṭha Upaniṣad*, 1.3.14.

a seeker is immersed in Self, do their actions also disappear. The point is that all these preparations, all these battles are to alight on the knowledge that there is nothing else but Self. Even after this knowledge is experienced, feelings of non-Self can return. This is not a demonic state, it is like a skin that a snake has shed, it can no longer bite. But it is definite that when some self-realized persons act in this world, they have at that time, moved from the nature of Self. But, this movement does them no harm as their ignorance or the knowledge of non-Self is gone.

Verse 22.

śiraścaṇḍasya kālī ca gṛhītvā muṇḍameva ca|
prāha pracaṇḍāṭṭahāsamiśramabhyetya caṇḍikām||

Verse 23.

mayā tavātropahṛtau caṇḍamuṇḍau mahāpaśū|
yuddhayajñe svayaṁ śumbhaṁ niśumbhañca haniṣyasi||

Translation:

Taking the heads of *Caṇḍa* and *Muṇḍa* in hand, *Kālī* went in front of *Caṇḍīkā* and laughing uproariously said, "In this ceremonial battle, I present you the great animals *Caṇḍa* and *Muṇḍa*. You will destroy *Śumbha* and *Niśumbha* yourself."

Explanation:

Taking the heads of *Caṇḍa* and *Muṇḍa*, *Kālī* presented them at the feet of *Caṇḍīkā*. A spiritual seeker should not forget that she who was before understood to be *Kouṣikī* was now residing in the Himālayās as *Amvikā*. It is her anger appearing in a destructive form, expressed as *Kālī*, that comes to present the heads of *Caṇḍa* and *Muṇḍa*. My Mother *Amvikā* is very enraged, so she is called *Caṇḍīkā*. She is the focus of *Devī Māhātmya*. When supreme nature is expressed, all states are destined to disappear. It is this dissolution that is described to be a result of her anger. The power that destroys all states is *Kālī*. In all these great acts, all this destruction, all these battles, *ātmā*, my Mother is eternally unchanging, blissful, always smiling. There is no change in her, yet they all point to her, it is by her spirit that these hosts of demons are destroyed.

This happens to all spiritual seekers. Before the nature of Self is revealed, the power of Self appears in the form of dissolution and removes all obstacles to its appearance. That is why the mantra says that *Kālī* said to *Amvikā*, 'you will yourself kill *Śumbha* and *Niśumbha* in battle.' A suggestion or reflection cannot be expressed without the basis or specificity of something. Without the basis of mind, intelligence, spirit, ego body, or inclination and disinclination, there cannot be anything like a suggestion of spirit. Just as no shadow can be cast in bare space, without some basis, there is no reflection of existence. Only *cit* remains. Only the power of existence can destroy its reflection *Śumbha* and *Niśumbha*.

There is something else. *Kālī* presents the heads of *Caṇḍa* and *Muṇḍa* at the feet of *Caṇḍīkā*. The bodiless upper end of inclination and disinclination remained at the feet of *Amvikā*. They will remain, but they will not be the reason for any knowledge of duality. Before this, they had been described as obstacles to a perception of nonduality, so they were described as demons. But now they are without their bodies, that is, lifeless heads. What has been said before about the returning faculties of inclination and disinclination are clearly stated by the presentation of the heads in this mantra. This is the final perception of those who realize Self. There is a little more mystery here. The heads are presented at the feet of Mother. After finding Mother, inclination and disinclination remain as shells. They are offerings for the feet of Mother. After finding Mother, all actions of inclination and disinclination follow the wishes of Mother. The sense that, 'I am the doer, I have duties' disappears.

Verse 24.

ṛṣiruvāca|
tāvānītau tato dṛṣṭvā caṇḍamuṇḍau mahāsurau|
uvāca kālīṁ kalyāṇī lalitaṁ caṇḍikā vacaḥ||

Verse 25.

yasmāccaṇḍañca muṇḍañca gṛhītvā tvamupāgatā|
cāmuṇḍeti tato loke khyātā devī bhaviṣyasi||

*iti mārkaṇḍeya purāṇe sāvarṇike man*vantare|
devī māhātmye caṇḍa muṇḍa vadho||

Translation:

The sage said, seeing that *Caṇḍa* and *Muṇḍa* had been brought to her (as presents, being dead) the beneficent Goddess *Caṇḍīkā* said sweetly to *Kālī*, "Because you have arrived with *Caṇḍa* and *Muṇḍa*, O Goddess, from today you will be known in this world as *Cāmuṇḍā*."

Here ends this episode of the destruction of *Caṇḍa* and *Muṇḍa*, in the *Devī Māhātmya*, in the era of *Sāvarṇi*, in the *Mārkeṇḍeya Purāṇa*.

Explanation:

It is for the destructive force to remain especially expressed that the Goddess bestows this blessing. Because she has destroyed *Caṇḍa* and *Muṇḍa* she is named *caṇḍāmuṇḍā* or *Cāmuṇḍā*. The word *Cāmuṇḍā* is formed by adding the root '*ā*' to *caṇḍamuṇḍa* signifying destruction. According to the grammatical *Pṛṣodarādi sutra*, the word *caṇḍāmuṇḍā* becomes *Cāmuṇḍā*. Whatever it is, because of the blessings of Goddess *Caṇḍīkā*, this destructive force of *Cāmuṇḍā* remains to end inclination and disinclination. Even now, every year, during the *Durgā pujā* ceremony, special worship for her is carried out at the junction of the eighth and ninth lunar dates.

Look! All over this world, there is this divine play of *Cāmuṇḍā*. The sorrow and unhappiness you see in this world are all wild games of *Cāmuṇḍā*. If you want to be free from the grasp of death of this terrible *Cāmuṇḍā*, if you want to be free of the fear of death and take shelter on the lap of fearless nectar, if you want to receive peace blessings of divine nectar while in this noisy, dying world, then worship this power of *Cāmuṇḍā*. Seat yourself on a corpse in this great cemetery of life, at the juncture between worldly persons with supreme Self. Then, finding existence that remains inside great death, establish on it a naked form of your 'I.' Established in great truth, only focusing on the pure nature of awareness, offer flowers of life with the seed mantra of *Ādyā*. If you can do this, it will be the worship of *Cāmuṇḍā*. Those who cannot die while alive, cannot perform the worship of *Cāmuṇḍā*. Those who cannot worship *Cāmuṇḍā*, have difficulty finding her beneficence. Without it, the grim shadow of death is not removed. Those who know *Cāmuṇḍā*, those who recognize her as the power of death, those who know her terrible grasp as a refuge of Mother, only they can be free of her rule and arrive at the independent nature of Self.

O look! It is *Cāmuṇḍā* who is devouring the stores of joy of this world. It is *Cāmuṇḍā* who is sucking the blood from the hearts of beings. She destroys all enthusiasm and enterprise in this world. It has been said that the constituent and instrumental cause of this world is bliss. Bliss is the true nature of this world of beings. Yet the host of beings feeling a lack of bliss, go about here and there in search of it. The only reason for this is *Cāmuṇḍā*, the terrible grasp of death. In case we lose our 'I'-ness, in fear, beings are unable to enjoy bliss without any concerns. They cannot independently, with free spirits, storm the eternal store of bliss of my blissful Mother. It is *Cāmuṇḍā*, this fear of death, that strikes a blow at the stem of all bliss. But you are a spiritual seeker, a brave child of Mother, you should not be afraid of death. Seeing that death chases you, do not run away to be free of its clutches. Do not turn your back on death. Turn around, and calling on Mother, face death. Call on Mother and offer flowers of life at the feet of death. Crying 'victory to Mother', fall on the lap of the destructive force of *Kālī* with courage and strength. You will see that there is no such thing as death. What you were afraid of as a terrible witch, is a beneficial, affectionate form of Mother, who holds you and brings you immortality.

Not only in this world of spiritual enterprise, but in the daily world, those who are very fearful of death can never accomplish anything. But that is something else.

Come, let us say, "*Kālī, Kālī, Mahākālī, Kālike papahāriṇī*[6]" and bow at the feet of Mother. Let us offer ourselves at the feet of the one, by the grace of who, stored tendencies of many lifetimes, the inclination and disinclination of demons are destroyed. Let us see the mysterious play of Mother and look at the destruction of *Raktavija*. May Mother shower us with her beneficence.

Here ends this explanation of the destruction of *Caṇḍa* and *Muṇḍa*, in *Sādhan Samar* or *Devī Māhātmya*

---

6 one who removes sins

Chapter 8

Destruction of *Raktavija*

Verse 1.

ṛṣiruvāca|
caṇḍe ca nihate daitye muṇḍe ca vinipātite|
bahuleṣu ca sainyeṣu kṣayiteṣvasureśvaraḥ||

Verse 2.

tataḥ kopaparādhīnacetāḥ śumbhaḥ pratāpavān|
udyogaṁ sarvasainyānāṁ daityānāmādideśa ha||

Translation:

The sage said, *Caṇḍa* and *Muṇḍa* having fallen and many warriors destroyed, the king of demons, the powerful *Śumbha,* in great anger, ordered all demon warriors to prepare for battle.

Explanation:

Seeing the death of inclination and disinclination together with their followers, ego was angered and prepared for battle, ordering all the warriors and generals of the monster clans to go and fight. The perceptions of duality are monsters (*daitya*). They are innumerable. Distorted knowledge of 'I am my thoughts' is the cause of perceptions of duality. Initially, this distorted knowledge had to appear, and in this final character, the destruction of *Dhumralocana* as distorted knowledge is described first. Then the great supports of the perception of duality, inclination and disinclination, in the form of *Caṇḍa* and *Muṇḍa* were destroyed. Seeing this, ego applies all its remaining effort. This is the mystery of the great battle preparation of *Śumbha*. They will all now be destroyed. The mantra says that all the warriors prepared for battle. *Śumbha* has to sacrifice himself with *Niśumbha*. This great preparation is only an indication of that. A spiritual seeker has to remember that all this is the grace or attraction of Mother.

Remember the words of *Gitā* in the Universal view, 'just as insects are destroyed flying precipitously into a burning flame, so are beings destroyed entering into your mouth'[1]. The demons by the great attraction of Mother are getting ready to sacrifice themselves in battle in the manner of insects. Remember, can this transpire by spiritual enterprise? Can such an opportunity come without the grace of Mother? My Mother is *Kṛṣṇa*. Without her strong attraction, can the perceptions of duality rush to be immersed in the spirit of the nondual? You have surrendered at the feet of Mother and sit there without any concern, just as a silent witness. The affectionate attraction of Mother destroys all your percepts of duality and brings you to the supreme bliss of nonduality. Even the thought of this brings immense joy to the heart.

As long as you reside outside the territory of the attraction of Mother, can you realize the immense grace of self-sacrifice in these demonic states?

Verse 3.

adya sarvabalairdaityāḥ ṣaḍaśītirudāyudhāḥ|
kambūnāṁ caturaśīti niryāntu svabalairvṛtā||

Verse 4.

koṭivīryāṇi pañcāśadasurāṇāṁ kulāni vai|
śataṁ kulāni dhaumrāṇāṁ nirgacchantu mamājñayā||

Verse 5.

kālakā daurhṛdā maurvāḥ kālikeyāstathāsurāḥ|
yuddhāya sajjā niryāntu ājñayā tvaritā mama||

Translation:

By my order, let all the warriors prepare for battle and move quickly. Let all eighty-six of the *Udāyudh* clan, eighty-four of the *Kambu* clan, fifty of the *Thekoṭivīryā* clan, a hundred of the *Dhumra* clan and those of the *Kālak*, *Dourhṛta*, *Mourya* and *Kālakeya*, surrounded by their warriors, go forward for battle.

1 *Bhāgavat Gitā*, 11:29

Explanation:

In a spiritual view, the eight clans of demons are known as the eight bondages. It is mentioned in the *Kulārnava Tantra* that 'hate, shame, fear, anxiety, reproach, these five, and clan, class, race are bondages.' Worldly persons are bound by these eight bindings. When freed of these eight bondages, beings (*jiva*) become *Śiva*. 'Beings are wrapped by bondages. When free of bonds, one is *Śiva*.' These are also words from *Tantra*. After so long, beings are landing in the state of *Śiva* by the grace of Mother. Ego, *Śumbha*, is sending these eight bondages to Mother. When these are destroyed, the material supports of *Śumbha* will be gone. We will enter this beautiful mystery. Here let us try to learn a little about these demons.

1) *Udāyudh*: one whose weapons are raised. With spiritual insight, this is hatred. Truly, hatred is a raised weapon. To harbor hate or disregard for someone, one has to raise one's ego. I am pure and elevated. The other one is impure and low. It is from such a view that hatred appears. So, it can be called the *Udāyudh asura*. They are eighty-six in number. In the waking state, based on the fourteen faculties, one can express hatred for the four kinds of living things, so, there are fifty-six kinds in the waking state. In the dreaming state, based on the four inner faculties, one can express hatred at the four kinds of beings, so there are sixteen kinds. Ego trying to be established in itself has a natural dislike of the fourteen faculties. In this fashion, one can see eighty-six different kinds of demons in the *Udāyudh* clan. This has been declared in the mantra.

2) *Kambu*: the word means a conch shell. This is the second binding of beings. Its nature is shame. The limbs of animals who live in shells are hidden. With the advent of anything painful, they hide. Humans react similarly when shamed. So that no weakness is expressed, people withdraw and hide. To express shame, one thinks of these shelled creatures. Shame is also a binding. This shame

or withdrawal appears from divisive knowledge. One has to notice that before we had bowed down to this as a form of Mother saying 'one who is established as shame.' That is why, today, the divisive knowledge of shame, or a self-withdrawing shell has come in the form of a demon to sacrifice itself. They are eighty-six in number. They are expressed by the fourteen faculties based on the six-layered body. When these numbers are multiplied, they give eighty-six. In this way, shame is of eighty-six different kinds. So *Śumbha* says 'eighty-six *Kombu* clans' in his order.

3) *Koṭivīryā*: *koti* (ten million), that is one of unlimited valor. This is fear, the third bondage of people. Fear is truly *Koṭivīryā*, very powerful. The fear of the destruction of one's existence prevents people from enjoying this world. It does not let them freely carry out spiritual exercises. It is because supreme spirit is not expressed, that this fear of self-destruction in the form of *Koṭivīryā asura* appears. They are fifty in number. The ten senses and five shells are their sites of expression. Multiplied together they are fifty. In the same way, the bondage of fear is of fifty kinds. So, the mantra says 'fifty of the *Koṭivīryā* clan.'

4) *Dhoumra*: The descendants of the *asura Dhumra* are called *Dhoumra*. This *Dhumra* is no other than *Dhumralocana*. It is from distorted knowledge that all anxiety appears. So, these are demons of the *Dhoumra* clan. This is anxiety, the fourth bondage. There is a difference between fear and anxiety. Fear is the expectation of the destruction of oneself. Anxiety is a mental alteration due to the expectation of material damage. In simpler words, fear is that due to death. Anxiety is the expectation of a loss of wealth and progeny. These appear from perceptions of divisiveness, so they are bondages. They are one hundred in number. These demons are based on the ten senses, the five *tanamātrās* and the five elements. Multiplied, they are a hundred. In this way, anxiety or the *Dhumra*

demons are one hundred in number. So, the mantra says 'a hundred of the clan.'

5) *Kālak*: the dark-colored demons. The word is formed by adding '*ka*' at the end of '*kāla*.' This is reproach, the fifth bondage. Ignorance is dark. It is from ignorance that the perception of multiplicity or divisiveness is nurtured. It is from divisive knowledge that reproach or criticism appears. As long as spiritual seekers do not land on nonduality, they cannot be free of the grasp of this *Kālak asura* or reproach.

6) *Dourhṛta*: these are the descendants of the *asura Durhṛta*. Because they bring wicked (*duṣṭa*) states, they are named *Durhṛta*. This is the pride of lineage, the sixth bondage. Even after a seeker has heard the advice about the unique spirit of *Brahmaṇ* a hundred thousand times, one is not quickly relieved from the ignorance of the pride of one's lineage. So, this too is a demonic state.

7) *Maurya*: these are the descendants of the *asura Mūra*. In a spiritual view, these are *śīla*, the seventh bondage of beings. The meaning of the word *śīla* is natural behavior or nature. In landing on the knowledge of nonduality, specific knowledge of one's nature is a great obstacle. It has been said that one's nature generates a person. Those who practice this truth, only they, arriving at the knot of *Rudra*, will see that this innate nature is leaving and ushering in the discovery of blissful, nondual spirit. If one cannot call one's nature Mother, one cannot discover the nature of this universe. Without finding the nature of this universe, one cannot arrive at that which is beyond this universe, the pure nature of Self.

8) *Kālakeya*: these are the descendants of the *asura Kālaka*. This is race, the eighth bondage. This pride of race is fed by ignorance or divided knowledge. So, these may be called *Kālaka* or the children of the ignorance natured, or dark-colored *asura Kālakeya*. We have said about this

pride of race in the explanation of the destruction of *Caṇḍa* and *Muṇḍa*. Its destruction was also described there. It is hoped that a generous reader will not be disturbed by the fault of repletion that is seen here. Because there, the race that was mentioned was about the origins of specific clans. Here, it is about the united human race. These perceptions of lineage, nature and race are very intractable. Even after being destroyed many times, they repeatedly reappear. It is to destroy the root of these perceptions, that Mother is making these final arrangements.

The eight bondages mentioned are firm bindings for beings. If they cannot be broken, one cannot meet Mother. Or, without meeting Mother, these bondages are not removed. One can see spiritual seekers take recourse to different procedures to free themselves of these bindings. To remove the tendencies of hatred and shame, they carry out opposing practices. Alas! On one hand, these bondages are not removed, on the other, because of such reverse actions, new tendencies are created. One has to remember that bondage and liberation are but variations of knowledge. Until pure perception arises, these eight bindings of ignorance are not uprooted. This is what Lord *Kṛṣṇa* advised *Arjuna*. When one starves or controls the senses, the matters of this world may cease, but the subtle tendencies of their desires remain. Only by meeting supreme spirit is the divisive desire for worldly things, the subtle tendencies, completely shut off.[2]

Only seekers, who from the beginning of their effort, can hold all their states, good or bad, in front of Mother, are by her grace freed from these eight bondages and immersed in an ocean of supreme bliss. At the beginning of *Sādhan Samar*, in the explanation of the first mantra for 'eighth *Manu*', this freedom from the eight bondages was raised. One has to remember that what was indicated in the beginning, has now after so many changes in circumstances, after so many events, about to come to fruition. A seeker who has pierced the knot of *Rudra* and resides calmly

---

2 *rasa varjaṁ raso pyasya paraṁ dīṣhṭvā nivartate*, *Bhāgavat Gitā*, 2:59.

on the lap of Mother can observe this. By the great attraction of Mother, one by one, bondages go forward to be destroyed. What seemed to require severe enterprise to be freed from, what seemed impossible, are now ready to leave by themselves.

Can you not believe this? Truly, if you call on Mother with simplicity, if you truly surrender at her feet, if you are truly keen to climb onto her lap, then all your bondages will go away with ease. Mother will come and remove all the bindings of her favorite children. Taking you to her heart, she will land you in the golden temple of freedom. For a long time, you have stayed away from the land of freedom and accepted the bonds of worldly life. Affectionate Mother will remove these imaginary bonds forever. She will merge your spirit into undivided, blissful, pure, conscious formed spirit of *Brahmaṇ*, where there is no bondage or sense of difference. Saying 'I am *Brahmaṇ*' you will go beyond this worldly state. Your human life will be worthy.

Verse 6.

ityājñāpyāsurapatiḥ śumbho bhairavaśāsanaḥ|
nirjagāma mahāsainyasahasrairbahubhirvṛtaḥ||

Translation:

The powerful king of demons *Śumbha*, giving these orders, went into battle himself, surrounded by many warriors.

Explanation:

Ego is the king of the demons. As the shelter of all the perceptions of duality, he is very powerful. No one can disobey his orders, because all perceptions of duality are his different expressions. This has been mentioned before. He was not satisfied by just sending all his generals to battle. He went out with the other warriors. It is needless to say that *Niśumbha* also went out with *Śumbha* for battle. Ego and attachment go out together on the battlefield. All tendencies of a state as worldly persons have been destroyed. The tendencies of godhood remain. These have been called the warriors accompanying *Śumbha* and *Niśumbha* to battle. This will later become clearer.

Verse 7.

āyāntaṁ caṇḍikā dṛṣṭvā tatsainyamatibhīṣaṇam|
jyāsvanaiḥ pūrayāmāsa dharaṇīgaganāntaram||

Translation:

Seeing that terrible army approach, the Goddess *Caṇḍīkā* covered the earth and sky with the strumming sound of her bow-string.

Explanation:

Truly there is tremendous preparation by these warriors. All tendencies of duality are going to battle. Seeing this army from afar, Mother began making a sound with her bow-string. It filled the earth and skies. The sound of the bow-string is *Praṇava.* This has been explained before with examples from the scriptures. A spiritual seeker must remember that as long as Mother does not sound this *Praṇava*, demons are not frightened. As long as it was the sound of *Praṇava* from you, the host of demons was not afraid. Then, when you surrendered at the feet of Mother, when your authority was removed, action by Mother, the sound of her bow-string began. Although during the chanting of *Praṇava*, sound emanates from your voice box, you now understand that the sound is not from you. It is a powerful, attractive primal sound (*nāda*) from the supreme power. When you pay attention to this sound, you see that it fills heaven and earth. All directions are filled with primal sound. There is nothing else. The universe is unending primal sound. Life and death, the journey through many wombs, joy and sorrow, are all various waves of this eternal sound. However powerful may be the strength of the demons, when this sound arises, there is an end to fear. All states are filled by this flow of sound. How sweet yet sedate is this all-filling note.

Verse 8.

tataḥ siṁho mahānādamatīva kṛtavānnṛpa|
ghaṇṭāsvanena tānnādānambikā copabṛṁhayat||

Translation:

O king! At this time, the lion roared repeatedly. The Goddess *Amvikā* ringing her bell raised the volume of this primal sound.

Explanation:

The carrier of the Goddess, the lion, that is the worldly person, was at this time, ready to apply its effort (*puruṣkār*). Knowing that this is the final attempt, beings prepare to do everything, to oppose the duality of perception. This mantra mentions the roars of the lion, pointing to this action, this severe effort, this intense interest. Let no one be under a false impression that those who have surrendered at the feet of Mother have no human effort left in them. In reality, it is only those who have surrendered and succeeded in yoga, who know the true nature of effort. They are never overcome by the stasis of dark tendencies. As long as there is a difference between Mother and child, there is some human effort left. Only when a pure state, without relation between Mother and child is reached, can there no longer be any effort. How can there be effort where there is no longer any sense, mind or intellect? That is why I say that from the beginning of spiritual enterprise, one has to have intense effort, and has to hold on to it to the end. When all states end, then all human effort stops and one resides in the nature of humanity. *Pātañjali* calls this the residence in the nature of the seer, *Gitā* calls this '*brāhmi sthiti.*' The devotional scriptures call this being overwhelmed by love. But that is something else.

We were speaking of the great sound from the lion. When demons begin their torture, spiritual seekers cry 'victory to *guru*' or 'victory to Mother' or other such words, and roar. These are useful in the kingdom of spiritual enterprise. Mother *Amvikā* with the sound of her bell, enhances these lion roars from a spiritual seeker. The unvoiced primal sound (*anāhata*) uniting with the voices of the seekers makes this more intense. The mystery of this primal sound has been explained in Volume Two. There the explanation was particularly about *vaikharī nada*. In this final character, it is especially about subtle, middle and *parā nada*. There are no more doubts if one understands this. Just as a seeker rises into more subtle planes, primal sound enters subtler stages.

Verse 9.

*dhanurjyāsiṁhaghaṇṭānāṁ śavdāpūritadiṅmukhā\
ninādairbhīṣaṇaiḥ kālī jigye vistāritānanā||*

Translation:

The strumming of the bow-string, roars of the lion and ringing of the bell mingled together and filled the horizons. Then, wide-eyed *Kālī* with her terrible roars drowned out even those sounds.

Explanation:

The sounds from *Kālī* are terrible roars of destruction. They drown out all other sounds because all sounds merge into these roars of dissolution. Just as the preparation of battle by *Śumbha* was terrifying, so are the sounds of victory from Mother. There is the need not only of subtle sounds but also of these physical ones. When pain due to the state of duality makes a seeker weak and hopeless, then one has to seek the help of this primal sound. The unvoiced sound of *Praṇava*, inner sound from *Anāhata*, the physical sound of 'victory to Mother', and this all-destroying great roar, when these all appear together, the weakness of a seeker and ennui, disappear within a short time. One then appears in this spiritual battle with new energy.

Verse 10.

*tanninādamupaśrutya daityasainyaiścaturddiśam
devī siṁhastathā kālī saroṣaiḥ parivāritāḥ*

Translation:

Hearing these sounds, the demon warriors surrounded the Goddess, the lion and *Kālī* from all directions.

Explanation:

The goddess *Amvikā* is the power of awareness. Her carrier is a lion, the worldly person, and *Kālī* a great destructive force. The innumerable demon warriors saw them from afar. The all-encompassing sounds of destruction that emanated from them, surprised these warriors. Because they could not imagine how the sounds of battle from only the three of them could be so loud and pervasive. The demons, the before mentioned eight-fold bondages, or binding tendencies, attacked from all sides, to engulf them.

When a spiritual seeker approaches that eternally pure spirit beyond all states and characteristics, many worldly tendencies arise to prevent this movement. They do not want to give any opportunity to taste the uninterrupted flow of bliss of nonduality. At every step, thousands of tendencies appear to prevent the progress of a seeker. Tendencies of duality stored over many lifetimes, come forcefully to prevent a move into nonduality. This is the mystery of the demon warriors attacking from all sides. Those who are spiritual seekers will understand this in their bones.

Verse 11.

*etasminn*antar*e bhūpa vināśāya suradviṣām*|
bhavāyāmarasiṁhānāmativīryabalānvitāḥ||

Verse 12.

brahmeśaguhaviṣṇunāṁ tathendrasya ca śaktayaḥ|
śarīrebhyo viniṣkramya tadrūpaiścaṇḍikāṁ yayuḥ||

Translation:

O king Suratha! At this time, to destroy these enemies of the gods, and for the benefit of the divinities, the magnificent powers of *Brahmā*, *Śiva*, *Kārtikeya*, *Viṣṇu* and *Indra*, emerged from their bodies (of *Brahmā* and others), and taking form, appeared in front of goddess *Caṇḍīkā*.

Explanation:

The great sage Medhasa here addresses Suratha as 'king.' Beings have now found the ability to rule over the earth principle, that is inertness. Now that Suratha has realized that physical materials are nothing but consciousness, Medhasa addresses him in this manner. As disciples advance from level to level, the *guru* encourages them. This encouragement from the *guru* is a provision for the advancement of a disciple. Medhasa will now introduce an intractable mystery. In case Suratha is shielded by his state as a worldly person and cannot pursue this mystery, he is addressed as a king, a conqueror of inertness.

When the demon warriors came and surrounded the Goddess from all sides, the powers of the divinities appeared for her assistance. We saw in the destruction of *Mahiṣāsura* that the gods donated their powers to encourage the supreme energy. They understood that their weapons, that is their energies, were the energies of *Mahāmāyā*. *Mahiṣāsura* was easily destroyed. But now, the demons are much more powerful, much more invincible. This time, one cannot succeed by donating power. At this time the specific powers appear as special forms.

Here, is a mystery of spiritual effort that spiritual seekers have to know. First, one has to offer one's individual powers to the supreme power. That is, one has to understand and realize that it is the one conscious supreme power that flows as different powers of our faculties to see, hear, receive and think. Then, one has to feel that this supreme power is expressed as the visible world. If one does not understand different perceptible energies as various pleasures of the supreme power of Mother, one cannot understand the energy flow in this world as one non-different power of consciousness.

When one merges one's energies, then minuteness and specificity vanish. In this state worldly persons perceive godliness. Then, one has to empower the specific energies offered to the supreme one and bring them back to remove the bondages of being. It is as if, before they are offered to supreme force, individual energies are weak. But now, coming in contact with God-energy. they are empowered. That is why the mantra says 'very powerful' (*ativīryabalānvitāḥ*). Because they are very powerful, they can help *Caṇḍīkā* in the destruction of these demons. The *śrutis* also say that the 'power of *paramātmā* is superior (*parā*), great and varied'[3]. If one understands that the various powers emanate from a superior power, then one can easily understand the appearance of the various forces of divinities from *Caṇḍīkā*. Just as one container with sight, hearing, movement and other powers is called a human, in the same fashion, what can be observed or perceived as a combined expression of all energies, is a superior force, or expression of the power of *paramātmā.*

Explanations of portions of this mantra will be found in those for the following ones. We need to discuss a bit about 'exiting from the body' (*sharīrebhyo viniṣkramya*). Commonly, it seems that the powers of *Brahmāṇī* and other powers appeared from the bodies of *Brahmā* and the others. Seeing the plural used for the word 'bodies' makes this seem appropriate. But, later in the section on the destruction of *Śumbha*, it will be seen that these powers of *Brahmāṇī* and others disappear into the body of the Goddess. The source from which some action appears, disappears in the same causal entity. This is an undisputed rule and conclusion. So, it is correct to conclude that these powers appeared from the body of *Caṇḍīkā*. On the other hand, there is no harm in thinking of them as appearing from the bodies of *Brahmā* and others, because their bodies are not different from that of the Goddess. We will here understand that the various powers emanated from the body of *Caṇḍīkā*. Although her body is one, the plural 'bodies' is used aimed at her unlimited size.

Previously, in the destruction of *Mahiṣāsura*, the offering of weapons or powers of the gods was seen. Here we again see the emergence of the specific energies that were offered. During the

3 *parasya saktir vividhaiva sruyate, Svetaśvatara Upaniṣad* 6.8

destruction of *Mahiṣāsura*, the goal was achieved by offerings. There it was the unexpressed stored tendencies which were relatively weak. In this case, it is prior tendencies (*prāravdha saṁskāra*) who are ready to fruit. They are very powerful. Now the host of gods has to appear specifically in battle.

Dear seeker! Do you remember? It has been said that whatever is offered to Mother, becomes empowered by her and comes back to the one who offers. See, the gods, defeated by the demons, had one day offered their weakened powers at the feet of Mother. Today, those powers have magnified and emerged from the body of *Amvikā* as divine powers to destroy these demons. In this manner, whatever you offer with an open heart at the feet of Mother, however small or dull it be, if you can do it right, you will see the offerings come back to you, bright and abundant.

Verse 13.

yasya devasya yadrūpaṁ yathā bhūṣaṇavāhanam||
tadvadeva hi tacchaktirasurān yoddhumāyayau|

Translation:

Whatever the form, adornments and carrier of a divinity, the energy of that divinity appeared for battle with the same form, attire and carrier.

Explanation:

Whatever was the form and shape of a god, that is, whatever be the specific resident consciousness, appeared for battle as its energy. The word 'adornment' (*bhuṣaṇa*) means wealth or a special energy. Whatever the special energy of a god, is the adornment of that divine energy. The word 'carrier' stands for the support of that energy. The principle of carriers was explained in Volume One, and that of adornments in Volume Two.

We need to say something about the divine energies. Each divinity has specificity. This specificity is the resulting action of that energy. Energy is a causal-natured, invisible substance.

When energy appears as action, then the spirit of energy is perceived, otherwise, energy is not observable. For example, the inflammatory power of fire is understood by its actions of heat and light. Otherwise, the nature of the power of fire is not perceived by the senses. This knowledge about the principle of energy is the final knowledge for beings. One is honored by understanding that this universe, body, mind, intelligence and senses, all that is seen or perceived are all manifestations of a higher energy. Beings generally see the emergence of energies or actions and are engrossed by them. They do not want to know the true nature of energy and so never realize it. But it is also true that if energy does not appear to one, there is no method or trick to catch or understand it. So, I often say, my Mother, although she is everywhere and well reflected, is invisible, undiscovered and unreceived. She is beyond words and thought.

There is something else that has to be said about the principle of energy. A statement in the *Brahma Sutras* acknowledges the nature of the energy of *paramātmā*. 'That from which the birth, stasis and end of this universe transpire is *Brahmaṇ*' (*janmādysya yataḥ*). By these words, the nature of *Brahmaṇ* as energy is established. We cannot completely agree with those who do not acknowledge this energy nature of *Brahmaṇ*, who fear that its attribute-less (*nirguṇa*) nature is disproved by it. We have understood what the energy-formed Mother has expressed in our hearts, that the 'one and only' is nothing else but the energy of awareness. It is by actions in this universe, that its nature as energy can be specially understood. When actions as this universe are absent, there is no longer a difference between Self and non-Self. When only pure perception is revealed, then it may not be termed energetic or non-energetic. But, as long as the energy nature of the *paramātmā* is perceived, the greatness of its state of being or Godhood can be seen. In a state as a worldly person, the three kinds of differences, similar, foreign and self (*sajātiya, bijātiya* and *svagata)* may be observed. In the God-state, only self-difference remains. By spiritual effort and by the practice of knowledge or devotion one can reach a state of God-principle. Because the state beyond this is not within the reach of any spiritual effort or attempt, the scriptures and the sages are silent about it. It is definite that when beings, as a result of spiritual effort, or by the grace of Mother arrive at this state of Godhood, that is on the energetic nature of Self, only then is its pure nature revealed. Without a taste of this state of Godhood, if one speaks of this pure state, if one pretends to be a knower of Self by analyzing great statements like 'I am *Brahmaṇ*', then we have to understand that one is far from the real principle. Arriving at that purest of states, if one calls it energetic, there is no loss, if one calls it without energy, there is also no loss. Saying it is both is fine too. It is everything, or it is beyond anything. It is so blissful that it cannot be described by words.

Whatever it is, in both the states, with and without characteristics, acceptance of the nature of energy in *paramātmā* makes the spiritual path easier. If after this, one has to accept an unknown vessel as a container for both, there is no argument. But, one has to remember something. That which is the container for energy, cannot be very different from the nature of energy itself. We have moved away from our topic under discussion. Where is a place for arguments about that which may be directly perceived?

Verse 14.

haṁsayuktavimānāgre sākṣasūtrakamaṇḍaluḥ|
āyātā brahmaṇaḥ śaktirbrahmāṇī sāhabhidhīyate||

Translation:

Riding on a vehicle drawn by swans, holding a rosary and water pot, the power of *Brahmā* appeared on the battlefield. She is known as *Brahmāṇī*.

Explanation:

In seven mantras from here on, the energies of the different gods are described in detail. The power of creation is *Brahmāṇī*. The portion of an undivided ocean of awareness in which the action of creation is expressed is called *Brahmā*. That is, where *ātmā* takes pride in the act of creation, is called *Brahmā*. The power of action that is expressed by the establishment of creation is called *Brahmāṇī*. So, in the context of spiritual enterprise, no difference may be observed between *Brahmā* and *Brahmāṇī*. If energy could have a separate nature not based on awareness, then we could accept a difference and perceive it. If the whole of energy is awareness or consciousness, then there is no error in naming energy as awareness. What is the error in calling fire the ability to burn? In the subtleties of logic, there could be many arguments, but those who are spiritual seekers, see no harm in the knowledge that power and the one with power are the same. Then, if there is any difference, it would be perceived. One would not need to seek the help of the scriptures. Self is directly perceptible, so there is no need to accept anything blindly.

The swans (*haṁsa*) are worldly persons. The rosary is a garland of letters. The water pot is a store or great stock, for seeds of action. Let me say more explicitly, and try to understand. Just as you have an individual mind, so do other beings. This individual mind is but part of the universal mind. Let us call that universal mind, great mind. This is *Brahmā*. The characteristic of the mind is imagination. This world is the imagination of the great mind. Imagination is a power, it is a *dharma* of mind or nature. This power of imagination is called *Brahmāṇī*. She rides on a swan. The expression of the universal mind is seen in the resolutions of individual beings, so they conduct creation. The power of creation is expressed based on beings. Without beings, there would not be a way to know the power of creation. So, the carriers of the goddess *Brahmāṇī*, the power of creation, are worldly persons. There is another significance in calling worldly persons *haṁsa*. Each day and night, they chant *Haṁsa* mantra, twenty-one thousand and six hundred times with their breath. This is called *ajapā*. This has been mentioned before.

The rosary is formed by the letters of the alphabet. Imaginations are encoded by sounds. This world is formed by specific sounds or words. Words are groups of letters. The fifty letters of the alphabet form the rosary of *Brahmāṇī*. The letters of the alphabet mentioned before as the garland of skulls of *Kālī* were unable to generate perceptions, so they were a garland of skulls. Because at each moment, they can generate innumerable states, the garland of letters of *Brahmāṇī* is a rosary. From the water-pot, due to seeds of creation of previous eons, novel creations reappear. This store of seeds of creation is the water-pot of *Brahmāṇī*. It is not necessary to discuss this again.

Verse 15.

māheśvarī vṛṣārūḍhā triśūlavaradhāriṇī||
mahāhivalayā prāptā candrarekhāvibhūṣaṇā|

Translation:

Riding a bull, holding a trident, wearing bangles of serpents, adorned with the crescent Moon, *Māheśvarī* appeared for battle.

Explanation:

Māheśvarī is the power of dissolution. The portion of the undivided ocean of consciousness in which a state of dissolution appears is called *Maheśvara*. That is, the place where Self prides itself as dissolution is named *Maheśvara*. The power of action that appears from this establishment of consciousness is called *Māheśvarī*. She rides on a bull. The word '*vṛṣa*' (bull) signifies *dharma*. The power of knowledge is directed based on *dharma*. Without acquiring the scriptural rules of *dharma*, the power of knowledge does not emerge. The explanation of carriers in Volume One should be consulted. The trident is three-fold knowledge. This has been discussed in Volume Two. The bangle of serpents (*mahāhivalayā*) is *Kuṇḍalinī*. It encircles the self-emergent *lingam* like a bangle. Why the *Kuṇḍalinī* is called a serpent has been explained before. The word '*candrarekhā*' means the phase of the Moon. Of the sixteen parts of the Moon phases, fifteen emerge as lunar days. The remaining part is called *amā*. This part resides on the forehead of knowledge-formed *Māheśvarī*. In giving the meaning of the word '*amā*', ancient authors have explained it as the inexplicable power of *māyā*. This *amā* or *māyā* is a specific expression of the power of knowledge. The great power of knowledge, based on which the play of *māyā* is carried out, appeared for assisting *Caṇḍīkā* for the destruction of the demons, as *Māheśvarī*.

Verse 16.

kaumārī śaktihastā ca mayūravaravāhanā|
yoddhumabhyāyayau daityānambikā guharūpiṇī||

Translation:

The Goddess *Amvikā* in the form of *Kārttikeya*, as the power form of *Kaumārī*, with weapons in hand, riding on a peacock, appeared for battle.

Explanation:

Kaumārī is the power of *Kārttikeya* that defeats the demons. She is the conductress of divine warriors. The mystery of the powers of demons and gods has been described in detail in Volume Two. The demon defeating power that suppresses the nature of demons and conducts the forces of gods is the energy *Kaumārī*. The power of the senses established in it is called *Kumāra* or *Kārttikeya*. Its carrier is a peacock. The peacock is a bird that kills serpents. Serpents move sinuously. Normally, the senses move sinuously towards material things. When spiritual seekers acquire the ability or strength to destroy this, they become of the nature of peacocks. Such a peacock-natured being is the carrier of the *Kaumārī* power. The area of the Self in which a state of divinity arises to suppress the demons is called *Kumāra* or *Kārttikeya*. The power that resides in this, to conduct divine forces is *Kaumārī*.

Verse 17.

tathaiva vaiṣṇavī śaktirgaruḍopari saṁsthitā
śaṅkha cakra gadā śārṅga khaḍgahastābhyupāyayau

Translation:

Vaiṣṅavī power riding on the bird *Garuḍa*, with conch, discus, mace, bow and scimitar in hand appeared on the battlefield.

Explanation:

The spirit of consciousness that has pride in its power of maintenance is *Viṣṇu*. Maintenance or preservation is by his authority. The conch, discus, mace, bow and scimitar have been explained before. The bow represents *Praṇava* and a scimitar means nondual knowledge that removes the perception of duality. The word '*Viṣṇu*' signifies immensity. The all-encompassing nondual knowledge that on rising, removes all perceptions of duality, is a scimitar in the hands of *Viṣṇu*. The word '*Garuḍa*' has been explained before in the discussion about carriers. *Vedas* convey the power of *Viṣṇu*, so the *Vedas* are *Garuḍa*. This is not an imaginary explanation created by us. *Vyāsadeva* said something very similar in the *Śrimat Bhāgavat*. Those who think of God as some specific figure or form, or think of *Śri Kṛṣṇa* as a specific figure when listening to the divine plays of the suppression of *Kāliya* or the games during *Rāsa*, should read *Śrimat Bhāgavat* with close attention. *Vyāsadeva* has clearly said that God only takes on specific forms to express spiritual mysteries in this worldly plane. Remember that if one is not aware of the mystery of nature without form, one cannot understand that of nature with form. So, it is necessary to know about the nature of the principle that takes various forms. The reason that *dharma* shows signs of decline today is a lack of understanding of matters of form and form-less. Let the intellect-formed *guru*, God the establisher of *dharma*, remove this ignorance and rid this land from a decline of *dharma*.

Verse 18.

yajṅavārāhamatulaṁ rūpaṁ yā bibhrato hareḥ|
śaktiḥ sāpyāyayau tatra vārāhīṁ bibhratī tanum||

Translation:

The power of *Hari* which takes on an incomparable beauty as a ceremonial boar, appeared in that form on the battlefield.

Explanation:

One of the figures of the power of *Viṣṇu* is *Vārāhī*. It is described in the *Purāṇa* that *Viṣṇu* took on the form of a boar (*varāha*) and lifted this world from destruction with his tusks. *Varāha* is another name for *Viṣṇu*. The spiritual meaning of the word *'varāha'* is a limiting period of time. The root '*vara*' means best or Self. One who covers it (*āhanan*) is *Varāha*. It is the nature of time that first covers Self, that is, it is time that is first imagined in Self. Time is the first covering of the Self. At present, in this world, it is the time period of *Varāha* that is in progress. One such period (*kalpa*) is formed by fourteen *manvantaras*. In this current *kalpa* of *Varāha*, six *mahāyugas* have passed. The twenty-seventh period of *Kali* of the seventh *manvantara* is now in progress. After a long period in this *kalpa*, our earth was formed. Before creation, everything was immersed in the waters of dissolution. The *Purāṇa* describe that this Earth was once saved by *Varāha*. For a long time, Earth resides in the *kalpa* of *Varāha*, so it stays on the tusks of the great form of *Varāha*. The difference between the power of *Kālī* and that of *Vārāhī* is this, *Kālī* is the combined destructive power of great Time. *Vārāhī* is the power of Time for one *kalpa*. Because this power is a container for this world, it is also a power of *Viṣṇu*. The power for maintenance and that for containment are nearly the same. The great container of time in which our universe resides is *Varāha* and so the world holding power is called *Vārāhī*.

Verse 19.

nārasiṁhī nṛsiṁhasya bibhratī sadṛśaṁ vapuḥ|
prāptā tatra saṭākṣepakṣipta nakṣatrasaṁhatiḥ||

Translation:

Taking on a shape like *Nṛsiṁhadeva*, *Nārasiṁhī* appeared on the battlefield. The stars were thrown around by the swirling of her mane.

Explanation:

Nārasiṁhī is also one of the powers of *Viṣṇu*. *Nṛsiṁha* is the knowledge of Self-nature. When knowledge of Self arises, humans become superior. The root '*nṛ*' means human and the word '*siṁha*' (lion) stands for greatness. *Nṛsiṁha* is the one who destroyed *Hiraṇyakaśipu*. It is known from the *śrutis* that the word '*hiraṇya*' signifies *ātmā*. The one who denigrates *hiraṇya* or Self, that is expresses it as a pride of material things, is *Hiraṇyakaśipu*. Only the proper knowledge of Self can destroy this *asura*. So, the word '*Nṛsiṁha*' means knowledge of Self-nature. It is by the hands of *Nṛsiṁha* that *Hiraṇyakaśipu* was destroyed. As long as humans do not realize their true nature, they cannot become lions, that is, be superior. The description of the destruction of *Hiraṇyakaśipu* given by ancient authors is a beautiful story filled with principles of knowledge. By his intense austerities, he was endowed with a boon from *Brahmā* that no one, god, demon, celestial, human or animal would be able to defeat him. Truly, as long as any knowledge of specificity remains, *Hiraṇyakaśipu* cannot be destroyed. Without non-alternate knowledge, the *asura* of alternate knowledge cannot be destroyed. The child of *Hiraṇyakaśipu*, *Prahlāda*, is blissful knowledge of *Brahmaṇ*. On its expression, ignorance tries different means to destroy it. In time, by the visions of *Prahlāda*, by influence of a view of *Hari*, that is true knowledge, in earth, water, sky and fire, the figure of *Nīsiṁhadeva* appears. Knowledge of Self is properly aroused. Only then is divisive knowledge or *Hiraṇyakaśipu* destroyed.

Spiritual seekers can look and see that in their hearts, the young child *Prahlāda*, the expression of bliss of a state of *Brahmaṇ* grows day by day. Materially engrossed mind, *Hiraṇyakaśipu*, tries to destroy it. Bearing this torment, your blissful child, knowledge of truth, firmly tries to practice the establishment of truth everywhere. One day, this knowledge of truth will tear apart the crystal pillar of material knowledge and appear as pure sense of perception. You will be overcome by a vision of the form of *Nṛsiṁha*. Your *Hiraṇyakaśipu* mind will be destroyed.

The power of *Nṛsiṁha* is *Nārasiṁhī*. Knowledge of *Brahmaṇ* is the power *Nārasiṁhi*. Because, it is by the influence of this knowledge that beings become *Nṛsiṁha*, that is, become established in the nature of Self. It is by its appearance that the demons of specificity are destroyed. It is to explain this, the words 'stars were thrown around' are used. The significance of the word '*satākṣepa*' is the effect of one's power. There is a purpose in calling specific knowledge to be stars. The material things that we accept daily, that is, the specific knowledge that we move in, have in them faint expressions of light or Self. Without self-expression, there can be no specific knowledge. The power of knowledge or *Nārasiṁhī*, appears on the battlefield and removes the specificity of this knowledge. If you have truly surrendered at the feet of Mother, you will see that on the battlefield of your heart, your imaginary stars of specific knowledge are being removed by the power of learning and are making way for the appearance of pure perception.

Verse 20.

vajrahastā tathaivaindrī gajarājoparisthitā|
prāptā sahasranayanā yathā śakrastathaiva sā||

Translation:

In the same fashion, *Indrānī*, with beauty similar to *Indra*, lightning bolt in hand, riding an elephant, with a thousand eyes, appeared for battle.

Explanation:

The ruler of the gods is *Indra*. His power is *Indrāṇī*. The explanations of a lightning bolt and riding an elephant have been given in Volume Two. Here, if we try to understand the mystery of a thousand eyes, we will be able to understand this mantra. The word thousand stands for innumerable. The word eyes (*nayana*) means the power of expression. One whose state of expression takes on innumerable descriptors and is expressed in innumerable ways is thousand-eyed *Indra*. His power of expression is *Indrāṇī*. The significance of the words, ruler of the gods, is an expression of one's power through all the gods. In stories in the *Puraṇas*, it is said that because of the sin of taking the wife of his *guru*, a thousand wounds appeared on the body of *Indra*. By severe austerities, these wounds turned into eyes. The only *guru* is *paramātmā*. Self-expressed energy is taken over by *Indra*, the ruler of the host of consciousnesses installed in the senses, and as a result, is divided into many parts. When by austerities, the eye of knowledge is opened, then in all these many states, expression of Self can be seen. Then *Indra* has a thousand eyes. A spiritual seeker can also see that the power of the *guru* is stolen by the senses all the time. In enjoying the power of expression in innumerable ways, you suffer many wounds. Then by the practice of establishment of truth and life force, you see the one power of expression through innumerable wounds. Your wounds turn into eyes.

Verse 21.

tataḥ parivṛtastābhirīśāno devaśaktibhiḥ|
hanyantāmasurāḥ śīghraṁ mama prītyāha caṇḍikām||

Translation:

After this, *Īśāna*, surrounded by the powers of the gods, said to the Goddess *Caṇḍīkā*, "Now, for my pleasure, let these demons be destroyed."

Explanation:

The eight powers spoken of up to now are *Brāhmī*, *Māhesvarī*, *Koumārī*, *Vaiṣṅavī*, *Bārāhī*, *Nārasiṁhī*, *Indrāṇī* and *Cāmuṇḍā*. To specifically explain that *Brahmā*, *Maheśvara*, *Kārttikeya* and other special consciousnesses are nothing but energy, the appearance of these eight powers on the battlefield is described. Spiritual seekers finally alight on this principle of energy. That is why the scriptures say, those who are twice-born, that is, those who by initiation have a second birth, are spiritual seekers and are all energy. All communities, *Śaiva*, *Vaiṣṇava,* etc. all worship this energy. But, as long as they do not discover this energy, they do not want to identify themselves as worshippers of energy (*śakti*). Then, by the grace of the *guru*, as the eye of knowledge is opened, they see that knowingly or unknowingly they have been worshipping energy. It is by knowledge of this energy that doors of liberation for beings are opened. Energy and the one with energy, that is established consciousness and its established energy are the same. That established consciousness is nothing but energy, is easily understood when one enters into the principles of *Caṇḍī*. It has been said that understanding *ātmā* as energy natured, simplifies the spiritual path. But in particular, understanding perception natured *ātmā* as energy natured is very difficult. So, the great sage Medhas first tries to explain the powers of *ātmā*, independent delights of Self, as energies. That is why here he describes them as *Brahmāṇī* and the other principles of *śakti*. A spiritual seeker must remember that these energies are not different from consciousness.

Let us now try to understand the meaning of this mantra. The mantra says that *Īśāna* being surrounded by the before-mentioned powers, prayed to *Caṇḍīkā* for the destruction of the demons. The combined established consciousness in which *Brāhmī*, *Māheśvarī* and other energies are expressed is *Īśāna*. He is the god of destruction, the pure perception of *Maheśvara*. The eight powers are established in *Īśāna*. Now, ṭhis eight-powered *Īśāna* requests *Caṇḍīkā* to destroy the demons. That is, the intellect-formed *guru*, lord of all beings, encourages the power of awareness to destroy all these states. Today, perceiving himself as the establishment for the eight powers, and seeing them ready to destroy the demons, he tries to rouse the power of awareness.

Let a spiritual seeker look at his heart. Your knowledge formed *Maheśvara* is lying like a corpse. One cannot understand how he could have any effort or action. All kinds of energies were trampling him under their feet and dancing with the enjoyment of material things, of multiplicity. Today the forces have especially risen, to remove multiplicity and unite with an undivided power of awareness. Spiritual seekers are honored. Honored are their efforts and their human life. Today, the *guru* in your heart, *Īśāna* is prepared to destroy the demons. Until now, you tried to prevent the demons on your own. Today the *guru* is ready to free you. You need to have no more fear. You will soon taste the nectar of undivided supreme bliss.

Īśāna said. 'for my pleasure.' If the demons are destroyed, *Īśāna* is pleased. The *Gitā* says, 'all actions *Pārtha*, end in knowledge.' All actions, that is, all flows of energy, end in knowledge, that is in *Īśāna*. When the demons are destroyed, then *Īśāna* becomes all-powerful and is established in his nature. So, he is pleased by the destruction of these demons.

Verse 22.

tato devīśarīrāttu viniṣkrāntātibhīṣaṇā|
caṇḍikā śaktiratyugrā śivāśataninādinī||

Translation:

From the body of the Goddess, emerged the very terrifying power *Caṇḍīkā,* together with hundreds of furiously screaming jackals.

Explanation:

The merciful *guru Īśāna* prayed that 'the demons be destroyed quickly.' In answer to this prayer from *Īśāna*, the Goddess did not offer any reply. She only let forth from her body the terrifying power of *Caṇḍīkā* and hundreds of furiously screaming jackals. The word '*caṇḍīkā*' used in the previous mantra, has to be understood as being applied to the Goddess *Amvikā*, because in this mantra, the terrifying *Caṇḍīkā* is said to emerge from the body of the Goddess. *Caṇḍīkā* is a very angry, destructive force. My Mother *Amvikā* is eternally unperturbed, so she has no anger. That is why this terrifying power named *Caṇḍīkā* emerges.

The awareness formed *Amvikā* is without alterations,

unperturbed, the nature of pure consciousness. She does not do anything, yet in her, all states arise, continue and are then dissolved. All prayers, complaints and requests are made to her. Although she does not do anything directly, in incredible and indirect ways, she fulfills the prayers of seekers in some manner or the other. Look. *Īśāna* prays to her, but she says no words. But it is seen that from her body emerged the angry force of *Caṇḍīkā* and hundreds of jackals. From this, it may be understood that even if she did not carry out any direct actions from the prayer of *Īśāna*, she acted indirectly to fulfill it. But she does not give any hint about this beforehand. My Mother deceives in this manner. A spiritual seeker may bang his head, cry for Mother, may shed tears to wet his chest, may scream his grievances, yet she may not give any hint that she hears anything. Thousands of screams or your anxieties do not seem to move or disturb that unmoving, tranquil, quiet heart of Mother. My Mother stands in her unmoving form as if she knows nothing. Then, one day, you see that all your needs are fulfilled, all your hopes satisfied.

This is what happens. My Mother seems to deceive in this fashion. I will here relate briefly a story described in the *Mahābhārata*. When the *Pāṇḍavas* were forest dwellers, the sage *Durvvāsā* with six thousand disciples came to their residence as guests. At this time *Draupadī* had finished her meal, so a divine feeding vessel given to them by the Sun was without any food remaining in it. It was a grave danger. There was a chance of annihilation due to condemnation by the sage. Being in such deep trouble, she sought to seek help from their savior, *Śri Kṛṣṇa*. The *Pāṇḍavas* were tired and sleeping. Only *Draupadī* was awake. Suddenly *Kṛṣṇa* appeared. He said to her, "Dear *Draupadī*, I have not had news of *Dharma Rājā*[4] for a long time, so going this way, I came in to find out. Another thing, I am very hungry, please give me something to eat."

Do you understand the condition of the mind of *Draupadī*? The ruler of this universe, the dearest one of our hearts, the one

4 the eldest *Pāndava* brother. *Yudhisṭira*.

who feeds this world, *Śri Kṛṣṇa* is hungry and asking for food, but there is nothing in the house. Her heart was breaking up. From her eyes, not tears but blood welled up. She forgot everything else, even that the *Pāṇḍavas* could be destroyed by the condemnation of a sage. If in exchange for everything else, she could satisfy the hunger of *Kṛṣṇa*, she would not turn back. But there was no way she could feed him. So, like a fallen log, she sank at the feet of *Kṛṣṇa* and began to say, "Lord, you who knows all, who feeds this world, why do you pain me today? Who else will understand my pain? Lord of my heart? Today, you are hungry and I can do nothing to give you any food." (I cannot write any more.)

Śri Kṛṣṇa remained unmoved. He said with a serious voice, "I am very hungry. Let me have whatever you have. Don't look at the quantity. Only offer it to me with respect." Then, finding a tiny morsel of food in the vessel, with great pain in her heart, she offered it to Lord *Kṛṣṇa*. Saying "I am satisfied" *Śri Kṛṣṇa* disappeared. After some time, when *Draupadī* was calmer, she did not understand what had transpired. Then she learned that *Durvvāsā* and his six thousand disciples had felt so full and satisfied that blessing the *Pāṇḍavas*, they had left. Can a spiritual seeker fathom these divine plays of God? Whatever that is, we now see that in *Devī Māhatmya*, without giving any answers to the request by *Īśāna*, my Mother *Amvikā*, in practice, fulfilled his request. We will see this in time.

It has been said that *Amvikā* is the undisturbed power of awareness. This may raise doubts as to how hundreds of jackals could appear out of an unmoving power. That from which something appears cannot remain unchanged. In answer, one has to say that such change is not of any supreme form, it is in an imagined or operative form. Being the residence of an infinite universe, *Brahmaṇ* remains without characteristics (*nirguṇa*). Even though hundreds of jackals and the power of *Caṇḍīkā* appear from *Amvikā*, there is not the tiniest change in her. Transformations of things are changes. The power of awareness, under no conditions, becomes anything else. Even with innumerable differences, its unity and uniqueness remain.

śivāśataninādinī - The power of *Śiva* is *Śivā*. Where all beings lie in dissolution is *Śiva*. This is the meaning of the etymology '*śiva*.' Although the common meaning of the word '*śivā*' is a jackal, we have to understand it as the expression of the force of dissolution. From the body of *Amvikā* appeared innumerable forces of dissolution. They began to howl or make sounds of devastation. Or, the part '*śataninādinī*' can be separated from *śivā*. Then it would mean the dangerous roars of *Śiva*, the destructive force. Such an explanation is also acceptable.

Verse 23.

sā cāha dhūmrajaṭilamīśānamaparājitā||
dūta tvaṁ gaccha bhagavan pārśvaṁ śumbhaniśumbhayoḥ|

Verse 24.

brūhi śumbhaṁ niśumbhañca dānavāvatigarvitau||
ye cānye dānavāstatra yuddhāya samupasthitāḥ|

Verse 25.

trailokyamindro labhatāṁ devāḥ santu havirbhujaḥ|
yūyaṁ prayāta pātālaṁ yadi jīvitumicchatha||

Verse 26.

balāvalepādatha cedbhavanto yuddhakāṅkṣiṇa|
tadāgacchata tṛpyantu macchivāḥ piśitena vaḥ||

Translation:

At this, the invincible Goddess *Caṇḍīkā*, said to dusky locked *Īśāna*, "O Lord! Go to the proud *Śumbha* and *Niśumbha* as a messenger and tell them with all the other demons gathered there for battle, to let *Indra* resume the rule of the three worlds, let the gods receive the rightful portions of their offerings, and if they want to stay alive, to descend into the nether lands. On the other hand, if they wish to battle, then let my jackals be satiated with their flesh."

Explanation:

The goddess *Caṇḍīkā* who had emerged from the body of *Amvikā* appointed *Īśāna* as a messenger. *Īśāna* is the resident consciousness of the eight powers. He is the determining controller, the god of knowledge *Śiva*. The action of knowledge is understanding of what is transitory and eternal, the analysis of right and wrong. During wrongful acts, it is *Īśāna*, who in the heart of beings, as conscience, tries to prevent them from carrying out wrongful actions. He has now appeared as a complex, smoky figure. By a mixture of the dark, black shade of destruction and the pure white of knowledge, *Īśāna* shedding a dusky force all around, is going to *Śumbha* and *Niśumbha* as a messenger. He is told by *Caṇḍīkā* what he has to say there to the demons.

First, let *Indra* resume as the ruler of the three worlds (*trailokyamindro labhatāṁ*). It was said that *Śumbha* was now the ruler of the three worlds. She tells *Śumbha* to end this rulership. Ego had thought itself to be the ruler of the three worlds. Now it has to end that state. The three worlds have to be returned to their rightful owner. That *Indra, paramātmā* is the true ruler of the three worlds has to be realized. In the *śrutis*, with the words '*indra māyāviḥ*', *paramātmā* is indicated by the word '*indra.*' One has to understand that only *ātmā* is the ruler of creation-maintenance-dissolution of these three worlds and ego cannot be its ruler. This is the first order by Mother through her messenger.

Then the second command '*devāḥ santu havirbhujaḥ.*' Let the gods receive their portions of rightful offerings. The demons of ego that are occupying the portions of divine offerings, that is consciousness, have to let them go. Only then can the gods be reflected as features of consciousness. This mystery of the stealing of offerings has been discussed before.

The third order by Mother is that the demons should move into the nether lands (*yūyaṁ prayāta pātālaṁ*). Ego, attachment and their followers cannot have any more place in heaven. They have to move down into the inert plane, into visible physical levels. For so long, ego used to consider itself as the viewer, that as a reflection of awareness in intelligence, viewed as Self. This cannot continue any longer. Now one who is the true visionary will reside in its own state. Ego and others will dissolve into what is observable. There is a mystery in Mother *Amvikā* ordering *Śumbha* and *Niśumbha* to go into the underworld. Even after the nature of Self is illuminated, as long as past actions are not eroded, ego, attachment and others stay on as following states. As long as a seeker resides in the nature of Self, they are not visible. When a seeker moves from Self, they reappear. Even with this reappearance, they cannot arouse perceptions of duality. Because, after meeting Self, any sense of personality is gone.

The fourth part of the message from Mother said that if they were proud and wanted to fight, then let them come so her jackals could feed on their flesh. If ego, attachment and their attendants do not want to disappear, then the destructive powers that have appeared from the body of Mother will remove them in no time. The jackals, the destructive powers were starved for so long without anything to devour. Now they will satisfy their hunger by destroying ego and the other forces. They will be satisfied.

The power of *Caṇḍīkā* emerged from the body of *Amvikā* and sent *Īśāna* as a messenger to *Śumbha*. *Amvikā* did not do anything directly. She is by nature without characteristics (*nirguṇa*). Yet, based on her, and powered by her consciousness, different states carry out their actions. That actions taken by the messenger would not be successful was known to *Caṇḍīkā*. She knew very well that *Śumbha* would not go into the nether worlds. Yet she does this out of duty. This is the divine play of Mother to show beings that one does not have to aim at goals but carry out actions as indicated, so as to travel on a path of peace. Before the battle of *Kurukṣetra*, *Śri Kṛṣṇa* also went as a messenger to *Duryodhana* and asked for five villages for the *Pāṇḍavas*. His wish was not fulfilled. He was to be insulted by *Duryodhana*. Did *Kṛṣṇa* not know that the great battle was inevitable? Yet he tried to prevent that battle. What you understand to be duty, you need to carry out, without an eye on results. To show the purpose of the beautiful mantra of *Gitā*, 'you have rights to actions but not to their fruits'[5], the Goddess *Caṇḍīkā* may have sent *Īśāna* as a messenger.

There is something else to note. When we carry out some action, God in our heart, conscience-natured *Īśāna*, in silence, orders us about duty and non-duty. When we can carry out the orders of this *guru* in our hearts without argument, then we come closer to resurrection. When knowing that an order of a *guru* to be right, we still choose attraction of desire and neglect what is right, we move backward. Here, *Śumbha*, *Niśumbha* and others neglected the words of *Īśāna* and were destroyed.

Lord, we know that following your orders, your signals, is the only path to find what is good for us. But where do we follow your advice without argument? You are *Īśāna*, you are the director, you are the end of this and the next life. We cannot hold this thought in our hearts. Only you can remove this weakness of ours. You are the only means to bring faith and reliance on you. For a long time, for many lifetimes, it is only because of this weakness, that we reside so far away from the safety of your sanctuary. No more. I do not want to do this anymore. Take me now. Only instructions and showing the right path do not work anymore. I am without any movement, without power. What will instructions do? You have to come and take me by my hand. Do not just sit in my heart and advise me silently. As the power of carrying out that advice, you have to appear.

In this manner, with simplicity, a spiritual seeker has to surrender at the feet of *Īśāna*. By his grace, strength will come. The power to carry out the instructions will come. Then one can with ease, enter the dense mysteries and go beyond life and death. The serious spiritual effort of many lifetimes will be successful.

---

5 *Bhāgavat Gitā*, 2.47.

Verse 27.

yato niyukto dautyena tayā devyā śivaḥ svayam||
śivadūtīti lokehasmiṁstataḥ sā khyātimāgatā|

Translation:

Because Goddess *Caṇḍīkā* engaged *Śiva* as a messenger, she was known in these worlds as *Śivadūtī.*

Explanation:

Someone for whom *Śiva* is a messenger is *Śivadūtī*. By her encouragement, an all-knowing entity resides in the hearts of all beings and controls unruly movement. By her inspiration, *Īśāna* resides in the hearts of all as conscience, discerns between the eternal and temporary. She is *Śivadūtī.* Only the power of awareness has the ability to employ *Śiva*, the intellect-formed *guru* to be a messenger. So, goddess *Caṇḍīkā*, emerging from *Amvikā* engaged *Īśāna* to be her messenger. Because the power of awareness is beyond all states, energies sheltered by her or generated from her accomplish all actions.

As long as an intellectual formed teacher does not appear as a messenger, with an ambrosial message from the power of awareness, what is the ability of worldly persons to be able to disregard mere games of this world and search for divine nectar. It is the *guru* who with great eagerness, goes to Mother and says, 'for my pleasure, destroy these demons.' It is by the wishes of the *guru* that demons are downed by *Caṇḍīkā*. Until the desire for the destruction of the demons arises in the *guru*, so long *Caṇḍīkā* does not rise to destroy them. Do you want to know what arouses this wish in the heart of the *guru*? Then listen. When disciples have no wishes of their own, when every wish in the heart of the disciple reflects that of the *guru*, then one has to understand that it will not be long before encouragement for the destruction of the demons is going to come from the *guru*. You do not see the *guru*? This world is the material form of the *guru*. You do not see the *guru*? The *guru* resides inside as perception, as knowledge and a sense of right and wrong. Even then you do not see? Then listen.

One who is the material form of this world, the subtle form of knowledge, in his mercy, appears in human form. The intellectual formed *guru* becomes dense and appears as a human. The *guru* is not human, and humans are not the *guru*. The *guru* is eternal *Īśāna*, *Maheśvara* of all beings. When Mother appears as respect in the heart, one can understand the *guru*.

Spiritual seeker, this sense of discrimination between eternal and transient, this conscience, is the grace of the *guru*. One cannot truly learn it just by listening or by oral discussion. If one does not move in that which is eternal, one cannot know what is transient. If one does not know the true nature of things, interest or renunciation does not appear. Only the grace of the *guru* is the true cause for this knowledge. If the seat of *guru* is established in the heart, beings are able to have this knowledge.

Whatever that is, we see that *Īśāna* goes to *Śumbha* with this good advice. Spiritual seekers should watch and see if in each of their actions, whether *Īśāna* appears or not.

Verse 28.

tehapi śrutvā vaco devyāḥ śarvākhyātaṁ mahāsurāḥ|
amarṣāpūritā jagmuryatra kātyāyanī sthitā||

Translation:

Hearing the words of the Goddess described by *Īśāna*, the demons in great anger moved to where the Goddess was residing.

Explanation:

When the time comes, opposite ideas appear to worldly persons. People whose life spans are ending, do not listen to counsel from well-wishers. The demons did not contradict these sayings. They were getting ready to visit a house of annihilation. They disregarded the three orders of the Goddess as relayed by *Īśāna*. Disregarding these orders, they wanted to fight. So,. the fourth statement of Mother is to become successful. Soon her jackals will be satiated with the flesh of these demons.

Although we can understand by logic and argument that ego is not *ātmā* and that intelligence is not awareness, our actions are carried out in reverse. In practice, we accept ego as Self and intelligence as awareness. So, the advice of *Īśāna*, a voice of conscience is not effective. We cannot accept this pure nature of consciousness, in case we lose our favored 'I.' But now there is hope. These demons, blinded by anger have come to *Kātyāyanī* for battle and so their destruction is inevitable.

In this mantra, Goddess *Amvikā* is called *Kātyāyanī*. The root '*kātya*' means one who knows *Brahmaṇ*. Where such a person resides is *Kātyāyanī*. One knowing *Brahmaṇ* always resides only in the power of awareness or in Goddess *Amvikā*. So, my Mother, soon to be famous to those who know *Brahmaṇ* is called *Kātyāyanī*.

Verse 29.

tataḥ prathamamevāgre śaraśaktyṛṣṭivṛṣṭibhiḥ|
vavarṣuruddhatāmarṣāstāṁ devīmamarārayaḥ||

Verse 30.

sā ca tān prahitān bāṇāñchūlaśaktiparaśvadhān|
ciccheda līlayādhmātadhanurmuktairmaheṣubhiḥ||

Translation:

After this, the angry demons, rained arrows and other weapons at the Goddess She easily ripped them apart with great arrows from her bow.

Explanation:

Those who throw the first weapons in battle are the attackers. Those that use weapons later are defenders. This is declared in the texts about warfare. In the battle of Kurukṣetra, *Kauravas* first sounded conch shells and engaged in battle. That is why they were the attackers and *Pāṇḍavas* are described as defenders. Here too we see that the demons are the first to throw weapons at Mother. They want to kill Self, so they are attackers. The texts say that attackers should be killed. So, my Mother will destroy them soon and bring her children to safety.

Now we will try to understand the mystery of the weapons used by the demons. Disgust, shame, fear, race, lineage and the other tendencies are special encirclements of ego. By their individual states, they try to characterize their sense of self. These are the weapons thrown at Mother by the demons. The mentioned special states are so mixed with the sense of Self that even though by repeated analysis they are determined to be separate from Self, they repeatedly characterize it. Self, always unique is characterized by the weapons of these demons.

Udhāyudh and the other demons threw their weapons at the pure body of the power of awareness. My Mother fired great arrows from her bow and began to destroy them. A secret of worship in the *Upaniṣads* is a simile about the firing of a great arrow from a bow. One has to fire an arrow of Self from the bow of *Praṇava*, repeatedly aiming at *Brahmaṇ*. With this, Self resides in *Brahmaṇ* and all states of fear and others are removed. Because Self is seen as separate from *Brahmaṇ*, one has to tolerate the weapons of demons. Only by a serious effort of firing the arrow of Self is its special nature revealed.

Take all the demonic states of eight-fold bondages collected over lifetimes and throw them at Mother. By her grace, you will soon be freed. Your state as a worldly person will end, you will discover the state of *Śiva*. And, if you have in every fashion, surrendered at the feet of Mother, you do not have anything more to do. Like all seekers who enter into a sacred battle, Mother will free you from the eight-fold bonds.

Verse 31.

tasyāgratastathā kālī śūlapātavidāritān|
khaṭvāṅgaprothitāṁścārīn kurvatī vyacarattadā||

Translation:

Kālī pierced the enemies with her lance and buried them with her club, pacing in front of *Amvikā*.

Explanation:

Now the separate powers of the gods in destroying the demons will be described. First is *Kālī*, the power of *Cāmuṇḍā*. She pierced some of them with her lance and crushed some with her club. Although during the emergence of *Kālī*, no mention was made of a lance, only a sword, club and net, one has to understand that as the eight powers were different expressions of *Īśāna*, a lance, his special weapon, is with all of them. An explanation of this weapon, a lance was given in Volume Two. The word '*śula*' usually means a trident (*triśula*). Three-fold knowledge is a trident. There is no other more potent weapon for the destruction of demons. From *Mahiṣāsura* to *Śumbha*, all the chief demons were destroyed by this weapon. In Volume Two, one understood the trident to mean three-fold knowledge. Here, one has to understand it as three-fold bliss. Bliss, the perception of bliss and a preceptor of bliss are three-fold bliss. Bliss is always vibrating as this triad. When this is realized, demons are destroyed. So, I have said that it is a very effective weapon in destroying demons.

Kālī, force of destruction, applying this three-fold bliss, killed the sixteen hundred demons of the *Udhāyudh* clan and strode in front of the Goddess *Amvikā* in joy. It has been said that the force of destruction resides in front of the power of pure awareness. Until all states are dissolved, the sense of *paramātmā* does not rise. So, the mantra says, 'moving in front of her.' Although this mantra does not describe the death of the *Udhāyudh* clan, we have to understand that the eight clans of demons that set out for battle at the command of *Śumbha*, those that we understood as the eight bondages of shame, etc. are being destroyed by the eight powers that came out of *Amvikā*. Of them, the power *Cāmuṇḍā* killed the *asura Udhāyudh*, that is the bondage of hate. When beings realize that there is nothing else but the undivided nature of bliss, then their sense of divisiveness disappears. When this takes place, hate is removed. In this manner, a seeker is released from the first bondage and moves closer to a state of *Śiva*.

Verse 32.

kamaṇḍalujalākṣepahatavīryān hataujasaḥ|
brahmāṇī cākarocchatrūnyena yena sma dhāvati||

Translation:

Moving about rapidly on the battlefield, *Brahmāṇī*, by sprinkling water from her water pot, made the enemies lose their hope and vigor.

Explanation:

The force by whose effect, nonmanifest seeds become ready to emerge, is the power of life for created beings. This is water from the water pot of *Brahmāṇī*. By sprinkling this water, *Brahmāṇī* made the demons weak and lose effort. *Brahmāṇī*, by sprinkling water, removed the ability of the seeds to emerge as new states. Remember that as long as Mother does not appear in this form as *Brahmāṇī* and remove the store of seeds of creation, the flow of life and death does not stop. This does not happen by effort from a spiritual seeker. We do not and cannot know, what tendencies lie hidden under our pile of desires. Only the keen sight of Mother can see them. It is action by the power of *Brahmāṇī* that exposes these hidden tendencies and destroys them. Spiritual seekers will notice that as one progresses on a spiritual path, opposing tendencies arise every so often to prevent passage. From these effects, many become weak and lose all hope. It is at this time, that one needs to be near a *guru* who can explain that there is no reason to lose hope. It is a precursor of the loss of power of these demons. When one understands this mystery of the sprinkling of water by *Brahmāṇī*, spiritual seekers do not have to lose hope and vigor. Although it is not specifically mentioned in this mantra, one has to understand that it is by the power of *Brahmāṇī* that the fourteen hundred demons named *Kambu* were destroyed. In this manner, Mother removes the second bondage of divisive shame. As a spiritual seeker loses disruptive knowledge and moves towards nondual spirit, all divisive knowledge and their tendencies begin to disappear. There is nothing impossible or unusual in this.

Verse 33.

māheśvarī triśūlena tathā cakreṇa vaiṣṇavī|
daityāṇ jaghāna kaumārī tathā śaktyātikopanā||

Translation:

Māheśarī with her trident, *Vaiṣṅavī* with her discus, and *Kaumārī* with her power weapon, in great anger, began to kill the demons.

Explanation:

The energies *Māheśarī*, *Vaiṣṅavī* and *Kaumārī*, using the trident, discus and power weapons, destroyed the demons named *Kotivirya*, *Dhaumra* and *Kālaka* respectively. The explanation of the trident, discus and power weapons have been given previously. The three demons mentioned are the third, fourth and fifth bondage of fear, anxiety and reproach. My Mother, appearing in her intellectual form as *Māheśarī*, using a trident, that is three-fold bliss, removes the very strong tendency of fear of death. As *Vaiṣṅavī*, she appears as the life-formed power of stability and with her discus (*sudarśaṇa*) that is, divine sight, destroys the fourth bondage of anxiety. Anxiety, that dear ones or things may be lost may be seen even in advanced seekers. My Mother, appearing in her form as *Vaiṣṅavī* destroys this too. In the same fashion, *Kaumārī*, the energy of *Kārttikeya*, the leader of divine warriors, destroys any divisive tendency of reproach. As divisiveness diminishes, the desire for secrecy and hesitancy are destroyed. Look, as Mother removes these bondages and offers a state of *Śiva*, she removes all these bonds with her hands. Those who have surrendered at the feet of Mother, find these opportunities and good fortune. So, I say, apply all your effort to surrender at the feet of Mother.

Verse 34.

aindrī kuliśapātena śataśo daityadānavāḥ|
peturvidāritā bhūmou rudhiraughapravarṣiṇaḥ||

Verse 35.

tuṇḍaprahāravidhvastā daṁṣṭrāgrakṣatavakṣasaḥ|
vārāhamūrtyā nyapataṁścakreṇa ca vidāritāḥ||

Verse 36.

nakhairvidāritāṁścānyān bhakṣayantī mahāsurān|
nārasiṁhī cacārājau nādāpūrṇadigambarā||

Translation:

With her lightning strikes, *Indrāṇī* pierced hundreds of demons and felled them to the ground. Blood streamed from their bodies. The power *Vārāhī* downed the demons with her tail, injured their chests with her tusks and pierced them with her weapons. The power of *Nārasiṁhī* damaged the demons with her claws and with loud roars filling the skies, striding about the battlefield began to devour them.

Explanation:

In these three mantras, the destruction of the demons by *Indrāṇī*, *Vārāhī* and *Nārasiṁhī* are described. Of the eight demons sent for battle by *Śumbha*, only three are left. They are *Dourhṛta*, *Maurya* and *Kālakeya*. Appearing in the forms of *Indrāṇī*, *Vārāhī* and *Nārasiṁhī*, my Mother destroys these three. Spiritually they have been described as lineage, nature and race. These are the sixth, seventh and eighth bondage of beings. To get rid of these bondages, spiritual seekers forsake signs of caste, pursue renunciation (*sannyāsa*), forgo rules of food and home, and try so many other methods. But only a very few can truly get rid of these. To be rid of them is to be free. Mother truly frees whoever she wishes. Then we see that Mother frees her children in many different forms. Freed from these eight bonds, you are ready to be in a state of *Śiva*. Your surrender at the feet of Mother is fortunate.

The tendencies (*saṁskāra*) of these eight bondages are very strong among prior tendencies (*prāravdha*). It is not that they do not occur in the stored and future tendencies, but, by the grace of Mother, these have been destroyed and are without power. The strong prior tendencies are a special obstacle to arriving at a knowledge of nonduality. So, Mother destroys them using different methods. Some by fulfilling the desires, some by control and some through dreams. It is difficult to say how a specific tendency is destroyed. Little is noticed by a seeker as to how the great wishes of Mother are expressed and how they remove bondages of the children. Whatever that is, we see here that Mother appears in many forms and figures, eroding the various tendencies.

Verse 37.

caṇḍāṭṭahāsairasurāḥ śivadūtyabhidūṣitāḥ|
petuḥ pṛthivyāṁ patitāṁstāṁścakhādātha sā tadā||

Translation:

The terrible laughter of *Śivadūtī*, (the goddess *Caṇḍīkā* appearing from the body of *Amvikā*), made some demons faint and fall to the ground. She devoured them.

Explanation:

Śivadūtī, that is, the goddess *Caṇḍīkā*, together with the eight *mātṛkās* eroded the *asura* tribes. Loud laughter is a weapon in this battle. The loud laughter of dissolution, induced such fear in the hearts of some demons that they fainted and fell to the ground. She began to devour them. All divisiveness and error are demons to be destroyed by *Śivadūtī*. By whose inspiration, the intellect formed *Maheśvara Īśāna* became a messenger, that *Śivadūtī*, knowledge formed, supreme power is today ready to destroy the demons. What is so unusual that divisiveness and error disappear with her appearance? Divisiveness is of five kinds, differences between, 1) beings and *Brahmaṇ*, 2) beings and God (*Īśvara*), 3) between beings, 4) beings and inert objects and 5) between inert things. These demons, with the light of the knowledge of nonduality, soon faint and fall. Mantras like 'One and only' and 'I am that', and the briefly expressed, bright laughter of nondual knowledge, quickly destroys these demons. Before this, they were established in the spirit of knowledge. They did not appear to be ignorance. Now that undivided spirit is expressed, they faint. They will all be devoured by *Śivadūtī*. This is declared in the mantra.

A spiritual seeker should notice that as the light of knowledge appears, ignorance and demons of divisiveness begin to be removed. So, I have been saying from the beginning, do not try to remove ignorance. Keep your eyes on the appearance of knowledge. The purpose of life is not to remove ignorance. Viewing the light, or finding knowledge is the aim of life. When knowledge arrives, ignorance disappears.

Verse 38.

iti mātṛgaṇaṁ kruddhaṁ mardayantaṁ mahāsurān|
dṛṣṭvābhyupāyairvividhairneśurdevāri sainikāḥ||

Translation:

Seeing that these forms of Mother were destroying them, the other demon warriors fled, that is, they disappeared.

Explanation:

Although Mother is without a second, today, as different powers like *Brahmāṇī*, she attacks the percepts of duality. As a result, these demons are destroyed. Notice that at the appearance of pure perception, percepts of duality are destroyed one by one. In this manner, by the grace of Mother, the five-fold sense of divisiveness and eight-fold bondages disappear. When perception is expressed by itself, that is, only expresses itself, then divisive knowledge or their tendencies disappear. Spiritual seekers should look and see where Mother has brought them. From a kingdom of mind to that of intellect, then from intellect to one beyond mind. One has had to do nothing. You only had to remain on the lap of Mother, a naked child, calling for Mother. What one has to do next, how one can remove a difficult mound of tendencies of lifetimes, one does not have to attend to any of that. Your only job is to pay attention to the games of Mother. Do not think even in error that this can be carried out by severe spiritual enterprise or firm devotion. If that were true, then any spiritual seeker or devotee would find liberation. Remember, 'it is not found by instruction, study or hearing. It is found by those to whom it reveals itself.'[6] It is found by those who accept it, make it their only goal and surrender to it.

Verse 39.

palāyanaparān dṛṣṭvā daityān mātṛgaṇārditān|
yoddhumabhyāyayau kruddho raktabījo mahāsuraḥ|

Verse 40.

raktabinduryadā bhūmau patatyasya śarīrataḥ|
samutpatati medinyāstatpramāṇastadāsuraḥ||

Translation:

Seeing the demons fleeing from the assault by these mother figures (*mātṛkās*), a very angry demon named *Raktavija* arrived for battle. From each drop of blood that fell from him on the ground, another demon of the same size would arise from the soil.

Explanation:

Raktavija is the last general of *Śumbha*. After this, only *Niśumbha* is left; he cannot be called a general. The character of *Raktavija* is very mysterious. One has to enter this principle gently. Blissful Mother of supreme power, appear to us as intelligence, come as revealing intellect. Let your very deep mystery of play alight on our lean intelligence. By your grace and great affection,

---

6 *Muṇḍaka Upaniṣad* 3.2.3

let us be honored to drink the nectar of intellectual bliss from this store. Let people of this world know of this mystery and with simplicity learn to call you Mother. Let this sorrowful world be established in bliss.

The feeling that 'I am a worldly person' is *Raktavija*. When 'I', that is a seed of the form of Self, is colored by a descriptor as being, it can be called *Raktavija*. The seed is only *paramātmā*, Mother. When it is colored by the sense of a worldly person, by duality, then pure perception becomes divided into Self and non-Self. This outer coloring of the pure seed is *Raktavija*. It is the characteristic of *Raktavija*, that as a drop of his blood falls on the ground, another *Raktavija* is generated. When blood, the feeling of being colored, falls or comes on the sense of this world, it again rises as a seed. As long as the feeling of being colored remains, it will fall to the ground and it will color any pure seed. Thousands of spiritual attempts, thousands of discourses and thousands of percepts cannot completely remove the feeling 'I am a worldly being.' By proper practice of statements from *śrutis*, 'one and only', '*ātmā* is *Brahmaṇ*', 'I am that', when a seeker prepares to meet *Brahmaṇ*, that is, go beyond divisiveness and error, *Raktavija* appears and expresses itself as 'I am a worldly person.' This ignorance as a being obstructs movement towards nonduality. Seekers feel this in their lives all the time. Without the grace of Mother, this terrible demon is not destroyed. Only those who are close to the principle of nonduality, those who have recognized that awareness reflected in ego or intelligence is also a demon, only they can understand the mystery of *Raktavija*. Even if one destroys the sense of 'I am a being' by analysis thousands of times, it reappears again and again. Not only analysis, even if one controls one's spirit by yoga, one cannot be relieved of this demon *Raktavija*. As soon as one stops restraining the spirit, this feeling comes back. Again that 'I' even if one is near the Self by supreme devotion, the feeling comes back. As a worldly person, one moves far away from *ātmā*. One thinks oneself to be very different from *Brahmaṇ*. This is the torment of *Raktavija*. In this manner, by whatever path you progress, analysis, yoga or devotion, you will see this attack by *Raktavija*. It is not destroyed. He does not want to be destroyed. Those who seek to unravel the knot of *Rudra* can feel in their hearts this torment by *Raktavija*. To others, this appears to be a puzzle.

Listen. When you speak, you say *jivātmā* (worldly person) and *paramātmā.* In reality, there is only one *ātmā*. It has no adjectives as worldly or supreme. When a state as a worldly person is imagined in *ātmā*, it is expressed in its colored form. When there is no color of any state, it is referred to as eternal *paramātmā.* In reality, *ātmā* can have no names or adjectives. As long as *ātmā* expresses a state as a worldly person, one has to understand that *Raktavija* has not been destroyed. As long as there is a body, mind and senses, so long *Raktavija* exists. Although this is true, when one is immersed in the nonduality of Mother, the nature of *Raktavija* disappears. It becomes tenuous and dissolves. We will hear about this soon.

O Mother, all this time we did not see *Raktavija*. We did not understand that this unknowable *asura* resided in our hearts and grew by sucking our blood. When I comprehend by your grace, that I am Mother, I am you, I am *ātmā*, as this understanding appears in my heart, the torment by this *asura* hurts me especially. I am clear, I am pure, free and great. I am eternally free. I am pure perception. I have no distinctions, no dullness. I am not connected to any tendencies, I have no birth, death, illness or sorrow. I have no earthly life, heaven or hell, no *dharma* or *adharma*. The state of *Brahmaṇ* is my true being. I am *Brahmaṇ* and nothing else. Even after we hear all this a thousand times and think of it, we again turn into worldly persons. O, Mother! Why do we have to turn back from our real nature? Why do we have to suffer the torment of these demons? Why although we are *Brahmaṇ*, do we have to remain small and dim? Why even though we are with complete knowledge, do we have to reside as beings with little knowledge? We who are eternal and whole, why do we have to live with disease, sorrow, birth and death? O Mother, as long as I did not understand this, I did not feel the pain. Now I cannot tolerate this for a moment more. O, my Mother! Seeing and feeling the difference between a state as a worldly person and *Brahmaṇ*, I do not want to stay here for even one more moment. I wish to go where your state as a blissful, pure spirit resides. O Mother, take me there. Free me forever from this torment by demons, from the bondage of being. I have no one else but you. I see no one else but you. Only you are everything, you are mine, take me along. I cannot move forward alone. Suffering the torment of *Raktavija* for so long, I have taken it as my desire. Such is my habit that I have left you and stayed with *Raktavija*. Come and hold me by my hands and lead me on. Let me be free forever from *Raktavija*. Let me find a place of stability in *Brahmaṇ*. Let my calling you Mother be worthwhile.

If a spiritual seeker understands the torment of *Raktavija*, then one has to weep in this fashion. Then Mother will appear and destroy *Raktavija*.

Verse 41.

yuyudhe sa gadāpāṇirindraśaktyā mahāsuraḥ|
tataścaindrī svavajreṇa raktabījamatāḍayat||

Verse 42.

kuliśenāhatasyāśu bahu susrāva śoṇitam|
samuttasthustato yodhāstadrūpāstatparākramāḥ||

Translation:

The great *asura Raktavija*, mace in hand began to fight the power of *Indra*. *Indrāṇī* injured him with her bolts of lightning. Hit by it, blood poured from the body of *Raktavija*. From that blood demons of the same shape and power began to rise.

Explanation:

Here, the battle of the eight powers, of the *mātṛkās* with *Raktavija* is described. First a fight with *Indrāṇī*. She hits him with her bolts of lightning. It has been mentioned before that the ruler of the organ of the hand is *Indra*. The word '*pāṇi*' means the power to receive and '*vajra*' means electrical energy. The feeling that 'I am a worldly being' is expressed in relationship to the sense organs. When by spiritual effort, by the grace of Mother, powers of the senses are imbued by the state of *paramātmā*, then the state as a worldly person becomes lean. This is described as *Raktavija* bleeding from the weapon of *Indrāṇī*. Although the mantra does not describe all the sense organs, all of them have to be understood, represented by the hands. The main issue is that a state as a worldly person is based on all the senses. By the grace of Mother, as they lose power, the state as a worldly person also begins to shrink. But, it has to be noted, that as much as they become lean, a state as a worldly person lingers. It does not end just by one sense becoming lean. Not only that, even if the senses are dissolved, that is if the state as a worldly person is attacked by intellect, this feeling of 'I am a being' does not want to end.

Verse 43.

yāvantaḥ patitāstasya śarīrādraktabindavaḥ|
tāvantaḥ puruṣā jātāstadvīryabalavikramāḥ||

Translation:

As drops of blood fell from the body of *Raktavija*, demons with powers and abilities similar to *Raktavija* were generated from them.

Explanation:

As soon as powers of the hand and other organs begin to merge into a state of *paramātmā*, this battle of *Indrāṇī* and the other powers begins with *Raktavija*. *Indrāṇī* and the other forms of Mother have now emerged as forces of dissolution. They are ready with various weapons to kill *Raktavija*. The force of lightning from *Indrāṇī* destroys the power of acceptance. As *Raktavija* is injured, his blood, that is his ability to color is divided into many. Not that it did not occur before this, but it had not been so noticeable. Now that a light of intellect is lit, even this most subtle of demons is visible. We have said how from every drop of blood, similar powerful demons are generated. The meaning of the word '*virya*' is influence, power, physical ability and enthusiasm. However, it is not necessary to complicate the issue. The feeling that 'I am a worldly person', is repeatedly weakened but in the next moment regains its power. It is because this feeling arises, that a spiritual seeker is forced to reside far away from *Brahmaṇ*. If we pay attention to this one idea, the mystery of this battle with *Raktavija* will be easy to understand.

Verse 44.

te cāpi yuyudhustatra puruṣā raktasambhavāḥ|
samaṁ mātṛbhiratyugra śastrapātātibhīṣaṇam||

Verse 45.

punaśca vajrapātena kṣatamasya śiro yadā|
vavāha raktaṁ puruṣāstato jātāḥ sahasraśaḥ||

Translation:

The demons arising from the blood, fought with the *mātṛkās* using great weapons. *Indrāṇī* damaged the head of *Raktavija* with her lightning bolt. He was bleeding and from his blood, thousands of demons were generated.

Explanation:

The demons fought with strength. The significance of their great weapons is the relationship and strong association with duality. When seekers begin to understand Self to be separate from intelligence, then tendencies as worldly persons, of divisiveness, arise repeatedly and move a seeker from a spirit of nonduality. This is the mystery of the terrible battle with *Raktavija*.

The power of *Indra* strikes with lightning bolts, and the limbs of the demons are injured and they bleed. From this, innumerable demons are generated. The significance of this is that, in whatever manner the sense of 'I am a worldly person' is damaged, it does not want to be destroyed. It multiplies a thousand-fold. Although this increase is not much compared to a state of ignorance, as a light of knowledge becomes brighter, one feels the danger of a state of worldly being more firmly. The mantra says that thousands of demons were generated. If spiritual seekers pay attention to the feeling of 'I am a worldly person', they will notice whether thousands of *Raktavijas* are generated or not. As the knowledge of Self brightens, the number of *Raktavijas* increases. How can these matters of feeling be described by words?

Verse 46.

vaiṣṇavī samare cainaṁ cakreṇābhijaghāna ha|
gadayā tāḍayāmāsa aindrī tamasureśvaram||

Verse 47.

vaiṣṇavī cakrabhinnasya rudhirasrāvasambhavaiḥ|
sahasraśo jagadvyāptaṁ tatpramāṇairmahāsuraiḥ||

Verse 48.

śaktyā jaghāna kaumārī vārāhī ca tathāsinā|
māheśvarī triśūlena raktabījaṁ mahāsuram||

Translation:

As *Indrāṇī* was attacking the *Raktavijas* with her lightning bolts, the power of *Vaiṣṅavī* attacked them in battle with her discus and beat them with her mace. The blood flowing from the bodies of *Raktavijas* injured by the discus of *Vaiṣṅavī* generated similar great demons, who filled this world. Then, *Kaumārī* with her power weapon, *Vārāhī* with her sword and *Māheśvarī* with her trident began to kill all these *Raktavijas*.

Explanation:

The mystery of the power of *Viṣṇu* and the mace and discus have been explained before. When the various expressions of the power of awareness stand against a state as a worldly person, then by a great attractive force it is broken into a thousand pieces. Because of tendencies of uncounted lifetimes, they do not easily disappear. Based on them, ego tries to keep its special state intact.

The blood that flowed from the body of *Raktavija* generated innumerable *Raktavijas* and filled the battleground of this world. As the feeling of 'I am a worldly person' begins to shrink with the light of intellect, it seems to acquire more power and fill this world. Until now, no other feelings were apparent. Whatever you call it, a light of knowledge or principle of intelligence, all were expressed through a feeling as a worldly person. Until now it was felt as one. Now, by the grace of Mother, pure perception is rising. Like a ray of lightning, nondual knowledge is for a moment removing any state as a worldly person. Now one can see these different feelings to be separate. Now when one sees these feelings as worldly persons, they appear powerful and innumerable. Although it is one, because it arises at each moment, it appears as many and fills this world. Wherever we look, whatever feeling we receive, it expresses that of the state as a worldly person. So *Raktavija* appears as many.

Although the number of *Raktavijas* increased in this manner, the powers of Mother used their weapons to destroy them. The goddess *Kaumārī* used her energy weapon, *Varāhī* used her sharp sword of nondual knowledge and *Māheśvarī* a trident of bliss to destroy the *Raktavijas*. My Mother appeared as many different figures, in different shapes of power to try to pierce the feeling of many lifetimes of the state as a worldly person. Great is the kindness of Mother. It cannot be expressed in words. It is true motherhood. Who but Mother would take so much care to remove all my divisiveness, all my errors and keep me forever on her lap. O, we are but unclothed children on the lap of Mother.

Verse 49.

sa cāpi gadayā daityaḥ sarvā evāhanat pṛthak|
mātṛḥ kopasamāviṣṭo raktabījo mahāsuraḥ||

Verse 50.

tasyāhatasya bahudhā śaktiśūlādibhirbhuvi|
papāta yo vai raktaughastenāsañchataśohasurāḥ||

Translation:

The great *asura Raktavija* becoming angry, began to hit the powers of Mother with his mace. On the other hand, from the blood flowing from him because of all the injuries, hundreds of (innumerable) demons were generated.

Explanation:

The energies of the divinities, *Aindrī*, *Vaiṣṅavī* and *Māheśvarī* had all risen separately to remove any state as a worldly person. They tried to kill *Raktavija* with their weapons. *Raktavija* refused to be annihilated. By applying special effort, although it is nonmanifest for some period, when it rises again, feelings of 'I am a worldly person' return. Due to the great attraction by the eight *mātṛkās* keeping attention on the pure nature of perception, feelings as worldly persons disappear for a little time into a nonmanifest arena, but they emerge again. This is the use of a mace by *Raktavija*. The root '*gad*' means expressed words. The ancient commentator Gopāl Cakravarttī has given the same meaning here. The *mātṛkās* separately tried to kill *Raktavija.* He too tries to express himself to them repeatedly. Instead of being able to kill him, the blood flowing from his body generates innumerable demons. The mystery of this appearance of demons has been given in the previous mantra. As much as one tries to end a state as a worldly person, it does not want to be removed. Instead, it becomes bigger and stronger. It is nearly impossible to remove it by applying effort. It is different when Mother applies effort.

Verse 51.

taiścāsurāsṛkśambhūtairasuraiḥ sakalaṁ jagat|
vyāptamāsīttato devā bhayamājagmuruttamam||

Translation:

Seeing that this world was filled by these innumerable demons generated from the blood of *Raktavija*, the gods became very fearful.

Explanation:

The deities, the awareness resident in the senses, seeing the spirit of *Raktavija*, were afraid. In whatever direction one looks, wherever one pays attention, one notices the torment by innumerable *Raktavijas*, the feeling of duality that one is a worldly person. When after much effort, one cannot be rid of this feeling, then great fear and hopelessness come in. Through this fear and hopelessness, there appears in the heart of a spiritual seeker an intense sense of separation. This separation feels very strong. When one sees that one cannot unite with the dearest one, one cannot merge into the heart of the dear one, then this pain becomes unbearable. One can see the dear one through a transparent wall of intelligence. One has to be satisfied seeing it behind a shade of intelligence. The wish to find the dearest increases daily, yet one cannot break this wall of intelligence to offer oneself at the feet of the dearest. So, this pain of separation increases and the state as a worldly person becomes intensely painful. Oh! This is very holy, very pure, it is beyond all feelings, it is my dear, loving Self, my blissful partner of life. How will I merge with it? It is *Brahmaṇ*, I am a tiny being. How can I merge into it? Can two unequal things unite? As long as the feeling of 'I am a being' does not disappear, one cannot merge into this dear one who is beyond intelligence.

Some modern *Vaiṣṇava* groups have declared that it is impossible and wrong for a devotee to be united with divinity. If they would pay special attention to great Vedic statements such as 'I am that' (*tattvamasi*), they would understand that in these statements, supreme love is indicated. Honored are those sages in whose hearts, these incredible feelings first arose, who offered themselves at the feet of their great love and arrived at their great peaks of love. Understanding that as long as even the tiniest bit of divisiveness remained, this love did not find completeness, the sages of the *Upaniṣads*, saying 'Self is *Brahmaṇ*'[7], merged their spirit into the ocean of *Brahmaṇ*. Today, hearing their great

7 *Māṇḍukya Upaniṣad*, Verse 2.

statements and following in their footsteps, after so many ages, people discover supreme love and are honored in this life. Until one arrives here, one cannot know the love of *Rādhā* and the *gopis* that is described in the *Vaiṣṇav* literature.

As long as a spiritual seeker does not realize 'I', Mother, Self, as long as one does not see the nature of Mother expressed, so long pain of separation will not be removed. As long as the perception of duality as a worldly person remains, one cannot be united. Remember that knowledge of nonduality is union and divisiveness is separation. Those who have never united with the dearest one, cannot understand this pain of separation. But that is something else.

The *Upaniṣad* says that 'fear comes from another.' Fear comes from the knowledge of duality. So, this mantra says that the gods were afraid to see the innumerable *Raktavijas*. If one can arrive here, if one acquires the power to be at this battle with *Raktavija*, then one can understand the meaning of the *Upaniṣad* statement, and realize what is fear. The fear that you see in this world is not great. It is just an outline of fear, only a distant shadow. One can know true fear when one arrives here. Differences and duality are not removed. So, fear does not go away.

There is some mystery in '*bhayamājagmuruttamam.*' Here, fear is called superior. Worldly fear is inferior. Only the fear that appears from divisive knowledge as a worldly being, at the union of beings with *Brahmaṇ*, is called superior fear. When will you forsake body and mind by the great attraction of the dear one, and arrive at this intellectual arena? When will you be engrossed by seeing the nature of *paramātmā* next to it? When will you remember the one who bestows fearlessness, learn the nature of fear, and be established at her feet?

Verse 52.

tān viṣaṇṇān surān dṛṣṭvā caṇḍikā prāhasatvara|
uvāca kālīṁ cāmuṇḍe vistaraṁ vadanaṁ kuru||

Translation:

Seeing the gods downcast, *Caṇḍīkā* quickly said, (O, gods, do not be sad), then said to *Kālī*, "O, *Cāmuṇḍā*, open your mouth wide."

Explanation:

The feeling 'I am a worldly person' does not want to be removed. One cannot immerse in the ocean of *Brahmaṇ*. Seeing this, the gods were downcast. So, my Mother said to them, 'do not be sad' and reassured them. In this manner, when the gods are tormented by the knowledge of duality, Mother in the form of knowledge of nonduality removes sorrow from their hearts.

Having the two words, '*prāha*' and '*uvāca*', of similar meaning in the mantra, some commentators have inserted '*mā viṣīdat*' (do not be sad) and given the meaning as above. *Tattva Prakāśikā* has taken '*prāhasatvara*' together, and given the meaning of '*prāha*' as 'battle.'

On one hand, Mother reassured the gods and on the other arranged for the death of *Raktavija*. She first asked *Cāmuṇḍā* to open her mouth wide. The need for this is explained in the next mantra.

Verse 53.

macchastrapātasambhūtān raktabindūn mahāsurān|
raktabindoḥ pratīccha tvaṁ vaktreṇānena vegitā||

Verse 54.

bhakṣayantī cara raṇe tadutpannān mahāsurān|
evameṣa kṣayaṁ daityaḥ kṣīṇarakto gamiṣyati||

Verse 55.

bhakṣyamāṇāstvayā cogrā na cotpatsyanti cāpare||

Translation:

Take all the blood shed by my weapons and the demons generated from the blood into your (wide open) mouth. Roam around the battlefield devouring the demons arising from the blood. *Raktavija* losing blood will be destroyed. Being devoured by you in this manner, no demons will remain and new demons cannot rise.

Explanation:

The Goddess *Caṇḍīkā* ordered the power of *Kālī* to open her mouth wide and devour the drops of blood and demons arising from them. Truly, if the destructive force does not devour the feelings of a worldly person, there are no other means for destroying *Raktavija*. Even the seeds of a state as a worldly person have to be devoured. Although, as long as *Śumbha* is not killed, subtle seeds of a state as a worldly person remain. Still, expressing feelings that keep a seeker in a state as a worldly person, separating him from *Brahmaṇ* has to be removed. This is the order from Mother to *Cāmuṇḍā*. If destructive force devours the drops of blood in this manner, then the blood cannot fall on the ground. New demons will not be generated. Then, *Raktavija* will weaken and be destroyed.

Let me explain. It has been said that the perception 'I am a worldly person' is the seed and the state as one is blood. Because some special feelings remain, the seed of 'I' is colored by blood as a worldly person. If now, by her grace, destructive Mother *Cāmuṇḍā* devours all our distinctiveness and does not let feelings of lifetimes as worldly persons be connected with distinctness, then this state or *Raktavija* cannot grow. (Being connected to distinctiveness is the shedding of blood.) Before feelings as a worldly person can arise in the shelter of anything distinct and so color 'I', it enters the wide mouth of *Cāmuṇḍā*. *Raktavija* will cease to exist.

This is a deep mystery. The '*yusmad* and '*asmad*' (you and I) perceptions and (superposition) of perceptor and perceived that are described in the *Śāririk Bhāṣya*[8] becomes apparent to a spiritual seeker arriving at this battle with *Raktavija*. Before, when the nature of things perceived by ego are expressed, they appear as

---

8 *Brahma Sutra* commentary by *Śankaracārya*.

non-Self. Even after thousands of attempts, one cannot be relieved of this perception as non-Self. This is the battle with *Raktavija*. Imagine that you are ready to land on the nature of nonduality. At that time, due to past tendencies, you have to descend from pure awareness to special consciousness. Whether that specialty is subtle, like mind or intelligence, or physical, like body and form, you have to come down from a pure arena to a special one. You cannot remain in nonduality. 'Seeing Mother', 'meditating on the other', 'meeting *paramātmā* ', all are in the realm of duality. They too are states as worldly persons. Because the subtle sense of 'I am separate from *paramātmā'* remains, divisive knowledge remains. They are *Raktavijas*. To destroy them, all such states have to be removed. Otherwise, if any distinctiveness remains, it will color 'I.' In whatever fashion possible, these colorations, these drops of blood have to be removed and one has to reside as pure Self, as unformed seed, alone. Only in this manner is *Raktavija* destroyed. Only ego and attachment remain. Come, let us shout "Victory to *Kālī*" and seek refuge in the power of *Cāmuṇḍā*. She will open her mouth wide and devour all the blood and all *Raktavijas*. Then will we be relieved of a state as a worldly person and land on nonduality. Our flow of birth and death will cease forever.

Verse 56.

ityuktvā tāṁ tato devī śūlenābhijaghāna tam|
mukhena kālī jagṛhe raktabījasya śoṇitam||

Translation:

Giving this instruction to *Kālī*, *Caṇḍīkā* struck *Raktavija* with her lance. Goddess *Kālikā* opened her mouth wide and drank all the blood

Explanation:

The significance of the striking of Mother's lance is a strike by the light of knowledge. The meaning of this world '*śula*' (lance) has been explained before. It is the chief weapon of Mother. The demons of dual perceptions cannot be removed by anything else but the light of pure knowledge. Do not think that within moments of expression of knowledge, all ignorance will vanish forever. That does not happen. Knowledge appears incrementally, it begins to strengthen and ignorance is slowly removed. The significance of saying that 'darkness of a thousand years in a room is removed by lighting a single lamp' is that once a light of pure knowledge is expressed, beings can never again be immersed in the darkness of ignorance. Day by day, with vigor, they advance in the light of knowledge. They are no longer bemused by delusions of false knowledge.

The words of the Lord also prove that ignorance is removed slowly. He has said that 'just as the ceremonial fire consumes all its fuel, a fire of knowledge turns to ashes all actions, all ignorance'[9]. What we have to notice in this, concerning our present discussion, is that just as all the fuel is not immediately burnt when a fire is lit, it takes some time to complete, the fire of knowledge also burns the fuel of ignorance a little at a time. Those who do not agree with this should think about it. As long as a stance of this body and this world remains, until then, even if a little, even as a suggestion, ignorance remains. One has to agree that it is not completely removed. But, there is a very bright place of knowledge. On arriving there, any stance of body and all else no longer remain. The *Yogā Vāśiṣṭa* has named it the sixth state *padārthābhāvinī* and the seventh *turīyaga*. Although today, seekers at such high levels are very rare, one has to say that such states are not impossible. By the grace of Mother and by intense effort and renunciation of a seeker, expression of such bright knowledge is very possible.

Whatever it is, we have moved away from our topic. Let us get back to it. We have said that by blows of the lance of Mother, the body of *Raktavija* was injured. The destructive force *Kālī* opened her mouth wide and received all the blood from his wounds. Truly, this occurs. On one side, the light of nonduality injures the intelligence of worldly persons, on the other, an all-encompassing force of *Kālī* devours all perceptions and feelings. When the blood

---

9 *Bhāgavat Gitā*, 4.37.

of a state as a worldly person remains, *Raktavija* is regenerated. But now, Mother in the form of *Kālī*, devours any flow of blood and the end of *Raktavija* is inevitable.

Verse 57.

tatohasāvājaghānātha gadayā tatra caṇḍikāṁ|
na cāsyā vedanāṁ cakre gadāpātohalpikāmapi||

Translation:

Thereafter *Raktavija* hit Goddess *Caṇḍīkā* with his mace. But it did not hurt the Goddess.

Explanation:

Before this, *Raktavija* had attacked the eight *mātṛkā* forces with his mace. Now he attacked Goddess *Caṇḍīkā* with it. But, such is the glory of Mother, that it did not pain her even a little. As much as demonic feelings may be expressed, as much as a feeling 'I am a worldly person' may arise, they do not give rise to any sensation in the body of Mother, in the nondual field. They are not expressed in the nature of awareness. My Mother remains eternally pure, supreme and unmoved as she always is. No decay can touch her. Characteristics of the field of intelligence cannot appear in a field of awareness. The word '*vedanā*' (pain) means special sensation. However strong the state of being may be, as much as it may try to engross Self, it does not produce any disturbance in the arena of pure *paramātmā.* So, the mantra says that Mother did not feel any pain.

I have been speaking of this pain or perception from the beginning. One has to advance in the spiritual arena holding on to perception. Perception is *ātmā*, it is Mother. First, one has to advance with the help of special percepts. Then when one reaches the knot of *Rudra*, any specialty of perception is removed, only perception remains. Perception is undivided bliss, it has no distinctiveness.

If you are used to the establishment of life force, then you understand what is pain or perception. I will tell you an easy way of realizing this vision. Hearing, thinking and all matters of senses, earth, water, energy and all matters of form and flavor are varieties of perceptions. One has to go from perception to matter and from matter to perception. After practicing in this manner for some time, matters of attention and senses become perceptible. Then one will see vision as a perception of vision or hearing as a perception of hearing. When this feeling matures, one can discard the special feelings of vision and hearing and try to hold on only to perception. In the beginning, one has to back off from trying to hold on to this perception without characterization. A violent electric force will move one away from this place. Then one has to try repeatedly and cry to Mother, saying 'take me on your lap.' Then by her grace, one can reside there for a few moments. One will understand what is 'only a figure of knowledge' (*jñānamurtti*). What I have said before about the distinctiveness of perception is the knot of knowledge (*Rudra granthi)*. To unravel or pierce this knot, one needs intense effort and the grace of Mother. I do not need to write about what happens when this knot of *Rudra* is pierced. A spiritual seeker will understand. I only say that whatever you have read or heard about freedom while alive, will be realized. But all that is something else.

Verse 58.

tasyāhatasya dehāttu bahu susrāva śoṇitam|
yatastatastad vaktreṇa cāmuṇḍā sampratīcchati||

Verse 59.

mukhe samudgatā yehasyā raktapātānmahāsurāḥ|
tāṁścakhādātha cāmuṇḍā papau tasya ca śoṇitam||

Translation:

From the wounds in the body of *Raktavija* that bled (injured by the lance of Mother), *Cāmuṇḍā* took all the blood into her mouth. The demons generated in her mouth from the blood were devoured by her and she drank all their blood.

Explanation:

Wherever there is bleeding, there is a wide-open mouth of *Cāmuṇḍā*. As soon as pure perception is colored by a state as a worldly person, *Kālī* with her mouth wide open devours that feeling. As a light of intellect falls from one direction, feelings as worldly persons terminate. To state this clearly, it is repeated in several mantras. There is no error because of this repetition. This matter of intellectual light and dissolution of the sense of non-Self occurs repeatedly.

Blood streaming from the body of *Raktavija* injured by the lance, fell into the mouth of *Cāmuṇḍā* because she kept it wide open. The demons generated from the blood in her mouth were also devoured by her. One can argue here, that it was said that only when the blood fell to the ground, were demons of the form and power of *Raktavija* generated. But, here it says that demons were being generated from the blood that fell into the mouth of *Cāmuṇḍā*. How can this be right? The answer is that the generation of demons in the mouth of *Cāmuṇḍā* is possible. The words '*raktavinduryadā bhumou*', only pointed towards distinctiveness. By it, *Raktavijas* would be generated. Or, the word '*bhumou*' signifies an earthly body. With this meaning, there should be no argument. As long as an earthly body remains, a state as a worldly person will always arise. It is because of the relationship to this worldly state, that pure awareness is reflected as a distinct or worldly person. Mother has appeared and opened her wide mouth, not letting the blood of *Raktavija* fall to the ground. She is not letting a sense as a worldly person be connected with the physical body. Although she devours any sense of a worldly person as it rises, still, a tiny bit, a little distinction related to a physical body is expressed. As long as it remains, a small amount of the blood of *Raktavija* will fall to the ground. At the time blood enters the mouth of *Cāmuṇḍā*, and a worldly being enters dissolution, one is still connected to a sense of a physical body. So, the mantra says that demons were also generated in the mouth of *Cāmuṇḍā*.

Verse 60.

devī śūlena vajreṇa bāṇairasibhirṛṣṭibhiḥ|
jaghāna raktabījaṁ taṁ cāmuṇḍāpītaśoṇitam||

Translation:

When *Cāmuṇḍā* had drunk the blood of *Raktavija*, the Goddess *Caṇḍīkā* with lance, lightning, arrows, sword and *ṛṣṭi*[10], injured *Raktavija*.

Explanation:

Now *Raktavija* is going to be destroyed. On one hand, a light of intellect, as the lance and other weapons of Mother is being applied, on the other, feelings as a worldly person, as they appear, are devoured by powers of dissolution. The five weapons, lance, lightning, arrows, sword and *ṛṣṭi,* mentioned in the mantra, represent faith, feeling, logic, scriptures and grace. These five are the proper weapons for destroying *Raktavija.* The great *asura* cannot be killed by any one of them. They have to be used together. On one hand the use of these weapons and on the other, the attraction of destructive force. When *Raktavija* is attacked in this manner, then his end is inevitable.

A spiritual seeker has to first establish very firm faith in 'beings are *Brahmaṇ* and nothing else' (*jivo brahmaiva nāparaḥ*). This is the first weapon. Then residing in the principle of intelligence, one has to repeatedly pay attention to the self-expressed power of awareness. That is, holding on to specific perceptions, try to arrive at a general perception. This is the second weapon. Then, with the help of logic, understand that there is only the power of awareness. All that is reflected in the form of visible, knowable specifics, are all applied utilities, without the spirit of Self. What is just usage, cannot be. There is no separate existence of what is only a utility, in any of the three time periods, cannot be. With this and other arguments, try to destroy special states. If analysis of *Brahmaṇ* in *Vedānta* is brought into battle with *Raktavija*, it becomes useful. Otherwise, before one has acquired any rights, entering into these

10 Evil influence of a star or planet.

arguments are usually problematic. They impede the progress of a spiritual seeker. Remember that it is only for the destruction of *Raktavija* that one needs the consistent weapons of analysis of *Brahmaṇ*. Whatever that is, this is the third weapon.

Then, try to realize the nature of nonduality with the help of the scriptures. It is very necessary for a seeker to see if realizations that arise are comparable to evidence given by the scriptures. Using the four great statements like 'I am that' (*tattvamasi*) and the great statements of unity like 'one and only' (*ekamevādvitiyam*), one has to try and realize the complete nondual nature of Self. This is weapon number four. The fifth weapon is the grace of Mother. Keen prayers from the beginning, for the grace of Mother, have to continue to the end. Grace is an inevitable result of a state of seeking sanctuary. The grace of Self is the chief provision for discovering Self. Once grace is received, the rest is easy. It is often seen that the previous five, come about in reverse order. That is, first, one feels the grace of Mother. Then faith is firmly established. Then the meaning of the scriptural statements becomes clear. Then one acquires the aptitude for logic and reason. Finally, following one's perceptions, one acquires the ability to arrive at non-defined nature. Understanding these five methods, the five weapons mentioned above gives one an understanding of the mystery of this mantra.

There is something to be said here, especially about '*Cāmuṇḍā* drinking blood' (*cāmuṇḍā pītaśoṇitam*). As long as *Cāmuṇḍā* does not drink the blood of *Raktavija*, no one has the ability to uproot him. So, one has to keep one's attention on this destructive power. One has to remember that efforts by a spiritual seeker are expressed by the grace of Mother.

Verse 61.

sa papāta mahīpṛṣṭhe śastrasaṅghasamāhataḥ|
nīraktaśca mahīpāla raktabījo mahāsuraḥ||

Translation:

O king! In this fashion, being injured by a swarm of weapons and losing blood, the great demon *Raktavija* fell to the ground.

Explanation:

Being injured by the weapons of faith, feeling, logic, scriptures and grace, *Raktavija* fell to the ground, turning inert. He was dead. Inertness and visibility are the same thing. A feeling as a worldly person was until now connected with 'I' formed matter and acting as the ruler and enjoyer. What was essentially inert or visible, had until now appeared as conscious, as the viewer. But today, the true nature of consciousness having been revealed, the viewer has turned into the view. On the other hand, 'I' is no longer just the viewed or only a seed. 'I' is now the viewer, consciousness. Until now distorted knowledge remained, so Self was expressed as a worldly person. But Mother having first destroyed *Dhumralocana* removed distorted knowledge. As an inevitable result, feelings as worldly persons began to disappear.

Listen. In reality, there is no separate identity as a worldly person. There is nothing separate as a view, never was, or will be. Only pure matter of perception is present. It is completely blissful, always sweet and ambrosial. In the complete and continuous substance of bliss, there is no ignorance or sorrow, never was, never can be. To be firmly established in this knowledge is the end of *Raktavija* because when such knowledge arises, a state as a worldly person cannot remain. Then 'I' is no longer colored by a state as a worldly person. It is because of ignorance that the inert seems to be mixed with what is conscious. By the grace of Mother, ignorance has been removed. Consciousness has been established. So, nothing appears as a worldly person.

The great sage Medhasa addresses king Suratha here as '*mahīpāla*' (protector of the earth). A seeker has to also become *mahīpāla*. The nature of consciousness is expressing its earthliness (*mahī*) or inertness in your shelter. You are the one protecting *mahī*, which is sustaining ignorance. When you understand this, you will see that there is no such thing as *mahī*, only the nature of consciousness. Monarchy or engagement was not part of you, is not and will not be. When will you, like Suratha leave the false arrogance of inertness and become a true *mahīpāla*? When will the demon *Raktavija* be destroyed? When will you be established in unending bliss?

Verse 62.

tataste harṣamatulamavāpustridaśā nṛpa|
teṣāṁ mātṛgaṇo jāto nanartāsṛṅmadoddhataḥ||

iti mārkaṇḍeyapurāṇe sāvarṇike manvantare devīmāhātmye raktabījavadho|

Translation:

O king! Then the gods found great happiness, and the *mātṛkās* danced vigorously with enjoyment after drinking blood.

Here ends this episode on the destruction of *Raktavija*, in *Mārkeṇḍeya Purāṇa,* in the era of *Sāvarṇi,* in *Devī Māhātmya.*

Explanation:

Truly the joy of the gods today is incomparable. The gods have been cleansed of contact with the dreariness of the state as worldly persons, which had been stored over many lifetimes. Contact with inertness has been removed. The light of Self has arisen. Special consciousness having found a relationship with an undivided, blissful spirit is greatly pleased. *Brahmāṇī* and other *mātṛkās* danced with joy after drinking blood. The word '*asṛk*' means blood. It is wine or joy. The blood of a state as a worldly person, that is colorations has been separated from the blissful power of awareness. The play of destruction of the powers of Mothers has been worthwhile. So, they are dancing vigorously. That is, the flow of pure perception of the various powers is being expressed.

The state as a worldly person resides in bliss-natured *Brahmaṇ*. It is as if *Brahmaṇ* was evident as a worldly person. A spiritual seeker had been used to moving about in such knowledge. But now, by the grace of Mother, one has arrived where one cannot feel one's state as a worldly person. Divisiveness in the state as a worldly person that limited bliss has been removed by the death of *Raktavija*. Any division in bliss is removed with his death. One does not have to find bliss drop by drop, separately in individuality. Discarding all specialties, the bliss of Self is expressed everywhere. There is bliss over all the world. There is nothing else but bliss. The bliss-natured 'I', the most loved 'I', an ambrosial 'I' is expressed everywhere. There is no beginning and end to my bliss, no movement. I am great, still, steady. A spiritual seeker alights on this perception. In this condition, beings and world, birth and death, illness and sorrow, Sun and Moon, sky and stars, all seem to be filled with a dense spirit of bliss. Deities resident in sense awareness, find great joy. Even *mātṛkās* dance vigorously in joy. Let a spiritual seeker discover this place, and be honored. You have been established in truth and in life force, now be established in bliss and finding your undivided nature of bliss, go from door to door in this world, distributing bliss. May the blessings of the *guru* be on you and inspire you to do good to this world. May joy return to this sorrowful world.

Here ends the explanation of the destruction of *Raktavija* in *Sādhan Samar* or *Devī Māhātmya*.

Chapter 9

Destruction of *Niśumbha*

Verse 1.

rājovāca|
vicitramidamākhyātaṁ bhagavan bhavatā mama|
devyāścaritamāhātmyaṁ raktabījavadhāśritam||

Verse 2.

bhūyaścecchāmyahaṁ śrotuṁ raktabīje nipātite|
cakāra śumbho yatkarma niśumbhaścātikopanaḥ||

Translation:

The king (Suratha) said, "Lord, you have described this extraordinary tale of the greatness of the Goddess in connection with the destruction of *Raktavija*. (Because of this) I would like to hear, how the very angry *Śumbha* and *Niśumbha*, acted after this."

Explanation:

Truly the destruction of *Raktavija* is extraordinary. Hearing of this incredible greatness of the character of the Goddess, seekers keen to end their state as worldly persons will surely be bemused. In this character, the unique Mother appears as multiple powers and sends a state of being towards dissolution. Mother, who is without attributes, with a lance and other weapons attacks demons. She removes mounds of past tendencies of innumerable lifetimes. One is stilled by wonder when one hears about this incredible character. So, king Suratha conforms this astonishing character with his statement (*vicitramidamākhyātaṁ*). Not only is the greatness of the character of Mother extraordinary, its narrator is also extraordinary and so are the listeners. More so is one who realizes this. It is said in the *Upaniṣad*, 'extraordinary is the speaker, expert the listener.' The Lord has said, 'some see it as incredible, others say it is incredible'[1]. Truly, speakers and

1 *Bhāgabat Gitā,* 2.29.

listeners of these principles are extraordinary. But, the subject of this discourse is even more extraordinary and inexplicable. One has to be surprised that to discover something so simple, easy and self-evident, one has to go through such an incredible series of events. It is surprising that one has to go through so many changes in condition, to find one who alone exists, who is always manifest and is simple. 'I am' is simple, natural and easily expressed. Blissful Mother is similarly simple, natural and self-manifest. Yet, to manifest to us her nature, she has to express an assortment of divine plays. She is great, who is so self-evident, yet so hidden. To find that which is always expressed, to perceive the nature of what is self-evident, there are thousands of books, advice, teachings and spiritual enterprises that are prevalent in this world. Great is she and the incredible mystery of her divine play.

Whatever it is, what remains after the destruction of *Raktavija*, how this all ends, is of interest to a seeker. So, the king expresses eagerness to hear about the destruction of *Śumbha* and *Niśumbha*. When king Suratha, having lost his kingdom, first met the great sage Medhasa, he addressed him as 'O Lord (*Bhagavan*).' It began with the proper address to a *guru*. The use of the word '*bhagavan*' here is the beginning of a true vision of God. In this manner, as the disciple advances, a vision of God in the *guru* is acquired. As the establishment of truth in *guru* as God increases, disciples advance.

Verse 3.

ṛṣiruvāca|
cakāra kopamatulaṁ raktavīje nipātite|
śumbhāsuro niśumbhaśca hateṣvanyeṣu cāhave||

Translation:

The sage said, when *Raktavija* and the other demons were killed in battle, *Śumbha* and *Niśumbha* expressed great anger.

Explanation:

The chief supports of *Śumbha* and *Niśumbha*, (ego and attachment) have one by one been destroyed. There is no one left who can give them refuge. Under this condition they should be hopeless, weakened and sad. But that does not happen. Immense anger appears. This anger is truly incomparable. Anger that results in the expression of Self, what can be compared to it in this world? The Lord has said, anger arises from desire (*kāmāt krodhohbhijāyate* [2]). *Śumbha* and *Niśumbha* desire *Amvikā*. Their desire is unfulfilled and repeatedly repelled. So, anger appears. This anger will bring their end in every manner. How anger appears from desire, and how it slowly changes to finally come to destruction, has been clearly stated by the Lord. Anger gives rise to engrossment (*krodhāt bhabati sammoha*). Seeing self-expression and bliss of Self, ego becomes engrossed by it. It becomes eager to acquire Self, even by sacrificing itself. This is engrossment. From engrossment appears distortion of intelligence. Becoming completely engrossed by the supreme nature of *paramātmā*, the memory of one's separate existence disappears. When one loses this memory, intelligence fails. From this comes complete destruction (*praṇāsh*). This is true dissolution, any separate existence of the ego from *ātmā* is destroyed. It has been said before that ego and intelligence (*buddhi*) are non-different. So, the destruction of intelligence and that of ego are the same. It is from anger that this destruction of intelligence begins. The sage says that *Śumbha* and *Niśumbha* expressed great anger. Anger that brings this culmination is incomparable in this world. With this, the feeling that 'I am a worldly person', a final attempt to overcome *ātmā* is expressed in the field of ego. The external manifestation of it is anger. Instead of *ātmā* being overcome by ego, ego is overtaken by *ātmā*. We will see this later.

Verse 4.

hanyamānaṁ mahāsainyaṁ vilokyāmarṣamudvahan|
abhyadhāvanniśumbhohatha mukhyayāsurasenayā||

2 *Bhāgabat Gitā*, 2.62

Verse 5.

tasyāgratastathā pṛṣṭhe pārśvayośca mahāsurāḥ|
sandaṣṭauṣṭhapuṭāḥ kruddhā hantuṁ devīmupāyayuḥ||

Translation:

Seeing his great warriors slain, *Niśumbha* was very angry and went to battle with his army. In front, behind and on both sides, angry demons bit on their lips and moved in, to kill the Goddess.

Explanation:

Of the two brothers, *Niśumbha* went first into battle. Of ego and attachment, the second one approaches first to find Self. It gets ready to take *Amvikā* saying, 'this is mine.' In front of *Niśumbha* or attachment is a desire for Self, behind him desire to enjoy this world and on either side, desire for unlimited wealth. This is the army of demons. They moved towards the Goddess for battle, biting their lips in anger. One can question that, before this, with the death of *Raktavija*, all states as worldly persons have ended. Then where do these demons of desire come from? The answer is that starting from *Madhu* and *Kaitava*, up to *Raktavija*, all demons that have been destroyed, have all been explained as the end of a state as worldly persons. Now we will speak of the ending of tendencies (*saṁskāra*) of a state of Godhood. So, all these demon warriors in front, behind and on side of *Niśumbha*, should be understood as tendencies of Godhood. One has to remember that in the destruction of *Śumbha* and *Niśumbha*, the erosion of the tendencies of Godhood is to be described. Just as *saṁskāra* of a state as a worldly person is an obstacle to reaching *paramātmā*, so are tendencies of Godhood. One can only find *Amvikā* by ending all the states as worldly persons and also divinity. Those who are truly seeking freedom, who truly seek to get rid of fruits of action, that is, those who reject even a state of Godhood, only they can meet with the nondual, ambrosial nature of *ātmā*.

Whatever it is, *Niśumbha* with his compatriots appeared for battle. Saying 'my *ātmā*', still trying to maintain his distinctiveness, maintained a relationship with *ātmā*. His purpose was that if one could sustain a relationship with *ātmā*, one could attain Godhood. One could independently, as a free spirit enjoy all wealth of this universe. This is the mystery of the battle expedition by *Niśumbha*.

Reaching this point, a spiritual seeker will understand what is Godhood and what is true devotional love. The manner in which we generally discuss it is not true devotional love. As long as one cannot say 'my *ātmā*', like *Niśumbha* and have a relationship with *ātmā*, you just get a hint of the nature of *ātmā*. There is no opportunity to discuss devotional love. One only has the ability to say 'my *ātmā*' when one does not have anything else to call mine. As long as all states are not destroyed, as long as the flow of feeling in spirit is not stopped, one cannot experience the worth of things like, my God, my Mother, or my *ātmā*. When Self is the only goal, nothing else arises in the field of perception, then one acquires the ability to form a relationship with Self. Then one acquires the ability to truly find the wonderful taste of devotional love.

Look, *Niśumbha* has lost nearly everything. Yet saying, 'I want *Amvikā*', he is going forward with speed. You too have to go forward with keen interest. Do not harbor greed for Godhood. Do not keep track of gain and loss. Only try to be engrossed by love. Like *Niśumbha*, saying, 'my *ātmā*, my Mother', go forward. You will find Mother, you will forget the word 'my' and be immersed in the nature of Self.

Verse 6.

ājagāma mahāvīryaḥ śumbhohapi svabalairvṛtaḥ
nihantuṁ caṇḍikāṁ kopāt kṛtvā yuddhaṁ tu mātṛbhiḥ

Translation:

The very powerful *Śumbha*, surrounded by his warriors also appeared (on the battlefield) to destroy the *mātṛkās* and *Caṇḍīkā* in battle.

Explanation:

Ego also goes to battle with attachment. It has been said before that attachment and ego are of similar states. Being surrounded by *asura* warriors, the various godlike powers, *Śumbha* and *Niśumbha* appear on the battlefield in anger. *Śumbha* desires the hand of *Caṇḍīkā*. If the *mātṛkās* who have emerged from the body of *Caṇḍīkā* can be destroyed, she will be alone. Then the desire of *Śumbha* may be fulfilled. This is what the mantra says.

Listen. There is something separate from the ego that is *ātmā*, which is truly God (*Īśvara*). Being able to acquire it is to truly find a state of Godhood. It is by understanding this, that ego is so eager, so firm in its effort. Ego tries to understand itself as *ātmā* or God. By occasionally seeing a hint of the nature of pure *ātmā*, it feels the deficiency of its nature. It tries to find *ātmā* and fill this emptiness. Its intention is that something that is the state of 'I' separate from itself, should not exist. That 'I' should merge in me and become one, or I will merge with it forever. One cannot tolerate the existence of these two 'I's. Before arriving in the field of ego, a spiritual seeker cannot comprehend this. As long as one does not have a hint of the nature of Self, ego appears as Self. One cannot at first understand that it is not Self. Slowly as one reaches closer to Self, one has an interest in trying to acquire it.

Verse 7.

tato yuddhamatīvāsīddevyā śumbhaniśumbhayoḥ|
śaravarṣamatīvograṁ meghayoriva varṣatoḥ||

Translation:

Thereafter, a terrible battle began between the Goddess, *Śumbha* and *Niśumbha*. Like rain falling from heavy clouds, they began to speedily shower arrows.

Explanation:

Saying 'my *ātmā*', attachment tried very hard to make Self its own. Saying 'I am *ātmā*', ego tried to properly end Self. This is the mystery of this battle by *Śumbha* and *Niśumbha*. Those who are used to thinking and practicing great statements like '*tat tama asi*', will be able to notice the subtle but very terrible attacks by attachment and ego. A seeker cannot rest and be peaceful, until that, which has been truly understood as the final and supreme abode, is brought near. This is why spiritual seekers, arriving here, expend tremendous effort. The yoga sutras of *Pātañjali* have mentioned that it is by 'seekers with intense effort' that *ātmā* can be found. And in reality, in the arena of perception, it is seen that this intense effort appears naturally. When a river meets the ocean, the currents become swift. The closer seekers get to Self, the more intense becomes their effort. This is the mystery of a great shower of arrows from *Śumbha* and *Niśumbha*. In this mantra, they have been compared to rain from the clouds. There is a purpose to this. Just as clouds by showering rain, lose their existence, by their intense effort, ego and attachment will also lose their selves. Then, only Self will remain. There will be nothing left of ego and attachment. We will come on this later.

Verse 8.

cicchedāstāñcharāṁstābhyāṁ caṇḍikāśu śarotkaraiḥ|
tāḍayāmāsa cāṅgeṣu śastraughairasureśvarau||

Translation:

Goddess *Caṇḍīkā* with her arrows began to splinter those thrown by the demons, and with various weapons began to injure their bodies.

Explanation:

Śumbha and *Niśumbha* fired many arrows, but they all failed because my Mother *Caṇḍīkā* destroyed them with her arrows. On top of this, the bodies of the demons were injured by her weapons. The mystery of the firing of arrows has been explained before but bears retelling. The great lesson on the firing of arrows, as told in the *Upaniṣads*, '*Praṇava* is the bow, Self the arrow, *Brahmaṇ* the target'[3], is seen in this battle by *Śumbha* and *Niśumbha*. As spiritual seekers fire arrows of Self with bows of *Praṇava* at *Brahmaṇ*, their separate states become weak. As one discovers proper spirit, the roots of one's separate state as a worldly person are destroyed. This is the significance of the failure of the arrows and the bodily injuries of these *asura* leaders. If one understands the arrows from *Caṇḍīkā* as repeated, transient expressions of the spirit of awareness, then one can understand this message. This Self, Mother, this eternal, unperturbed Self, the more one tries to make it one's own, the more one is weakened. As the pure nature of *ātmā* brightens, attachment and ego become weak. If a seeker pays attention to this, the mystery of this battle by *Śumbha* and *Niśumbha* will be understood.

Verse 9.

niśumbho niśitaṁ khaḍgaṁ carma cādāya suprabham|
atāḍayan mūrdhni siṁhaṁ devyā vāhanamuttamam||

Translation:

(Then) *Śumbha* with shining sword and bright shield, hit the lion, great bearer of the Goddess, on its head.

Explanation:

In the battle with *Mahiṣāsura*, we have seen a similar attack on the head of the lion. With a sharp sword and shied, *Niśumbha* also attacked the lion on its head. His purpose is to disable the conductor of power of Mother, the lion-formed worldly person. His aim is that if this worldly person is disempowered, *Amvikā* would acknowledge the rule of *Niśumbha*.

One can argue here, as to where this lion as a worldly person comes from? The state as a worldly person ended with the destruction of *Raktavija*. A point to note is that awareness reflected in intelligence is the proper state of a being. This is described here as *Śumbha* and *Niśumbha*. Then where does the

3 *Muṇḍaka Upaniṣad*, 2.2.4.

carrier of the Goddess, the lion appear from? This argument is not wrong. The answer to it is that, although in a practical view, there is nothing more to a worldly person than awareness, yet, as long as ego and attachment remain, there is a force, although lacking pride of 'I am a worldly person', that is a special expression of Self. This has to be acknowledged and is here as the lion, a carrier for the Goddess.

There is an adjective, '*uttamam*' (the best) used for the lion. The carrier of the Goddess before this was relatively materialistic. It is now a very subtle flow of energy in the blissful sheath (*ānandamaya koṣa*). There is no expression of a material state. So, it is called an excellent carrier. During dreamless sleep (*suṣupti*), beings reside in the blissful sheath. At that time, they have no knowledge of material or subtle matters. But if it can be recalled that knowledge of ignorance remains, then one may comprehend this mystery.

Verse 10.

tāḍite vāhane devī kṣurapreṇāsimuttamam|
niśumbhasyāśu ciccheda carma cāpyaṣṭacandrakam||

Translation:

When her carrier was injured, the Goddess with the weapon *kṣurapra*, broke the great sword and shield which was marked by eight moons, of *Niśumbha*.

Explanation:

Seeing her great carrier, the lion injured, the Goddess used her *kṣurapra* weapon and destroyed the sword and the shield *Niśumbha*. The *kṣurapra* is a hoof-shaped sharp weapon. Its spiritual meaning is a power expressing the nature of Self. The power by which, the disturbances of a state of godhood are prevented, is described as the weapon *kṣurapra*. The prevention of disturbances described in Volume Two, in the destruction of *Cikṣura*, were disturbances of a state as a worldly person. The prevention of disturbances in this arena of the ego has to be understood as disturbances of a state of godhood because in this place there is no chance of disturbance as a worldly person. Whatever it is, the Goddess with her weapon destroyed the sword and shield of *Niśumbha*. One has to understand divisive knowledge as a sword and power covering the nature of Self as a shield.

There is a mystery in the mantra saying that the shield was marked by eight moons. The last subtle seeds of eight bondages, the destruction of which have been described before, are here described as a shield marked by eight moons. This shield is another name for a concealing force. When the self-expressed power of *ātmā* is ready to destroy *Niśumbha* or attachment, it tries to cover itself by a subtle force of concealment. This is of the nature of attachment. Mother destroys this too.

Verse 11.

chinne carmaṇi khaḍge ca śaktiṁ cikṣepa sohasuraḥ|
tāmapyasya dvidhā cakre cakreṇābhimukhāgatām||

Translation:

When his sword and shield were broken, the *asura* threw his energy weapon. When it approached the Goddess, she destroyed it with her discus.

Explanation:

Seeing his sword and shield broken, *Niśumbha* applied his energy weapon. The Goddess divided it with her discus. It is needless to say that the formerly mentioned powers of concealment and disturbance arise from the energy of root ignorance. The nature of the energy of ignorance has been acknowledged in Vedic scriptures. When the concealing and disturbing powers expressed from root ignorance are destroyed, then *Niśumbha* makes a final attempt. He holds on with all his might to root ignorance. This is described in this mantra as the use of an energy weapon. Mother disables it with her discus (*cakra*). The word '*cakra*' represents '*sudarṣana cakra*' or the 'circle of this universe.' The mystery of the *cakra* has been explained before. Whatever it is, when attachment goes forward to acquire *ātmā*, saying 'it is mine', then Mother holds the circle of this universe in front of it to prevent its action. The significance of this is that, a seeker out of ignorance, tries to get hold of *ātmā*, saying 'it is mine', but does not get hold of it. The powers of Self, the god-natured tendencies appear in front, and one grows an attachment to them. Attachment to feelings of non-Self has been completely removed. By the influence of high renunciation, powers of the states as worldly and divine are understood to be not accepted or rejected. Attachment only seeks *ātmā*, nothing else entices it. When Mother holds the circle of this universe in front of it and tries to stop his advance, it tries with greater energy to move towards *ātmā*. Although this attempt is usually a failure, there is some utility in this effort. As a seeker, by the force of root ignorance, tries to make *ātmā* one's own, feelings of attachment weaken. So, the mantra says that by the *cakra* of Mother, *Niśumbha* weakened. This is felt by the subtle senses of a seeker. Those who have attained these higher states will be able to understand this mystery.

Verse 12.

kopādhmāto niśumbhohatha śūlaṁ jagrāha dānavaḥ|
āyātaṁ muṣṭipātena devī taccāpyacūrṇayat||

Verse 13.

āvidhyātha gadāṁ sohapi cikṣepa caṇḍikāṁ prati|
sāpi devyās triśūlena bhinnā bhasmatvamāgatā||

Verse 14.

tataḥ paraśuhastaṁ tamāyāntaṁ daityapuṅgavam|
āhatya devī bāṇaughairapātayata bhūtale||

Translation:

Thereafter, being angered, the demon *Niśumbha* threw his lance. As the lance advanced, the Goddess, shattered it with her fist. Then *Niśumbha* twirled his mace and threw it at *Caṇḍīkā*.

It was shattered by her trident. Then the Goddess injured the approaching demon who had a double-edged axe (*paraśu)* in his hand and threw him to the ground.

Explanation:

The use of various weapons by *Niśumbha* and the Goddess is described in these three mantras. When *Niśumbha* threw his lance, the Goddess shattered it with her fist. When *Niśumbha* threw his mace, the Goddess broke it too. When he tried to use his double-edged axe. She injured him with her arrows and felled him to the ground. The lance is knowledge of the nature of self, a mace is the application of explicit words, recitation of hymns and praises. A *paraśu* is the perception of dual states. It is not necessary to repeat the spiritual significance of these weapons. The broad idea is that attachment repeatedly tries to keep its special identity and make Self its own. This feeling that 'I remain and you be only mine' is described as the wielding of various weapons by *Niśumbha*. If in a life of spiritual effort, this feeling truly appears, then one can freely say that one is honored. This is indeed the greatest state in the practice of devotional love. But, one cannot linger here. One has to move forward. We see that as much as *Niśumbha* tries, as much as he practices devotional love, attempts to taste Self and keep his own identity, Mother makes him fail. We see that *Caṇḍīkā* with her various weapons, that is, repeatedly throwing the light of nondual knowledge, removes any special identity of attachment. As a result, by the force of self-revealed *ātmā*, any special expressions of attachment weaken and lose identity. Perception of duality is lost for some duration. When attachment is unaware of any separate identity, it faints. This is also described in *Vaiṣṇav* literature. Fainting is the last state of the eight-fold *sattvik* states described in devotional scriptures. Saying 'mine, mine', and trying to get hold of *ātmā*, when the sense of 'me' disappears, only the nature of Self is lit up, only then proper love will appear. Do not think of the word 'faint' here as a loss of consciousness. Beings cannot be without consciousness when near the nature of consciousness. If you see that someone has lost consciousness when singing praises to God, then understand that one has not realized the nature of consciousness, let alone move close to it. Understand that those who become unconscious when remembering one who is consciousness, have not risen above the arena of the mind.

Verse 15.

tasminnipatite bhūmau niśumbhe bhīmavikrame|
bhrātaryatīva saṅkruddhaḥ prayayau hantumambikām|

Translation:

When his brave brother fainted and fell to the ground, *Śumbha* becoming very angry and moved to kill *Amvikā.*

Explanation:

Niśumbha is very brave. One day, it was attachment, who in this world, was attracted by wealth and lust. With severe effort and time, one moves it from such attractions toward *dharma.* Then attachment accepted *dharma* as its own. A long time after that, by the grace of Mother and inspiration of *guru*, one rids it of tendencies of *dharma* and brings it into the arena of spiritual enterprise (*sādhanā*). Then it understands this to be its own. Then, as a result of much good effort, it discovers the nature of Self and recognizes *ātmā.* Look where attachment has reached. Discarding all enticement, leaving behind all material and subtle states, it has arrived at the causal principle. It has come from lower levels to a much higher one. Yet, attachment has not been able to change its habit. Now it does not want anything but *ātmā.* It has discarded this world and is now prepared to acquire *ātmā.* But this too is divisive knowledge and Mother will destroy it. It has to be remembered here that when one reaches the knot of *Rudra*, all divisiveness that is mentioned is internal (*svagata*). There can be no divisiveness between similar or different distinctions. By the expression of the nondual nature of Mother, *Niśumbha* faints. There is no more expression of attachment. *Śumbha*, ego, moves in quickly to kill *Amvikā.* If Self can be destroyed, then the two brothers, ego and attachment can both remain safe. But alas, that is not possible.

Verse 16.

sa rathasthastathātyuccairgṛhītaparamāyudhaiḥ|
bhujairaṣṭābhiratulairvyāpyāśeṣaṁ babhau nabhaḥ|

Translation:

The demon *Śumbha*, on his chariot, holding great weapons in his eight hands, resplendent, filled the skies.

Explanation:

Śumbha is on his chariot. The chariot is the body. The body is three-fold, physical, subtle and causal. One has here to understand it as a causal body because the physical and subtle ones that held pride of self have been destroyed. The eight arms are the eight-fold states of right attribute (*sattva*). The sky is the space of intellect. Ego was displayed, in the sanctuary of a causal body, in the eight-fold states of *sattva*, filling intellect. By the practice of devotional love, eight-fold characteristics of right tendency, tremors, tears, etc. may be seen. A spiritual seeker must remember that these are not on a physical plane but in an ultra-natural one. 'Filling the skies' is the true nature of ego. When a spiritual seeker arrives in this arena of ego, this state may be observed. A very transparent, all-filling space of awareness is expressed as 'I.' One does not have the perception of physical or subtle bodies. The sense of 'I' seems to drown in a sense of unique, indefinable bliss. Characteristics of the right tendency are expressed. Arriving there, one perceives from a distance, the supreme form of *ātmā*, Mother *Amvikā*. A sense of 'I' entwined with percepts cannot witness the nature of *Amvikā*. Until one is bereft of all percepts, until one is a naked 'I', one cannot climb onto the lap of the unadorned Mother. But that is something else.

Verse 17.

tamāyāntaṁ samālokya devī śaṅkhamavādayat|
jyāśabdaṁñcāpi dhanuṣaścakārātīva duḥsaham||

Verse 18.

pūrayāmāsa kakubho nijaghaṇṭāsvanena ca|
samastadaityasainyānāṁ tejovadhavidhāyinā||

Translation:

Seeing him (*Śumbha*) approach, the Goddess sounded her conch shell and twanged her bow loudly. She filled the horizons with the sound of her incredible hand-bell, which drained the power of the demon warriors.

Explanation:

Seeing ego covering everything, the Goddess created sounds with her conch shell, bell and bowstring. The conch shell and bell are unvoiced sounds (*Anāhata nada*), the bowstring, *Praṇava nada*. *Nada* here is not the voiced (*vaikhari*) sound but subtle ones like *madhymā* and *paśyanti*. As long as there is the perception of duality, *nada* remains. The differences are in physicality or subtlety. This subtle *nada* is especially of use in destroying the valor of demon warriors. When one is tormented by demonic feelings, if attention is focused on unvoiced *nada*, and *Praṇava* is chanted, then any attack is calmed. This has been mentioned in *Devī Māhātmya* from the beginning. Physical demons, lust or anger, and subtle ones, like ego, are all overcome by unvoiced *nada*. Their power diminishes. It has been said, that Mother went into battle. This is clear in these mantras. When one begins to meditate or tries to subdue demonic tendencies, spiritual seekers who have sought refuge will see that from inside, Mother conducts the right spiritual enterprises. It is as if these methods appear by themselves. Remember, she is directing this. This is her battle.

Verse 19.

tataḥ siṁho mahānādaistyājitebhamahāmadaiḥ|
pūrayāmāsa gaganaṁ gāmtathopadiśo daśa||

Verse 20.

tataḥ kālī samutpatya gaganaṁ kṣmāmatāḍayat|
karābhyāṁ tanninādena prāksvanāste tirohitāḥ||

Translation:

Thereafter, the lion began uttering terrible roars that destroyed the great pride of the elephant, and filled the sky, earth and all ten directions. *Kāli* rose to the skies and with her palms, beat on the earth. This sound obscured all the previous ones.

Explanation:

The roars from the lion, which is the joyful sound of success by worldly persons, mixed with unvoiced *nada* and *Praṇava*, filled heaven and earth. That is, from the principle of earth to that of space, all of them were perturbed. This mantra points to very subtle conditions of the five material elements. There is an adjective used for the sound of the lion, 'destroyed the great pride of the elephant.' The word '*ibha*' means elephant, that is mind. The great pride of mind, that is, its constant movement, was removed by roars of the worldly person as a lion.

When spiritual seekers see that subtle unvoiced *nada* is arising with subtler *Praṇava*, then they too can raise shouts of joy and destroy unconquerable disturbances of the mind elephant. Your hopes will be fulfilled. When this combination of sounds filled the earth and skies, *Kālī* with her palms began to beat on the ground. That is, she removed any expression of the earth principle. By this noise, all previous sounds were drowned out. It is because of the earth principle that other feelings and sounds are expressed. When it is beaten by the palms of *Kālī*, other sounds are drowned out. A spiritual seeker has to realize a material expression of feeling by ego with the words 'earth principle', then these mysteries may be easily understood.

Verse 21.

aṭṭāṭṭahāsamaśivaṁ śivadūtī cakāra ha|
taiḥ śabdairasurāstresuḥ śumbhaḥ kopaṁ paraṁ yayau||

Translation:

There was loud, ominous laughter from *Śivadūtī*. These sounds made the other demons fearful, but *Śumbha* was angered.

Explanation:

The one who had previously sent *Īśāna* (*Śiva*) as a messenger to stop *Śumbha* from engaging in battle, that Goddess *Caṇḍīkā*, laughed loudly. This was inauspicious for the demons. This loud laughter made the demons wary but angered *Śumbha*. Laughter is an expression of blissful nature. The laughter of *Śivadūtī* is like a ray of lightning, a momentary expression of supreme Self that is beyond words and mind. This laughter is inauspicious for the demons because it destroys their own state. They become very fearful of a momentary expression of *paramātmā* because they lose their identities. This is a fearful state. When demons tend to lose their nature, they grab on to it.

In this manner, as Mother laughs, any separate state as a worldly person disappears and demonic tendencies are frightened. On the other hand, the center of all the demonic states, *Śumbha* or ego is angered. He becomes determined to destroy any expression of Self that is about to destroy his special state.

Verse 22.

durātmaṁstiṣṭha tiṣṭheti vyājahārāmbikā yadā|
tadā jayetyabhihitaṁ devairākāśasaṁsthitaiḥ||

Translation:

"O wicked one, wait." As *Amvikā* said this to *Śumbha*, the gods gave shouts of victory in the sky.

Explanation:

Mother addresses *Śumbha* as 'wicked.' Ego, reflecting *ātmā*, wants to be known as the nature of *ātmā*. This is the evilness of ego, so Mother addresses it as 'wicked.' Mother says, 'Wait in a little while you will be destroyed.' When Mother begins the destruction of *Śumbha* within a short time, the deities of special consciousnesses, residing in the intellectual skies, give cries of victory. They will soon be rid of the torment by demons and will no longer be under the control of the terrible ego-natured *asura*. The great day for enjoying the nature of Self is near. The joyous gods shout for victory.

When a spiritual seeker sees these auspicious signs on a road to progress, they can be sure that before long, their hopes will be fulfilled. As long as the gods do not face Self, as long as consciousness established in the senses does not desire to enjoy *ātmā* with great joy, until then, Self cannot be found. When one sees that senses, mind, life force and intelligence are tuned together, and moving towards Self with great joy, then obtaining Mother is inevitable. Just cry for Mother and say, 'come close to me, hold my hands and take me on your lap. I will dance with arms raised and return to my home.' If you say this with simplicity, Mother will appear and the gods will help. Your 'I'-ness will disappear, you will be united forever with the heart of Mother.

Verse 23.

śumbhenāgatya yā śaktirmuktā jvālātibhīṣaṇā|
āyāntī vahnikūṭābhā sā nirastā maholkayā||

Verse 24.

siṁhanādena śumbhasya vyāptaṁ lokatrayāntaram|
nirghātaniḥsvano ghoro jitavānavanīpate||

Translation:

Approaching the Goddess, *Śumbha* applied a terrible power weapon with tongues of fire. Coming like a conflagration, it was disarmed by the *maholkā* weapon from the Goddess. Then, *Śumbha* filled the three worlds with his lion-like roars. But, O king, great sounds like thunder from the Goddess overcame his roars.

Explanation:

The change in the fate of *Śumbha* is described in these two mantras. Both his power weapon and his lion-like roars fail. Ego wants to apply its power and bring *ātmā* into a worldly state to enjoy it. This is the mystery of the power weapon of *Śumbha*. This power appears like a great conflagration because when it is expressed, the all-pervading nature of 'I' covers Self. But, the nature of Self is even more dense and bright, so when it even momentarily falls on Self, ego is overcome. This is the secret of the *maholkā* (great comet) weapon of Mother. Whenever ego tries to raise its special nature with enterprise, *ātmā* lights up momentarily. So, all applications of power fail.

Seeing his power weapon fail, *Śumbha* roared like a lion. The sounds of thunder from Mother drowned them out. Truly, the sounds of 'I'-ness of *Śumbha* fill the three worlds. Ego sees that 'there is nothing else but me, all states are me.' This is the lion roar of *Śumbha*. But, O king Suratha, now his nature is overcome. Now sounds of thunder in the skies have overcome the lion roars of *Śumbha*. These sudden sounds of thunder are nothing but momentary, lightning-like emanations of *ātmā*. By its expression, ego is weakened. It doubts its existence. The feeling of 'I am' is doubting its existence. A hint of knowledge as to whether it is me or Self appears. As this knowledge appears, ego is weakened. If eternal existence appears even for a moment, reflected existence is weakened. Spiritual seekers will realize this in their hearts.

Verse 25.

śumbhamuktāñcharān devī śumbhastat prahitāñcharān|
ciccheda svaśarairugraiḥ śataśohatha sahasraśaḥ||

Verse 26.

tataḥ sā caṇḍikā kruddhā śūlenābhijaghāna tam|
sa tadābhihato bhūmau mūrcchito nipapāta ha||

Translation:

The Goddess cut down thousands of arrows shot by *Śumbha* with her own and *Śumbha* did the same to thousands of arrows from the Goddess. Angered by this, the Goddess hit *Śumbha* with her lance. Injured, *Śumbha* fainted and fell to the ground.

Explanation:

The battle between *ātmā* and ego is a battle between object and image. A spiritual seeker should notice that 'I'-ness connected to feelings does not want to lose itself in any manner. It wants to save 'I' in a sanctuary of all states. These are the thousands of arrows shot by *Śumbha*. On the other hand, the power of awareness of the Goddess expresses its nature and destroys these sanctuaries of ego. This is the mystery of the battle between *Śumbha* and Mother.

After this, being struck by the lance from Goddess *Caṇḍīkā*, *Śumbha* fainted. The significance of the words, 'hit by the lance' is the expression of the spirit of knowledge. This has been said before. The striking with a lance is pointing to the fact that 'I' is of the nature of knowledge, it does not have the nature of knower or known. The moment this perception appears, ego faints or disappears. Momentarily, universality and spread of ego are lost, such is the self-expression of Mother. When she is expressed, all other states disappear. Nothing remains. What remains, cannot be expressed by words. It is 'I' without 'I', or the true nature of 'I.' It is the true 'I', the 'that I am' (*sohahaṁ*), *ātmā*. It cannot be expressed by 'the Sun, Moon, or stars, lightning is not expressed there, nor fire'[4], only 'I' exists, pure, blissful *ātmā*. When it is expressed, ego faints.

Verse 27.

tato niśumbhaḥ samprāpya cetanāmāttakārmukaḥ|
ājaghāna śarairdevīṁ kālīṁ kesariṇaṁ tathā||

4 *na tatra sūryo bhāti na candra . . . Kaṭha Upaniṣad*, 2.2.15

Verse 28.

punaśca kṛtvā bāhūnāmayutaṁ danujeśvaraḥ|
cakrāyudhena ditijaśchādayāmāsa caṇḍikām||

Translation:

Thereafter, *Niśumbha*, regaining consciousness, took his bow and injured *Kālī* and the lion with his arrows. The ruler of *Danu*, son of *Diti*, *Niśumbha*, spread his ten thousand hands and showered *Caṇḍīkā* with *cakra* weapons.

Explanation:

So long, *Niśumbha* had been unconscious. When *Śumbha* lost consciousness from being hit by the lance of Mother, *Niśumbha* regained consciousness and taking his bow, aimed arrows at *Kālī* and the lion. This is how ego and attachment torment a spiritual seeker. When one is weakened, the other extends its influence. The mystery of attachment firing his arrows is progress towards *ātmā* saying 'it is mine.' The anger of *Niśumbha* is towards destructive power and the carrier of the Goddess. It is because of the destructive power that nothing remains. It is *Kālī* who has not left anything to be called one's own, having devoured all. The lion always damages the state as a worldly person. *Niśumbha* fires arrows at both of them.

In this mantra, *Niśumbha* has been called the ruler of *Danu* and the son of *Diti*. They are the names of the same person, the wife of *Kaśyapa*. The words '*danu*' and '*diti*' come from the divisive root '*do*.' The power that divides undivided perception, that is, holds on to divisiveness is *diti* or *danu*. The word '*kaśyapa*' means seer (*paśyaka*). By rules of grammar, the word '*kaśyapa*' transposes letters to become '*paśayka*.' This is not an imaginary explanation given by us, but explained by Vedic authors of *Nirukta*[5]. The wives of *Kaśyapa* are *Diti* and *Aditi*. All-expressive *Brahmaṇ* has twin powers, one external and one internal. The sons of *Diti* or *Danu* are demons (*dānava*)and those of *Aditi* are the *adityas* or deities. One faces inside, the others outside. One divides the nature of Self, the other unites with it.

---

5 Texts of etymology and interpretation of words in *Vedas*.

The knowledge of 'mine' is the first seed of divisiveness. That there is nothing else but 'me' is true knowledge. But, for whatever reason, on that undivided 'I', there appears a sense of 'mine.' Then there appears a sense of a second, other than 'me.' That is, one perceives a nature of something other than Self. This is the nature of all demonic feelings. So, the demons are called children of *Diti* or *Danuja*. Because attachment is the refuge of all divisive knowledge, *Niśumbha* has been called the ruler of *Danuja*.

Spreading ten thousand arms, *Niśumbha* covered *Caṇḍīkā* with his *cakra* weapons. This is something to think about. The final attack by attachment is a feeling of affection for *ātmā*. It is from this feeling of affection that modern *Vaiṣṇava dharma* was established. Saying my lord, my father, my companion, my friend, my consort, spiritual enterprise is begun by connecting to *paramātmā* with these various relationships. It ends here with the destruction of *Niśumbha*. Nothing remains that is 'mine', everything becomes 'I.' As long as saying 'mine' keeps something else other than *ātmā*, till then the word 'mine' is not used correctly. When all feelings are destroyed, when self-expressed *ātmā* appears in front, only then does true affection towards *ātmā* emerge. Any feeling of affection that is seen before this is only a beginning. This proper attachment applies the *cakra* weapon with ten thousand arms to cover *Caṇḍīkā*. With innumerable feelings, through the senses, it tries to establish affection with *ātmā*. Feelings that are vested on *ātmā* by attachment, return to attachment. They are sent back to *ātmā* but again return to perceptions of attachment. It is aimed at this circular movement that the mantra mentions a *cakra* (discus) weapon. When proper meditation occurs, the truth of this is realized in viewing *ātmā*, hearing its call and receiving its sweet odor and taste. It is by these sense pathways, that one approaches *paramātmā*, which is without sight, sound, form or flavor. It is by spreading ten thousand arms that one has to attack nature that is beyond feeling. In the language of the *Vaiṣṇava*, all this is in a territory beyond nature. Although subtle principles of ego and attachment are in the arena of nature, they are so imbued with consciousness, that there is no harm in saying that they are beyond nature. It is unnecessary to tell a smart seeker that here, these matters of sight and sound are not of the usual senses organs.

Verse 29.

tato bhagavatī kruddhā durgā durgārtināśinī|
ciccheda tani cakrāṇi svaśaraiḥ sāyakāṁśca tān||

Translation:

The Goddess who removes the sorrow of people who are in trouble, became angered and shattered the cakras thrown by *Niśumbha*, with her arrows.

Explanation:

Children who are in trouble have called for Mother. Seeing no relief from torment by these demons, they have called on the all-providing Mother. They called on *Durgā* with simplicity. So, *Bhagavatī* Mother, in six-fold grandeur, in the form of angry *Caṇḍīkā*, has made the weapons of attachment fail. Her weapon is her arrows, arrows of Self. Shooting arrows of self-expression moment by moment, when Mother appears, all weapons and enterprises by the demons fail. Such is the nature of *ātmā* that when it appears, no one else can be found. It is the expression of the nature of Self that destroys all other states. Flows of divisiveness of attachment weaken. The yoga scriptures call this 'a condition of weakened burdens' (*prakṣiṇa kleśāvasthā*). Those who have stopped inclinations of spirit, and try to weaken the burden of attachment and other pains, use special techniques. However, we have found an old, but ever-new path. We have understood that when my Mother expresses herself, burdens become weak. Mother is easily expressed by our feelings of seeking refuge. The establishment of truth and life force is the foundation of this spiritual effort. But these are away from the discussion here.

Verse 30.

tato niśumbho vegena gadāmādāya caṇḍikām|
abhyadhāvata vai hantuṁ daityasainyasamāvṛtaḥ||

Verse 31.

tasyāpatata evāśu gadāṁ ciccheda caṇḍikā|
khaḍgena śitadhāreṇa sa ca śūlaṁ samādade||

Translation:

After this, surrounded by demon warriors, with mace in hand, *Niśumbha* moved forward to kill *Caṇḍīkā*. With her sharp scimitar, *Caṇḍīkā*, broke the mace in the hand of *Niśumbha*. Then *Niśumbha* took up a lance.

Explanation:

The meanings of mace, lance and the other weapons have been explained before. Attachment wants to take *ātmā* as 'mine'. *Caṇḍīkā* with her sharp scimitar, the expression of her nature, destroys all attempts by attachment. Here, expression of nondual knowledge that destroys divisiveness may be called a sharp scimitar. In ancient texts, special knowledge (*vijñana*) has been called a sword. If knowledge of 'one and only' is expressed even momentarily, all divisive knowledge is disarmed. Then, attachment takes up his last weapon, a lance. The nature of knowledge in which ignorance of attachment is established has been here called a trident. Tri-fold knowledge is a trident. The inner difference that exists in a state of 'I am meeting Self' is the lance of *Niśumbha*.

Verse 32.

śūlahastaṁ samāyāntaṁ niśumbhamamarārdanam|
hṛdi vivyādha śūlena vegāviddhena caṇḍikā||

Verse 33.

bhinnasya tasya śūlena hṛdayānniḥsṛtohaparaḥ|
mahābalo mahāvīryastiṣṭheti puruṣo vadan||

Translation:

Seeing the heroic *Niśumbha* approaching with his lance, *Caṇḍīkā* quickly threw her own lance at his heart. His chest was split by it, and a very powerful man came out from it crying "Wait, Wait."

Explanation:

My mother *Caṇḍīkā*, with her lance, broke the lance of *Niśumbha*, making his tri-fold knowledge fail. By expressing her nondual nature, she pierced his heart. If the heart is not pierced in this manner, if knowledge of duality is not torn apart, if nondual knowledge is not lit up, we have no other means for success. O Mother, today you have arrived at the gates of a temple of freedom and pierced the heart of nondual knowledge of divisiveness with your lance. This action began in ancient times. From time immemorial the heart has been wounded, yet it did not wake us up. Mother, when with great affection, I embraced wealth as 'mine', I did not understand that it was you as wealth. With divisive knowledge, I held them as material things, and you with a painful lance of knowledge would move them away from me. I would cry, 'I am lost.' Then, when I held my spouse, children and friends as 'mine', I did not realize that they were nothing but you. You would move them away with your lance and tear my heart apart. In this manner, not one day, but for so many lifetimes, I have taken wounds of your lance to my heart. I have cried and endured terrible pain, yet again and again have been engrossed by divisive knowledge and forgotten you. You have struck me with your lance repeatedly to wake me up. I have endured your attacks on my injured heart. Yet, I did not see your figure of grace and did not understand. Being engrossed by delusions of inertness, I ignored your grace and ran around outside. At that time, the action of your lance was very painful. But today, I accept the injuries to my heart as very necessary. I have nothing more to say. My voice chokes up, crying 'Mother, Mother.'

Whatever it is, attachment is first expressed based on physical materials, then in material-based consciousness and later in pure consciousness. When attachment seeks pure consciousness, then proper devotion or the *dharma* of love can be practiced. Then, as the love of Self deepens, attachment is shielded. Only when pure, perception natured Self is expressed, is attachment destroyed. This is briefly the mystery of the death of *Niśumbha* by piercing with the lance of *Caṇḍīkā*.

There is another issue in this mantra. When *Niśumbha* was killed, a powerful man emerged from his heart. This person is none else but consciousness established in attachment. The nature of consciousness in which a special feeling of attachment is expressed is the person emerging from the heart of *Niśumbha*. When the feeling of attachment is destroyed, the consciousness established in it is not destroyed. On emerging, it asks the Goddess to wait. He intends that as long as I am here, even if you destroy *Niśumbha*, I can create a thousand of him again when I wish. If seeds remain, how long will they take to germinate?

Verse 34.

tasya niṣkrāmato devī prahasya svanavattataḥ|
śiraściccheda khaḍgena tatohasāvapatadbhuvi||

Translation:

Laughing loudly the Goddess severed the head of the man emerging from the heart of *Niśumbha* with her scimitar. He fell to the ground.

Explanation:

Caṇḍīkā, with a stroke of her scimitar, by the light of the knowledge of nonduality, severed the head of consciousness established in attachment. The end of pride that 'I am attachment' is the severing of the head of the man emerging from the heart of *Niśumbha*. The pride of *Śumbha* regarding *Niśumbha* is destroyed in this manner. The thought in the mind of *Śumbha* that 'I have a brother' is removed. Attachment is but a special feeling of ego. By expression of the nature of Mother, by appearance of a sharp sword of nondual knowledge, it is removed. Attachment is gone forever. Now *Śumbha* is without any other support.

A spiritual seeker has been told that if one is not completely alone, one cannot find the 'supreme one.' Look, after all this time, *Śumbha* is properly alone. So now, it will not be long before he alights on nondual principle. Attachment is at the root of all divisive knowledge that brings sorrow. Now that root has been destroyed. So, it is possible to alight on the nature of bliss. Dear seeker, sing in joy. The world is filled by bliss. I see only a blissful world. Mother has let us discover her pouring out bliss. My Mother is the blissful one, I am her affectionate child. I see a world full of bliss, removing all sorrow.

Verse 35.

tataḥ siṁhaścakhādogradaṁṣṭrākṣuṇṇaśirodharān|
asurāṁstāṁstathā kālī śivadūtī tathāparān||

Translation:

Thereafter, the lion piercing the necks of warriors of *Niśumbha* with his sharp teeth, began to devour them. *Śivadūtī* also began to devour the other demons.

Explanation:

The excellent carrier of the Goddess, this worldly person in the form of a lion, began to chew on the followers of attachment. The goddess *Śivadūtī* also began to devour other demonic percepts. It is needless to say that as attachment is destroyed, other tendencies residing with it are easily destroyed. I have said that tendencies of divinity are the warriors of *Śumbha* and *Niśumbha.* A wish to reach a God-like position and a desire for immense powers were inherent in attachment. Now, by expression of pure, nondual principle, any special longing to reach a state of Godhood is destroyed. To destroy these tendencies, spiritual seekers, *Śivadūtī* and the other eight powers all work together. They are able to destroy the demon warriors within a short time. The next mantra describes the destruction of demons by the eight powers.

Verse 36.

kaumārīśaktinirbhinnāḥ kecinneśurmahāsurāḥ|
brahmāṇīmantrapūtena toyenānye nirākṛtāḥ||

Verse 37.

māheśvarītriśūlena bhinnāḥ petustathāpare|
vārāhītuṇḍaghātena keciccūrṇīkṛtā bhuvi||

Verse 38.

khaṇḍaṁ khaṇḍañca cakreṇa vaiṣṇavyā dānavāḥ kṛtāḥ
vajreṇa caindrīhastāgravimuktena tathāpare

Translation:

Some of the great demons were pierced by the power weapon of *Kaumārī*. Some others were disabled by sacred water from *Brahmāṇī*. Some by the trident of *Māheśarī*, some by tusks of *Vārāhī*, fell to the ground. Then *Vaiṣṅavī* cut them into pieces with a discus. *Indrāṇī* killed some demons by shooting bolts of lightning.

Explanation:

Attachment has fallen. His *asura* followers are subdued by the *mātṛkās*. Although the mantra mentions six powers, *Kaumārī*, *Brahmāṇī*, *Māheśarī*, *Vārāhī*, *Vaiṣṅavī* and *Indrāṇī*, from the circumstances, eight-fold powers have to be understood. They are the ones who previously, in the destruction of *Raktavija*, killed the eight-fold demons of the eight bondages like hatred and shame. Here again, they end the eight-fold god-like wealth of subtle tendencies, like atomicity and the others. Even pride of Godhood is an obstacle to the knowledge of Self. Without renunciation to a state of Godhood, the *asura* of attachment, *Niśumbha* is not destroyed. Many spiritual seekers, after arriving here, are engrossed by desires for eight treasures, by a desire for Godhood. Understanding pure knowledge of Self to be an inert state like dreamless sleep, (*suṣupti*), they stop. By good actions from the past, by unconditional grace of *guru* and incomparable love from Mother, a seeker may be saved from this enticement of Godhood.

As long as attachment remains, it is natural to be attracted by a desire for Godhood. Without the grace of Mother, until she appears as the eight-fold powers, the attraction of the eight treasures is not removed. Renunciation of the state of a worldly person is not difficult. It has been enjoyed for innumerable lifetimes. One can renunciate with ease what has been enjoyed for a very long. But a state of Godhood is rare. Until one is established in the principle of wholeness, in the supreme, one cannot perceive the nature of godhood. When a seeker travels focused on the nature of *paramātmā*, then on the journey, an incredible opportunity to enjoy Godhood appears. There are very few in this world, who can consider this to be of no importance and ignore it. Only those, in whose hearts, the great power of Mother is established as supreme strength and great renunciation, may be relieved of this very powerful inducement. Seekers in spiritual battles have from the beginning sought sanctuary at the feet of Mother. They do not know the state of worldly persons or that of godhood, liberation or bondage, knowledge or devotion. They only know Mother. Under all conditions, they are unclothed children on the lap of Mother. So, Mother appears for them y, divides herself as eight-fold powers, and removes the enticement of the eight-fold treasures. They are freed from the danger of a state of godhood and considering this world to be not important, in great joy, move towards the supreme state of *paramātmā.* This is clearly stated by the principles of *Caṇḍī.*

Verse 39.

kecidvineśurasurāḥ kecinnaṣṭā mahāhavāt|
bhakṣitāścāpare kālī-śivadūtī-mṛgādhipaiḥ||

iti śriimārkaṇḍeyapurāṇe sāvarṇik manvantare devīmāhātmye niśumbhavadho|

Translation:

Some of the demons were killed in battle, some disappeared from the battlefield, and the rest were devoured by *Kālī*, *Śivadūtī* and the lion.

Here ends this episode of the destruction of *Niśumbha*, in *Devī Māhātmya*, in the era of *Sāvarṇi*, in *Mārkeṇḍeya Purāṇa*.

Explanation:

All the demons other than *Śumbha* were destroyed. In this mantra, describing the plight of these demons, the sage says, some of the demons were killed, some ran away and others were devoured by *Kālī*, *Śivadūtī* and the lion. Among these, those that were killed will not reappear. The significance is that some demonic tendencies will disappear forever. They will not reappear as fixed habits. Some other tendencies, (like eating and movement), will reappear when one is awake. These are noted in the mantra as warriors that fled from the battlefield. This has been mentioned before, but there is no harm in repetition. These principles are very difficult. A realization of nonduality is challenging. So, it is necessary to discuss them repeatedly.

All tendencies are destroyed when one alights on the principle of nonduality. When one awakens from it, some tendencies of a worldly state reappear. As long as a physical body remains, they continue, but they can no longer do any harm, that is, they cannot again establish false knowledge. Their aptitude is destroyed. Some tendencies remain, (establishment of *dharma*, distribution of knowledge, teaching) being conducted solely by the wish and direction of Mother. These actions are not expressed without the special inspiration from Mother. It is aimed at these that the mantra speaks of demons being devoured by *Śivadūtī*. Those who were devoured by *Śivadūtī*, if needed, that is, if inspired by supreme power, those tendencies could come back. They would no longer be harmful because they follow supreme wishes. They cannot engross the seeker. The point is that, once one meets nondual principle, divisiveness, error, fear of bondage and death of a seeker are removed forever. Then, as long as a physical body remains, a seeker waits for the erosion of prior tendencies. At the end of this, one attains liberation beyond a body (*videha kaivalya*).

Come, let us seek the feet of Mother and try to understand the destruction of *Śumbha*. As long as strong prior tendencies remain, *Śumbha* is not destroyed. The true principle of nonduality is not revealed. Let us cry for Mother. Come, let us be eager to see Mother. Let us leave even the desire for Godhood and be overcome by unconditional love. Mother will surely pick us up and carry us to that kingdom of purity. All our hopes will be fulfilled.

Here ends the explanations on the destruction of *Niśumbha*, in *Sādhan Samar* or *Devī Māhātmya.*

Chapter 10

Destruction of *Śumbha*

Verse 1.

ṛṣiruvāca|
niśumbhaṁ nihataṁ dṛṣṭvā bhrātaraṁ prāṇasammitamḥ|
hanyamānaṁ balañcaiva śumbhaḥ kruddhohabravīd vacaḥ||

Verse 2.

balāvalepaduṣṭe tvaṁ mā durge garvvamāvaha|
anyāsāṁ balamāśritya yuddhyase cātimāninī||

Translation:

Seeing his dearest brother slain and his warriors destroyed, *Śumbha* was very angered and said, "O, *Durgā*! Because of pride of power, you have risen too much. Do not be proud. Because, even though you are so proud, you are fighting in the shelter of the powers of others."

Explanation:

The dear brother of *Śumbha* has been slain. Attachment, the close ally of ego, with all the tendencies of duality have been destroyed. Now ego is without support, alone. Yet, he is not without hope, not tired, he has enthusiasm and a deep desire for revenge and sacrifice. That is why the mantra says that *Śumbha*, in anger, said to the Goddess, 'O you are so appalling with your power, so full of pride and arrogance. I see that you are full of pride, but do not see anything that you have to be so proud of. Your power is that of others. You are fighting with the power of *Brahmāṇī* and the other *mātṛkās* and so were able to destroy all these demons. What is your greatness in this, that you are so proud?'

The words of *Śumbha* to the Goddess are beautiful. *Ātmā*, my awareness-formed Mother is truly very proud. There is no one else. There is nothing that can diminish the pride of *ātmā*. *Ātmā* is the true 'I.' Pride is the nature of one who is the true 'I.' Why she is so proud, Mother will say in the next mantra. The 'I' that was to be searched for at the beginning of *Sādhan Samar*, in the *Devī Sukta*, after many changes in fortune, we have arrived at that 'I.' Now we can see the undivided influence and glory of 'I' natured Mother. We have to progress slowly.

One is the reflection of 'I', the other, the reflected 'I.' One is ego, the other *ātmā* or power of awareness. One, is the state of awareness, the other, awareness itself. After all this time, the two face each other. After untiring spiritual efforts of innumerable lifetimes, no, by the intense attraction of love of Mother and *guru*, one has arrived in front of Mother *Amvikā*, *ātmā*. One is honored. Honored is the child.

Listen, it is the nature of the ego that it wishes to see itself as supreme God. It understands *ātmā* to be without any physical characteristics, without any physical state, something very unusual, very strange. It analyzes and concludes that there is no harm in considering this which is beyond words and thought, to be inert. What is there of which this can be proud? But, how can one call *ātmā* inert? One can see that all energy is established in it. If there are no powers, if there is no expression of energy, then it could be inert. Maybe it can be overcome. It is with this thought that *Śumbha* says that the Goddess is empowered by others. His thought is that if the power of awareness took the help of other powers to destroy the demons, it can be overcome.

The words that *Śumbha* spoke to the Goddess also reveal a deeper aspiration. *Tattva Prakāshikā* has also mentioned this. Taking individual words forming the mantra, one can say, she is the one who can weaken the powerful (*balābale*). Mother who can weaken any strong feelings of pride is truly powerful. One who removes all wicked sentiments is '*apaduṣtā*.' The word '*durgā*' means one who brings relief from danger or the one who is difficult to know. '*tvaṁ mā*', means you are Mother. Because you hold all feelings, maternity is expressed by you. So, you are the only one who can be proud (*tvaṁ garvaṁ āvaha*). All feelings are expressed by you. They are given spirit by your spirit. They are empowered by your consciousness. So, you are the only one who can be proud.

You battle with the power of others. You are without any change, without characteristics or results. When you battle you have to use the power of others, you use these other natures (*parā prakṛti*). In *Bhāgavat Gitā*, the Lord called this other power *ātmamāyā* or nature of Self.[1] When pure *ātmā* without characteristics, has to battle, when it has to come into duality, it has to take refuge in other powers of itself. Just as we have to seek the help of the power of sight to discern the shape of something, or of the power of hearing to receive sound, pure *ātmā*, to come into a realm of feeling, needs power. These powers are expressed in the shelter of *ātmā* and arise from it. This has also to be understood as the emergence of *Caṇḍīkā* and the other powers from the body of the Goddess. Our Mother, who is the source of all powers, refuge of all energies, why will she not be proud? The root '*mān*' means worship. My Mother is to be worshipped, to be honored. No one else has the right to be proud. All pride is with 'I.' When 'I' is only Mother, when no one else is 'I', when no other has the right to say 'I', then the one who is 'I' has to be honored, can be proud.

Does the reader understand why those who find Mother, those who have discovered Self, why they do not have pride? When one finds one who is truly the figure of pride, then false pride, reflected pride is gone forever. So, *Brahmaṇ*-realized persons are without pride. Remember that without seeing Mother, pride can never be removed. Do not try to think of yourself as poor and low to get rid of pride. Even that has pride hiding in it. Look upon true Self, false pride will go away.

Verse 3.

devyuvāca|
ekaivāhaṁ jagatyatra dvitīyā kā mamāparā|
paśyaitā duṣṭa mayyeva viśantyo madvibhūtayaḥ||

1 *Bhāgabat Gitā*, 4.6.

Translation:

The Goddess said, "In this universe, only I exist. Who else is there second to me? O wicked one, look, my powers enter back into me."

Explanation:

After all this time, my Mother expresses her real nature. Whatever scriptures may be discussed or severe spiritual exercises conducted, as long as Mother does not express her nature, no one can discover her spirit. To find Mother, to understand her nature, to receive her, one has to surrender at her feet. Just as a bride receives a groom, one has to surrender to Mother. Then she expresses her real nature. This has been said in different ways in many places. For those who have practiced this with all their effort, Mother has expressed her nature to them. Whatever it is, 'in this universe, only I exist, who else is there second to me?'

Seeing the expression 'in this universe', different commentators have given different meanings. We will not go into any discourse on all the finer meanings. We will try to understand this in simple language. All that which is experienced as 'this universe' is Mother. As long as there is the perception of a universe, understand it to be nothing else but Mother. Truly this universe has no other nature but that of 'I.' This universe is the physical expression of 'I.' One has to understand mind, intelligence, etc. by 'universe.'

By the words, 'who else is there second to me.' all duality is negated. Just as the words of *śrutis*, 'one without a second' (*ekamevādvitīyam*), signifies one without any similar or dissimilar division, the words of Mother are the same. Although, there is something special here. Discussing the previous word from *śrutis*, one can understand the spirit of something without any divisions, but one cannot make out its nature. To understand its nature, one has to use indirect statements, 'not big or small', 'truth, knowledge, bliss' and direct ones like 'I am *Brahmaṇ*' and 'you are that.' But in this self-description by the Goddess, direct words, 'only I', express both spirit and nature together. One is not satisfied just saying that Mother is beyond words and thought. A child wants to see, understand and hold Mother. So, one is not satisfied with 'not small, not big.' Mother expresses directly as 'I.' Even the very wicked will know and feel this. Mother does not hide from anyone. So, the *Gitā* says that even the most wicked are fit to worship God.

'I' (*ahaṁ*) that was mentioned at the beginning of *Devī Sukta* in the mantra '*ahaṁ rudrevi*' and others, through many percepts, and through the establishment of truth, life force and bliss, continue to be explained in different ways. But until now, the true nature of the *ahaṁ* has not been appreciated. Mother by her grace is removing this ignorance. She expresses her nature. What the *śrutis* have called 'One', Mother says 'only.' That *ahaṁ* without second is of the nature of energy is expressed clearly by using the feminine gender '*ekā*.' Its nature as energy in this universe is established. These are not only our words, *śrutis* and the philosophies accept this as the power of awareness. We have discussed this before. Let us now instead of debating, accept the words of Mother. As long as we are in this universe, that is, as long as knowledge of this universe is expressed, we have to understand Mother as formed of energy. This energy is not multiple, it is one without a second. She is expressed in all beings as *ahaṁ*. It is unique, without a second. Why only that, look at every tree, every leaf, every grain of sand, they are all unique. Even coming into the material zone, in divisiveness, the uniqueness of Mother is not diminished even a tiny fraction. When we leave this material world and enter one of consciousness, not a trace of divisiveness can be seen. In the physical, subtle, or causal, Mother is one and only. This is her nature.

Another meaning can be drawn from 'who is second to me' (*dvitīyā kā mamāparā*). All that is perceived as second to me is minor, to be discarded (*dvitīyā mamāparā kā*). All that is perceived other than *ahaṁ* ('I') can be discarded because they are not substance, they are applications of *ahaṁ*. The only substance is *ahaṁ*. All else that appears to be with *ahaṁ* is usage. Usage cannot be substance. Just as your eating and moving are not substances, so is the visible world using *ātmā*, Mother. *Vedāntins* do not accept the nature of this universe, only a functional state. Truly, this universe does not have an existential nature.

Let us try to understand the other half of the words. She says, 'O wicked one, look, my powers enter back into me.' Being a reflection, ego wants to take over the actions of the reflected. Without being 'I', it wants to be known as 'I.' This is wickedness, so Mother calls him so.

My powers, '*madbibhūti*', are powers of Self. All multiplicity, all other powers are those of Self. These powers cannot have any independent nature. Just like the ability of speech of a great speaker, that cannot have any existence separate from the speaker but is a function of the speaker. When the unique *Amvikā* appears with her powers, she is seen as many. She is one and only.

With these words, the Goddess also tells *Śumbha*, 'I am the only I, there is no second. How could you, *Śumbha,* be separate?' When *Śumbha* seeing all her powers doubts her uniqueness, my Mother by her grace, withdraws them all into herself and tells him, 'See, all my powers enter back into me.'

Verse 4.

tataḥ samastāstā devyo brahmāṇīpramukhā layam|
tasyā devyāstanau jagmurekaivāsīttadāmbikā||

Translation:

Thereafter, *Brahmāṇī* and the other powers merged into the body of the Goddess. *Amvikā* alone remained.

Explanation:

At the wish of Mother, the eight powered forms of her glories merged back into her body. The different powers emerging from awareness went back into their cause, that is, into awareness. Their utility had ended. Now Mother is one and only, without any differences, complete, of the nature of bliss. But yet, *Śumbha* remains and the words of the Goddess remain. Do not be anxious about duality here. When Mother is brought within the bounds of words, to explain or be understood, she appears to be dual. There is no duality. How the one, undivided matter of the nature of bliss, appears as many while keeping its nature intact, has been explained before. Here, we cannot agree with present proponents of the theory of *māyā*. They have called this multiplicity from the glory of Self to be error or false. We understand it as the glory of Self. As long as any perception of duality remains, it cannot be blown off as an error. When nondual nature is revealed, there is nothing left to be called error or false.

Therefore, as long as there is spiritual effort, there is realization, there is a discussion of great scriptural statements, there is something left to be understood. Instead of calling it error, considering it to be divine play, will bring overall congruency. The *Upaniṣads* and the *Brahma Sutras* have also explained this multiplicity as an expression of divine play. They have not used words like error or false. It never did strike in their hearts, as to how there was the luxury of divine play in that which was without characteristics. Who can say, what can be in it, and what cannot?

Remember this wonderful message of *Devī Māhātmya*, the spiritual path will be easy. Remember this universe, this multiplicity to be the glory of Self. It is the wish of 'I' that is expressed as many, the 'I' viewed as many. When 'I' views itself as one, then there is no longer anything left as many. All divisiveness merges into 'I'. This is the right and true knowledge.

Verse 5.

devyuvāca|
ahaṁ vibhūtyā bahubhiriha rūpairyadāsthitā|
tat sahnhṛtaṁ mayaikaiva tiṣṭhāmyājau sthiro bhava||

Translation:

The Goddess said, I am withdrawing the many glorious forms in which I was residing. Now I reside alone. (O, *Śumbha,* you), focus on this battle.

Explanation:

Even when the Goddess is one and only, her words are not impossible. What they are like, those who envision these principles will understand. Although my Mother is eternal, beyond word, touch, form and flavor, even then her speech and a battle with *Śumbha* are not impossible. When perception of Self is withdrawn into supreme principle and focused on awareness formed *Amvikā*, then a light of intellect from her appears in the reflected space of awareness. These are words of Mother and her acts of battle. With each ray of light from intellect, many riddles are solved, many demons are killed and many incredible things may be discovered.

Whatever it is, the Goddess said to *Śumbha*, 'I am withdrawing the many glorious forms in which I was residing. Now I am alone. But be careful, you must focus on this battle.' The significance of these words is very clear. She said, because you were trying to see multiplicity, I appeared as many according to your desire. All this time, you did not ask for me, you sought my glories, you wanted to decorate your imagined 'I', so I existed as many different figures. I had to take multiple forms, to fulfill your desires. But, after all this time, your desires are fulfilled. Your need for multiplicity has ended. Today you have even discarded Godhood and want only me. There is so much love in your heart. You are honored for wanting only me, for myself. Look, now I have withdrawn my many forms and express my unique self. Now you must stay still and fight.

There is a mystery in the words of Mother, 'stay still'. Arriving here, being near this uniqueness, it is very difficult to remain still. All specialties weaken. Although multiplicity has been removed, the specialty of ego remains, it has not yet been removed. Arriving near *ātmā*, that specialty also tends to disappear. It is not easy to remain still. So, Mother affectionately says 'be still.' As long as ego can be still, it can keep its specialty. By the pleasure of Mother, these acts of the spiritual battle can continue. It is necessary to remain still. But for how long?

Verse 6.

ṛṣiruvāca|
tataḥ pravavṛte yuddhaṁ devyāḥ śumbhasya cobhayoḥ|
paśyatāṁ sarvadevānāmasurāṇāñca dāruṇam||

Verse 7.

śaravarṣaiḥ śitaiḥ śastraistathāstraiścaiva dāruṇaiḥ|
tayoryuddhamabhūdbhūyaḥ sarvalokabhayaṅkaram||

Translation:

Thereafter, in front of the goeds, a terrible battle began between *Śumbha* and the Goddess. In this dreadful fight, great volleys of arrows and the many sharp weapons, filled these worlds.

Explanation:

There is a terrible battle between the Goddess and *Śumbha.* On one side, ego wants to maintain its specialty, on the other *ātmā* by its self-expression is ready to end it. One is the reflection, the other reflected. There is always a great battle between these two. As long as the reflection does not understand itself to be so, it competes with the reflected to maintain its separate identity. So, a severe battle is inevitable.

The battle between the Goddess and *Śumbha* is terrible for all these worlds. On one side, ego is attempting to keep its identity intact, on the other, self-expressed *ātmā* is ready to destroy this distinctiveness. Truly this battle is terrible for all worlds because the nature of the ego is that of all these worlds. Without ego, there is nothing left. Although before this, destruction of all demonic states has been described, one has to understand that if ego remains intact, it does not take long for demonic states to reappear, because they are expressions of ego. Up to now, it was determined by the destruction of these demonic tendencies, that they did not have any special identity. The various expressions being destroyed, they dispersed into ego. But, if ego remains, there is a chance of their reappearance. It is aimed at this condition, that a text in *Pātañjali* philosophy has said, 'those that dissolve into nature, can arise again.' Until this nature is not destroyed, true Self is not expressed and worldly beings cannot be liberated. The end of ego or nature (*prakṛti*) is the same thing. The subtlest seed state of supreme principle (*mahat*) is *prakṛti* of *Sāṅkhya* philosophy. The state of all feelings resides in this most subtle nature. The nature of ego that we see here, can be called a balanced condition of the three attributes (*guṇas*) of *prakṛti*. In the language of *Sāṅkhya*, this battle between the Goddess and *Śumbha* may be called the flight of *prakṛti* from the front of *puruśa*. In the language of *Vedānta*, this may be called the end of the assignment of *māyā*. The language of devotion calls this the close union of God and devotee. Whatever it is, this is a furious and terrible battle for all these worlds.

Verse 8.

divyānyastrāṇi śataśo mumuce yānyathāmbikā|
babhañja tāni daityendrastatpratīghātakartṛbhiḥ||

Verse 9.

muktāni tena cāstrāṇi divyāni parameśvarī|
babhañja līlayaivograhuṅkāroccāraṇādibhiḥ||

Translation:

Thereafter, hundreds of divine weapons thrown by *Amvikā*, were shattered by opposing weapons of the demon king *Śumbha*. The weapons hurled by the demon king were also easily broken by the supreme Goddess, with her roars and other means.

Explanation:

The weapons of *Amvikā* were divine and expressed by themselves. As the nature of Self is expressed more and more, ego, afraid of losing its state, becomes anxious. Under this condition, it tries different means to keep its nature intact. That is, it tries in different ways to prevent the expression of Self. The weapons of the Goddess fail. A worldly person does not immediately wish to accept the state of *Brahmaṇ*. It tries very hard to maintain its special status, its sense of difference. When ego focuses on Self, even for a moment, observing its expression, it loses its nature. When it focuses on its own special existence, then the expression of Self is obstructed. This is the mystery of the battle between the Goddess and *Śumbha*. In the next few mantras, this is described as the deployment of various weapons. If the previous discussion is kept in mind, it will not be difficult to understand the secret of the battle between the Goddess and *Śumbha*.

The mantra says that the Goddess roared and destroyed some of the weapons of *Śumbha*. The roar (*huṅkāra*) is the seed sound of destruction. This has been mentioned before. Although in the supreme arena, there is no special expression of destructive power, by its nature it destroys divisive knowledge. When self-expressed *ātmā* is revealed, destruction of ego is inevitable. So, the mantra says that the Goddess destroyed the weapons of *Śumbha* with her roars. When reflection focuses on the reflected, it loses its identity. When it focuses on itself, the reflected one is shielded from it. This is the mystery of the weapons used against each other.

Verse 10.

tataḥ śaraśatairdevīmācchādayata sohasuraḥ|
sāpi tatkupitā devī dhanuściccheda ceṣubhiḥ||

Verse 11.

chinne dhanuṣi daityendrastathā śaktimathādade|
ciccheda devī cakreṇa tāmapyasya karesthitāmḥ||

Verse 12.

tataḥ khaḍgamupādāya śatacandrañca bhānumat|
abhyadhāvata tāṁ devīṃ daityānāmadhipeśvaraḥ||

Verse 13.

tasyāpatata evāśu khaḍgaṁ ciccheda caṇḍikā|
dhanurmuktaiḥ śitairbāṇaiścarma cārkakarāmalamḥ||

Translation:

Then the demon showered the Goddess with hundreds of arrows. The Goddess being angered, broke the bow of the *asura* with her arrow. His bow being broken, the king of demons took a power weapon, but the Goddess destroyed this with her discus. Then the demon king raced towards the Goddess with a scimitar and a very bright shield named 'a hundred moons.' As he ran towards her, she shattered his scimitar and bright shield, with her sharp arrows

Explanation:

These four mantras describe the weapons used by the Goddess and the great *asura Śumbha* against each other. First, *Śumbha* showered her with hundreds of arrows. Being angered, the Goddess breaks his bow. Putting arrows of the sense of Self, on the bow of *Praṇava*, ego aimed them at *Brahmaṇ*. Although this has been described before as a great spiritual effort, it is here said to be a weapon used by a demon. In this statement about aiming an arrow of Self with the bow of *Praṇava*, there is a perception of duality. So, the recitation of *Praṇava* and arrows of Self, are here stated to be demonic torment. My Mother, will not leave any remnant of divisiveness. So, with her arrow of self-expression, she breaks the bow of *Praṇava* of the demon. The efforts of *Śumbha* fail. Similarly, when a spiritual seeker tries to maintain individuality with special enterprise, my Mother destroys it.

After this, *Śumbha* took his power weapon. Holding on firmly to the feeling 'I am Self' is the power weapon of *Śumbha*. Alas, the Goddess broke this too. The true expression of Self is so pervasive that even the tiniest shred of divisiveness cannot remain. With the discus of divine sight, that is, by expression of the all-pervading nature of the Goddess, the sense of ego was overcome. Losing all hope, *Śumbha*, holding his scimitar and shield, advanced toward the Goddess. With her arrows, she shattered his weapons. The scimitar is divisive knowledge, the shield is concealment. This too has been mentioned before. When ego cannot reside in front of the expression of Self, while maintaining its own identity, it takes recourse to divisiveness and concealment. On one hand, it abandons its aim towards *ātmā*, on the other, it tries to hold on to its own difference. This is the mystery of the scimitar and shield of *Śumbha*. The stance of ego is this, 'let *ātmā* be present, I agree that I am expressed by it, still, why should I discard my existence? I am fine. I will enjoy the beauty of *Amvikā* from a distance. Why go near her and merge my existence with her?'

Many spiritual seekers arrive here and stop their movement. They do not want to merge into God. They think that enjoyment in the proximity of God is the greatest achievement. This enjoyment is also an impediment to liberation. This enjoyment is one of the obstacles to knowledge of Self that is described in the scriptures. Although this was mentioned during the destruction of *Niśumbha*, there is no harm in repeating it. *Śumbha* and *Niśumbha* are the two manifestations of the same percept. If one holds enjoyment of the supreme as a final achievement, then the principle of nonduality is not revealed. When beings are not established in the nondual principle, they are not liberated. Those who say that love of God is the goal, not liberation, do not know that until one is free, there can be no true love. A single-pointed devotion is true love. But these are way from this topic. Those who have practiced the yoga of surrender, arrive here to an arena of awareness, and residing as ego, try to maintain their identity. My loving Mother defeats their efforts. Until her adored children are completely overcome, she does not leave them. This is the mystery of the repeated failure of the weapons by *Śumbha*.

The shield named 'a hundred moons' used by *Śumbha* is said to have been as pure as the rays of the sun. Truly, in this field of the ego, the covering the nature of Self is very bright. Before this, *Mahiṣāsura* and others also used scimitars and shields, but those of *Śumbha* are even brighter. Because there is very only a small difference between ego and Self, only a suggestion of difference, it may appear as non-different. So, the shield is said to be bright and pure. A flame within a glass container heats and lights the glass. From a distance, the glass may appear to be the flame. The proximity of ego to Self gives it some of the nature of Self and makes it appear as Self. It is to convey this impression that the mantra says a very bright shield. If a seeker pays attention to his perceptions, this mystery may be envisioned.

Verse 14.

hatāśvaḥ sa tadā daityaśchinnadhanvā visārathiḥ| [2]
jagrāha mudgaraṁ ghoramambikānidhanodyataḥ||

Verse 15.

cicchedāpatatastasya mudgaraṁ niśitaiḥ śaraiḥ|
tathāpi sohabhyadhāvattāṁ muṣṭimudyamya vegavān||

Translation:

Without his horses, bow broken, without his charioteer, holding a heavy mace, the demon readied himself to kill *Amvikā*. As he came forward, the Goddess destroyed the mace with her sharp arrows. Despite this, *Śumbha* ran towards the Goddess with his fists raised.

Explanation:

The sense horses, the bow of *Praṇava* and the charioteer of intelligence have all been destroyed. All attempts have failed. Although the senses are specialized encirclements of ego, they do not come to its aid. The recitation of *Praṇava* and other mantras has been silenced. The charioteer, definitive intelligence, is no longer expressed. Only when there are subject matters, can one perceive the expression of intelligence. There is nothing here that is any of any matter. Intelligence is extinct. Without no other recourse, the *asura* picks up his heavy mace. Ego is taken over by a sense of inertness. 'I will not go to *ātmā*. I will not surrender to it. I will stay as I am. I will not merge with *ātmā*.' It is aimed at this firm resolve of ego, that the mantra says that *Śumbha* picked up his mace. 'Remaining in an inert state, my special state will

2 a *mantra* line before this verse, seen in many texts of *Devī Māhātmya*, is not present in the Bengali edition of *Sādhan Samar*

remain in existence.' It is aimed at this feeling that the mantra uses the term 'destroy *Amvikā*.' The attempt to keep the nature of Self concealed is termed this attempt to kill *Amvikā*.

Even though ego wants to keep itself under a cover of ignorance, Mother does not let it be. With her sharp arrows, that is, by expression of Self, which destroys all perceptions of duality, she destroys the heavy mace, the ignorance of *Śumbha*. My Mother is now furious, her anger is roused, so she will not let ego remain separate. Although ego tries its best to maintain its identity, my *Caṇḍīkā* Mother will defeat it. One day, 'I' was ready to surrender at the feet of Mother. As long as that surrender is not completed, she will not let it be. One day, whether in danger, or by being weakened, or without understanding, one had sought refuge at the feet of *ātmā*, Mother. Nothing else can save one now. True Self will appear. It will destroy any imaginary 'I.' This is the grace of *Caṇḍī*. The ignorance of ego, the mace of *Śumbha*, is broken by the self-expressed power of *Caṇḍīkā*.

With all these failures, 'I'-ness is not inactivated or without hope. The mantra says that when his mace failed, *Śumbha* raised his fists and ran towards the Goddess. The fist is symbolic of the power of disruption. Ego wants to keep *ātmā* away. When Self is away, ego can be established. The disruption mentioned here is not in the arena of spirit (*citta*). It is in ego, it is very subtle. The death of *Cikṣura*, the disruptive demon of *citta*, was described in the battle with *Mahiṣāsura*. Here there is no trace of disruption of material vibrations. In the language of *Sāṅkhya*, this disruption may be called a condition of the subtlest seed of a resultant state of *prakṛti*. In the language of *Vedānta*, it is the subtle seed of the assignment of *māyā*. When a subtle seed of divisiveness remains, it can condense and reappear in the material field. So, Mother does not let even the subtlest seeds remain. She inspires *Śumbha* to raise his fists and run toward her. That is, she inspires the subtle seed of disruptiveness in *Śumbha*. Nothing can hide from the self-expressed nature of my Mother.

Verse 16.

sa muṣṭiṁ pātayāmāsa hṛdaye daityapuṇgavaḥ|
devyāstañcāpi sā devī talenorasyatāḍayat||

Verse 17.

talaprahārābhihato nipapāta mahītale|
sa daityarājaḥ sahasā punareva tathotthitaḥ||

Translation:

The demon hit the Goddess over her heart with his fist. The Goddess too hit him on his chest with her hand. Being hit, the demon king fell to the ground but got up again.

Explanation:

Disregarding strong attraction towards Self, residing in the subtlest power of distraction, the attempt of ego to maintain its state of non-Self is the blow by his fist to the heart of the Goddess. Ego aims to keep *ātmā* away. But, this does not work. The more ego tries to keep *ātmā* away and attack it, *ātmā* comes closer. When *Śumbha* hits the Goddess, she also hits him back with her hand. They hit each other over their hearts. By 'heart', one has to understand here a center. The center of infinite energy is the heart of Mother. The center from which ego is expressed is the heart of *Śumbha*. As long as these two are not unified, any perception of divisiveness is not removed. Until these hearts are united, separation does not end. *Vedānta* philosophy gives the meaning of 'heart' as *ātmā*. The perceived Self is felt in the heart. So, another name for *ātmā* is heart (*hṛdaya*). Union of hearts means the union with Self. As long as one is not merged with *ātmā*, until hearts are united, separation does not end.

O, Mother! From how long have we been running, to merge our hearts with you. We have suffered many million births and deaths, illness and sorrow to come and merge in your heart; but we have failed. We have not been overcome by you. O, our eternal rest, our eternal peace, we have not been able to merge into you. We suffer the pain of separation and our hearts burn. We have not attained the ability to find peace of merger into your heart. O, Mother, end this now. Fulfill this desire for union. After this long interval, let us be one. There is nothing left to understand in this pain of separation. Hit us over our hearts, like that of *Śumbha*. Let all darkness in our hearts vanish. Let it be hallowed by your sacred touch. Today, *Śumbha* is honored. Honored is this game of war. Today you have laid your hands over the heart of *Śumbha*. He will no longer be expressed separately. With your holy touch, he will be hallowed and merge with you. He truly wants you for yourself, everything else is gone. He wants you. That is why this grace flows from you.

Ego truly wants *ātmā*. By merging with *ātmā*, it will find true peace. The repeated use of weapons that is seen in this war game, is the subtle expression of strong tendencies of divisiveness stored from the past. It is also seen in this world that when one wants to be united with someone most dear, on coming close, one at first, draws away. Engrossed by the beauty of *Amvikā*, ego truly wants to surrender to *ātmā*, but cannot let go of the store of past tendencies. So, love appears as a battle. There is great beauty in all this.

A spiritual seeker can see that they too hit Mother over her heart and try to prevent her. But as soon as they step back and turn from her, there is pain in their hearts. They are again drawn by the attraction of Mother. They are again keen to see her great beauty. They turn her away in anger with their violence. They close their eyes saying 'we will not look at you.' But then are eager to see her again. They cannot refrain from looking at her. Why is this? It is the attraction of Mother. Mother does not leave you. Even if you leave her, she wants to merge with you, that is why these events occur.

Whatever that is, it is aimed at the expression of Self in ego that the mantra describes as the Goddess beating it with her hand. I will mention something about spiritual effort over here. When one unites one's heart with that of a *guru*, one can understand these blows over the heart, of the Goddess and *Śumbha*. Truly, the joy of union becomes unbearable. When this joy becomes painful, then it cannot but be called blows of joy. A perceptive seeker will understand this.

Verse 18.

utpatya ca pragṛhyoccairdevīṁ gaganamāsthitaḥ|
tatrāpi sā nirādhārā yuyudhe tena caṇḍikā||

Verse 19.

niyuddhaṁ khe tadā daityaścaṇḍikā ca parasparam|
cakratuḥ prathamaṁ siddhamunivismayakārakam||

Translation:

Having risen, *Śumbha* with the Goddess resided in the sky. *Caṇḍīkā* continued to battle him there. Then, the demon and *Caṇḍīkā* fought each other in such a manner, that even the Self-realized sages were amazed.

Explanation:

When ego found that it could not overcome *ātmā*, but was himself overcome, seeing no other alternative, it rose with the Goddess into the skies. That is, it tried to feel emptiness as *ātmā*. There is no such thing as *ātmā*. It is emptiness, the nature of it is absence. That which is without mass, size or length, which is only described by negation, whose nature is the absence of all percepts, what can it be but emptiness? (This is a Buddhist principle discussed before.) Seekers who come here, think of Self as deep slumber, understanding it to be of the nature of absence. They think that residing in this state of absence of all percepts is a great achievement, of realizing Self, of *Brahmaṇ*. It is aimed at this, that the mantra says that *Śumbha* rose into the skies with the Goddess. Alas! Even here *Śumbha* is not relieved. The Goddess battles with him in the skies. Even if *ātmā* is negated as emptiness or absence, the knower of it that remains is expressed as Self. One is not comforted by calling it emptiness. *Ātmā* is needed to declare that there is emptiness. Ego wants to negate *ātmā*, but *ātmā* is the knower of emptiness, residing as wholeness, negating any state of negativity. This is the mystery of the battle between *Śumbha* and the Goddess in the skies.

This battle in the skies is truly incredible. On one side, *ātmā*, designated as emptiness, is expressed as wholeness. On the other side, ego which has no supreme state resides to appear by itself. So, this battle is amazing. Although, it may not be so for everyone, those who are realized, the sages, that is, those who have achieved Self, the yogis, to them this battle is incredible. So, the mantra says, that 'even the self-realized sages' (*siddhamuni*) 'were astonished' (*vismayakārakamḥ*). Truly, who but realized seekers will understand the mystery of this battle? Once it appears that *ātmā* is emptiness, then it appears that *ātmā* is not empty but whole.

Verse 20.

tato niyuddhaṁ suciraṁ kṛtvā tenāmbikā saha|
utpāṭya bhrāmayāmāsa cikṣepa dharaṇītale||

Verse 21.

sa kṣipto dharaṇīṁ prāpya muṣṭimudyamya vegitaḥ|
abhyadhāvata duṣṭātmā caṇḍikānidhanecchayā||

Translation:

Thereafter, battling with him for very long, Goddess *Amvikā* raised *Śumbha* and twirling him about, threw him to the earth. The wicked *Śumbha*, fallen to the ground, again raised his fist and swiftly ran forward, to try to kill her.

Explanation:

This aerial battle, this riddle of emptiness goes on for very long. Most seekers think that this entity beyond words and mind is something of the nature of deep slumber, ignorant and empty. That *ātmā* is something self-expressed, that even if we negate it a thousand times it remains as knower, even though not understood in the beginning, is realized later by most seekers. When *ātmā* is expressed in its full blissful form, the riddle of emptiness ends. From that day, ego becomes suspicious of its existence. Is there nothing opposed to *ātmā*, is there then nothing that is 'me'? In this fashion, doubts appear as to one's existence. This is described in the mantra as *Śumbha* being twirled in the sky. The condition of ego at this time becomes like a dizzy person. 'What a calamity! I do not exist! Then like this material world, am I just visible, imaginary?' It is aimed at this that the mantra says that he was thrown to the ground. When Self is expressed, this feeling comes to the heart of all spiritual seekers.

Whatever it is, this is the final attempt by *Śumbha*. Being thrown to the ground by the Goddess, that is, becoming visible like the material world, inconsequential, to maintain his identity, the wicked one, again raised his fists to kill *Caṇḍīkā*. It is his wish to destroy her. If in some fashion, ego can negate Self, then it can maintain its status. So, the mantra says that *Śumbha* again raised his fists. Although it is impossible to kill *Caṇḍīkā*, still the farther away he can stay from her, the better is his purpose served. That is why *Śumbha* raises his fists again. Needless to say, this is his final attempt.

Verse 22.

tamāyāntaṁ tato devī sarvadaityajaneśvaram|
jagatyāṁ pātayāmāsa bhittvā śūlena vakṣasi||

Translation:

When the king of all the demons advanced (in this manner), the Goddess pierced his chest with her lance and felled him to the ground.

Explanation:

The end of *Śumbha* comes after all this time. Because ego is the shelter for all perceptions of duality, he has been called the king of all demons. That all perceptions of non-Self are in the shelter of 'I', can be understood by anyone, by steady thought.

Although, generally, when we say 'I', one thinks of something from the material body to intelligence, with sin, piety and *dharma*, those who are seekers in the arena of ego, can discern a specific 'I' entwined with all this perception. As long as a hint of the nature of an all blissful 'knower' does not appear, this 'I'-ness is not expressed. By the store of good actions of many lifetimes, by unconditional grace of *guru* and incomparable affection of Mother, a spiritual seeker appears at pure perception and is forever freed from false pride, the demon ego. This is the mystery of the destruction of *Śumbha*.

The great *asura Śumbha* was felled to the ground, being hit by the lance of the Goddess. The expression of the bliss-natured perception is the blow of the lance of the Goddess. Before, the lance was explained to be a tri-fold state of bliss. Here one has to understand the lance to be a blissful state of the knower, without any tri-fold state. By its expression, ego and all seeds of non-self are destroyed. Mother throws *Śumbha* to the ground. Just as there is nothing visible, material, never was, never will be, so there is no 'I'-ness, never was, never will be. What is, and is perceived to exist, is not 'I' but *ātmā*. The 'I' that was perceived all this time as ruler of all, as the knower of all, is no longer there, was not ever there.

This is the destruction of *Śumbha*. The 'I' with which you have suffered the load of millions of births and deaths, with which you have traveled through so many heavens and hells, that you have decorated in so many ways, that you thought was bound, you have tried to free by so much severe spiritual enterprise, look and see now, there is no 'I', never was in any of the three time frames. You are eternally pure, free *ātmā*. You are fearless, divine ambrosia, truth. You are *Brahmaṇ*. There is no birth and death in you, no bondage and freedom. You are eternally free, this is great prosperity. This is a great achievement. I have said that unless one loses oneself, one cannot find Mother. After all this time, 'I' has been lost, it has fallen and the nature of Mother, of Self is revealed. This is finding Mother.

Listen. The meaning of the word *Śumbha* is 'ever destroyed'. The meaning of the root '*śunv*' is beauty. The root '*śunv*' has another meaning, 'to be killed.' The one who is already destroyed, one eternally killed, who has no existence is *Śumbha.* In terms of philosophy, *Śumbha* may be said to be the impossible future. 'I' and this universe supported by 'I' are impossible items. There is nothing in *Brahmaṇ* that is a universe. This is truth. To reside in this truth is proper 'establishment of truth', or 'residence in *Brahmaṇ*' (*brāhmī-sthiti*).

One has to say here briefly what *Vaśiṣṭhadeva* said in the *Yogavaśiṣṭha* text, in reply to *Śri Rāmachandra*'s query about the nature of this universe. In a kingdom without any king, there lived an unmarried king whose two wives were childless. Their two sons entered a treeless forest to hunt, and so on. Just as this makes no sense, just words to quieten active child on the lap of a nurse, in the same manner, this universe, this 'I', this space of awareness, this ego, none of them are. Only *ātmā*, Mother is. It is existence, it is awareness, it is bliss. There is nothing else.

One day a spiritual seeker was engrossed by hearing the words from the mouth of the great *guru*, 'seek refuge in me.' You had surrendered your 'I' at his feet. After all these days you see the worth of that. Look, how by that surrender, Mother has moved you through so many states and purified, merged it into Self. Your surrender has had proper fruition. Worldly persons are established in the state of *Brahmaṇ*. Say, 'honored is our successful life. Honored is our clear sense of *Brahmaṇ*. Honored is our end of sorrow. Honored is the removal of ignorance. Honored is our end of duties. Honored is our achievement.'

Verse 23.

sa gatāsuḥ papātorvyāṁ devīśūlāgravikṣataḥ|
cālayanḥ sakalāṁ pṛthvīṁ sābdhidvīpāṁ saparvatām||

Translation:

Being severely wounded by the lance of the Goddess, the

demon lost his life and fell to the earth, perturbing the oceans, islands, mountains and all this world.

Explanation:

When *Śumbha* fell, wounded and killed by the lance of the Goddess, the earth with all its oceans, islands and mountains was shaken. This is the literal meaning of the mantra. It has been mentioned, that the interaction between attributes (*guṇas*) because of their differences, results in seven categories. They are the seven oceans. *Mulādhāra* and the other centers of perception are seven islands. Physical, inert feelings are mountains. All of them are shaken by the death of ego because they are all different expressions of 'I'-ness. How can their spirit remain still as 'I'-ness is destroyed?

As long as stored actions are not completely depleted, these bodily perceptions, that is, the feelings of non-Self return. When a seeker resides in the nature of Self, there is no longer any sign of them. When he is not there, they come back.

When the error of a rope as a snake is removed, when the knowledge about the rope is definite, even then, fear, tremors and other signs from the temporary cognizance as a snake remain for a time. By the expression of Self, any appreciation as non-Self is discontinued. Yet, as long as a store of actions remains, they return. This is why a physical body persists, and teaching, advice, writing texts, establishing *dharma* and other such acts continue. Yoga philosophy describes this as 'results of a spirit of action.' That is, a Self-realized person, creates a spirit from the residuals of ego, for the good of this world and in its shelter carries out actions for the welfare of all. *Vedānta* has called this '*vādhitānuvṛtti*.' There is no conflict between these two. When a spiritual seeker is ready to forego even ego and is ready to enter into the nature of Self, then truly earth, oceans, islands and mountains, that is, physical, subtle and causal bodies are shaken, because they are forever going to lose their nature. In some seekers, this may be seen in the physical body just before *samādhi*.

Whatever it is, as long as there is no continuous residence in the nature of Self, the body and other things reappear as non-Self. When stored actions are completed, then the seeker attains liberation beyond a body. The portrayal of non-Self ends. Among stored tendencies, those that are high obstacles to knowledge of Self have been called strong stored tendencies. When these are eroded, the knowledge of Self is illuminated. In the language of spiritual enterprise, this is called piercing the knot of *Rudra*. The perception is that this universe, this body and all else are of an intellectual form (*vijñāna*). This is the knot of *Rudra*. Truly there is nothing that remains as universe or body, there is nothing that is non-Self, never was, never will be. The spirit of this universe is not there in any of the three frames of time. Unique *ātmā*, my Mother is eternally present. There is nothing else but *ātmā*. This realization is the piercing of the knot of *Rudra*. That which is the nature of awareness does not have awareness in it. That which is the nature of perception does not have anything perceptible in it. In the nature of *paramātmā*, there is no creation, maintenance and destruction of any universe. The *ātmā* is eternally clear, eternally unstained, eternally pure.

Do you understand? One can mistake a rope to be a snake, but there is nothing that is a snake in the rope. Just as there is no snake-ness in the rope, there is no sense of the universe in *ātmā*. After this realization, in an awakened state, the natural affection for *ātmā* is unconditional love. In the first chapter of *Śrīmad Bhāgabat*, the verse about the self-satisfied sages describes this unconditional love. The love towards *ātmā* and firm knowledge about this universe turns a seeker to be completely without desire. One renunciate this world. In this manner, by the grace of Mother, knots of *Brahmā*, *Viṣṇu* and *Rudra* are pierced. A seeker is liberated while alive, all bondages are removed, one tastes eternal freedom.

Verse 24.

utpātameghāḥ solkā ye prāgāsaṁste śamaṁ yayuḥ|
sarito mārgavāhinyastathāsaṁstatra pātite||

Translation:

When the demon *Śumbha* was felled, the clouds and meteors that before appeared to be inauspicious, disappeared, and rivers flowed in the proper directions. (Before this, they had reversed.)

Explanation:

'I' has disappeared, so there is no more aggravation. The heavy load of concerns about this world that was there before has been removed because of the absence of 'I.' Let alone this world, there was much worry about spiritual enterprise. How this unconquerable mind and senses could be tamed, how one could succeed, how the store of actions of innumerable lifetimes could be eroded and so many others. Those clouds of worry were combined with meteors of hopelessness, lack of faith and suspicion. Now it is calm. There is nothing more to worry about, nothing more to do, there is no more hopelessness, no more need for hope. With the end of 'I'-ness, all these have ended. So, the mantra describes the clouds of annoyances to have disappeared. The rivers, that is, the flow of energies in the body, followed their usual paths. Before this, because of spiritual effort, or because of worries about this world, they flowed in reverse. Now there are no more worries, so they are calm and follow their usual paths. After the end of 'I', the body of a seeker is also calm. As long as *Śumbha* remained, as long as there was the effect of ego, all kinds of disturbances remained and much misbehavior was seen. When they are end, all becomes calm. The signs that appear in a seeker after meeting with Self, are described in this and the next mantras. Perceptive seekers will be able to recognize these signs.

Verse 25.

tataḥ prasannamakhilaṁ hate tasminḥ durātmani|
jagat svāsthyamatīvāpa nirmalaṁ cābhavannabhaḥ||

Translation:

At the death of the wicked *asura*, the whole world was pleased, this universe regained its health and the skies turned pure.

Explanation:

When ego is destroyed, the whole world becomes truly pleased. Before, wherever one turned one's eyes, one saw some degree of unruliness and misbehavior because there was a sense of 'I am the ruler.' Now that is no more. On all sides, one finds feelings of satisfaction. If one exists in a realization that only the nature of Self is illuminated, then there is no more discontent. When the 'I' of a spiritual seeker is destroyed, then one sees that this world is also pleased.

This universe becomes healthy. To reside in Self is to be healthy. This feeling of Self is health. Self is expressed everywhere, so this universe resides in health. There is nothing separate as the universe, it is all Self.

The skies are pure. There is no longer any murkiness in intellectual space. Before, because of the cover of multiplicity, the sky was dark. With the end of the ego, any sense of multiplicity has been removed, so the sky is clear.

Verse 26.

tato devagaṇāḥ sarve harṣanirbharamānasāḥ|
babhūvurnihate tasminḥ gandharvā lalitaṁ jaguḥ||

Verse 27.

avādayahnstathaivānye nanṛtuścāpsarogaṇāḥ|
vavuḥ puṇyāstathā vātāḥ suprabhohabhūddivākaraḥ||

Translation:

The gods were very pleased with the demon being killed. The *gandharvas* began to sing sweetly. Some others played musical instruments and the *apsarās* danced, holy breezes blew and the Sun came up bright.

Explanation:

At the fall of *Śumbha*, deities, celestial and angelic beings, the Moon and the Sun were all pleased. They each expressed their joy according to their abilities. The deities established in the senses were no longer anxious, the senses were quiet. The kingdom of consciousness was intact. There was no longer the danger of ceremonial offerings to the gods being stolen. All were joyous. The *gandharvas*, senses established in primal sound, played pleasing music. Singing songs of bliss, they extended their joy. Until this time, these celestials were overcome by *Śumbha*, so they were tormented by sounds without pitch and rhythm. Now, consciousness established in sound is calm, they are well-modulated.

Listen. After Self is found, sounds pronounced by a seeker become sweet. There is a sweet attraction in their voices. The way words were pronounced before, may not have been attractive to all. But now, even when they are rebuking someone, they sound sweet. Those who are being scolded do not feel sad, they feel happiness in their hearts. This is a result of the joy of the celestials.

Apsarās, divine angels, danced. They expressed feelings of excitement and limb movements. At the beginning of yoga, these can induce disturbances of spirit and so are obstacles to a spiritual effort. Now, after the end of ego, body movements that occur when alighting on the nature of Self are joyful. They are not obstacles. There is no disturbance of *ātmā*. Disturbance is a characteristic of the spirit. But even if body movements are seen at this time, they are not detrimental to the realization of Self. Instead, they are blissful.

Holy breezes blew. After a meeting with Self, air truly appears to be holy and blissful. Nectar-like, blissful, dear nature of *ātmā* is reflected everywhere. So, in tune with the sages who envisioned the Truth, we like to say, 'air flows like nectar, oceans release nectar.'[3] I have heard a song saying, 'when my mind is engrossed in you, then this world becomes nectar.'

3 *madhu vātā ṛtāyate madhukṣaranti sindhavaḥ|*

In this manner, not only does the outer air become holy and blissful, but the inner five breaths also turn holy and full of bliss. Before this, we have not had a chance to speak about *prāṇa* and the other five breaths, so even though not pertinent here, we will mention it briefly. There are five inner airs, *prāṇa*, *apāna*, *vyāna, udāna* and *samāna*. Commonly they are known as breaths or airs. Air is only their physical form. Here, we will not discuss the physical forms, because that nature, action and location are known by many. I will only try to speak about the realization of their nature from a spiritual view.

The five breaths are special natures. Beings have two kinds of natures, inner and outer. The four inner natures are mind, intelligence, spirit and self-importance (*ahaṁkāra*). The outer nature is three-fold, organs of senses, organs of action and the five breaths. The three-fold natures arise from the three *guṇas*, right, active and passive (*sattva*, *rājasa* and *tāmasa*). Just as natures from right tendency, are mainly expressed in organs of the senses, those of active ones are expressed in organs of action. Any obstructive nature of breath is from *tāmasa*, the passive *guṇa*. When one speaks of *prāṇa*, it means an embrace of feelings from outside. That is, internal feelings that arise from contact with external objects. Their establishment is an action of *prāṇa*. For example, say you are drinking water because you are thirsty. In this case, contact of external water with your throat results in a feeling of satisfaction of thirst. The force that holds this feeling is *prāṇa*.

The action of *apāna* is to establish a power to eliminate waste from the body. The action of *vyāna* is the power for moving the limbs. Similarly, the action of *udāna* is the force to move body fluids and blood. The action of *samāna* is the power to form the body from food and drink. It is by these five-fold holding powers that the body is formed, maintained and destroyed. When they are in decline, the body is terminating. Like the organs of sense and actions, they are expressions of ego. The five breaths are the proper natures of the five sheaths (*koṣas*).

Whatever it is, after meeting Mother, that is, when one awakens in the nature of Self, not only does the spirit become quiet, from the satisfaction of spirit, the organs of senses and actions are satisfied, so also are the five breaths. As a result, the physical body is felt to be condensed bliss. One perceives that each molecule of the body is a particle of bliss. This is the sign of all the airs in the body being sanctified.

O! When one lands on Self, once one gets onto the lap of affectionate Mother, this takes place. Mind, life, senses and even the physical body becomes imbued with incredible sweetness. This nectar is other worldly, one has never tasted it before, wondrous is the mystery of this union. Continuous bliss is its nature.

Verse 28.

jajvaluścāgnayaḥ śāntāḥ śāntā digjanitasvanāḥ|
svavasti śrīmārkaṇḍeyapurāṇe sāvarṇike manvantare devīmāhātmye śumbhavadh||

Translation:

The ceremonial fires were lit, they burned calmly, and all signs of disturbances were quietened.

Here ends this episode on the destruction of *Śumbha*, in *Devī Māhātmya*, in the era of *Sāvarṇi*, in *Mārkeṇḍeya Purāṇa*.

Explanation:

Ceremonial fires are the principle of energy in a body. Before this, they caused many disturbances. Now they are calm. Before, hits by desire, happiness or sorrow would keep a spiritual seeker in turmoil. The principle of energy in the body would be always moving and cause disturbances. Now all is calm. 'I'-ness is absent. All disorderliness has gone. Before this, this world ceremony, this ceremony of actions was established on the sense of 'I'-ness. Everything was unruly, disturbed, and brought danger. Now that the nature of Self is illuminated, everything is turned into a ceremony of *Brahmaṇ*. Now, all action is offered to *Brahmaṇ*, the fire, offerings, worshipper and results are all *Brahmaṇ*. All is Self. So, the ceremonies of actions are no longer perturbed.

The sense of 'I' has been removed, Self is illuminated. There is nothing but auspicious *ātmā* everywhere. Inauspicious sounds are calmed. Before, there was the analysis of worldly results and the good and bad thereof. Now, that is no longer present. Everything is auspicious. Everything is imbued by Self, blissful.

This is the establishment of bliss. These five mantras describe the expression of bliss. When blissful Self is encountered, everywhere, only blissful spirit is experienced. As long as any special knowledge as 'I' exists, this bliss cannot be found. When *Śumbha* is destroyed by the grace of Mother, a seeker finds continuous bliss. Under no circumstances is this bliss removed. Whatever may come, movement of spirit, desire or renunciation, illness or sorrow, one is not moved from bliss. It has no beginning or end, undifferentiated completeness, yet ever new. Even though one enjoys it continuously, the novelty does not disappear. It is very beautiful. In the language of a *Vaiṣṇava*, it is the dark one in eternal *Vṛindāvana*, always young, always desirable. This bliss is *puruśa* of *Sānkhya*, the *Brahmaṇ* of *Vedānta*, *ātmā* of *Upaniṣads*, *Kṛṣṇa* of *Gitā*, *Caṇḍīkā* of *Devī Māhātmya*, our Mother.

Look. You are bliss, your universe is bliss. Your mind, *prāṇa*, senses and body are all bliss. You and this universe are formed of bliss. Bliss is the ingredient of both you and this universe. Under no circumstances have you moved from bliss. You are honored. Say, 'I am *sadcidānanda,* forever free.'

Here ends the explanations on the destruction of *Śumbha*, in *Sādhan Samar* or *Devī Māhātmya*

Chapter 11

Praises to *Nārāyaṇī*

Verse 1.

> *ṛīṣiruvāca|*
> *devyā hate tatra mahāsurendre*
> *sendrāḥ surā vahnipurogamāstām|*
> *kātyāyanīṁ tuṣṭuvuriṣṭalābhād*
> *vikāśivaktrāstu vikāśitāśāḥ||*

Translation:

The sage said that in that battle, the greatest of the demons, *Śumbha* having been destroyed by the Goddess, *Agṇi* and other gods, together with *Indra*, joyously singing praises to *Kātyāyanī*, illuminated the horizons.

Explanation:

When one resides in a spirit of pure feeling, by the absence of any perception of duality, hymns and praises may not appear to be possible. When one comes out of it, from habit, a sense of non-Self of the body arises again. Then, the singing of praises is feasible and very natural.

Śumbha has been destroyed. The goal of deities established in the senses has been fulfilled. They have recovered their portions of ceremonial offerings that had been stolen. There is no end to their joy. Now, although they are special consciousness, they are united with undivided consciousness. They are able to realize the nature of undivided bliss. So, their faces express their feeling of exultation.

Although *Indra* is the chief of gods, in this case, *Agṇi* (god of fire) is in front. *Agṇi* is the ruler of the organ of speech. Hymns are groups of sentences. So, keeping consciousness established in the organ of speech in front, singing of praises may be accomplished properly. Because of this, the gods keep *Agṇi* in front for singing this hymn. If the residing deity of speech is not satisfied, recital of hymns cannot be imbued with truth and life force.

Whatever it is, the sound of hymns sung by the gods sanctified all directions. The horizons were lit up by the pure rays of right tendency (*sattva*). The gods devotedly sang praises to *Kātyāyani*. *Kātyāyani* - Goddess of this universe. Because she is the shelter of those who realize *Brahmaṇ*, she is known as *Kātyāyani*. She is *Brahmaṇ* with characteristics (*saguṇa*). Hymns are sung to *saguṇa Brahmaṇ*.

Verse 2.

devi prapannārtihare prasīda
prasīda mātarjagatohakhilasya|
prasīda viśveśvari pāhi viśvaṁ
tvamīśvarī devi carācarasya||

Translation:

O, Goddess! O, remover of sorrow of those who seek refuge! You who are Mother of this universe, be pleased. O, Goddess of this world, be pleased. O, Goddess! You protect this world! You are the (only) ruler of this world.

Explanation:

Mother. You remove the sorrow of all who seek your refuge. Those, who know you as their only sanctuary, seek refuge at your protective feet. However wicked they may be, however ignorant, you remove all their sorrow, all grief, and failings. Mother! Be pleased with us. May we be able to take refuge at your feet. We do not have power or faith in our hearts, to be able to leap onto your lap knowing you as our only refuge. Despite this, you give us sanctuary. Why would we still nurture an imaginary 'I' in the refuge of material things? Do what is needed so that we seek refuge only in you. Be pleased with us.

You are the Mother of this universe, so you are pleased with us. Just because we are terrible children, you cannot be a terrible

Mother. We do not, cannot call you with open hearts. But because of that, you do not push us away. You are our Mother. O Mother of this world! When you are pleased, all our desires are fulfilled. For how many lifetimes, only to please you, we have suffered so much conflict, so much oppression. But we did not realize that you are eternally pleased, eternally satisfied. As long as we see you expressed by multiple perceptions, how will we realize your satisfaction? O Mother! We have waited for so long, hiding hopelessness in our hearts, looking at your face, just to hear a word from you. We have suffered many blows, knowingly and unknowingly, truthfully or untruthfully, with or without desire. We have called you Mother. Be pleased, O Mother. Tell us, 'I am not many, I am One.' Our lives will be honored if we can hear one word from you. Bondages of lifetimes will vanish. Your pleasure will be felt by us.

Mother, you are the Goddess of this world, you protect it. This world, not seeing you, not feeling your spirit, not understanding your satisfaction, moves outwards. Day by day they move toward destruction. Save us, protect us. Save this world from its rapid, external movement. Save it from destruction. Why not? You are the only ruler of this world. All that is here, is under your control. Who will save this world if you do not? That is why we say to you, save this world by destroying *Śumbha* inside us.

Verse 3.

ādhārabhūtā jagatastvamekā
mahīsvarūpeṇa yataḥ sthitāsi|
apāṁ svarūpasthitayā tvayaita
dāpyāyate kṛtsnamalaṅghyavīrye||

Translation:

You are the vessel that holds this world, as you exist as earth. As water, you satisfy all this world. Mother, your valor is insurmountable.

Explanation:

Mother, that you are of the nature of the power of this world, we can understand a little by seeing it as your form. As earth, like a mother, you hold everything in your heart. There is no change from eternal time, no alternatives. In a form as earth, you have held this world of beings. Not only that, in the form of water, you greet all beings, you bring them relief. Satisfying their hunger as crops, their thirst as water, you show your nature as Mother. Just as a mother holds a child at her breast and satisfies its thirst and hunger, you hold this world of beings as earth and as water, to nurture them. Mother, the manner in which you embrace and maintain this universe and show your influence, cannot be surpassed by God. Mother, you are of insurmountable valor.

Your nature is Self. You are *ātmā*. Yet, you are with the nature of earth and water. You are *ātmā* that goes beyond any physical matter. Yet, you separate yourself to be earth and water, to sustain this world. Mother, truly, your valor cannot be overcome.

Verse 4.

tvaṁ vaiṣṇavīśaktiranantavīryā
viśvasya bījaṁ paramāsi ṁāyā |
sammohitaṁ devi samastametat-
tvaṁ vai prasannā bhuvi muktihetuḥ||

Translation:

You are *Vaiṣṅavī* power, of infinite valor, you are the seed of this world, supreme *māyā*. O, Goddess! You keep this world of beings mesmerized. On the other hand, when you are pleased, you are the cause of liberation for this world.

Explanation:

Mother! You are the power *Vaiṣṅavī*, the all-encompassing, great power of stability. Every atom of this universe resides in you. You are of infinite valor. There is no end to the wealth of your valor. Mother! When you reveal yourself as the power of

Vaiṣṅavī to your children, then truly you appear as infinite valor. At that time, it seems that overcoming the power of your valor is impossible. It is not only that you are *Vaiṣṅavī* power of the expression of this universe, you reside as the seed of this world, the unaltered, primal cause of creation. You are the supreme seed, and as *Vaiṣṅavī*, you are known as *māyā*. As the implicit seed of creation, you are supreme *māyā*. *Sānkhya* has called this supreme spirit, prime nature (*mūlprakṛti*).

Mother, in your twofold nature, we see two kinds of actions. When you appear in the figure of *māyā*, that is, when you appear in your explicit form as this universe, then you mesmerize all. When you appear in your supreme form, you being pleased are the cause of liberation for this world. In one form you are the enjoyer, in the other, the liberator. In your nature as *māyā*, you keep all this world engrossed. You do not let your Self be perceived. At that time, seeing your figures of *māyā*, beings try to acquire them. Those who are engrossed by form and flavor, desire and wealth, material things, are mesmerized by you directly. Those, who instead of seeking your refuge, carry out much spiritual enterprise, may also be engrossed by accomplishment, power, fame and establishment. Just as people, bind weaker ones with their charms and magic, so have you held all beings from what eternal time. They cannot ask for you. They think that their lives are meaningful with your costumes and toys. They cannot even think that there is a need to ask for you. Such is the overwhelming delusion. Mother, you are unconquerable. If it was anything else but you that came in this form of delusion, beings would have been able to remove it with severe effort. But, it is you, unconquerable Mother, who standing as delusion, keeps the eyes of beings from a view of Self. Mother, how long will you keep all of us turning around like blindfolded oxen? O Mother, remove these coverings from the eyes of your children, let them seek the shelter of your feet and make their lives worthwhile.

O Mother! It is you, who is with this mesmerizing form! It is you who appears every day in the shape of material things, as desire and wealth, and engross us. When we get to hold you, your engrossing form disappears, your eternally pleased figure appears. Then there is no more danger, no more fear. It is you, who then appears as affectionate Mother and carrying your favored children, take them to a temple of freedom. This is why we see that the gods, in singing your praises, on one hand, seeing your world bemusing figure say 'you mesmerize all these worlds', and on the other, seeing your figure of liberation, say, 'when you are pleased, you grant freedom to all.' Mother, be pleased. Let us understand that in your eternally delighted form, you hold us at your heart all the time. Like the gods, let us cry 'Mother' and alight on the door of the temple of liberation.

Verse 5.

vidyā samastāstava devī bhedāḥ
striyaḥ samastāḥ sakalā jagatsu|
tvayaikayā pūritamambayaitat
kā te stutiḥ stavyaparāparoktiḥ||

Translation:

O Goddess! In this universe, everything is knowledge. All these are your divisions, that is, different forms. Only you, as Mother, fill this world. How can there be praises sung for you? You are established beyond praises and words (or, praises by words about you are not possible).

Explanation:

It has been mentioned in the previous mantra that when Mother is satisfied, the path to liberation of a spiritual seeker is unfettered. In what manner a seeker perceives this world when Mother is pleased is described in this mantra.

O, Goddess! Resplendent one. All this universe is knowledge (*jagatsu vidyā samastā*). *Upaniṣads* say that by which eternal *puruśa* can be known is knowledge. In infinite universes, everything is knowledge. '*jagatsu*': infinite worlds. Those who are true seekers, those who have the great fortune to see your figure of satisfaction, see forms of knowledge everywhere. What is known in this world as not-knowledge (*avidyā*), is also nothing else but knowledge. It is knowledge expressed in a muted manner and is called *avidyā*. Only your children who can envision your principles understand this. So, saying 'all is knowledge', they fall at your feet, as the form of all knowledge. One can question that if all is knowledge, what have scriptures labeled as *avidyā*? In answer, the gods said, 'all that is disunited with you' (*tava devī bhedāḥ*). What is *avidyā* is only a division from your figure as knowledge. They are all your different forms. Only you, undivided appear as all, reside eternally as this universe. Mother, this universe appears as figures of your divided self. So, for the gods, everything is illuminated as knowledge *. They do not see anything opposed to knowledge.

[*Note by Author: We have no conflict with those who take the meaning of knowledge here to be the eighteen *vidyās*. Their meaning is intensive, ours is extensive.]

All that is experienced as this world is feminine, they are your energy (*striyaḥ samastāḥ*). As pure consciousness, only you are supreme *puruśa*. What is perceived as all of this universe is feminine, all is *prakṛti*, your energy, your wish, your nature. Just as energy is united with the one with energy, so is this world of nature united, undivided from you, the supreme being. In the language of *Vaiṣṇava*, it is the union of *Rādhā* and *Kṛṣṇa*.

Mother, all this is eternally existent with your parts (*kalā*). As spirit, as consciousness, as appearance and existence, it is you that is everywhere. This is why the gods say, all that is perceived is all you (*sakalā*). If it is not existing as you, if it is not illuminated by your consciousness, there is nothing that exists. Although there are no divisions in you, you are eternally whole, you are undivided, still, as long as there is a perception of specialty, so long they have to be called divisions. So, *śrutis* say that this universe exists as one part of you.

Mother! Those who are used to seeing this world, not as the world, but as knowledge, are used to seeing all of this as your divided forms, as parts of your nature. Only to them is your form as the satisfied Mother revealed. Then they loudly say, 'you as Mother, fill this world.'

A spiritual seeker has to remember about spirit in the folds of energy mentioned in Volume One. Look and see that there is only one undivided spirit in this universe. There is a tree, a fruit, a flower, I am, you are, all these divided entities, all of them are evidence of that one undivided existence. That undivided existence is the power of awareness, *puruśa* or Mother. That spirit is unknowable, yet the nature of knowledge, is not receivable, but the nature of a receiver. When we try to understand it specifically, then with that undivided spirit, we see energy in the figure of a woman. 'A tree is', here 'tree' is the energy and 'is' *puruśa*. It is the same elsewhere. This energy is that of *puruśa*, not something different. The spirit of energy, or energy of spirit. Now look, That tree, in a form with a name, is energy or Mother who fills this universe. Look around, there is nothing but Mother. 'You fill this world.' If you can view it in this manner, that is, as the sentient, supreme power, as Mother, then you will realize its satisfaction. If you understand the satisfaction of Mother, you will see that Mother is the only cause of liberation in this world. It is Mother who will take you on her lap and land you in a temple of liberation. Your life will be honored.

Singing her praises in this manner, the gods saw the form of Mother in all this world. They were forced to say, '*kā te stuti*.' How can one sing your praises? There is nothing else but you. You reside beyond all praises and hymns. One cannot describe your nature, or ascribe characteristics to you by singing praises because you are above all of it. Not only that, to sing praises, one has to use words, but you exist beyond words. Not seen by words, 'where words cannot reach' (*na tatra vak gacchanti*). So, whichever way we take it, praises are not possible. O Mother! To cleanse our speech, like children, we have to sing about the greatness of your nature. You have to forgive us.

Verse 6.

sarvabhūtā yadā devī svargamukti pradāyinī|
tvaṁ stutā stutaye kā vā bhavantu paramoktayaḥ||

Translation:

Mother, when you are manifest as all forms, offer freedom of heaven when you are eternally praised, what hymns are conceivable that are proper speech, that is, with proper words?

Explanation:

Mother! For humans, the assignment of great character is a hymn of praise. There is no lack of any characteristics in you that have to be assigned and described. For the gods, singing about their natures are praises for them. For you, that is not possible, because no one knows or can know your true nature. There is no one other than you, who can know your nature. So, singing your praises is not reasonable. You are the nature of all, manifest and offer freedom of heaven, you are inherently praiseworthy. What praises can be sung to you? You are beyond words and mind. Whatever we may say about you, are not 'supreme words.'

Verse 7.

sarvvasya buddhirūpeṇa janasya hṛdi saṁsthite|
svargāpavargade devi nārāyaṇi namohastu te||

Translation:

O Goddess *Nārāyaṇī*! You reside in the hearts of all beings as intelligence. You offer heaven and liberation, we bow down to you.

Explanation:

O Mother! We are unable to sing your praises. So, we act as if we bow to you. Only you know when we will be able to truly bow down to you. Only you know, when, on bowing down to you, we will not return to this body and mind, when in bowing down to you, we will find a place in your supreme home. Even though we cannot truly bow down to you, we will act as if we are doing so. Then, when you wish, you will make us truly bow down to you.

Mother, you reside inside all beings as intelligence (*buddhi*). The definite intelligence that on one hand takes tendencies of this world and on the other a shadow of *ātmā* without characteristics, that is also you. To find you as intelligence, three times a day, *brāhmiṇs* pray to you for intelligence saying '*dhiyo yo naḥ pracodayāt*[1].' When this intelligence is pure, of right tendency (*sattva*), it offers, on one hand, heaven, that is knowledge, renunciation and greatness, on the other, it reveals the nature of liberation. Liberated seekers reside in this intelligence enjoying heaven and also a hint of what is beyond heaven. You are Mother who as intelligence offers heaven. You are *Nārāyaṇī*, in each human (*nara*). You reside as intelligence in all beings. You are *Nārāyaṇī*, in whose shelter, all humans reside. You are *Nārāyaṇī*, so we are *nara*. We bow down to you with our bodies, minds and words. Mother receive our obeisance.

Verse 8.

kalākāṣṭhādirūpeṇa pariṇāmapradāyini|
viśvasyoparatau śakte nārāyaṇi namohastu te||

Translation:

As divisions of time, you conduct the results of this world. You are the destructive power in this world, you are *Nārāyaṇī*, we bow down to you.

Explanation:

Mother, in the form of time, you are always directing results, that is, changes in this world. The divisions of time are imaginary parts of your undivided form as time. Eighteen *nimeṣ* forms one *kāṣṭhā* and three hundred *kāṣṭhā* form one *kalā*. In this fashion, there are seconds, days, weeks, months, seasons, years, ages, and so many imagined divisions. Mother, although your form

---

1 may it guide our intelligence, *Gāyatri* mantra.

as time is undivided, to perceive its nature, we have segmented it into many. As undivided time, you carry out changes in this world. In this form as time, through change, you perform the dissolution of this world. You are the destroyer of *Brahmā*, *Viṣṇu* and *Maheśvara*. To you, any indifference in this world does not matter. Even though you are with extreme power, you reside in the individual as *Nārāyaṇī*, and globally as Mother. Being Mother of all, you are also Mother of each individual. You are *Nārāyaṇī*, we bow down to you.

Verse 9.

sarvamaṅgalamāṅgalye śive sarvārthasādhike|
śaraṇye tryambake gauri nārāyaṇi namohastu te||

Translation:

You are one beneficial to all, you are beneficence, you fulfill all wishes. You give shelter, you are three-eyed, you are fair *Gourī*, you are *Nārāyaṇī*, we bow down to you.

Explanation:

There are many meanings of the word beneficial (*maṅgala*). The achievement of what is desirable is *maṅgala*, that which is beneficial to all, or all that is beneficial in this world. The one who is beneficial to all is *sarva-maṅgala-māṅgalye*. There are eight things beneficial in this world, *brāhmiṇs*, cattle, fire, gold, *sarpiḥ* (clarified butter), the Sun, water and a king. These eightfold benefits are intended by *sarva-maṅgala*. My Mother is beneficial to all of these eight. Or, the word *sarva* could mean *Śiva*. She is his beneficial aspect.

We have understood another meaning in this. Everything is beneficial, she is beneficial to all. What is perceived as everything, be it false, be it error or inert is nothing but awareness (*cit*). When a seeker realizes this, everything appears to him as beneficial. Only *cit* is beneficial, nothing else is. Because they are conscious when alive, beings are with beneficial natures. That is why *Śri* is used before the name of someone alive. Those who are not alive are not beneficial. When everything is illuminated as that nature of awareness, then they are all beneficial. There is nothing detrimental. The one who determines that by whom everything is expressed, is being called by us *sarva-maṅgala*. With the entry of *sadcidānanda*, everything is turned beneficial. She is beneficial. The gods address her as *Śive*. Mother, when people understand you to be the one who is beneficial to all, you appear as the one who fulfills all desires. All their goals and desires are fulfilled. They merge into you.

Mother! You are the one to seek help from, the only shelter of beings. You are three-eyed, with the Sun, Moon and fire as your three eyes, expressed as physical, subtle and causal, you exist for all time. Again, as memory, imagination and hope, as present, future and past. You see all three periods of time with your three eyes. You exist for all time. Mother, you are *Gaurī*, the fair one, enchanting, very beautiful, peaceful. You are *Nārāyaṇī*, we bow down to you.

Verse 10.

sṛṣṭisthitivināśānāṁ śaktibhūte sanātani|
guṇāśraye guṇamaye nārāyaṇi namohastu te||

Translation:

Mother, you are the power of creation, maintenance and dissolution. You shelter the three attributes (*guṇas*), you are the shelter for the three attributes. You are *Nārāyaṇī*, we bow down to you.

Explanation:

Consciousness formed Mother! That your nature is energy, can be understood by looking at everything in this world, in your form as creation-maintenance-dissolution. If there is anything to hold you or understand you, it is this three-fold expression. You are ancient, you are eternal. Even though you are by nature nonmanifest, you are revealed everywhere in the form of creation-maintenance–dissolution. *Purāṇa* and *Tantra* literature describe your figure as *Mahākālī*. You appear as *Brahmā*, *Viṣṇu* and *Maheśvara*. Mother, from you, appear the three-fold powers of creation-maintenance-dissolution. These three are not separate, but three-fold vibrations of the energy of awareness. Although the nature of the energy is not explicit, it is by these three-fold vibrations, that its nature is perceived. Mother, it is aimed at this nonmanifest nature of energy that the gods said that you are the nature and refuge of all attributes (*guṇas*). It is based on the three attributes of *sattva*, *rājasa* and *tāmasa* that these three-fold vibrations appear. Or, your three-fold powers are called the three *guṇas*. When the three *guṇas* are expressed in your refuge, then you being the nature of the attributes, in that form of *Nārāyāṇī*, hold us on your lap. Mother, we bow down to you. Mother, take us from this three-fold condition of *guṇas*, into your eternal nature, where there are no longer movements of creation-maintenance–dissolution. Mother, take us there, take us there.

Verse 11.

śaraṇāgatadīnārta-paritrāṇaparāyaṇe|
sarvasyārtihare devi nārāyaṇi namohastu te||

Translation:

Mother, you are the savior of all who seek your refuge, who are weak and needy. You are the relief of all, you are *Nārāyaṇī*, we bow down to you.

Explanation:

Mother! When beings seek refuge at your feet, are weak and feel your absence, are needy because they are separated from you, then they may perceive your three-fold energy and attribute formed nature. Then you appear in your form as a savior and remove all their needs. Then the pain of life and death and sad cries of innumerable lifetimes end.

When beings can seek shelter at your feet, they can be aware of your first power, your nature as right attribute (*sattva*). Knowing that you are the only refuge, that your nature is the nature of this world, they try to forsake all *dharma* and seek refuge only in you. They realize your figure as the nature of *sattva*.

They learn to be humble. Beings realize their small stature after viewing your infinitely rich forms, the empress of billions of worlds, your divine play. They understand how weak and poor they are. Understanding my Mother to be the empress of a billion worlds, is to realize your second nature of active attribute (*rājasa*). When we understand our low status, we may feel the wealth of Mother. No, feeling the wealth of Mother lets one know lowliness. Mother appears in this form as active attribute, to show her children her figure of awareness (*cit*).

After this are feelings of distress. To realize the nature of your continuous form of bliss, beings have to feel weak. That there is no joy in materials of this world, that the only source of bliss is you, an external sign of this understanding is a feeling of distress. A feeling of separation from you is real distress. When this feeling appears, beings meet your figure of bliss, the form of your inert attribute (*tāmasa*), and are honored to go beyond sorrow.

Mother, when we say 'we are without shelter, save us' and feel unprotected, we accept your existence, seek your sanctuary, we understand that we are truly sheltered by you. Then, your nature as existence (*sat*) is revealed to us, we are established in truth. When we perceive your infinitely great, divine play in all this universe, realize our small stature, and desire to acquire your great wealth, then your form as awareness (*cit*) is revealed. Then we perceive you everywhere as life force (*prāṇa*), as consciousness. We are then established in life force. When disturbances of birth and death, this body raise distress in the heart, then we see you appear as a dense, eternal figure of bliss. There is no dearth of bliss in you or us. We are eternally still, eternally blissful. O my Mother, O *Nārāyāṇī*, O remover of distress, we bow down to you. You first make us seek shelter, weak and distressed, then establish us in truth and life force. Let our respect for you be worthy. As long as these three-fold features are not expressed in us, we cannot perceive your form as savior. Make your children ready for revelation, make them seek shelter and humility.

Verse 12.

haṁsayuktavimānasthe brahmāṇīrūpadhāriṇi|
kauśāmbhaḥkṣarike devi nārāyaṇi namohastu te||

Verse 13.

triśūlacandrāhidhare mahāvṛṣabhavāhini|
māheśvarīsvarūpeṇa nārāyaṇi namohastu te||

Verse 14.

mayūrakukkuṭavṛte mahāśaktidharehnaghe|
kaumārīrūpasaṁsthāne nārāyaṇi namohastu te||

Translation:

Mother, seated on a celestial craft, drawn by swans, you take the form of *Brahmāṇī* and from your water-pot sprinkle sacred water. You are *Nārāyaṇī*, we bow down to you. Holding a trident, the Moon and serpents, you ride a great bull and appear as *Māheśvarī*. You are *Nārāyaṇī*, we bow down to you. You appear as the great power *Kaumārī*, decorated with peacock feathers. You are *Nārāyaṇī*, we bow down to you.

Explanation:

Mother, you are *Brahmāṇī*. As the great mind, you hold the imagination of this world. The individual mind is your craft drawn by swans. You sprinkle holy water from your water pot. Just as you inspire the power of determination in the supreme storehouse of work, so does work appear from the individual workshops of beings. Whatever action you confront them with, they take pride in that action. Without this holy water sprinkled by you, the thirst for action would be unsatisfied. You are the self-expressed Goddess *Nārāyaṇī*, we bow down to you.

Mother. In the form of *Māheśvarī*, with a trident of tri-fold knowledge, the Moon of mind, and the serpent of *kuṇḍalinī*, you appear, riding on the bull of *dharma*. You appear to each person with this form. O *Nārāyaṇī*, we bow down to you.

Mother, you are adorned with resplendent peacock feathers. (The word '*kukkuta*' means feathers or greatest.) Mother. When worldly persons have the nature of peacocks, when they are ready to destroy wicked serpents, then you appear as *Kaumārī* adorned with peacock feathers. Taking leadership of the divine warriors you are ready to destroy the demons. Your children are then relieved of the fear of demons. Mother, you are sinless, so when they see you, your children are sinless. The knowledge of divisiveness is '*agha*'. The sense of duality is sin. On viewing you, the sense of duality is removed. Worldly beings become *Brahmaṇ*. Evil is destroyed. You are *Nārāyaṇī*, we bow down to you.

Verse 15.

śaṅkhacakragadāśārṅgagṛhītaparamāyudhe|
prasīda vaiṣṇavīrūpe nārāyaṇi namohastu te||

Verse 16.

gṛhītogramahācakre daṁṣṭroddhītavasundhare|
varāharūpiṇi śive nārāyaṇi namohastu te||

Verse 17.

nṛsiṁharūpeṇogreṇa hantuṁ daityān kṛtodyame|
trailokyatrāṇasahite nārāyaṇi namohastu te||

Translation:

Mother. As *Vaiṣṅavī*, holding great weapons, a conch shell, discus, mace and bow, be pleased. O, *Nārāyaṇī*, we bow down to you. In the form of a boar, you hold a terrible discus and with your tusks have rescued this earth. O, *Śive*, O, *Nārāyaṇī*, we bow down to you. Taking the form of terrifying *Nṛsiṁha*, you were ready to destroy the clan of demons. You are *Nārāyaṇī*, the one who saves the three worlds, we bow down to you.

Explanation:

Mother, in your three forms as *Vaiṣnavī*, *Vārāhī* and *Nārasiṁhī*, we see you as special expressions of the power of *Viṣṇu*. As the figure of the supreme power of maintenance, you hold a conch shell, discus, mace and bow. That is, by the attraction of loving *Praṇava*, you draw this explicit and implicit circle of life towards liberation. The divine ones view your worldwide supreme feet as the space-filling power of direction. Spiritual seekers by their water ceremony (*ācamana*) try to unite their perceptions with your supreme state. You are *Nārāyaṇī*, all persons (*nara*) are sheltered by you. We bow down a million times at your feet. Mother, be pleased.

Mother. If in your form as *Varāhī* you had not rescued this world from the flood waters of destruction, if you had not brought out the nonmanifest seed of this world, then this world would have been sleeping in ignorant darkness, who knows for how long? It is your grace, that beings, knowingly or unknowingly holding on to their physical perceptions are moving toward liberation. You are *Śivā*, the beneficent *Nārāyaṇī*, we bow down to you.

O Mother! In your form as *Varāhī*, your nature as *Nārasiṁhī* appears in our memories. Oh! What a cruel figure it is! The demons were destroyed and you severed the body of *Hiraṇyakaśipu* into pieces. The three worlds were saved from demons.

Mother, one day, by the influence of the strength of truth in *Prahlāda*, you had expressed your conscious nature, emerging out of a crystal pillar. Today, in this age of inertness, in these times of heartless action, appear again in your form as truth. Emerge from the crystal pillar of the inert sense of beings and reveal your Self. Let doubts of worldly persons disappear. Let them forego any enchantment of inertness and be established in consciousness. Let the tide of truth, life force and bliss flood this world again. Let this world, like the gods, see you as *Nārāyaṇī* everywhere, and saying '*namohastu te*', bow down to you. Mother, when will the hopes of your child be fulfilled?

Verse 18.

kirīṭini mahāvajre sahasranayanojjvale|
vṛtraprāṇahare caindri nārāyaṇi namohastu te||

Verse 19.

śivadūtīsvarūpeṇa hatadaityamahābale|
ghorarūpe mahārāve nārāyaṇi namohastu te||

Verse 20.

daṁṣṭrākarālavadane śiromālāvibhūṣaṇe|
cāmuṇḍe muṇḍamathane nārāyaṇi namohastu te||

Translation:

Mother, wearing a crown, holding a great lightning bolt, adorned with a thousand eyes, you are *Indrāṇī*, destroyer of *Vṛtra*. You are *Nārāyaṇī*, we bow down to you. Taking the form of *Śivadūtī*, you destroyed demon soldiers. You are dangerous and roar loudly. You are *Nārāyaṇī*. O *Cāmuṇḍe*, we bow down to you. Your teeth are frightful, you are adorned with skulls, you destroyed the *asura Muṇḍa*. You are *Nārāyaṇī*, we bow down to you.

Explanation:

Mother. The jewel of pure knowledge crowns your head. You hold a great lightning bolt. The *śrutis* say 'raise the great fear of lightning.' Because you hold a lightning bolt of great fear, the Sun comes up and the air flows, fire gives heat and death rides on. This world is ruled by you. This is the nature of your figure holding a bolt of lightning.

You have a thousand eyes. You have innumerable eyes. Every being, each tiny atom is illuminated by your eyes, your sharp vision. There is nothing unseen by you. Mother, let your loved children know that they may not be moved from truth, into a shelter of untruth, hidden from you. Knowing that you are the eyes of this world, that your vision goes into the deepest heart, they will not travel on paths of untruth. They will be truthful. Restrictions of their hearts will be removed.

Mother, you are *Indrāṇī*, destroyer of *Vṛtra*. The demon *Vṛtra* in the form of a sense of non-Self is destroyed by your lightning bolt. Your lightning bolt is built from the bones of *brāhmiṇs*. A *brāhmiṇ* is a living form of *Brahmaṇ*. Your lightning bolt cannot be built without the bones of a *brāhmiṇ*. Even the tiniest part of the material body of a *brāhmiṇ* is illuminated by the light of knowledge of *Brahmaṇ*. So, not only do *brāhmiṇs* hold this world with a knowledge of *Brahmaṇ*, the bones of their material body can destroy demons, do good for this world. Is it only to explain this that you built your lightning bolt from the bones of *brāhmiṇs* and destroyed the demons? It is true that without the bones of *brāhmiṇs*, a lightning bolt to destroy the demons would not be created. Only a *brāhmiṇ* can destroy demons in this world. As custodians of knowledge of *Brahmaṇ*, to destroy demonic percepts, *brāhmiṇs* exist in this world. Mother, a *brāhmiṇ* is a glory of this created world of yours. You are Mother, so in this world, your *brāhmiṇ* children declare and spread the word that you are *Indrāṇī*, you are *Nārāyaṇī*. We bow down to you.

Mother, you are *Śivadutī*. Before the destruction of *Śumbha*, you sent *Śiva* as a messenger and so became known in this world as *Śivadutī*. In the great battle with demons, you destroyed innumerable demons. Because of your terrible figure and deafening roars, demonic feelings are quickly removed. You are *Nārāyaṇī*, we bow down to you.

Mother, you are *Cāmuṇḍā*, destroyer of *Caṇḍa* and *Muṇḍa*. Demons of knowledge of duality enter your mouth with its fearsome teeth and clear the way for seekers of the knowledge of nonduality. You wear a garland of fifty skulls. The fifty maternal alphabets (*matṛkā varṇas*) are hung around your neck as a garland of skulls. You are *Nārāyaṇī*, we bow down to you.

Mother, you appear as *Brāhmī*, *Māheśvarī*, *Koumārī* and the other eight powers and remove the demons of our eight bondages of hatred, diffidence and others. You also trample the desire for eight-fold glories, remove the desire for a state of Godhood and bring us to the principle of nonduality, to the nature of pure perception. The expression of your eight-fold powers, tears our eight-fold bonds, makes eight-fold glories insubstantial and lands us at a golden temple of liberation. You appear in each person as a loving Mother, so you are *Nārāyaṇī.* We bow down a million times at your feet. We hope that one day, you will be visible in the hearts of all beings in your form as *Nārāyaṇī.*

Verse 21.

lakṣmī lajje mahāvidye śraddhe puṣṭi svadhe dhruve|
mahārātri mahāmāye nārāyaṇi namohastu te||

Verse 22.

medhe sarasvati vare bhūti bābhravi tāmasi|
niyate tvaṁ prasīdeśe nārāyaṇi namohastute||

Translation:

You are *Lakṣmī*, modesty, great knowledge, respect, nourishment, *svadhā*, tranquility, great darkness, and great *avidyā.* You are *Nārāyaṇī*, we bow down to you. You are intelligence *Sarasvati, Varā, Bhūti, Vābhravi* and *Tāmasi*. Goddess be pleased. *Nārāyaṇī*, we bow down to you.

Explanation:

Mother, you are *Lakṣmī*, the figure of life force, of beauty and wealth. You are modesty, one opposed to proscribed actions. You are great knowledge, *Kālī*, *Tārā* and all the ten *Mahāvidyās*, the supreme knowledge of *Brahmaṇ*. You are respect, dedicated to truth and a firm reliance on the words of a *guru.* You are nourishment the one who sustains the five sheaths. You are *svadhā*, the funeral rites and actions for forefathers. You are *dhrubā*, ever serene; *Mahārātri*, final destruction. As ignorance, you are great *avidyā*, knowledge of non-self. You are *Nārāyaṇī*, we bow down to you.

Mother, you are *medhā*, focused intelligence, one able to conceive the knowledge of *Brahmaṇ*. You are *Sarasvatī*, pure knowledge of *Brahmaṇ*. You are *Varā*, one granting great boons.

You are *Bhūti*, the nature of right attribute (*guṇa*), *Vābhravi*, the nature of active attribute and *Tāmasī*, the nature of dark attribute. You are *Niyatā*, one with definite attributes. Mother be pleased. You are *Īśā*, the Goddess. Being the creator, maintainer and destroyer of this universe, you reside in each being as *Nārāyaṇī*, we bow down a million times at your feet.

Verse 23.

sarvasvarūpe sarveśe sarvaśaktisamanvite|
bhayebhyastrāhi no devi durge devi namohastu te||

Translation:

O Goddess, you are the nature of all, the ruler of all, the one with all power. Relieve us from fear. O Goddess *Durgā*. We bow down to you.

Explanation:

Mother, the gods, singing your praises have bowed down to you repeatedly, naming you as *Brāhmī* and other eight-fold powers, as special forms as *Lakṣmī*, modesty and other. They have with tender hearts prayed to you for your satisfaction. Now, saying that you are the nature of all, ruler of all, they express signs of your satisfaction. The three natures of you that are expressed when you are satisfied, are remembered by them as they bow down to you.

Mother, you are the nature of all. Al this that is viewed by us, all this variety that we perceive all the time, all this is your first nature. This is your physical body. The children who truly see all this as your physical body, have revealed to them your second nature as ruler of all. You appear to them as creator-maintainer-destroyer of all. This is your subtle body. Your children, meeting your form as Goddess in this manner, are relieved of their states as worldly persons, of their illusions of minuteness. Then your third form as the nature of power is revealed. Unified energy is expressed as the form of all, as creator-maintainer-destroyer of all, as Goddess of all. Where there is no expression of energy, yet where all energy is combined, that is your third nature. By your grace, we have understood that all that is perceived is nothing but energy. Mother, this nature of yours as energy is your causal body. It is given other names, *Brahmaṇ* or *paramātmā*. All these three natures of you are equally true. The *śrutis* sing praises of these three bodies. *Bhāgabat Gitā* mentions your three forms as *kṣara, akṣara* and *puruṣottma*. Even though modern theories of *māyā* only accept your form without attributes, and says that your other natures are false, it does no harm. It is true that in your pure form, there is no such thing as this universe. The great commentator, to explain form without attributes, strongly downplayed the other forms. Whatever it is, Mother, to us, all three forms exist equally. You remove our fear, for all of us. Only you are able to remove the fear of all beings, who are afraid to live in this dangerous world. You are *Durgā*, one who removes sorrows Remove our sorrows of life. We bow down a million times at your feet.

Verse 24.

etatte vadanaṁ saumyaṁ locanatrayabhūṣitam|
pātu naḥ sarvabhūtebhyaḥ kātyāyani namohastu te||

Translation:

Mother, may your beautiful face, adorned with three eyes, protect us from all physical entities. O *Kātyāyani*, we bow down to you.

Explanation:

Mother, your beautiful face that expresses three worlds, adorned with three eyes that see three time-frames, is the nature of pure bliss. Save us from all physical entities (*bhutas*). May beings realize by your grace, that only you, the nature of bliss, is eternally expressed physically as all, as supreme ruler in the subtle and as all energy in the causal planes. Only then is the riddle solved. One understands that all these are not separate entities, that there is nothing as different physical entities. Once one realizes that you, the blissful one is expressed as all, then this is removed forever. Protect me and all of us from all these physical entities. Let us understand in our hearts that only bliss is expressed in everything. Mother, you are *Kātyāyani*, the shelter of those who know *Brahmaṇ*. Be pleased with us as you were pleased with the sage *Kātyāyan*. We bow down to you.

Verse 25.

jvālākarālamatyugramaśeṣāsurasūdanam|
triśūlaṁ pātu no bhīterbhadrakāli namohastu te||

Verse 26.

hinasti daityatejāṁsi svanenāpūrya yā jagat|
sā ghaṇṭā pātu no devi pāpebhyonaḥ sutāniva||

Verse 27.

asurāsṛgvasāpaṅkacarcitaste karojjvalaḥ|
śubhāya khaḍgo bhavatu caṇḍike tvāṁ natā vayam||

Translation:

O *Bhadrakāli*! May your trident, violent (with its terrible flames), that destroyed innumerable demons, relieve us from fear. O Goddess, may your motherly bell, that by its sound fills this world and drains the power of the demons, save us children from sin. May the scimitar in your hand, stained by the blood of demons be auspicious for us. O *Caṇḍīkā*, we bow down to you.

Explanation:

In these three mantras, prayers are made for relief from fear and beneficence, by the three weapons, the trident, bell and scimitar. Tri-fold knowledge, the unvoiced sound and the intellect that destroys the sense of non-Self, these three specifically destroy the percept of demons. The gods pray to them for beneficence.

Mother! You protect us. May your weapons protect your children. Before this, they have saved us from the prison of the state as worldly persons by destroying demonic natures. May they protect us from the demons until the end of the erosion of our stored actions. Mother! When you appear in the form of *Caṇḍīkā*, your weapons arise to protect us by destroying the demons. So, we bow down to you, in your figure as *Caṇḍīkā.*

It is not unnatural to pray in this manner to the specific weapons. In the Vedic ages, such prayers arose spontaneously in the hearts of the sages who envisioned Truth. They were not considered narrow-minded because them. Today, words about lack of desire induce laziness. Those who comprehend what a lack of desire truly is, can pray in this manner. The ignorant or desirous ones cannot offer proper prayers. It is prayer that created this universe, prayer that it resides in, and it is by prayer that this universe merges into the spirit of *Brahmaṇ*. Creation, maintenance, dissolution, bondage and freedom are all grounded on prayer. Prayer is not supplication. Those who believe in the spirit of God and who have unwavering faith in the supreme power of God can pray properly. If one prays correctly, it is bound to be successful. Prayer is not a hindrance to the spiritual quest. But these things are here beside the point.

Verse 28.

rogānaśeṣānapahaṁsi tuṣṭā
ruṣṭā tu kāmān sakalānabhīṣṭān|
tvāmāśritānāṁ na vipannarāṇāṁ
tvāmāśritā hyāśrayatāṁ prayānti||

Translation:

Mother, when you are pleased, you remove all illnesses. When you are displeased you destroy all objectives. When persons are in your shelter, they have no danger. Those sheltered by you, truly find shelter (they are a shelter for others).

Explanation:

Mother your pleasure and displeasure are both beneficial to us. When you are pleased, when we see satisfaction in you, who is eternally satisfied, then we are relieved from all disorders. Illnesses in a physical body are tri-fold, inner disbalances of the constituent elements, divine ones like heat, cold and rain, and physical ones like wild beasts and robbers. All these changes that happen to a body are three-fold illnesses. Diseases of the subtle body are mental. Changes that occur due to loss of intention and occurrence of harm are mental illnesses. Then are those of the causal body. Its nature is ignorance and the forgetting of Self. It is pointing to these three-fold disorders, that the gods say, all illnesses. Mother, as we see your pleasure, all these illnesses are removed. This is the result of visualizing your figure of satisfaction. Mother, those who do not have faith in these words, tell them that these are not just words, truly all illnesses are removed. When one perceives divine satisfaction, then all their affairs are beneficial. Success appears.

Mother, when you are displeased, all desires of beings are destroyed. The mantra uses two words of similar meaning. Present desires are called *kāmanā*, and future ones are called *abhīṣṭa*. When people notice your displeasure, are fearful seeing your angry, red eyes, then all their present and future desires are destroyed. Although in the general view, these are signs of your anger, if we consider it calmly, we can understand that when you are angered and destroy our desires, then we advance on a path of true beneficence. It is to free us from our many desires and wishes that your angry form as *Caṇḍīkā* is expressed. If our present and future desires are not destroyed in this manner, we would forever be bound in utter darkness. If your angry form did not remove desires in our hearts, we would never find the supreme benefit of your golden temple. I say, O Mother, your pleasure and displeasure are both beneficial for us. We have to say that if one seeks your shelter, beings have no more danger. Your satisfaction brings success to desires, your displeasure brings their end. Both are beneficial for us. Mother, it is because you express yourself in these two modes that there is so much variety in creation, so much beauty. Those that find shelter in you, not only have no more danger, but give shelter to others. Many find shelter with them. This is your specialty.

In this mantra, the term '*narāṇāṁ*' designates both male and female.

Verse 29.

etatkṛtaṁ yat kadanaṁ tvayādya
dharmadviṣāṁ devi mahāsurāṇām|
rūpairanekairbahudhātmamūrtiṁ
kṛtvāmbike tatprakaroti kānyā||

Translation:

O Goddess *Amvikā*! You have expressed yourself in many forms and destroyed the *dharma*-hating demons. Who else could have accomplished this but you?

Explanation:

Mother, even though you are unique and the nature of pure perception, you have expressed yourself in many forms. As *Brāhmī, Vaiṣṅavī, Māheśvarī, Kaumārī* and others, you have expressed yourself and destroyed those demons who were against *dharma*. Those who do not want to accept this, those who only accept your eternal form and brush away your expression in these many forms, have to know that as long as perceptions of this world remain, so long one cannot do away with your many forms. The *Upaniṣads* accept your many forms (*rupaṁ rupaṁ pratirupa babhuva*).

Because we try to understand you with our measure of intelligence, we cannot reconcile your many forms with the One and only. In reality, you exist as many although you are One. Who else is there but you? There is nobody, cannot be. That you are the one and only is true. Other than the one true thing, nothing else can express so many forms. So, you are as one and as many. The specialty is that in being expressed as many, your one Self is still one. Even when they are known as pots and plates, they retain their nature as clay. With our weak understanding, we cannot reconcile one-ness and many-ness. You are One while being many, many while One. If yogis can willfully divide their selves into many while retaining one-ness, then what is so strange that you who is the ruler of this universe, can be with attributes while retaining your state without attributes? So, the gods say that you express yourself with different forms. As Self you are One and only, as Goddess you are many. You protect us by destroying demons who are against *dharma*. We bow down a million times at your feet.

Verse 30.

vidyāsu śāstreṣu vivekadīpe
ṣvādyeṣu vākyeṣu ca kā tvadanyā|
mamatvagartehatimahāndhakāre
vibhrāmayatyetadatīva viśvam||

Translation:

Mother. On one side, are knowledge, scriptures, all prime statements, standing like lamps for conscience. On the other, is a dense, dark crevasse of attachment. Who else but you can make this world travel repeatedly in either direction?

Explanation:

Mother, only you can make this world travel in both knowledge and its opposite, above and below. On one side, *vidyā*, knowledge of *Brahmaṇ*, the scriptures and their practice, primal statements, *Veda* and *Upaniṣad* are like lamps for the conscience of Self and non-Self. On the other side, *avidyā*, a dense, dark crevasse of attachment that is deep ignorance. On both banks, who else is there but you? Mother, you as the viewer of non-Self, keep knowledge of attachment and travel for lifetimes in a dark, crevasse of the ignorance of Self. Then again, as *ātmā*, even though you are self-expressed, you travel, recite scriptures, learn *Vedas* and study conscience-based procedures. Mother! On one hand, I see you as a child, selfless and unaware. On the other, you are driven to find yourself. Mother, you are the sentient one who expresses everything, there is not a shred of covering over you. Still, this error, this imaginary travel through this universe is so full of variety. Mother, you are sought by both knowledge and its opposite. You are different from both, beyond words and mind. You move through this world as error of both *vidyā* and *avidyā*. On one hand, seated in the hearts of all as God, you make them travel in this world under the influence of *māyā*. On the other, as beings, you are crushed by the process of travel and express your sorrow. On one side, a bright light, a lamp of conscience, on the other, dense darkness, a crevasse of attachment. On both sides, we feel your absence, but there is only you. There is no absence anywhere. Blessed is your divine play.

Mother, in the word '*vibhrāmayati*,' we see another strange mystery. You seem bewildered, forget your nature, appear as various figures and go back to bewilder others, make them forget. You forget yourself, immersed in a darkness of ignorance, or lighting a lamp of conscience, you try to find yourself. This divine play by you, who is eternal, of the nature of knowledge, is very mysterious.

It will not be out of place here if I quote a song written a long time ago.

My truth, my Mother, my nurse, my life!
Why is your face sunken, why do you act as if in bound?
Why do tears come from your heart?
You are ever-free *Brahmaṇ*, you are universal truth.
Where are birth and death, where is bondage? 1
You are the eternal, supreme truth,
  you are the life of this universe.
You are pure, sinless, complete knowledge.
Bliss is your nature, you are Mother.
You have willfully become small
  and carry the woes of this world. 2
You are the Sun, you are the Moon,
  you are dressed as this world,
  you become the viewer and reside as 'I.'
You are the holy supreme light that reveals everything.
Then, not seeing yourself, willfully become darkness. 3
In a blink of your eye, you think for ages,
Self-expressed, being moved, you see all lands.

Time and direction expand from you,
 you are their subject knowingly.
By your own will you become bound,
 and carry burdens of sorrow. 4
O, my Mother, I cannot stand this game anymore.
Look at your children, poor because of imaginary needs.
O, my loving Mother, stand as the nature of your Self.
You are supreme *māyā*, drown my 'I'-ness in it. 5

Verse 31.

rakṣāṁsi yatrograviṣāśca nāgā
 yatrārayo dasyubalāni yatra|
dāvānalo yatra tathābdhimadhye
 tatra sthitā tvaṁ paripāsi viśvam||

Translation:

Mother, where there are demons, poisonous snakes, enemies, bandits, forest fires and in the middle of the oceans, you reside in all these places to protect this world.

Explanation:

O, Mother! Not only are you confusing this world in the former manner, but you also reside everywhere and protect it. We face demonic enticement from material things, poisonous serpents of jealousy and violence, the enemies, desire and anger, the robbers, pride, arrogance and resentment, forest fires of sorrow and pain, and this worldly life like an impassable ocean. In all these places where there is no one else to protect us, covered by ignorance, a terrible terror of loss of Self, an inevitable dark shadow of death, you emerge in the form of sustenance. You appear as the loving form of Mother and protect all beings, protect this world. In this physical world, full of demons, serpents, enemies, bandits, fires, impassable oceans, and terrible places in which your children fall, you save them miraculously. You protect them in surprising ways. We see it repeatedly, but do not understand you. Even if we understand, we do not accept your spirit. If we accept, we do not believe. We do not accept that you truly are and that you protect all beings. But even if we do not, there is no doubt that you are our protector.

On the other hand, those who fall into trouble and are not protected in our eyes, are also always in the protection of your loving care. There is no doubt or argument about this. Because '*tatra sthitā tvaṁ*', you are there. In any place of danger, in a place of destruction, only you are there. So, if your beloved children are in danger, and are going to be harmed, they are not hurt. They find a place on your lap of peace. O, you are everywhere, you are Mother who protects all. During safety and destruction, you protect this world. This is the definitive truth. Those who view you everywhere as protectress of this universe, are never destroyed.

The words 'you are there and protect this world', have hidden in them, a special mystery of spiritual effort that a seeker should know. When by the order of *Hiraṇyakapiśu*, *Prahlāda* was thrown into a burning fire, he did not call the Lord as 'dweller of the fire' or 'dweller of my heart', but as 'King of *Vaikuntha*'. When *Draupadī* was molested by *Duḥśāsana*, who tried to disrobe her in the court of the *Kurus*, she too did not call the Lord as 'King of my heart' but as 'King of *Dvarakā*.' In both cases, the Lord took a little time to appear, because *Prahlāda* and *Draupadī* had both for the moment forgotten the mystery of 'you are there and protect this world.' The Lord resides everywhere, is there as fire and as clothing, as Lord of the hearts of all beings. So, whatever danger one is in, it is Mother who is there as danger. If one can hold this firm belief in the heart, and remember Mother, then one is freed from all danger. Keeping this feeling firmly in the heart that Mother is everywhere, will keep one from not being swayed by any danger.

Verse 32.

viśveśvari tvaṁ paripāsi viśvaṁ
viśvātmikā dhārayasīti viśvam|
viśveśavandyā bhavatī bhavanti
viśvāśrayā ye tvayi bhaktinamrāḥ||

Translation:

Mother, you are lord of this world, so you protect it. The world is your body, so you hold this world. You are praised by the gods of this world. Those who bow down to you with devotion, become the spirit of support for this world.

Explanation:

Mother! It is not to be forgotten that you miraculously save beings from demons and other dangers. You are the Goddess, ruler of this world. Anyone who rules something protects it. Then why do the gods say 'you protect this world'? Only those who know that you are the ruler of this world understand that only you protect it. Again, it is not surprising that you support this world, because you are the spirit of this world. Saying 'the one became many', you expressed yourself as many. This world is your body, so it is your nature to hold it.

In connection to this, it may not be beside the point to say a few worlds about special nonduality (*viśiṣṭādvaityavād*). The followers of this philosophy say that this world is the body of God. Just as the totality of our physical body, mind, intelligence and soul comprises 'I', in the same manner, the explicit world, great mind and intelligence, in the sum total, comprises *paramātmā*, the only one to be worshipped. In the realm of spiritual enterprise, this principle is loved and accepted. This is not opposed by the *Upaniṣads*. In many places, *Upaniṣads* have said that this world is the physical body of *paramātmā.* But something about this line of thought needs closer attention. Followers of special nonduality say that the visible world is in principle, non-awareness. If this means that it is inert, it is against the *śrutis*, because they have sung about this inert world as the nature of *Brahmaṇ*. However, if non-awareness is taken to be a lower expression of awareness, then there is no controversy.

Mother, you are worshipped by this world. The gods, rulers of this world, that is *Brahmā* and the other deities, sing your praises all the time. They seek your support in every manner and because they seek support from you, they have ownership of this world. They who bow down in devotion to you, become shelters of this world. People of this world find shelter in them and find knowledge, devotion and peace.

Verse 33.

devi prasīda paripālaya noharibhīte
nrityaṁ yathāsuravadhādadhunaiva sadyaḥ|
pāpāni sarvajagatāṁñc śamaṁ nayāśu
utpātapākajanitāṁśca mahopasargān||

Translation:

O Goddess! Be pleased. Just as by killing the demons, you have freed us from a fear of enemies, protect us from our fear of them for all time. Relieve us from all the results of sins and troubles of this world.

Explanation:

Mother, be pleased. Let us understand that you are always pleased with us. Just as now, you have relieved us from fear by destroying the demons, so for all time, remove our fear of enemies, that is, dangers of lust and other tendencies, for all of us, all of our 'I'-ness that comes from ignorant imagination. Look after us.

Mother, your dear children are always tormented by a fear of enemies, lust and other desires. Listen to them. Being tormented by these enemies, some declare you to be unattainable, some scold you as harsh and stony. Others practice severe control and yogic methods to relieve themselves from their enemies. Mother, protect these children who are afraid of their enemies. Let them know that 'those who seek my shelter are relieved from the fear of enemies.'

Not only that, all that is known as sin, in all these worlds, is soon removed. Why do they feel sinful? Because they act as doers of action, the results of actions in the form of sins are entwined with them. (What is commonly known as piety, is also included in this.) Mother, if beings approach you for refuge, then soon, their sense of ownership is removed. There is nothing left as results of actions or sins. Let your dear children know, 'that sense of I, that is sin; leave your sense of I; that I is me, your Mother. Do not become the I without me. Keep your focus on me, seek my shelter. You will see that sins are removed.'

'*utpātapākajanitāṁśca mahopasargān*': signs of danger, meteors, the appearance of comets, darkness around the sun, etc. These dangers, famines, epidemics, floods and untimely deaths, are the direct results of sins. Acting with a sense of ownership, beings are thrown into such conditions. Mother, remove the sins of this world. Heal these ailments. Let children of bliss, discover bliss, find immortality and be relieved of all these illnesses.

Verse 34.

praṇatānāṁ prasīda tvaṁ devi viśvārtihāriṇi
trailokyavāsināmīḍye lokānāṁ varadā bhava||

Translation:

O Goddess! O reliever of this world. Be pleased with all who bow down to you. You are the one about who this world sings praises. Be beneficent to all people.

Explanation:

You are the Goddess, luminescent, self-expressed. You remove all affliction in this world; all afflictions of beings go away when they find you. It is your nature to be pleased with those who bow down to you. Or, those who can truly bow down to you, can see you are eternally pleased. Mother, today we bow down at your feet, truly bow down to you, our raised heads of our 'I'-ness is lowered at your feet, you have made us lower them. Now you will be pleased. Mother, dwellers of all three worlds, gods, men and celestials, in whatever manner they can, purify their voices by singing your praises. You are in the three worlds, you offer benefits to all. Mother, stand in your form as the beneficent one. Let your children be honored by receiving benefits from you. Let this world again be lit by a light of truth.

Verse 35.

devyuvāca|
varadāhaṁ suragaṇā varaṁ yaṁ manasecchatha|
taṁ vṛṇudhvaṁ prayacchāmi jagatāmupakārakam||

Translation:

The Goddess said "O gods, I will grant you favors. Whatever you wish for the good of this world ask from me, I will grant them."

Explanation:

As a result of a recital of praises by the deities, my Mother is especially pleased. She offers favors for the benefit of this world. Truly, this happens. Even now, in this age of disbelief, Mother appears. She glorifies her children by offering favors. This is beneficial for this universe because when the children are with this universal self, the good of this universe is their only goal. They do not pay attention to narrow individual ambitions. By the spiritual effort of seekers without personal desires, all people of this world benefit. The good of this world is achieved by the effort of these seekers.

It will not be beside the point to mention here, what scriptural authors have to say about such workers who are without desire. *Śrutis* say that those who support knowers of Self, acquire the results of their good actions. Those who resent them, receive the effects of bad actions. Those who are offspring or successors receive their accountabilities, that is wealth and properties. The *Upaniṣads* also advise seekers to worship knowers of Self. These knowers of Self appear in this world for its benefit. But that is something else.

Verse 36.

devā ūcuḥ|
sarvābādhāpraśamanaṁ trailokyasyākhileśvari|
evameva tvayā kāryamasmadvairivināśanam||

Translation:

The gods said, "O Goddess of this universe, the manner in which you have destroyed all our enemies, remove the dangerous obstacles of these three worlds in the same way."

Explanation:

Mother, we have nothing more to ask for, other than to remove all obstacles in these three worlds. O Mother, you are Goddess of all this universe. For so long, there has been sorrow in this world, severe obstacles. What is this I hear that this world is full of obstacles? Until all these obstacles are removed, we cannot find you. We see that only a few can discard everything. Those who do will sing that everything was an obstacle. Those who fail, declare that these material obstacles prevented them from finding Mother. But, these are not serious obstacles. It is only you who exists as all this. When beings are established in this truth, then they can realize your nature beyond all material obstacles. Until they can understand that all materials are Mother, then these stand as obstacles to finding Mother. So, I say, Mother, establish truth in this world, that you are expressed as all, as truth, let this be written in letters of gold in the hearts of beings. Let your children understand in their hearts that materials are not obstacles, it is the heart of Mother as matter that opens to receive the children. Let all establish this truth. Let them believe in your spirit. When they believe in your spirit, all obstacles are relieved. All grievances, wants and sorrows in this universe will be removed. This universe will find true beneficence.

Verse 37.

devyuvāca|
vaivasvatehantare prāpte aṣṭāviṁśatime yuge|
śumbho niśumbhaścaivānyāvutpatsyete mahāsurau||

Verse 38.

nandagopagṛhe jātā yaśodā garbhasambhavā|
tatastau nāśayiṣyāmi vindhyācalanivāsinī||

Translation:

The Goddess said "In the *Vaivasvata* era of *Manu*, in the twenty-eighth *yuga*, the demons *Śumbha* and *Niśumbha* will arise again. (Then) I will take birth from the womb of *Yaśodā*, in the house of the cow-herd, *Nanda* and residing in *Vindhyācala*, destroy those demons.

Explanation:

Being ready to grant blessings the gods have prayed for (remove obstacles from these three worlds), Mother reveals several mysteries over here. The three mysteries described in *Devī Māhātmya*, are here articulated by Mother. In this chapter, there are fourteen mantras given as words from the Goddess. Figuring out their significance is a difficult matter. But, by the grace of the one who speaks them, the removal of delusion in seekers can help determine the mysteries in these words. Come, dear seeker, let us bow at the feet of Mother and pray to her. "O Mother, let us take to heart the real meaning of your mysterious words. May we not be led into erroneous paths as 'the blind leading the blind.' Glory to Mother. May you be illumination".

'Vaivasvata Manu' - the seventh *Manu*. The duration of time occupied by one *Manu* is called a *manvantara*. Seventy-one *mahāyugas* make one *manvantara*. *Satya* with the other three *yugas* make one *mahāyuga*. Fourteen *manvantaras* make one *kalpa* or one period of dissolution. The name of this present *kalpa* is *Śvetavarāha*. Of the seventy-one *mahāyugas* of this *kalpa*, twenty-seven have passed. Of the twenty-eighth *mahāyuga*, *Satya*, *Treta* and *Dvāpara yugas* have gone by. Presently it is the *yuga* of

Kali. Its duration is four hundred and thirty-two thousand years. Out of it, only five thousand years have passed.

In this context, we draw attention to the Indian method of counting time. Those who in determining the duration of Indian civilization, conclude it to be four or five thousand, or ten to twenty thousand years, should pay attention to the previous method of calculating time. Those who say that '*Bhārata* has declined, it is forever occupied, bonded', should for once think that a thousand years is tiny, compared to the lifetime determined for this country. There is no reason to be concerned about the condition of this land. In a short while, these poor conditions will turn into a fairy tale. Although this is beside the point here, it is good to bring it up. It will bring new hope and strength to a weakened people. Another great benefit is the destruction of ego in people. Thinking about how tiny a duration this is compared to the infinite ocean of time, diminishes the ego.

Whatever that is, the mantra mentions that Mother said, in the twenty-eighth *yuga* of the era of the *Vaivasvata Manu*, the demons *Śumbha* and *Niśumbha* would reappear and she would be born in the womb of *Yaśodā*, in the house of *Nanda*. Residing in *Vindhyācala*, she would destroy those demons. The times mentioned by Mother here, are aimed especially at the present times. *Devī Māhātmya* is in *Svarociṣa* or era of the second *Manu*. At that time, this present time was far in the future. So, the mantra uses the future tense as '*utpatsyete*.' In the present time, most people are weakened by *Śumbha* and *Niśumbha*, which are ego and attachment. Mother will appear in the house of *Nanda*, in the womb of *Yaśodā* and destroy these two demons.

'Nanda gopa' is the blissful mind facing *Brahmaṇ*. The root '*go*' can mean senses. Because it maintains and protects the senses, the mind is called '*gopa*.' When this mind *gopa*, turns towards *nanda*, that is bliss, then it is called *'nanda gopa*.' The force that is expressed by the mind completely turned towards Self, that is, intellect by which ego and attachment are destroyed, may be called one who is born in the house of *'nanda gopa'*. It

is born of *Yaśodā*, one who brings eminence. When one attempts to find Mother, she takes beings onto her lap in a form that brings eminence. Then, unknown to them, their eminence radiates everywhere. The children ask her for fame, so Mother appears as *Yaśodā* and nurtures the power of *Nandā*. It is this blissful force nurtured in the lap of *Yaśodā* that destroys *Śumbha* and *Niśumbha*. It is named the power of *Nandā*. She resides in *Vindhyācala*, in the heart center. The Tantras term the head *Sumeru*, the *Vindhya* mountains the heart and the *Kula* mountains *Mulādhāra*.

The point is that Mother said, even in this age, when beings move away from truth, not finding me, are bemused by pride, I will appear in their hearts as the force of *Nandā*, born of *Yaśodā*, and destroying their pride, will bring them to an arena of truth. In the era of *Dvāpara*, my Mother appeared as *Śri Kṛṣṇa*, born in the house of *Nanda* from *Yaśodā*, destroyed the demons *Śiśupāla* and others, establishing a kingdom of *dharma*.

In the 'Mystery of Forms', goddess *Nandā* is described as *Lakṣmī*, the power of *Viṣṇu*. That she is the power of *Viṣṇu* was also mentioned during the destruction of *Madhu* and *Kaitava*. In that first character, the power of *Nandā* and the seed *Raktadantikā* are both mentioned. The issue about *Raktadantikā* is discussed in the next mantra. The power that was expressed then to destroy *Madhu* and *Kaitava*, will appear again in this age in the hearts of all beings to destroy *Śumbha* and *Niśumbha*.

Listen. Power is invisible but perceptible and of causal nature. When it appears as action, as what is visible, then it becomes the one with power, a substance of usefulness. Look at a tree. Although it is power, we use and feel it as the 'power of a tree.' There is no difference between power and the one with the power. In the same fashion, when the supreme, undivided power of awareness, or *Brahmaṇ*, expresses itself, then it is known by different names and forms. By this, its oneness is not impaired. That is why the people of this land, even after honoring three hundred and thirty million deities, are nondualists. The people of this honored land are viewers of power and consciousness, whenever they see a special expression of force, instead of viewing it as something inert, they worship it as a deity. The people of many other lands, not understanding the science and spirituality of this, ridicule it as idolatry. We have no resentment about that. It is these idolaters that were the first in this world to sound the victory drums of nondual knowledge with the words 'You are that.' Now, in these times of much disbelief, the people of this land, with the worship of many divinities, reach their goals and are entitled to the knowledge of nonduality.

Whatever that is, in this place, I remind readers of *Sādhan Samar* that although this book describes spiritual mysteries of gods and goddesses, we do not deride any special figures. Let no one think that there cannot be a special form of the power of *Nandā*, that it cannot be seen. If one keeps one's eyes on the words, '*Brahmaṇ* acquires form for the benefit of the seeker'[2], then doubts about form and formless may be removed.

Verse 39.

punarapyatiraudreṇa rūpeṇa pṛthivītale|
avatīrya haniṣyāmi vaipracittāṁśca dānavān||

Verse 40.

bhakṣayantyāśca tānugrān vaipracittān mahāsurān|
raktā dantā bhaviṣyanti dāḍimīkusumopamāḥ||

Verse 41.

tato māṁ devatāḥ svarge martyaloke ca mānavāḥ|
stuvanto vyāhariṣyanti satataṁ raktadantikām||

Translation:

I will return as a terrible figure and appear on earth to destroy the demons named *Vaipracitta*. By devouring the demons *Vaipracitta*, my teeth will be stained red like *Dārim* flowers. Then the gods in heaven and the people of this world will sing my praises and hail my name as *Raktadantikā*.

---

2 *sādhkānāṁ hitārthāya brahmaṇo rūpakalpanā*

Explanation:

Brahmiṇs, experts in the *Vedas* (*vedavit*) are called *vipra.* Those in whom the *Vedas* are expressed, in whom Self is perceived are *vedavit* or *vipra.* Their spirit is called *Vipracitta*, spirit of *vipra.* The feelings and natures expressed in them may be called the demons *Vipracitta.* Mother has to express herself as a very terrifying figure to destroy them. Because such beings are very powerful, Mother also has to appear as a terrible figure.

Before this, we have spoken of a spirit of construction (*nirmmaṇcitta*) in yogis. There is a statement in yoga scriptures that self-realized persons structure their spirits from ego. That is, after the dissolution of spirit, they rebuild a novel spirit. Their purpose is to benefit this world and its people. The source of action that yogis build for the good of this world, can be called the *asura vipracitta.* Mother appears at the right time, to destroy them, because they too are opposed to liberation, to *kaivalya.*

To destroy these *Vipracitta* demons, Mother has to express herself in another nature, as a flow of awareness of the active tendency (*rājasa*). One who was known as the force of *Nandā*, will now, after destroying the great *Vipracitta* demons, be known as *Raktadantikā* (one whose teeth are red). Teeth are the greatest means of destroying a flow of feelings. When the highest feelings are destroyed, then it truly appears that Mother opening her mouth with terrible teeth is swallowing them all. In the *Gitā*, *Arjuna,* during a vision of the Universal form, saw a wide-open mouth swallowing everything. The vision of all the kings entering the mouth like insects flying into a fire, in the *Bhāgavat Gitā*, and this mouth with reddened teeth, swallowing *Vipracitta* demons express the same feelings.

From this time, the gods and people will praise the power of *Nandā* as *Raktadantikā.* In whatever manner Mother expresses herself and carries out her actions, gods and men praise her in the same fashion. This is natural. She has been described previously as the power and seed for the destruction of *Madhu* and *Kaitava.*

Although that time, there was no mention of the destruction of *Vipracitta*, one has to understand that the destruction of desire for multiplicity, is the seed for the dissolution of spirit. When the desire for multiplicity is destroyed, then other demonic feelings are removed. At the appearance of the Goddess *Raktadantikā*, the *asura vipracitta* and constructive spirit of yogis are all destroyed. We have to acknowledge that the basis of constructive spirit is the subtle desire for multiplicity. Although it is not binding, it is divisive. Whatever that is, by the destruction of this divisiveness and establishing a seeker in a state of *kaivalya*, Mother *Nandā*, appears as *Raktadantikā*.

Verse 42.

bhūyaśca śatavārṣikyāmanāvṛṣṭyāmanambhasi|
munibhiḥ saṁsmṛtā bhūmau sambhaviṣyāmyayonijā||

Verse 43.

tataḥ śatena netrāṇāṁ nirīkṣiṣyāmi yammunīn|
kīrtayiṣyanti manujāḥ śatākṣīmiti māṁ tataḥ||

Translation:

Again, after a hundred years of droughts, this Earth will run out of water. After praises by the sages, I will appear immaculately in this world. At that time, I will watch over the sages with a hundred eyes. From then, people will sing of me as *Śatākṣī*, one with a hundred eyes.

Explanation:

Before this, the mystery of the first character of *Devī Māhātmya* has been explained as the powers of *Nandā* and *Raktadantikā*. Now the mystery of the middle character is ready to be expounded. The Goddess said, 'I will appear again.' Because of a drought of a hundred years, the earth will become parched, that is, because of a lack of the nectar of *paramātmā*, all beings will become dry and lifeless. They will play with the skeletons of spiritual effort. Then, sages and *brāhmiṇs* will sing my praises and

I will reappear on this Earth. I will remove any sense of inertness and establish a spirit of awareness and truth. At that time, I will look over the sages, mindful seekers, with one hundred eyes. They will see me as this world-ranging power of sight. At that time, people will joyfully sing of me as *Śatākṣī*, the one with a hundred eyes. Wherever they look, they will see my divine sight, my looks of affection. They cannot but sing of me as *Śatākṣī*. I will then express myself in earth, in inert things, as truth, as consciousness. My spirit will be illuminated everywhere. The children of *Manu*, seeing my special expression, will be very joyful.

Verse 44.

tatohahamakhilaṁ lokamātmadehasamudbhavaiḥ|
bhariṣyāmi surāḥ śākairāvṛṣṭeḥ prāṇa*dhārakaiḥ||*

Verse 45.

śākambharīti vikhyātiṁ tadā yāsyāmyahaṁ bhuvi||

Translation:

O, gods! At that time, until it rains again, I will sustain and nurture the life of all people with plants that will appear from my body. At that time, I will be known in this world as *Śākamvarī*.

Explanation:

The Goddess said, 'O, gods! *Śatākṣī* will again become famous as *Śākamvarī*. Because, in that time of drought, I will sustain people with plants that will appear from my body.' Nagoji Bhatta has determined that *Śākamvarī* will appear in the thirty-ninth *mahāyuga*. That time will come, after eleven more *mahāyugas* have passed after this present one. At that time, because of a long period of drought, there will be a lack of supply of grains and food. The affectionate Mother will grow plants from her body to protect her children until it rains again. It will be long before this sorrowful time will begin on earth. There is no danger in the near future.

Whatever it is, we will try to understand the spiritual meaning.

Plants from her body mean the sap of earth principle or energy of life. The earth is a body of the Self. The plants produced are life force. They will sustain people during the drought. The significance is that as long as it does not rain, until this world is not flooded by the intellect of *Brahmaṇ*, (one should understand all intelligence to be this world), as long as beings are not established in *Brahmaṇ*, Mother will appear as *Śākamvarī* and nurture this world with plants emerging from her body. By establishing life force, she will create a source of peace in the hearts of beings.

Listen. Let me explain clearly. Mother said, there will come a time in this world, when because of drought, that is, the absence of flow of the nectar of *Brahmaṇ*, beings will be very sorrowful and full of grief. They will not find the nectar of *ātmā* in this universe. Thinking it to be something unknowable, beyond this world, they will turn outside. Then she will appear in her form as *Śākamvarī*. She will explain to beings that this world is her body. They will find sustenance in the plants from her world-body. That everything in this world is imbued with life, that consciousness is the only ingredient of this world, will be understood by everyone. Wherever they look, they will see life-sustaining plants, discover consciousness and nurture themselves.

One can say in summary that *Śākamvarī* Mother will establish life force in the lifeless, sorrowful people engrossed by inertness. To view consciousness in inert materials is the secret to sustaining life with plants. We understand that Mother as *Śākamvarī* establishes life force for us. *Śākamvarī* has been described as the power of the second character of *Caṇḍī*. Because she sustains life with the plants, (*śāka*), she is called by this name. The word '*Śākamvarī*' has another meaning. *Kaṭhopaniṣad* has sung of worldly persons as grain and death as plants (vegetables). One who sustains death, or, one who with plants of death from her body sustains beings, who repeatedly with the nourishment of death nurtures beings, is *Śākamvarī*. Ambrosial *ātmā* is called *Śākamvarī*.

Verse 46.

tatraiva ca vadhiṣyāmi durgamākhyaṁ mahāsuram|
durgādevīti vikhyātaṁ tanme nāma bhaviṣyati||

Translation:

At that time, I will destroy a demon named *Durgama*. From then on, I will be known by the famous name of Goddess *Durgā.*

Explanation:

Mother said, 'In that figure as *Śākamvarī*, I will destroy a demon named *Durgama* and will be famed as Goddess *Durgā.*' A knowledge of Self that is very difficult to traverse (*durgama*), what *śrutis* have described to be as difficult as walking on the edge of a razor, to make that arduous knowledge of Self easy, I will appear as the power of *Śākamvarī.* I will establish life force and direct a path to Self. Then the fortress (*durga*) of a worldly person, the sorrow of their state as a worldly being, will be easily destroyed. From then, I, will become known as *Durgā.*

The destructive root '*ā*' after *durga*, gives the word *Durgā.* The meaning of *Durgā* is Mother who removes distress. She is the seed of the middle character of *Caṇḍī.* Her purpose is to remove distress. In the introductory verse of the middle character in *Devī Māhātmya*, the power of *Śākamvarī* and the seed *Durgā* are mentioned.

In some older texts, the second verse of this mantra is absent. Some previous commentators have also not mentioned it. Even though not seen in some texts, we perceive the appearance of Mother as *Durgā* in all beings. Whenever beings are in distress, are tormented by the demon *Durgama*, are unable to advance towards knowledge of Self, my Mother appears as *Durgā* and destroys the *asura Durgama*, removes the sorrow of her beloved children and eases the path towards Self-knowledge. It may be because of this, that in India and especially in Bengal, from ancient times, there has been the worship of Goddess *Durgā*. Even now, in this age of disbelief, people worship *Durgā*, reciting, 'all elements are *Durgā*, this world is *Durgā*, all women, men and animals are *Durgā*, all that we see is *Durgā*', and are honored seeing *Durgā* everywhere.

Verse 47.

punaścāhaṁ yadā bhīmaṁ rūpaṁ kṛtvā himācale|
rakṣāṁsi kṣyayiṣyāmi munīnāṁ trāṇakāraṇāt||

Verse 48.

tadā māṁ munayaḥ sarve stoṣyantyānamramūrtayaḥ|
bhīmādevīti vikhyātaṁ tanme nāma bhaviṣyati||

Translation:

Again, when I take on a terrible form and arrive in the *Himācala* (Himālayās) to destroy demons and protect sages, then the sages will humbly worship me. Then I will be famous as Goddess *Bhimā*.

Explanation:

According to the evidence in *Lakṣmī Tantra*, the appearance of *Bhimā avatāra* is in the fiftieth *mahāyuga,* in the era of *Vaivasvata Manu*. That time is far off. This is now just the twenty-eight *mahāyuga*. After twenty-one more *mahāyugas* will be the time for the arrival of *Bhimā*. However, we have seen the appearance of Mother as *Bhimā* even in this age. It is some time in the past that Mother appeared in the Western part of the Earth in her form as *Bhimā* and destroyed a large number of beings of demonic natures. When persons engrossed by inertness, are ready to take away the livelihood of others, we understand that Mother holds them on her lap in her demonic form. It is for the destruction of such beings that Mother has to appear in her form as *Bhimā*.

With spiritual vision, we see that the figure of *Bhimā* has to appear to protect sages. When *munis*, mindful persons, are tormented by demonic natures, Mother has to appear in her terrible form. She appears in *Himācala*. Worldly beings engrossed by inertness may be called *Himācala*. When they are engrossed by inertness, when their only goal in life is the success of inertness,

Mother appears in her form as *Bhimā*, expressing herself as famines, epidemics, civil wars, floods, hurricanes and severe earthquakes. Destroying those of demonic nature, protecting mindful ones, she reestablishes truth and *dharma*. It is for this that the sages humbly worship her form as *Bhimā*, for the good of this world. Satisfied by this, Mother discards her terrible form and reappears in her gentle one, as *Jagadhātrī* (one who bears this world), and removes all torment in this world.

Verse 49.

yadāruṇākhyastrailokya mahābādhāṁ kariṣyati|
tadāhaṁ bhrāmaraṁ rūpaṁ kṛtvāsaṁkhyeyaṣaṭpadam||

Verse 50.

trailokyasya hitārthāya vadhiṣyāmi mahāsuram|
bhrāmarīti ca māṁ lokāstadā stoṣyanti sarvataḥ||

Translation:

When the demon *Aruṇākṣya* will torment the three worlds, then for the benefit of the three worlds, I will take the form of *Bhrāmarī*, surrounded by innumerable bees, and destroy that demon. Then people will sing hymns addressing me as *Bhrāmarī*.

Explanation:

According to the words of *Lakṣmī* tantra, one understands that the time of this *Bhrāmarī avatāra* is after sixty *yugas* in this era of *Manu*. This time will come after thirty-one *yugas* have passed after this present one. It is in the very deep future. One cannot even imagine these timespans. In the description of this appearance, it is said that it will be surrounded by innumerable bees, or one with strange bee-like hands, and this figure will destroy the demon *Aruṇa*.

We will now try to enter the spiritual mystery of this mantra. The state before any knowledge of Self can be called the demon *Aruṇa* (dawn). Just as dawn appears before sunrise, before the rise of the sun of knowledge, the dawn of awareness *Aruṇa* appears. Seekers who think of this to be ultimate knowledge may be understood as being tormented by the demon *Aruṇa*. What has been called *Śumbha* in the final character, has another name, *Aruṇākṣya*. This demon *Aruṇa* is truly a tormentor of the three worlds. It is a barrier causing much anguish. Appearing as ego-self, it shelters control and action. So, my Mother appears as *Bhrāmarī*, as one that destroys error (*bhrama*) of self-awareness. The body of six shells is called *Ṣatpada* (six-legged, bee). Here '*pada*' means place. The error of Self appears in these six levels of non-Self. My sentient Mother is named as the one surrounded by *Ṣatapadas*. When *paramātmā* appears in the form of Mother and destroys this tremendous error, that is, destroys the demon *Aruṇākṣya* tormenting the three worlds, then all discover pure consciousness and are established in bliss. They all praise Mother as *Bhrāmarī*, destroyer of error. In verses by sages (*ṛṣīcchanda*), *Bhrāmarī* is described as the seed and *Bhīmā* as the power of the final character. One who destroys demonic nature is known as *Bhrāmarī* after she destroys the demon of self-awareness *Aruṇākṣya*. The establishment of bliss is the theme for the final character.

We will now try to understand the meaning of the previous mantras in brief. First, the power of *Nandā*, the seed *Raktadantikā* are principles for the destruction of *Madhu* and *Kaitava*, establishment of truth or piercing of the knot of *Brahmā*. Second, the power of *Śākamvarī*, the seed *Durgā* are principles for the destruction of *Mahiṣāsura*, establishment of life force or piercing of the knot of *Viṣṇu*. And third, the power of *Bhīmā*, the seed *Bhrāmarī* are principles for the destruction of *Śumbha* and *Niśumbha*, establishment of bliss or piercing of the knot of *Rudra*. These are three brief descriptions of the three mysteries in *Devī Māhātmya*. Not only did this happen in the past, but at present, Mother appears in the hearts of all seekers in this manner. Mother gives her word that she will do so in the future

The figures with which my Mother destroyed the various demons in these battles of a spiritual quest (*Sādhan Samar)*, she will carry out again in the future. At those times, the names and forms of demons and their actions will be different. This is the significance that may be drawn from the previous mantras. This is something to think about. In the distant future, worldly beings would still be bemused and of different natures than at present. Demonic tendencies may be more severe than at present. Ignorance may cover this world at that time. As the darkness of ignorance deepens, knowledge-formed Mother will become available. So, we see in the mantra, that in the future, first, she will destroy *Śumbha* and *Niśumbha* in the form of *Nandā*. Then, nurture this world with plants from her form as *Śākamvarī*, destroy the demon *Durgama* as *Durgā*, protect sages from the demons as *Bhīmā* and kill the demon *Aruṇa* as *Bhrāmarī*. These are future action plans of Mother.

Verse 51.

ittham yadā yadā bādhā dānavotthā bhaviṣyati|
tadā tadāvatīryāham kariṣyāmyarisamkṣayam||

iti śrīmārkaṇḍeyapurāṇe sāvarṇike manvantarīya
devīmāhātmye devyāḥ stutiḥ|

Translation:

In this manner, whenever there is any torment by demons, I will arrive and destroy those enemies.

Here end these praises to the Goddess, in *Devī Māhātmya*, in *Mārkeṇḍeya Purāṇa*.

Explanation:

This is the conclusion of the words of the Goddess. The gods had prayed for the removal of all the obstacles in these three worlds. Mother in granting all of it, spoke about various torment of enemies in the future. Finally, she said that, whenever there is any torment by demons, I will arrive and destroy them. All obstacles on the path of acquiring knowledge of Self, all torments that arrive, Mother removes all of them, for children who seek shelter at her feet. For us, these are words of hope and reliance. In

Gitā, the Lord has said this repeatedly. All responsibility of self-surrendered yogis is in the hands of Mother. So, they are confident, full of bliss, unclothed infants on the lap of Mother. Any obstacles that appear for them are removed by Mother. There is no change to this now, in the past or the future, never was and never will be. Come let us seek shelter at the feet of Mother. Mother will protect us from all torments of demons and establish us in the nature of *Brahmaṇ*. The principle of the *avatars* that Mother hints about here, is further explained in the mantras in the next chapter.

Here ends the commentary on the praises to *Nārāyaṇī*, in *Sādhan Samar* or *Devī Māhātmya*.

Chapter 12
Recital of Results

Verse 1.

devyuvāca|
ebhiḥ stavaiśca māṁ nityaṁ stoṣyate yaḥ samāhitaḥ|
tasyāhaṁ sakalāṁ bādhāṁ śamayiṣyāmyasaṁśayam||

Translation:

The Goddess said, 'Those who focus and sing my praises with these hymns, I will, without doubt, remove all their obstacles.'

Explanation:

After granting desired requests of the gods, Mother gives some words of advice. We have named these the recital of results. The first thing Mother says is '*ebhiḥ stavai*' (these hymns). This is aimed at the hymn by *Brahmā* after the destruction of *Madhu* and *Kaitava*, the one after the destruction of *Mahiṣāsura,* the '*namastasai*' hymn in *Deviduta saṁvāda*, and the hymn to *Nārāyaṇī* after the destruction of *Śumbha.*

The second, Mother says, '*samāhita*', focus and recite. If the spirit is focused, on Self, then only do results of recital of hymns appear. When one is totally centered in Self, there is no longer any recitation of hymns. In that condition, three-fold knowledge of knower-knowledge-known disappears. Here one is not speaking about such a state. Here we have to understand these words as keeping focus calmly on Mother. If one recites praises, looks on Mother, keeps tendencies of spirit on Mother, understands the proper meaning of hymns of praise, and is attuned to the nature of that meaning, then one is focused. Singing praises of greatness or a divine name is the same thing. There is no name that does not praise the greatness of Mother. Whatever name one may pronounce, *Hari, Kṛṣṇa, Rāma, Durgā, Śyāmā, Śiva or Śankara*, if one places one's focus on it, one can understand that each of these names signifies greatness. If with each name, the *guru* appears in a form as true knowledge, then each name, becomes filled with life force and greatness and aligns with the desired deity. Those who are seekers, when singing praises, become imbued with its spirit and taste. One has to become aware of the consciousness of mantra. Without it, hymns, worship, chants and rosaries all turn into lifeless ceremonies. Mantra consciousness was discussed in Volume One.

Mother truly removes all obstacles for those who can recite hymns with a focused spirit. Why does she do that? Say, your spirit is centered, with knowledge and simplicity say 'remove all sins.' With that, in your spirit, will surely rise, a feeling of the end of darkness and removal of sins. It will take place in action. The feeling that arises in the spirit, will within some time, be expressed as results. The manner in which spirit is molded brings about similar results. These things need not be understood by logic because their results can be observed. Whenever such actions are carried out, their truth may be perceived. It is no use to just know these words, without action results cannot be seen.

Verse 2.

madhukaiṭabhanāśaṁ ca ṁahiṣāsuraghātanam|
kīrtayiṣyanti ye tadvadvadhaṁ śumbhaniśumbhayoḥ||

Verse 3.

aṣṭamyāṁ ca caturdaśyāṁ navamyāñcaikacetasaḥ|
śroṣyanti caiva ye bhaktyā mama māhātmyamuttamam||

Verse 4.

na teṣāṁ duṣkṛtaṁ kiñcidduṣkṛtotthā na cāpadaḥ|
bhaviṣyati na dāridryaṁ na caiveṣṭaviyojanam||

Translation:

Those who with focused spirit, on the eighth, ninth, and fourteenth lunar days, sing praises of my greatness on the destructions of *Madhu-Kaitava*, *Mahiṣāsura* and *Śumbha-Niśumbha*, or those who listen to them with devotion, they do not have any danger from ill-actions, poverty or loss of goals.

Explanation:

In the previous mantra, the benefits of reciting hymns were mentioned. In this one, those of reading and listening to *Devī Māhātmya* is proclaimed. The spiritual significance of the eighth, fourteenth and other lunar days were explained in the explanation of the *Kilaka stotram* (Volume One) and is not repeated here. The results mentioned in these mantras are not just words. Truly these results transpire if a seeker keeps in mind the two issues mentioned by the Goddess.

The Goddess said, '*ekacetasaḥ*' and '*bhaktyā.*' First, focus on that which is one, which has no divisions. Second, recite with devotion. Unmoving belief in the words of the Goddess and focusing on her, these two things, brings the right results of reading or listening to *Devī Māhātmya*. Sinful actions are removed. If one keeps in mind the three characters of *Devī Māhātmya* that have been discussed and recites or listens to *Caṇḍī*, then the true nature of Mother is surely revealed to them. For them, there are no sinful actions. So, dangers due to them do not exist. Also, poverty, a feeling of want is removed. Anyone established in 'this is full, that is full' (*purṇamadaḥ purṇamidaṁ*), cannot have a feeling of want. So, the mantra says, 'no poverty in the future.'

One is never separated from one's cherished goals. *Paramātmā* is the true desired goal. One is never separated from it. One can think that it is not possible to be separated from *paramātmā*, so what is the use of calling this a result of reciting or listening to *Devī Māhātmya*? This argument is correct. The answer is that only those who recite or listen to *Devī Māhātmya* with focus and devotion can comprehend this.

Only Self is the cherished goal (*iṣta*) of everyone. Learned or ignorant, pious or not, the cherished goal of everyone is Self. Even those who think that wealth and desire are their goals, if they think a bit calmly, will understand that it is for the satisfaction of Self that one is addicted to wealth and desire. No one in this world wants Self because of material things, it is because of Self that they seek material things. I have said that Self is the only cherished goal. A spiritual seeker looking at the principles of *Devī Māhātmya* is never separated from Self.

In general terms, there is no harm in understanding the meaning of loss of cherished goals as the loss of dear ones, or earthly things. Because, a spiritual seeker of *Devī Māhātmya* can see dear ones who have passed, or lost things in the grotto of their heart. This is also mentioned in the *Cāndyogya Upaniṣad*. In practice, under no conditions, does a seeker lose cherished goals.

If one understands the meaning of the words as not having any sorrow for losing cherished goals, then it is wonderful. Śrutis say that those who are centered in Self, are forever relieved from the sorrow of the loss of cherished things (*tarati śokamātmavit*[1]).

Verse 5.

śatrubhyo na bhayaṁ tasya dasyuto vā na rājataḥ|
na śastrānalatoyaughāt kadācit sambhaviṣyati||

Translation:

One who reads *Devī Māhātmya* has no fear of enemies, robbers, kings, weapons, fire and floods.

Explanation:

In general, this is what happens. If one reads *Devī Māhātmya* with focus and devotion, enemies are subdued, robbers overcome, weapons, fire, floods and other dangers removed. Look at it from another angle. When a seeker reads or hears it in this manner, one discovers knowledge of Self. As a result, lust and anger and other enemies cannot do any harm and enchantment, a robber cannot steal the wealth of conscience.

As long as one does not find Self, there is always a danger

1 *Īśā Upaniṣad*, Verse 7.

of diversion in a spiritual quest from the strength of past actions. Many seekers fear that some day, hidden past tendencies will rob them of knowledge or devotion obtained after severe efforts. This fear of theft is a jest for those who have discovered Self. One sees that there is nothing but Self. What is fear or downfall for those who have envisioned truth?

Then there is the fear of rulers. The king of the senses is the mind. There is no more fear from it. Disturbances of mind or its turning towards material things are meaningless for those who know Self. Whether the mind is disturbed or still, whether it faces material things or Self, what does it matter to *ātmā*? 'I' am *ātmā*, Mother. What do 'I' have to fear from rulers or disturbances of mind? Those who do not know 'I', have not found it, have not understood, only they say that spiritual effort fails because of disturbances of the mind. Even between such disturbances, look at Mother, Self, for a little while. Within moments, life will turn worthy.

These words, not from weapons, fire or water, are like the words of *Gitā* saying, 'cannot be cut by weapons, not burnt by fire'[2]. One has no fear of weapons, fires and floods. What are teachings in *Gitā*, are experiences and joy in *Devī Māhātmya.*

Verse 6.

tasmānmamaitanmāhātmyaṁ paṭhitavyaṁ samāhitaiḥ|
śrotavyañca sadā bhaktyā paraṁ svastyayanaṁ hi tat||

Translation:

With spirit centered and with devotion, always recite and listen to hymns of my praises. This is high worship, most beneficial.

Explanation:

Whether it is people seeking material pleasure, looking for heavenly bliss in the afterlife, or those on a search, all should with devotion and focus, recite or listen to *Devī Māhātmya*. Just reading

2 *Bhāgavat Gitā,* 2:23.

it and saying that one has understood is not enough. The Goddess says that one should read and listen to it all the time. By repeated reading or listening, the principles of *Caṇḍī* will become a part of our lives and actions. Then one will see that the direction of one's life will move towards Self. Spiritual events of *Devī Māhātmya* are being acted out in our daily lives. Every day, these battles with demons are taking place. You will understand where the Goddess is asking us to go, by using the word 'constantly.' This is the greatest rite for security, the greatest good. All earthly benefits can be obtained by reciting or listening to *Devī Māhātmya*. Mother says that this is the means to find relief. Let no reader understand by this that one has to leave *Veda* and *Vedānta* and only read or listen to *Devī Māhātmya* to find benefits. That is not what is said here. If one takes the shelter of any beneficial scriptural text, be it *Veda* and *Vedānta*, or philosophies or *purāṇas*, can there be any harm? If one understands that all texts are saying similar things and there is no conflict between them, then reading of scriptures is meaningful. Vedic scriptures and *Brahmaṇ* are nondifferent. Another name for the *Vedas* is *Brahmaṇ*. Vedic scriptures have character. They have conscious forms. When scripture-formed Mother, by her grace, reveals truth in the hearts of devoted readers, they discover the mysteries of the scriptures. So, I say, to find the grace of the scriptures, one has to read them in a spirit of worship and with great respect.

When saying 'scripture', one should understand *śrutis* and *Upaniṣads*. The more other scriptures follow the *śrutis* the more is their glory preserved. Statements opposed to *śrutis* are not palatable. One should try to understand the meaning of apparently opposed statements, by following the meaning in the *śrutis*. The success of this attempt is a rite of great benefit. A unified understanding of the words of the scriptures brings great benefits by ending divisive doubts. Such unification is expressed in *Devī Māhātmya*. Reciting or listening to it is of great benefit.

In the everyday world, one can see that teachers and priests perform rites of worship for the peace and sustenance of disciples and worshippers by reciting the *Devī Māhātmya*.

Verse 7.

upasargānaśeṣāhṁstu mahāmārīsamudbhavān|
tathā trividhamutpātaṁ māhātmyaṁ śamayenmama||

Verse 8.

yatraitatpaṭhyate samyaṅ nityamāyatane mama|
sadā na tadvimokṣyāmi sānnidhyaṁ tatra me sthitam||

Translation:

My praises, subdue the effects of epidemics and three-fold disturbances. I never forsake the place where such praises are recited daily. I am always there.

Explanation:

Recital of *Devī Māhātmya* reduces epidemics and their symptoms. The common meaning of the word '*mahāmārī*' is an epidemic spreading over the land. These were mentioned in the praise to *Nārāyaṇī*. The point is that if one recites *Devī Māhātmya* with focus and devotion, then three-fold disturbances and epidemics are healed. With spiritual vision, the word '*mahāmārī*' can be taken to be repeated deaths. From the fear of death rises much distress. Birth following death is to suffer in a worldly purgatory, the inevitable pain of three worlds. Recital of *Devī Māhātmya* (by meeting Self), removes these ills.

Mother is close to a place, a home, in which the *Caṇḍī* is recited daily. This is the common meaning. In the spiritual sense, the place is the physical body, where one undergoes desires. Mother says, that 'in this place' where my praises are recited daily, those who read this with focus and devotion, I never leave them. I am always there. That is Mother resides inside and outside. This is what is said in *Gitā*, 'I am always there, where my devotee sings my praises.'

Mother! You said that you are close to where *Caṇḍī* is recited daily, are you not close to where it is not? Listen. There is no place where she is absent. So, there is no place that is without her. But, that 'I am always close,' can be understood by those who worship her with devotion, that is, recite and listen to *Devī Māhātmya*. This is the secret of this mantra.

Verse 9.

balipradāne pūjāyāmagnikārye mahotsave|
sarvaṁ mamaitanmāhātmyam uccāryaṁ śrāvyameva ca||

Verse 10.

jānatājānatā vāpi balipūjāṁ yathā kṛtām|
pratīkṣyāmyahaṁ prītyā vahnihomaṁ tathā kṛtam||

Translation:

In all sacrifices, worships, service and fire ceremonies, recite and listen to the words of these characters (*carita*). If knowingly or unknowingly, these ceremonies are performed in the proper manner, that is, with the recital of my characters, then I accept those actions with great pleasure.

Explanation:

It is necessary to recite and listen to *Devī Māhātmya* during prescribed acts like worship ceremonies, and in general acts like celebrations. When they are carried out in this manner, all these acts, prescribed and general are completed without difficulty. This is the common meaning of this mantra. Even now, this is how nearly all over the land, it is carried out in practice.

With a spiritual vision, one can see that if prescribed acts like worship ceremonies and general acts like celebrations are carried out directed at Mother, at *ātmā*, then they are accomplished easily and deliver proper results, because 'I am the only receiver and lord of all ceremonies.' If one carries them out without their eyes on me, they are ceremonies without *Śiva*. I am *Śiva*. I am eternally expressed as action, as ceremonies and results of action. If one keeps this in mind when carrying out these acts, then the practice of my characters occurs during all these acts. As a result, they are carried out with ease.

Those who know that through all actions, one worships me, are learned and know the rules. The word '*jānatā*' is used aimed at them. There is a saying about this, 'until the Self is united with meditation, rosaries, worship or chanting, they are ineffective', that is, they bring little result. The word '*ajānatā*' is for those who miss such an aim in prescribed acts. The Goddess said, for both of these, I receive the rightful acts they conduct, with pleasure. No one else but me has the right to accept the results of ceremonial worship. I accept the acts of everyone, with pleasure. But, there is a distinction. Only those with knowledge can understand my receiving results of ceremonies. Those who are without knowledge, that is, without their focus on me, cannot see this. When those with knowledge, offer me leaves, flowers, fruits, water and ceremonial fuel, they perceive that I am receiving it with pleasure. They find satisfaction with their actions. Those without knowledge are deprived of this. But, there is no doubt that I receive from both with pleasure.

It will not be beside the point to say something about sacrifice over here. Those who are fond of consuming meat may sacrifice goats or other animals. That would be all right for them. It is to reduce uncontrolled and useless consumption of flesh that the texts prescribed such sacrifice. Such sacrifice is not prohibited in *rājasa* worship. Those who have right nature, who have forsaken meat and fish, who see the presence of life in all beings, do not sacrifice animals. The mysteries of sacrifice have been discussed in detail in a book on principles of worship (*Pujā Tattva*). Here, if one understands the meaning of sacrifice as a gift for worship, then balance is maintained.

Verse 11.

śaratkāle mahāpūjā kriyate yā ca vārṣikī|
tasyāṁ mamaitanmāhātmyaṁ śrutvā bhaktisamanvitaḥ||

Verse 12.

sarvābādhāvinirmukto dhanadhānya samanvitaḥ|
manuṣyo matprasādena bhaviṣyati na saṁśayaḥ||

Translation:

There is no doubt that those who with devotion, recite and listen to my praises, during the yearly great worship ceremony in autumn, are freed from all obstacles by my blessings.

Explanation:

Even now, in most places in this land, a great worship ceremony is held in Autumn. But, the results said in the mantra are found only by a few. The reason is that these ceremonies are not conducted with focus and devotion. The issue is doubt in the words of the Goddess. Many cannot believe that recital of *Caṇḍī* during the great ceremony can remove all obstacles and bring prosperity. Because of such doubts and disbelief, prescribed acts in this age do not bear fruit.

Autumn is the season when the principle of the earth is especially expressed. The seasons express special principles. This is mentioned here in passing. Autumn — is the earth principle, Monsoons — water, Summer — energy, Spring — wind and Winter — space. When a principle is chiefly expressed, its action is seen in nature. Here we are speaking of Autumn. At this time, the earth principle, that is, dense inertness is specially expressed. Those who perform the great worship ceremony[3], take care to establish consciousness formed Mother during this rule of inertness. As part of this, they recite *Devī Māhātmya* and are relieved of all obstacles and torment by demons, finding peace and wealth. They find a wealth of love and a harvest of faith, that is, they find sustenance and progeny. Those who worship Mother and recite or listen to *Caṇḍī*, have no dearth of love. Their hearts are ever filled with a wealth of belief. They have knowledgeable children, who can relieve them from the cycles of birth and death.

---

3 *mahāpujā*: annual ceremonial service.

Verse 13.

śrutvā mamaitanmāhātmyaṁ tathā cotpattayaḥ śubhāḥ|
parākramañca yuddheṣu jāyate nirbhayaḥ pumān||

Verse 14.

ripavaḥ saṅkṣayaṁ yānti kalyāṇañcopapadyate|
nandate ca kulaṁ puḥsāṁ māhātmyaṁ mama śṛṇvatām||

Translation:

Hearing about my greatness and blessed appearance, people succeed in battle and find courage. Persons who hear of my magnificence, have their passions eroded, find beneficence and their kinfolks are joyous.

Explanation:

Various holy advents by the Goddess have been described in *Devī Māhātmya.* In answer to the question that king Suratha had asked about the Goddess, the sage Medhasa has described her many appearances. If one listens to these descriptions with attention, then one succeeds in battle, that is, one gains the power to subdue demonic natures. One also finds courage. *Ātmā* is the only fearless entity. The *Śrutis* always advise to find *ātmā*, that is of the nature of fearlessness. 'Child, find ambrosial *ātmā*, that is of the nature of courage.' These words of *Upaniṣad* are repeated in *Devī Māhātmya.*

The mantra says that those who listen to *Devī Māhātmya* have their passions (*ripu*) eroded. One has to understand by this, the domination of passions of lust and anger, etc. On the other hand, the natural resentment of a seeker towards these may be removed. By seeing Self everywhere, being free of attachment, one can enjoy them without conflict. One finds beneficence. The misfortune of birth and death are removed forever.

'*nandate ca kulaṁ*' - one's lineage is joyous. The ancestors of the lineage in which a knower of Self is born, dance in joy, because their path to liberation is made easy. The descendants find great beneficence by the grace and blessings of a liberated soul.

What is difficult for general people, is easy for such a lineage. The ancestors and descendants of a knower of Self are all joyous.

Verse 15.

śāntikarmaṇi sarvatra tathā duḥsvapnadarśane|
grahapīḍāsu cogrāsu māhātmyaṁ śṛṇuyānmama||

Verse 16.

upasargāḥ śamaṁ yānti grahapīḍāśca dāruṇāḥ|
duḥsvapnañca nṛbhirdṛṣṭaṁ susvapnamupajāyate||

Translation:

In all acts of peace, in nightmares and serious illness, listen to my great episodes. With these, all signs of trouble will be relieved, the effects of ill planets removed, and nightmares will turn to sweet dreams.

Explanation:

These are the results of listening to *Devī Māhātmya*. Before this, the words '*śrutvā*' and '*śṛnvatāṁ*' were about hearing. Listening is the first and chief spiritual enterprise. The more one's hearing is purified and immersed in truth, the quicker and more definite the attainment of results. The scriptures have also said that listening, reflection, and deep meditation are the greatest spiritual efforts. If the hearing is not pure, then contemplation is not purified. If contemplation is not right, then the results of deep meditation fail. The more one's hearing is purified, the greater the results are defined. What is the way to listen well? First, a listener has to be humble and respectful. Then, the speaker, that is, an advisor of the principle of Self, has to be error free. If by great fortune, such a proper speaker and listener meet, there is no doubt about results. If they do not have these abilities, then listening and spiritual effort fail. When a speaker is mute and listener deaf, both are in trouble.

The mantra mentions that in peaceful acts, on having nightmares and in planetary illnesses, one should listen to *Devī*

Māhātmya. Look. One has a lack of peace all the time. At all times one has nightmares of earthly action. Planets of the senses are tyrants. If you truly seek peace, want to be free of nightmares and be relieved of planetary illnesses, then listen to these great episodes. If you listen properly, then there will come reflection and deep meditation. Then you will be honored by finding knowledge of Self, you will have uninterrupted peace and the torment of the senses and worldly actions will be removed. These are the results of listening to my greatness.

Verse 17.

bālagrahābhibhūtānāṁ bālānāṁ śāntikārakam|
saṅghātabhede ca nṛṇāṁ maitrīkaraṇamuttamam||

Verse 18.

durvvṛttānāmaśeṣāṇāṁ balahānikaraṁ param|
rakṣobhūtapiśācānāṁ paṭhanādeva nāśanam||

Verse 19.

sarvaṁ mamaitanmāhātmyaṁ mama sannidhikārakam||

Translation:

The recital of my great episodes brings one closer to me. It brings peace to children afflicted by evil planets, removes conflict between people, brings friendship, drains the powers of evil and destroys ghosts and demons.

Explanation:

In these three mantras, the third is mentioned as the cause, so it should be considered first. Mother said, my glory brings proximity to me. It has been said that wherever *Devī Māhātmya* is recited, Mother is present. Being close to Mother, that is, when pure consciousness is expressed, all obstacles and dangers are removed. The word '*bāla*' means child or ignorance. All attacks of planets are mended. By the appearance of pure knowledge of *ātmā*, all sorrow of ignorance is removed.

'*saṅghātabhede ca nṛṇāṁ*': Any mutual sense of the difference between beings is removed and friendship is created. People see that the one 'I' is equally existent in all. Self is dear to all. It exists everywhere, so there is no divisiveness. Mutual friendship is naturally created.

All trouble makers are weakened. Those with ill will are weakened, but they are not destroyed. As long as they have a body, they have the nature of beings, but they are without power. Their demonic and evil natures are removed. Their material natures, the attractions to physical things and the sense of permanence in them are removed. This is the connotation of their destruction.

Verse 20.

paśupuṣpārghyadhūpaiśca gandhadīpaistathottamaiḥ|
viprāṇāṁ bhojanairhomaiḥ prokṣaṇīyairaharniśam||

Verse 21.

anyaiśca vividhairbhogaiḥ pradānairvatsareṇa yā|
prītirme kriyate sāsmin sakṛducarite śrute||

Translation:

Worshipping me with excellent sacrifices, flowers, incense, scents and lamps, with feasts for *brāhmiṇs*, fire ceremonies, inaugurations, and the offering of gifts, when carried out over the year for my pleasure, they all make me happy. I am equally pleased by one who even once, listens to my greatness.

Explanation:

Mother says that listening to her glory also has great results. One is purified by carrying out prescribed actions like worship ceremonies, feasts for *brāhmiṇs*, inaugurations and gifts. Letting one know of my nature brings one close to me. By listening to these great episodes of mine even once, people acquire equal purification of spirit, knowledge and proximity to me. By hearing of the mystery of nondual knowledge from a right *guru*, persons immersed in ignorant darkness discover a sense of momentary learning. Only by hearing this, can one have indirect knowledge of who I am, what this universe is, what is God and what are the relationships between them. This indirect knowledge is indicative of the love of Mother. Such signs of love appear where Mother expresses herself.

The purification of spirit that occurs by carrying out worship and fire ceremonies or offerings over long periods, is equal to that which occurs by hearing the words of a right teacher with respect, even once. Maybe because of an understanding of this, Ācārya Śankara gave more importance to listening and thinking than the performance of ceremonial actions. The words of the Goddess give the same indication. There is no doubt that listening to principles of knowledge even once is more effective than the performances of lifeless action bereft of principles of knowledge. But, it is also true that it is through the performance of ceremonial acts that respect, devotion and intelligence for holding on to principles of knowledge appear.

One may ask, are ceremonial acts to be discarded and only listening and thinking taken up? No. It is these ceremonial acts that produce abilities for listening and recounting. When one acquires the proper ability to discard ceremonial acts, then, their performance for the teaching of others is not to be criticized. They are necessary. These ceremonial acts are special features of Hindu worship. If these are allowed to go extinct, or their lack of necessity spreads in society, then one should be concerned that in the near future, this land will turn into a spiritual wasteland. Even if spiritual seekers truly rise above actions, they should still stand on a foundation of principles of knowledge and carry out acts imbued with life. This has been said by the Lord in *Bhāgavat Gitā*. Even if there is no duty, just for the maintenance of people, one should carry out prescribed acts. This is good for the land. Do not destroy what is there, try to protect it. Imbue lifeless acts with life. One will truly find beneficence.

One sees in this mantra that Mother says, with my love (*priti*). There is nothing that is not love for Mother. What is not pleasure for one who is eternally pleased? Although there is indeed nothing that is not her pleasure, only those who understand that she is eternally pleased, are those who listen to *Devī Māhātmya* with respect.

Verse 22.

śrutaṁ harati pāpāni tathārogyaṁ prayacchati|
rakṣāṁ karoti bhūtebhyo janmanāṁ kīrtanaṁ mama||

Verse 23.

yuddheṣu caritaṁ yanme duṣṭadaitya nibarhaṇam|
tasmin śrute vairikṛtaṁ bhayaṁ puṁsāṁ na jāyate||

Verse 24.

yuṣmābhiḥ stutayo yāśca yāśca brahmarṣibhiḥ kṛtāḥ|
brahmaṇā ca kṛtāstāstu prayacchanti śubhāṁ matim||

Translation:

When one listens to or recites descriptions of my birth and my emergence, sins of people are removed, they are healed and protected from the elements. Listening to the great episodes of my destruction of evil demons, one is freed of the fear of danger. (O gods), If people recite the hymns that you have sung and the one by *Brahmā*, they inspire beneficial counsel to people.

Explanation:

In these verses assuring results, the same kinds of words are repeated. For persons who are doubtful and with little knowledge, this is necessary. We will here explain only a few of these words. Sins are feelings of non-Self. As long as there is the perception of something other than *ātmā*, there is sin. By repeatedly hearing and reminiscing the greatness of Mother, one arrives at the knowledge of Self. So, all one's sins are removed.

'*tathārogyaṁ prayacchati*': one is cured of this worldly disease of repeated birth and death. '*bhayaṁ na jāyate*' when fearless, ambrosial knowledge of Self is gained, fear of death is removed forever. Besides this, Mother also says, if one is not able to recite or listen to the whole *Devī Māhātmya*, but only the verses of praise, then one finds beneficial counsel, that is, find knowledge of discovering Self.

Verse 25.

araṇye prāntare vāpi dāvāgniparivāritaḥ|
dasyubhirvā vṛtaḥ śūnye gṛhītovāpi śatrubhiḥ||

Verse 26.

siṁhavyāghrānuyāto vā vane vā vanahastibhiḥ|
rājñā kruddhena vāñjapto vadhyo bandhagatohapi vā||

Verse 27.

āghūrṇito vā vātena sthitaḥ pote mahārṇave|
patatsu vāpi śastreṣu sahngrāme bhṛśadāruṇe||

Verse 28.

sarvābādhāsu ghorāsu vedanābhyarditohapi vā|
smaranḥ mamaitaccaritaṁ naro mucyeta saṇkaṭāt||

Verse 29.

mama prabhāvāt siṁhādyā dasyavo vairiṇastathā|
dūrādeva palāyante smarataścaritaṁ mama||

Translation:

If one is lost in a forest or desert, surrounded by flames, helpless and under attack by robbers or enemies, chased in a forest by lions, tigers or wild elephants, bound or condemned by orders of an angry monarch, swept by storms on the great oceans, felled by weapons in battle, in all serious dangers and illnesses, if people remember my glories, then by my influence, wild animals, enemies and dangers are removed.

Explanation:

The benefits of hearing and reciting episodes of the glory of Mother have been described. If one is unable to hear or recite, if one just remembers them humbly, then people are saved from danger. In mentioning the reasons that bring sorrow to people, Mother mentions many things like forests, wild animals, fire and robbers. In *Bhāgavat Gitā*, the Lord also said that this world was transient and full of sorrow[4]. It always weakens people. If they call on God under these conditions, then they are saved from these dangers. On top of it, they acquire belief in God. When there are cries from stricken beings, my Mother appears.

People should notice, what comforts they live with. It is aimed at their conditions that Mother speaks of 'forests, and desert.' Look and see if your life is not spent in forests and deserts. Even though surrounded by many friends, in this desert of life, bemused by hopes of pleasure, you are constantly cheated. See if all around you, do there not burn fires of trouble? What you think to be peace, look at it calmly, you will see that it is mixed with trouble. See if your good *vrittis* are not stolen by these outward-facing robber traits, who are mesmerized by material things. See if those who you think of as friends, those enemies, lust and desire, do not break the banks of your rivers of peace. See if the dangerous beasts of terrible tendencies do not attack you daily. See if you are empty and alone. On top of this, there is the anger from the king. The one who is God, the ruler of this world, you cannot follow his orders and satisfy him, so you cannot appear in front of him. By his orders, you approach death and are bound by the chains of this worldly life. On this great ocean of life, your ship is constantly beaten by storms of fate. You are injured by great battles with your tendencies. You suffer from mental and physical illnesses. You are in deep trouble. Look at your life, and you will notice this distress. Looking at this, be sorrowful and remember me. The moment you remember me, you will be relieved of these misfortunes. Think of me repeatedly, and you will always taste this relief. Those who have not yet reached such trouble in life, do not have a chance to think of me. But my love for you places you in such states, gives you the chance to remember me. Today or tomorrow, or after some time, you will surely find this opportunity. When this

---

4 *anityamasukhaṁ lokamimaṁ prāpya bhajasva mām*, *Bhāgavat Gitā*, 9:33

fortunate chance comes, do not forget to remember me. If you do that, you will be relieved from danger and in time view me. This is my final message.

Verse 30.

ṛṣiruvāca|
ityuktvā sā bhagavatī caṇḍikā caṇḍavikramā|
paśyatāmeva devānāṁ tatraivāntaradhīyata||

Verse 31.

tehapi devā nirātaṅkāḥ svādhikārānyathā purā|
yajñabhāgabhujaḥ sarve cakrurvinihatārayaḥ||

Translation:

The sage said, 'the terrifying, powerful Goddess *Caṇḍīkā* disappeared from the view of the deities. Their enemies having been defeated, the gods, without fear, regained their rights to ceremonial offerings, as before.'

Explanation:

Mother disappears from the front of us. No one can hold on to her continuously. She appears by her own wishes and disappears at her own will. No one has the ability to interfere with her appearance or disappearance. But, there is one thing. When Mother appears in her form as terrifying *Caṇḍīkā*, persons are honored, their states as worldly beings end. Their treasured houses of play are torn down. Beings discover their true nature and are relieved of the enchantment of their worldly state forever. Then the gods are relieved of torment by demons and regain their rights to ceremonial offerings. They enjoy the bliss of *paramātmā.*

Verse 32.

daityāśca devyā nihate śumbhe devaripau yudhi|
jagadvidhvḥsini tasmin mahogrehatulavikrame|
niśumbhe ca mahāvīrye śeṣāḥ pātālamāyayuḥ||

Translation:

Śumbha, the very destructive and violent enemy of the gods, and powerful *Niśumbha* having been destroyed, the rest of the weakened demons entered the underworlds.

Explanation:

Both *Śumbha* and *Niśumbha* were destroyed. together with most of their followers. The rest of the demons entered the underworld. It was said in Volume Two that the seven levels of ignorance are the seven underworlds. When the Sun of knowledge arises, ignorance is uprooted. So, demonic tendencies due to ignorance of Self are automatically destroyed. Here, the Goddess destroys *Śumbha* and *Niśumbha*, demonic ego and attachment. The remaining weakened demons disappear.

This is what happens. When pure perception formed *ātmā* appears, all sense of duality due to ignorance ends. Then, on awakening, some of the previous ignorance and its actions return. Even so, the liberation of beings is not hindered. One enjoys this world with fragments of knowledge before it is completely expressed. A seeker too, moves in the previous world, in non-Self, by traces of ignorance. Then, when all stored actions end, when the body is gone, one attains liberation. One forever merges with *Brahmaṇ*. Such beings do not return. So, *śrutis* say that 'they do not come back.'

The adjectives used to describe *Śumbha* and *Niśumbha* have been explained before and are not repeated here.

Verse 33.

evaṁ bhagavatī devī sā nityāpi punaḥ punaḥ|
sambhūya kurute bhūpa jagataḥ paripālanam||

Translation:

O king, although she is eternal, the Goddess appears repeatedly in this manner to care for this world.

Explanation:

In this mantra, the great sage Medhas indicates to king Suratha the principle of incarnations (*avatāra*). Although before this, in the mantra '*itham̐ yadā yadā ...*' incarnations of the Goddess have been described, here, the sage repeats it to explain it to Suratha. 'To take care of this universe, the Goddess appears repeatedly.' It will not be beside the point to say a few words about such incarnations.

The word '*avatāra*' means descent. Pure awareness natured *ātmā* descends into pure intelligence. When beings can reside in the nature of pure intelligence, then the nature of *ātmā* is illuminated in that pure intelligence. This illumination of *ātmā* in pure intelligence is true descent or incarnation. By this, the absence of attributes of *ātmā* is not infringed. Although without attributes, it is reflected in pure intelligence like the Sun reflected by a clear mirror.

Self that is reflected in global intelligence, *Hiraṇyagarbha* or *Iśvara*, who is truth-pledged, self-fulfilled, who is love, affection and mercy, who is Lord and arbitrator, when it is reflected in intelligence, it may be called an *avatāra*. When people are tormented by demonic tendencies, when they are thirsty for knowledge, hope for peace, and pray for deliverance, then the source of kindness, the great *Īśvara* is expressed in intelligence. Then, people on a true quest, coming in contact with this viewer of truth are privileged. This is the mystery of incarnations.

Both *Gitā* and *Caṇḍī* speak alike about principles of incarnations. *Gitā* said 'to relieve the saintly, destroy the wicked, and establish *dharma* in all epochs.'[5] The *Caṇḍī* says 'whenever in future demons reappear, I will destroy them.' In the *Gitā,* the actions of an *avatāra* are destruction of the wicked and establishment of *dharma*. Expression of the Self and destruction of enemies are actions of an *avatāra* in *Devī Māhātmya*. In the former, the *avatāra* establishes *dharma*. In the latter, *avatāra* establishes Self. It is by the establishment of Self that *dharma*

5 *Bhāgabat Gitā,* 4:8.

is protected and this universe is cared for. Wherever an *avatāra* has appeared, they have protected truth. All incarnations are my sentient Mother. No one else but Mother can be an incarnation. It is the consciousness-formed Goddess who descends into a human body and is expressed as an *avatāra*. The one who is truly 'I' appears. Mother said, 'I come down' and destroy enemies.

Let me say something here in this connection. Mother establishes an unwavering belief in incarnations, in the hearts of those who are thirsty, who are truly seeking. If one has a firm belief in incarnations and has unqualified devotion, then there is right fortune. Ācārya Śankara believed in incarnations. In the introduction to his commentary on *Bhāgavat Gitā*, he said, 'as if, one has a body, is born, for the good of people.' The one who is without the conflicts of a physical body, the nature of pure perception of the *māyā* of God, appears like one with a body. Otherwise, beings covered by *māyā* cannot go near it. *Paramātmā* for the benefit of people expresses itself as an *avatāra*. It brings good fortune to people to believe this instead of trying to deny it. At the same time, one has to be careful about something. The figure of the *avatāra* is not God. *Paramātmā* descends sheltered in that figure. This is to be understood. An *avatāra* is not defined just by its form. One has to realize the true nature of the *avatāra*.

Verse 34.

tayaitanmohyate viśvaṁ saiva viśvaṁ prasūyate|
sā yācitā ca viñjānaṁ tuṣṭā ṛddhiṁ prayacchati||

Translation:

(O Suratha.) She keeps this universe bemused, she gives birth to this universe, when worldly beings please her by their prayers, she gives (them) intellect formed prosperity.

Explanation:

The sage Medhasa said, 'O, Suratha. Even though Mother is explicit, she remains unseen, because she keeps this world bemused. Is she an enemy of people? Even though she has the ability to give freedom to beings, she keeps them covered by delusion. Why is she not an enemy? No. No. She is Mother. She gives birth to this world (*saiva vishvaṁ prasūyate*). Can a mother wish ill of her children? Then why does she not reveal herself to her children? Who says she does not? When Mother is sought and satisfied, she offers the wealth of knowledge. That is, when one seeks her she may be seen. If you say, we seek her so much, why do we not see her? No. You do not seek her. What is sad is that you do not understand that you do not seek her. Truly I say, if you seek her, you will find her. When you seek Mother just for herself, then you will see Mother. Mother will give you indiscriminately whatever you ask from her. When you ask for nothing else, only ask for her, satisfied, she will give you a great treasure of intellect formed prosperity. By its influence, you will find Mother, know Self and discover the stability of *Brahmaṇ*. I repeat, if one seeks Mother, one finds her. This is the advice of Medhasa to Suratha.

Verse 35.

vyāptaṁ tayaitat sakalaṁ brahmāṇḍaṁ manujeśvara|
mahākālyā mahākāle mahāmārī-svarūpayā||

Verse 36.

saiva kāle mahāmārī saiva sṛṣṭirbhavatyajā|
sthitiṁ karoti bhūtānāṁ saiva kāle sanātanī||

Translation:

O king of men! One who at the time of dissolution is of the nature of a scourge, that *Mahākālī* covers this universe. In the time of dissolution, she is the destroyer. In creation, she is of the nature of the creator, and in the time of continuity, she protects and maintains all beings. Yet, she is without birth and is eternal.

Explanation:

The sage Medhasa is saying, O Suratha, king of men! Look.

Only destructive death-natured *Mahākālī* covers all this universe. All beings, all atoms, at all times, knowingly or unknowingly are moving towards dissolution, towards death and destruction. Look. Open your eyes of knowledge. This universe is a great ceremony of destruction. From the newborn infant in the nursery, to the sickly old person, all are to sacrifice themselves at this ceremony of destruction of *Mahākālī*. Childhood, youth, and old age that we see in people are but indicators of their path towards this ceremony of destruction. It indicates how far one has traveled towards destruction. Creation and maintenance are but preparations for dissolution. So, destruction natured *Kālī* is being named as creator and maintainer.

Where do you go and seek Mother? Look. This universe filling power of creation, maintenance and destruction is expressed as the eternal form of *Mahākālī*. Lord *Kṛṣṇa* had once described himself to *Arjuna* as 'I am time, the one who destroys.'[6] God in the form of Time can be sought and worshipped by people. The form beyond time cannot be sought. It is beyond words and mind. When persons surrender to the hands of Time, they conquer it, arrive at a state beyond time and overcome death. Come, let us all cry 'victory to *Kālī*' and leap into the heart of great Time. Mother will hold us to her heart and take us beyond Time. We will overcome death.

Existence-natured Mother, expressing herself in her three-fold nature of creation, maintenance and dissolution, is eternal. Even in all of this, she is not eroded, not changed. Leave yourself in her hands. Offer the sense of 'I' at the feet of *Mahākālī*. Knowingly or unknowingly, you are on the lap of *Mahākālī*. What will you do that is new? One is only asked to accept and understand what is true. If you can surrender, then you will discover her nature beyond Time. What *Sāṇkhya* called inert Nature, what *Vedānta* named false *māyā*, what *Vaiṣṇava* literature terms *lilā*, *Tantra* calls *Mahākālī*. It is the nature of existence, pure perception. If you surrender to it, you will understand how she is eternal and the

---

6 *kālohasmi lokakṣyakṛt*, *Bhāgabat Gitā,* 11:32.

nature of pure existence. She is expressed as the spirit of creation-maintenance-dissolution.

Verse 37.

bhavakāle nṛṇāṁ saiva lakṣmīrvṛddhipradā gṛhe|
saivābhāve tathālakṣmīrvināśāyopajāyate||

Verse 38.

stutā sampūjitā puṣpairdhūpagandhāadibhistathā|
dadāti vittaṁ putrāṁśca matiṁ dharma gatim śubhām||

iti śrīmārkaṇḍeyapuraṇe sāvarṇike manvantare devīmāhātmye phalasruti samāptaḥ|

Translation:

At the advent of man, she is *Lakṣmī* offering prosperity at home. Again, in the time of poverty, she is the all-destructive *Alakṣmī*. Being praised and worshipped with flowers and perfume, she gives wealth, children, and the beneficial intelligence of *dharma*.

Here ends the recital of results, in *Devī Māhātmya*, in the era of *Sāvarṇi*, in *Mārkeṇḍeya Purāṇa*.

Explanation:

When people acquire worldly or after-worldly benefits, one has to understand that it is consciousness formed Mother who has expressed herself as beneficence (*Lakṣmī*). When she holds her children on her lap in the form of the prosperity of *Lakṣmī*, then from all sides, prosperity, that is wealth, or elements of spiritual effort appear. Then in the times of poverty, when she holds beings in her form as *Alakṣmī*, destruction appears from all around. Everywhere the figure of Mother as *Mahākālī* is present. In whatever direction the wheel of great Time turns, beings are moved by that feeling. In whatever form the Mother holds them, they act in that role. Knowingly or unknowingly, beings are seated on the lap of *Mahākālī*.

The question may be, how can one please this power of great

Time? In answer, the sage says that chanting and worship (*pujā*) are infallible means for the affection of Mother. In services, these are present. Loud chanting of a name as advised by *Vaiṣṇava* literature is nothing but singing praises. A focus on God as advised by yoga is pointing to this worship. *Purāṇā* and *Tantra* texts also give similar advice. Even *Vedas* give counsel for praise and fire ceremonies.

In the abstract of the *Upaniṣads*, in the *Bhāgavat Gitā*, the Lord advised worship with offerings of flowers and leaves. We see in all scriptures, worship and hymns as the two great parts of service to God. Listening and reflection, restraint and rules, are all prescribed and followed to ensure the complete success of praises and worship. If one continues to perform what has been going on in these lands for ages, such practices in a spiritual quest pleases Mother and seekers to find what they seek. To please the eternally satisfied Mother, one has to take recourse of worship and hymns as advised in *Devī Māhātmya*.

What does one receive if Mother is pleased? The sage said, wealth, children and a beneficial sense of *dharma*. These are the results in the outer world. In the spiritual realm, one finds the wealth of devotion, a child of pure perception, and beneficent *dharma*, intelligence by which eternal bondage of beings are forever freed. So I say, do not turn away from worship and praises of Mother. No other procedure has such a beautiful combination of knowledge, devotion and action.

May Mother protect all her children from those who bewitch and cheat them by saying enchanting words that 'in this age of *Kali*, carrying out prescribed acts are useless.'

Here end the explanations on the recital of results, in *Sādhan Samar* or *Devī Māhātmya*.

Chapter 13

Epilogue

Verse 1.

ṛṣiruvāca|
etatte kathitaṁ bhūpa devīmāhātmyamuttamam|
evanprabhāvā sā devī yayedaṁ dhāryate jagat|
vidyā tathaiva kriyate bhagavadviṣṇumāyayā||

Translation:

The sage said, "O king, I have described to you this excellent glory of the Goddess. The Goddess who holds this universe has great influence. It is this Goddess *Viṣṇumāyā* who proffers knowledge of Self."

Explanation:

Guru Medhasa is concluding the narration of *Devī Māhātmya* to king Suratha. He spoke. O, king, you have conquered this inert world. O, pure one. I have described to you the glories of the Goddess, who is of the nature of knowledge of *Brahmaṇ*. By many pious acts and the blessings of sages, you have acquired proper respect and rights to hear about knowledge of *Brahmaṇ*. I have described to you these three principal characters of the Goddess. This is not very effective for those who do not have proper rights to it, who do not have a firm belief in the words of *guru* and scriptures. But, I hope this is very fruitful for you. Hearing this glory of the Goddess, do not hold doubts about any of it. There is nothing that is imagined or exaggerated. What is described is truth. One who is creator-maintainer-destroyer of this universe, that very powerful *Viṣṇumāyā*, has this authority. Do not hold doubts about the divine greatness of her character. It is Goddess *Viṣṇumāyā* who offers knowledge to beings like you, gives them knowledge of *Brahmaṇ* and lands them in the arena of freedom. Again, to those who seek, she expresses herself as liberation. My Mother has this authority.

Verse 2.

tayā tvameṣa vaiśyaśca tathaivānyevivekinaḥ|
mohyante mohitāścaiva mohameṣyanti cāpare||

Verse 3.

tāmupaihi mahārāja śaraṇaṁ parameśvarīm|
ārādhitā śaiva nṛṇāṁ bhogaśvargāpavargadā||

Translation:

You and the *Vaiśya*, others with and without conscience, are mesmerized by the Goddess, were in the past and will be in the future. O king, seek refuge of the Goddess. When she is worshipped, she fulfills all enjoyment (*bhoga*), offers heaven and liberation.

Explanation:

Child Suratha! One day, both you and this *vaiśya* said, 'even though we are knowledgeable, why do we have delusion?' But, today, you must know, that not only you and this *vaiśya*, but all others are bemused by the Goddess *Viṣṇumāyā*. This has appeared in the past and will be so in the future. My Mother is *Mahākālī*. Past, present and future, are all forms of Mother. As long as Mother appears in these three forms, that is, as long as she is reflected in the intelligence of beings as memory, hope and imagination, beings will be bemused by *Mahāmāyā*. One who has no imaginary divisions, who is undivided, complete, seeing her as divided is an act of delusion. This delusion is in all time frames. This delusion is the seed of this universe, of the variety of creation. One cannot play a game of blind man's bluff, without closing one's eyes. If one does not forget oneself, one cannot engage in divine play. All those with and without conscience have some degree of delusion, always had and will in the future.

O, Suratha! Even though you have lost everything because of your courtiers and family, your tenderness towards them, the sadness for your lost kingdom, is delusion. If you truly wish to be free of this, seek refuge at the feet of the Goddess. Seek refuge in *Mahāmāyā*.

Lord *Kṛṣṇa* says in *Bhāgavat Gitā*. 'If you want to be freed from this intense delusion of mine, then seek refuge in me.' Come to my shelter, the shelter of Mother. When one seeks the shelter of Mother, she is worshipped. When Mother is worshipped, you will feel her pleasure. She will offer you your desires, heaven and salvation. From the three figures of Mother, as creator, maintainer and destroyer, one obtains three-fold results. In her first form, Mother pierces the knot of *Brahmā*, as a result your engrossment with worldly matter ends. Enjoyments of this world come. This is the first gift. In her second form, she pierces the knot of *Viṣṇu* and as a result, one observes life force all over this world and acquires the rights to enjoy heaven or the arena of divinities. In her third form, she pierces the knot of *Rudra* and brings you into the nature of pure perception and knowledge of Self. Then you find liberation. In this manner, not only you, but all who seek refuge at the feet of Mother, find these three fruits of enjoyment, heaven and salvation.

What the scriptures call four-fold results are included in these three. Within enjoyment is *dharma* and wealth (*artha*), desire is part of heaven, and liberation and salvation are the same.

The use of the word '*nṛṇāṁ*' in this mantra, shows that all persons have a right to these three things. One may ask, why everybody does not find them. The answer is that they do not seek shelter at the feet of *Paramesvarī*. Remember that children who truly seek refuge at the feet of Mother, inevitably find these three.

Verse 4.

mārkaṇḍeya uvāca|
iti tasya vacaḥ śrutvā surathaḥ sa narādhipaḥ|
praṇipatya mahābhāgaḥ tamṛṣiṁ saṁśitavratam||

Verse 5.

nirviṇṇoatimamatvena rājyāpaharaṇena ca|
jagāma sadyastapase sa ca vaiśyo mahāmune||

Translation:

Mārkaṇḍeya said, "O great sage (*Krouṣṭuki*), hearing his (Medhasa) words, the sorrowful king of men, who had lost his kingdom, and the *Vaiśya*, disheartened because of his attachments, paid their respects to the intensely austere great sage (Medhasa) and departed, to carry out their spiritual practice."

Explanation:

The words of *Brahmaṇ* enlightened *guru* Medhasa end. *Devī Māhātmya* began with the first '*Mārkaṇḍeya* said.' Here near the conclusion, it also ends with '*Mārkaṇḍeya* said.' Until now, in this context, the words have been between Suratha and the sage Medhasa. Originally, *Devī Māhātmya* had been narrated by the intellect-eyed *Mārkaṇḍeya* to the material-prided, world-formed *Jaimini*.

Suratha having lost his kingdom is despondent. The *Vaiśya* hurt by his affection is also grieved and sorrowful. One desires his kingdom, the other wants to be rid of his affection, to seek his conscience. Both are very respectful of the words of the *guru*. As the sage said, 'you should seek refuge of the great Goddess', they saluted his feet and left, to carry out his orders to begin their spiritual practices. With spiritual vision, one can see that the worldly being of Suratha, in the company of Samādhi, hearing the words of the *guru* humbly and with respect, begins their best efforts towards concentration and meditation.

In the common view, Suratha seeks his kingdom, so is addicted to wealth, and the *Vaiśya* is affected by love for his wife and children, so is addicted to desire (*kāma*). The world is addicted to these two traits. These are the basis of the episodes of *Caṇḍī*. Both of them have been banished because of their circumstances. Yet, they are both engrossed by their longing for wealth and desire. By good fortune, they have found the right *guru*. Hearing *Devī Māhātmya* and by orders from the *guru*, they begin their spiritual effort to seek refuge at the feet of the Goddess. This is the general route for a life of *dharma*. Most people arrive at the kingdom of *dharma* in this manner. Those who from infancy are unattached to things and are seekers are different. They are ready from the very beginning.

Verse 6.

sandarśanārthamambāyā nadīpulinśaṁsthitaḥ|
sa ca vaiśyastapastepe devīsūktaṁ paraṁ japam||

Verse 7.

tau tasmin puline devyāḥ kṛtvā mūrtiṁ mahīmayīm|
arhaṇāṁ cakratustasyāḥ puṣpadhūpāgnitarpaṇaiḥ||

Verse 8.

nirāhārau yatātmānau tanmanaskau samāhitau|
dadatustau baliṁ caiva nijagātrāsṛgukṣitam||

Verse 9.

evaṁ samārādhayatostribhirvarṣairyatātmanoḥ|
parituṣṭā jagaddhātrī pratyakṣaṁ prāha caṇḍikā||

Translation:

The king and *Vaiśya* set up at the side of a river and began spiritual austerities to view Mother. They recited the very fruitful *Devī Sukta*, built a clay *murtti* of the Goddess and worshipped it with flowers and incense. They carried out fire ceremonies (*homa*) and fasted or had very little food. Residing with concentration, they made offerings tinged with their blood. In this manner, they worshipped for three years. One who is Mother of this universe, Goddess *Caṇḍīkā* was satisfied, appeared and spoke to them.

Explanation:

These four mantras describe the manner of worship by the king and the merchant. To have a vision of Mother, they both went away from human habitation, living on a lonely riverside, regularly recited *Devī Sukta* (*ahaṁ rudreviḥ . . .*); offered flowers and incense to a figure of the goddess made from clay, did fire ceremonies, lived with little or no food, concentrated and made offerings tinged with their blood. In this manner, not for a day or two, but three years, they carried out severe austerities.

Before this, near the end of Volume Two, much has been discussed about external worship, so it is unnecessary to repeat it here. I will just say a few words about the creation of figures (*murtti*). Texts of the *Purāṇā* and *Tantra* have much to say about this. However, those texts also say that making a figure out of clay, stone, metal or wood, and worshipping it brings no results. This has to be given consideration. If one builds a figure and worships it as God, one cannot truly find God. But, if one considers the figure to be a concentrated expression of the supreme power of creation-maintenance-dissolution, as a center of the nature of consciousness, as a reflection of Self, then it is never fruitless. In ancient times, sages worshipping different forms arrived at undifferentiated knowledge and reached a state of *Brahmaṇ*. They tasted liberation.

Some say that it is for the materially-minded that worship of a *murtti* is prescribed. This is not entirely true. It is by knowing the true mystery of form, and by the establishment in truth and life force, that a knower of Self is able to perform worship. Today, the style in which such worship is mostly carried out is more suited for those with lower abilities.

Although there may be milk in many parts of a cow, one can only collect it from its udders. In the same manner, to appreciate the special nature of universal consciousness, one has to take the help of special figures. Only those who have discovered spirit beyond the physical are truly worthy of worshipping a *murtti*. As long as one has a physical body, as long as one worships a lump of flesh with food, drink, dresses and ornaments, until then worship of forms will remain. Until one resides continuously in the nature of *paramātmā,* one knowingly or unknowingly worships form. So, discarding such worship before reaching such a state is a sign of disorderliness. In these times, by the worship of inert figures, inertness has come to this land. When we can establish life force in such figures and worship them, inertness will disappear. This has been discussed in another book 'Principles of worship' (*Pujā Tattva*).

Whatever it is, the mantra says that Suratha and Samādhi, not only worshipped a clay figure, they lived on limited food or fasted. The meaning of the word '*āhāra'* is receiving objects. Ācārya Śankara has said, that it is reception by the senses. When this is controlled, when it is covered by God (*Īśāvāsya*), when things are received as established in truth, one can be said to control food. Those who have stopped receiving such things could be said to be fasting. The word '*tanmanaska*' means to be withdrawn and focused. The root '*tat*' points to *Brahmaṇ*. When the mind is completely dissolved, then a seeker is in this state. Broadly, Suratha and Samādhi, together with reciting the *Devī Sukta*, and external worship, practiced withdrawal, concentration and meditation. Not only that, what is at the heart of spiritual effort, without which there is nothing, they practiced it also. They made offerings tinged with their blood at the feet of Mother. The spiritual meaning of 'own blood' is life. This meaning is not invented by us. *Upaniṣad* has called *prāṇa* nectar of the body (*angirasa*). This and one's blood have the same meaning. Whatever it is, Suratha and Samādhi took life force and offered it at the feet of Mother. As long as one cannot offer life, until then, sacrificial offerings should be tinged with one's blood, that is, imbued with life force, and offered at the feet of Mother as an envoy of life. Even today, another custom is prevalent in this land. Offerings are first worshipped with flowers before they are offered. Unfortunately, at this time this is just a ritual. Not many understand that there is a great principle embedded in such a simple custom. It is to tint the offerings with one's blood that this is carried out. If they are not tinged by one's blood, as long as they are not imbued with one's life force, they cannot be offered at the feet of Mother. Offerings have to be envisioned as one's life, established in truth and life force and then offered. It is because our individual lives are not merged with the universal one that we do not meet Mother. But, if we imbue our small offerings of fruits and flowers with universal life and get used to offering them at the feet of Mother, then one day, our tiny life will merge with the universal one. Then, one can meet Mother. King Suratha and Samādhi, having understood this mystery, carried out this practice. After three years of doing this, Goddess *Caṇḍīkā* appeared to them in her beneficent form.

The mantra mentions three years. This also has a great spiritual significance. The word '*varṣa*' does not only mean a year; it can also mean a location. In three years, means carrying out the spiritual effort at three levels. One is the mental plane, one of life force and one in the plane of knowledge. Spiritual effort in these three arenas is one carried out for three *varṣas*. When worshipped in this manner, my Mother is pleased and appears in her form as *Caṇḍīkā* and *Jagatdhdhātrī*. As a result, the three-fold knots of a seeker are untied. What manner of spiritual enterprise can achieve this goal quickly is shown by this description of the efforts by Suratha and Samādhi.

Verse 10.

devyuvāca|
yat prārthyarte tvayā bhūpa tvayā ca kulanandana|
mattastatprāpyatāṁ sarvaṁ parituṣṭā dadāmi tat||

Translation:

The Goddess said, 'O, king, O, child of your ancestors, you will get all that you ask from me. I am pleased and will grant you everything.'

Explanation:

Mother has appeared in her beneficent form and awards Suratha and Samādhi the blessings they seek. The next mantra will describe the benefits. Here, Mother addresses Suratha as king and Samādhi as the child of his lineage. By these, she prefaces their desires beforehand. Suratha is addressed as king (*bhūpa*) as ruler of the inert world (*bhū*). The *Vaiśya* is addressed as one who brings joy to his lineage (*kulanandana*). The lineage in which a knower of *Brahmaṇ* is born is truly blessed. Both the ancestors and the descendants are enthralled by the prospects of liberation.

Verse 11.

mārkaṇḍeya uvāca|
tato vavre nṛpo rājyamavibhranśyanyajanmani|
atra caiva nijaṁ rājyaṁ hataśatruvalaṁ balāt||

Verse 12.

sohapi vaiśyastato jñānaṁ vavre nirviṇṇamānasaḥ|
mametyahamiti prājñaḥ saṅgavicyutikārakam||

Translation:

Mārkaṇḍeya said, "King Suratha prayed for his kingdom in this one and the hereafter, his ability to defeat his enemies and recover his kingdom. The wise merchant, the *Vaiśya* harassed by worldly matters, prayed for knowledge of Self that destroys the ignorance of attachment for family, ego and body."

Explanation:

Suratha is the spirit of worldly beings. Whatever knowledge he finds, his natural tendency is towards desire. So, he asks Mother for the destruction of his enemies and recovery of his kingdom and a safe one in future lives. Formerly, being defeated by outgoing spirits and senses, beings had been defeated and lost the kingdom of Self. Now one asks for control over those senses and tendencies, may one not be tormented by them anymore. Let them be subdued and be elements of enjoyment in this world. May this be not only in this life but in future ones. This is the prayer by Suratha. Samādhi, who was dissatisfied with material things, prayed for knowledge of Self. By its effect, ties of ego and attachment would end forever.

When a seeker finds Mother, the mind wants uninterrupted enjoyment. The heart seeks eternal peace of liberation, to completely immerse in Self. When one meets Mother, seekers find both enjoyment and liberation. To make this point, the mantra speaks of Suratha asking for his kingdom and Samādhi seeking liberation. In the episode in the *Mahābhārata*, where *Kṛṣṇa* is feigning to be asleep, this may be seen. The mind-formed *Duryodhana*, seated at the head end of *Kṛṣṇa*, received the desire formed *Nārāyaṇī* warriors. The heart-formed *Arjuna*, seated at the feet of *Kṛṣṇa*, received the Lord himself, as the captain of the ship of his life. One was overwhelmed by the wealth of God, the other by the beauty of God, by love. In practice, worldly persons have both these two feelings. It has been said many times that love and the knowledge of Self are the same things. Whatever that is, here the rebirth of Suratha has been mentioned. There is nothing to doubt about this. It is not a physical rebirth, but the origin from the sun, to be in the state of *Manu*. This is desirable for all beings.

You are knowingly or unknowingly making these two prayers to Mother, for wealth and knowledge. Wealth is the state of all-powerful godhood and knowledge is pure perception. These are the inherent prayers of beings. Whether you understand or not, in all conditions, you are making these two prayers to Mother. Mother, through birth after birth, is slowly purifying you to make you eligible for this wealth and knowledge.

Look into your heart and see, Mother waits there in her form as encouragement. She smiles and waits to offer you wealth and knowledge. Be her child and stand in front of her and call her, praying for wealth and knowledge. Pray as a child does to Mother, like Suratha and Samādhi, you too will find both and be honored.

Verse 13.

devyuvāca|
svalpairahobhirnṛpate svarājyaṁ prāpśyate bhavān|
hatvā ripūnaskhalitaṁ tava tatra bhaviṣyati||

Verse 14.

mṛtaśca bhūyaḥ samprāpya janma devādvivasvataḥ|
sāvarṇiko nāma manurbhavān bhuvi bhaviṣyati|

Translation:

The Goddess said, 'O king, within a few days, you will recover your kingdom, and defeating the enemies, enjoy it without opposition. After your death, you will be reborn from the Sun, and be famous on earth as *Manu* of the *Sāvarnika* era.'

Explanation:

Spiritual seeker! Try to remember the state of Suratha who had lost his kingdom. After going through much distress and suffering many obstacles, by the grace of the *guru* he found Mother. Mother offers him the blessing of his unhindered kingdom. One has to understand one's kingdom as control over mind, intelligence and senses. Before this, the 'I' was a slave of mind and intelligence, one that was an 'I' of ego. Now 'I' reminds one of Mother, so the senses lose their power. This is the gift of getting one's kingdom. This is the first gift from Mother. Above this is a state of being *Manu*. So, Mother said, 'O, Suratha, in the future, you will be born of the Sun, and be known as the ruler of the era, *Sāvarnik Manu*; you will be established in the collective consciousness.' To discover this consciousness of *Manu*, one has to be a child of the Sun, that is, one has to merge into the spirit of supreme life. One has to be in the lap of the power of *Sāvarna*, creator-maintainer-destroyer. When spiritual seekers attain such a state of *Manu*, they shower blessings on people, which results in all seeking wealth of knowledge. The race of men advances by the grace of the ancestral *Manu*.

An old verse says, 'if one has to worship, one should worship the supreme, because one may achieve much more than one seeks.' An example of this is king Suratha. He prayed to Mother to seek his kingdom, but my Mother not only gave him back his kingdom, but also the state of *Manu*, a most joyous position.

We may see in this world that people ask God to be rid of some earthly or physical illness. As a result, not only are trivial problems relieved, but by the grace of Mother, one achieves abilities for knowledge and renunciation. This is the specialty of a spiritual quest. The young yogi *Dhruba* went through this.

Verse 15.

vaiśyavarya tvayā yaśca varoasmattoabhivāñcitaḥ|
taṁ prayacchāmi sansiddhyai tava jñānaṁ bhaviṣyati||

Translation:

O great *vaiśya*! I offer you what you asked for. You will find knowledge and as a result you will be liberated.

Explanation:

My Mother gives Samādhi the gift of Self-knowledge that brings liberation. Mother is a tree of wish fulfillment. Whatever one prays for with firm belief, she gives, a kingdom to Suratha and knowledge to Samādhi.

The realization of the nature of *Brahmaṇ* without attributes and the ability to reside in *Brahmaṇ* with attributes are signs of liberation in life. The *Śvetāśvatara Upaniṣad* says exactly the same thing. Persons who are able to reside in what is transient, eternal or the one beyond may be called liberated while alive. They are knowers of *Brahmaṇ*. When such a person resides in a physical body, one can see in it sometimes the spirit of a worldly being, sometimes of godhood, and sometimes pure nature. Those of them that are keen, or are able to enjoy special bliss, may reside most of the time in that pure state, in a sixth level of knowledge.

Something to take notice of here is that, the scriptures do not say that a liberated person is always a renunciate. As a result of stored actions, the conduct of a liberated person may be varied. *Vedānta* literatures have illustrated this variety of actions with the examples of *Sanaka, Sananda*, *Ṛṣi Janaka, Yājñavalka*, and *Vāmadeva*. But, in their manners of restraint and other behaviors they were very similar.

Verse 16.

mārkaṇḍeya uvāca|
iti dattvā tayordevī yathābhilaṣitaṁ varam|
babhūvāntarhitā sadyo bhaktyā tābhyāmabhiṣṭutā||

Verse 17.

evaṁ devyā varaṁ labdhvā surathaḥ kṣatriyarṣabha|
sūryājjanma samāsādya sāvarṇirbhavitā manuḥ||

*iti śrīmārkaṇḍeyapurāṇe sāvarṇike manv*antare *devīmāhātmye devīmāhātmyaṁ samāptam|*

Translation:

Mārkaṇḍeya said, in this fashion, worshipped by Suratha and Samādhi with devotion, and fulfilling their desires she disappeared. The great king Suratha, receiving the blessing of the Goddess, would in the future be born from the Sun, and be the *Manu* of the *Sāvarnika* era.

Here ends the *Devī Māhātmya*, in the era of *Sāvarṇi*, in the *Mārkeṇḍeya Purāṇa*.

Explanation:

It is in this manner that beings, in the company of Samādhi, powered by the energy of a right *guru*, and by his orders, carrying out chants and worship, and practicing withdrawal, concentration and meditation, meet Mother. They are established in truth, *prāṇa* and bliss. Mother disappears after proffering them their desires and freedom. As long as one has a physical body, Mother disappears like this. But one can again see her blissful affectionate nature if one wishes.

The mantra says that as a blessing from Mother, king Suratha of the great warrior caste, will become the ruler of the eighth era (*manvantara*) as *Sāvarnik Manu* born of the Sun. It is now the seventh era. When Suratha and Samādhi granted their wishes, it was the second era of *Svārociṣa*. At that time because it was in the deep future, the future tense '*bhabiṣyati*' is used. The one who was Suratha in the second era would be the *Sāvarnika Manu* in the seventh one. He would be the beneficent parent of all mankind and be there for their good. The spiritual meaning of all this was described at the beginning of Volume One.

This is not just the tale of Suratha and Samādhi. All spiritual seekers may be honored by meeting Mother in this manner. This is not impossible. There is nothing unnatural in this. It is very possible and natural. The grace of Mother is the chief provision for finding her. There is no consideration of worldly life or renunciation. In the kingdom of Mother, all have the same rights. Even the most wicked may worship Mother with one mind, seek her refuge. If worldly beings seek shelter at her feet, they will inevitably find her.

Where the *Bhāgabat Gitā* ends, *Devī Māhātmya* begins. When spiritual seekers forsake all religions and seek shelter at the feet of God, they find refuge in this unique assurance. How they progress through various conditions, is described in *Devī Māhātmya*. 'Forsaking all religions seek shelter only in me' is the beginning of *Sādhan Samar*; 'one never returns' is the end.

Come, let us all like the truth seeing sages of the Vedic times with pure voices and simple hearts sing together,

oṁ purṇamadaḥ purṇamidaṁ purṇat purṇamudacyate|
purṇasya purṇamādāya purṇamabāśiṣyate||
oṁ śāntiḥ, oṁ śāntiḥ, oṁ śāntiḥ|| hariḥ oṁ||
oṁ purṇam, oṁ purṇam, oṁ purṇam||

This is full complete, that is full complete. What is full arises from that which is full.

When that which is complete is taken from what is complete, what remains is complete'

Peace, peace, peace; Hari Oṁ.

❍ ❍ ❍

Here ends Volume Three of *Sādhan Samar*, commentary on the piercing of the knot of *Rudra* in *Devī Māhātmya*.

Brief Glossary[1]

ahaṁ- I embodied self, soul, sense of 'I'

ajñān- ignorance, absence of knowledge, incorrect or misguided understanding

akṣara- letter of the alphabet, imperishable, ever-lasting

amṛta- divine nectar, ambrosia, immortality

ānanda- bliss, joy, ecstacy, spiritual contentment; a principal attribute of *Brahmaṇ*

asat- not real, non-existence

asmitā- the sense of a divided 'I', individual ego

asura- those opposed to the gods (*sura*), those of demonic natures

ātmā- Self, *Brahmaṇ* expressed as individual

avatāra- incarnation, divine presence in the form (*rūp*) of an individual being

bhāva- perception or feeling, subjective state or affect, general sensation, aesthetics expressed by a form (*rūp*), the state of being or becoming

bhakti- devotion, love and adoration

bhoga- enjoyment, spirit of consumption and attachment to the material world

bhutas – the elements, the idea of five elements forming the material world, earth, water, energy, air and space (sky)

Brahmaṇ- supreme reality, the inexpressible entity with the characteristics of existence (*sat*), awareness (*cit*), bliss (*ānanda*)

budhi- intelligence, intellectual faculty that imparts self-awareness and oversees mind

1 For some of the *Saṁskṛta* and Bengali terms in the original Bengali text.

cit- awareness, consciousness, perception of self, a principal attribute of *Brahmaṇ*

dharma- literally that which keeps things together, a natural property of things, standard rule or law of truth and action, collective social religious and moral rule and conduct, ethical life of individuals

guṇa- attribute, natural mode or quality, the three modes of life: *sattva* (balanced, harmonious and right), *rājas* (kinetic, active and effortful), *tāmas* (static, inertial and ignorant)

guru- a guide and teacher who takes responsibility of the pupil's development

indriyas- organs, the sensory organs with which the external world is perceived and the effector organs that work on this world, presided by the mind

iṣta- deity, the adored form (*rūp*) of divinity for a particular devotee

jiva- worldly being individual human entity one embroiled with the material world

jñana- knowledge, true or correct concepts, inner perception of the truth

kāmana- desire, the mental state of attachment to this world; need to satisfy the senses

karma- action, work or function, the principle of cause and effect of actions

kirtaṇa –chant, hymns and verses in praise, repeatition of names (*nām*) of God or divinity

koṣa- shell, layer, the individual being formed of five super-posed shells, anatomical (*annamaya*), physiological (*prāṇamaya*), psychological (*manomaya*), intellectual (*vijñanmaya*) and blissful (*ānandamaya*)

lilā - play, game, drama, the cosmic play, divine enjoyment of this existence *mā*- mother, active feminine principle, creator manifesting herself as this universe

man- mind the faculty that perceives the information from the sense organs and presents them to intellect (*buddhi*)

mantra- word or phrase which is usually recited or repeated and of special significance for a devotee, sounds tuned to particular mental and spiritual states

māyā- creative principle, transient or illusory phenomena

moha- delusion, psychological state of belief or fascination with that which is of no lasting or real value

mokṣa- liberation, emancipation from the bondage of *karma*, freedom from the continued cycle of individual birth and death.

nām- name, a verbal representation of divinity

prakṛti- nature, the natural world, innate character of individual beings

prāṇa- life, phenomenon of being alive in contrast to dead or inert, breath that sustains life

pravritti- inclination, natural tendencies of beings, usually to involve in action

prema- love, unconditional and desireless adoration

pujā- worship, individual or communal ceremony conducted in honor of a divinity, activity in honor and adoration for a deity

ripu- passions, inner drives that impel beings into attachment to this world, desire (*kām*), anger (*krodh*), greed (*lobh*), delusion (*moha*), pride (*mada*), envy (*mātṣarya*)

ṛṣi- a seer or a sage, who experienced and visualized truth and transmitted them through the scriptures

rūpa- form, any particular manifestation perceived physically or mentally visualized

tattva- principles, fundamental or axiomatic truths which are experiential

sādhaka- spiritual seeker, an apprentice making a spiritual endeavor

sādhanā- practice, the pursuit of spiritual exploration and Self

sādhu - a renunciate who is devoted to a spiritual life, pious, righteous

saṁskāra- tendencies, results left over from previous births

śarira- body, existential being consisting of material (*sthula*), subtle (*śukṣa*) and causal (*kāran*) domains

śāstra- scriptures, the verbal material consisting of the direct knowledge of the seers (*śruti*), the histories (*smriti*), the philosophies and logic (*mimāṁsa*)

Śaivite- those who worship *Śiva*

śākta- those who worship *śakti*

śakti- energy or strength, sentient, feminine force that operates this universe

sohaṁ- identification of individual beings with ultimate reality.

satya- truth, reality that is neither be created or destroyed

saṁskāra- residual impressions, latent tendency to purify

śaman- emissary, a bailiff serving court orders; (also court papers or summons)

vairāgya- renunciation, non-attachment to the material world, personal relationships and social ties; inner detachment

viveka- faculty of discernment, awareness of polarities, the sense of 'conscience.'

vritti- faculty or inclination

yajña- sacrifice, ceremonial service to the gods, all action as such service

yoga- to join or add, individual being uniting with supreme reality, the teachings of *Pātanjali*

❍ ❍ ❍

Brahmarṣi Satyadeva

Brahmarṣi Satyadeva (Saratcandra Bandhopdhyāyā), was born in 1883, in the village of Navagrām in Bariṣāl district in what is presently Bāngladesh. He was given the honorific Brahmarṣi for his exalted spiritual attainment. Brahmarṣi passed away in 1932. Sādhan Samar is an enlightened and much-admired spiritual interpretation of Devī Māhātmyain Bengali. It was written by Satyadeva in the early 1900s and first published from Calcutta in 1920.